"...A brilliant guide to traditional Spanish cooking. The food is both authentic and accessible, with excellent introductions..."

—Taste Magazine, Britain

"...Whether you live in the United States, Germany, Iceland or Bahrain, I'm sure you'll find *Cooking in Spain* as fascinating as I did..."

—Stars and Stripes, W. Germany

"...The complete guide to the fascinating foods of Spain..."

—Costa Blanca News, Spain

"...A great source for tapa recipes, and those wonderful vegetable-and-seafood-rich dishes that distinguish the Spanish table...."

—San Francisco Examiner, U.S.A.

"...Much more than another book of recipes..."

—Anglo-Spanish Society Quarterly Review, Britain

"...Janet Mendel brings the flavour of Spain to your kitchen..."

—The Gibraltar Chronicle, Gibraltar

"...This book lends a hand to those who want to be seduced by Spain, by the best and quickest route: Spanish food..."

—Sobremesa Magazine, Spain

"...Janet Mendel is one hell of a good cook..."

—Lookout Magazine, Spain

This book is dedicated to the women of Mijas, who took me into their kitchens

COOKING
IN SPAIN

Janet Mendel Searl

A LOOKOUT PUBLICATION

First printing, August 1987
Second printing, December 1987
Third printing, October 1988
Fourth printing, July 1989

Text copyright © 1987 by Janet Mendel. Published by Lookout Publications S.A., Puebla Lucía, 29640 Fuengirola (Málaga), Spain. Tel. (952) 460950. No part of this book may be reproduced or transmitted, in any form or by any means, without permission in writing from the publishers.

Printed at Gráficas Jomagar. Pol. Ind. n.º 1. Arroyomolinos. MOSTOLES (Madrid).

D. L.: M. 23.536-1987   I.S.B.N.: 84-398-9986-6

Photography by AGE Fotostock, Barcelona

Illustrations by Heber Clewett

ACKNOWLEDGEMENTS

Many thanks to the many cooks, both professional and housewifely, throughout Spain, who have shared their recipes with me. Additionally, I would like to acknowledge my debt to several Spanish cookbooks which have been very helpful. These are *El libro de la cocina española* by Nestor Lujan and Juan Perucho; *Viaje por la cocina española* by Luis Antonio de la Vega; *Cómo conocer la cocina española* by Enrique Sordo; *Papeles de la gastronomía malagueña* by Enrique Mapelli, and *El libro de oro de la cocina española,* published by Ediciones Naranco.

    I wish to thank my sons, Daniel and Benjamin, who, having tasted their way through most of this book, recommended the sweets chapter be longer and the recipes for brain fritters and fish eggs be omitted entirely. Many thanks, too, to Linda Drate, who helped me with the recipe testing.

CONTENTS

Introduction

I learned about Spanish cooking in pueblo kitchens. Some twenty years ago, when I first came to live in an Andalusian village, I enjoyed tasting the local foods at a *tapa* bar, where a tiny plate of food was served free with every glass of wine.

One day, when I asked what flavoured the chicken dish, the owner sent me back to the kitchen to talk to his wife.

The women in the kitchen were delighted to talk about food. I returned day after day, watching the preparations, tasting, making notes, sometimes helping. One kitchen led to another and an enquiry about new dishes got me sent off to other homes. We would talk about recipes while the women of the house fanned the fire under the *olla,* the great soup pot set on a tripod in the hearth. In those days, very few village homes had butane-fuelled cookstoves and almost none had refrigerators. Against whitewashed walls hung pots and pans burnished to satin brilliance. Earthy pottery jugs, the family collection of glassware and colourful ceramic bowls lined the tile counters and mantel. Ropes of garlic bulbs and branches of laurel adorned these simple kitchens.

On travels throughout Spain I found that people everywhere in this country love to talk about food and are delighted to share their recipes. In simple bars and restaurants in small villages, I would soon be in the kitchen, absorbing the local culture and customs by way of food. In fine restaurants in the cities, where the cooks were most often men, I found the same generosity. A chef with a few minutes free would come and sit with me and share the secrets of his specialities.

Experimenting with the many new dishes in my own kitchen was also the best possible initiation into the Spanish marketplace. I slowly learned the names of fruits and vegetables, kinds of seafood, cuts of meat, spices, herbs and wines.

This book is intended both for residents in Spain who, like myself, shop here and cook here, and for those visitors who would like to reproduce some of the flavour of Spain in kitchens back home. More than just a cookbook, it's a cook's guide to good eating throughout Spain, to marketing and to cooking, with lots of recipes for favourite Spanish dishes.

This is a book about cooking in Spain and I hope you will enjoy your introduction to the Spanish kitchen as much as I have.

CHAPTER 1

The Flavour of Spain

Spanish food as I learned to cook it was without pretentions, simple fare. It was the subtlety of flavourings, the combinations of ingredients — sometimes truly inspired — and the freshness of the raw materials that made it very special.

Cooking in Spain today is still the traditional fare of the pueblo kitchen, but it has changed. Where once rang the sound of the brass mortar and pestle, now there is the whir of the electric blender. Fruits and vegetables which once came by donkey from nearby fields now are trucked in from far distant regions. In addition to the local fishermen's catch, there is frozen seafood from far-off seas. All this has greatly enriched Spanish cooking and, with prosperity, people today eat much better than they did 20 years ago.

The availability of produce beyond what is raised in local farms plus the talent of a new generation of cooks, both professional and housewifely, have led to *la nueva cocina española,* Spain's "nouvelle" cuisine, with its adaptation of traditional recipes to modern tastes and the imaginative use of old products in new ways and new products in old ways.

The growth of the tourist industry and the influx of foreigners come to live on Spain's sunny coastlines have also influenced the cooking. Restaurants offer a more or less "international" menu with a smattering of traditional Spanish dishes. Markets and supermarkets catering to new demands import everything from Norwegian smoked salmon to Chinese vegetables to Indian chutneys to English Christmas puddings.

This culinary cross-fertilization is nothing new in Spain. The Romans may have started it. They had a passion for Spanish olive oil, figs, grapes, wine and fish, which were exported to Rome and points beyond. In turn, the colonizers contributed dishes — such as the original *cocido,* a boiled dinner which could be considered the national dish of Spain.

The Moors, who ruled much of the Iberian peninsula for more than seven centuries in a Golden Age of science, literature, philosophy, art and gastronomy, left their culinary calling card which can still be savoured today. The Arabs, with complex systems of irrigation and water wheels, turned vast barren regions into rich agricultural lands and introduced into Spain the cultivation of rice and sugar cane, and many fruits and vegetables previously unknown. The cooking was vastly influenced by both the Moors and the Sephardim Jews who cohabited peacefully — exotic spices such as saffron, the use of fruits and almonds with savoury dishes, honeyed sweets and pastries. It is this Moorish flavour that makes Spanish cooking so distinctive from that of the rest of Europe.

Then came the discovery of the Americas. Though gold was of foremost interest to the *conquistadores,* the discovery of tomatoes, potatoes, peppers, beans, squash, avocados, corn and chocolate, which were introduced to Europe from Spain, were of longer-lasting importance. The famous *gazpacho,* of Moorish origin, didn't become the dish so well known today until tomatoes came from the New World.

A cook's tour of Spain

Many of us who live in Spain enjoy frequent travels throughout the country, discovering a wealth of art, history and culture as well as exciting foods, cheeses, wines and sweets, some very local indeed. For the traveller, this survey of regional specialities can provide suggestions of what to eat in Bilbao, Barcelona or Badajoz and, for the enthusiastic and adventurous cook, a culinary tour of this most fascinating country.

There are a few dishes without culinary frontiers — the *cocido,* a one-pot feast of meats, sausages and vegetables; the *tortilla* or Spanish omelette, made with eggs and potatoes, and *sopa de ajo,* garlic soup. Though each varies from region to region, incorporating local produce and flavours, they are all truly "national" dishes. Additionally, all three are simple to prepare, wonderful introductions for the novice into the complexities of Spanish food.

Regional variations are best characterized by the Spanish saying, referring to both climatic conditions and to cooking techniques: "in the north you stew; in the central region, you roast; in the east you simmer and in the south you fry." We'll start in the north.

Asturias. Green meadows and mists, thick forests of oak and chestnut, fat cattle and fast-running trout streams. Can this really be Spain? The Principality of Asturias might seem rather a corner of Brittany, Normandy or Ireland, which is not so extraordinary considering they were all settled by Celts.

Tucked away at the top of this subcontinent on the Bay of Biscay and behind the rugged slopes of the Picos de Europa, Asturias may actually be the most

Spanish of all Spain's regions. It was here the Visigothic kings fortified themselves and, through all those centuries, was the only one never conquered by the Moors. It was from the Asturias that the Christian reconquest of Spain began.

The Asturias has another claim to fame — the *fabada,* beans and sausages at their most elegant. To know the landscape of Asturias is to understand the fabada. Bitterly cold in the winter, all life centres around the warm hearth where the beans gently bubble on the fire. There is no winter growing season and summer harvests must feed the family until spring. Corn, grain, beans, vegetables are hung in sheds to dry. Pigs are slaughtered, salted and cured to provide meat for winter eating. No wonder that Asturias is famous for its cured meats — *morcilla,* black pudding; *longaniza,* smoked sausage; *chorizo,* paprika-flavoured red sausage, and hams, salt pork and bacon.

The rivers of Asturias provide excellent salmon and trout and the Bay of Biscay, a plentiful array of seafood. Also famous: 250 varieties of apples; a blue cheese called Cabrales, one of the best in Spain; lentils, chestnuts and cider. Little wine is produced in Asturias. Instead there is the "wine of the apple," *sidra,* which seems to contain the essence of the crisp and green countryside. Dispensed in the *chigres* or taverns, cider is good with seafood on a summer's day.

Besides fabada, excellent dishes are *caldereta de pescado,* a seafood stew; *sardinas trechadas,* boned and stuffed sardines, and trout fried with ham.

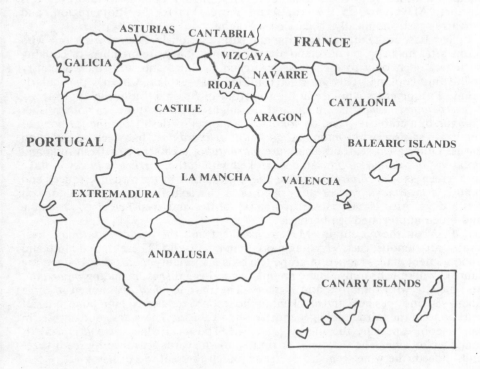

13

Basque lands. "Apalaurreaudiak," "txitxardiñak," "kokotxas" and "txangurro." It looks like a typewriter gone berserk, but those are actual words for culinary specialities in that crazy language, Basque. No one knows how the language originated. Though it has borrowed from both French and Spanish, the native tongue of the Basques has no relation to either. Or to anything else, though some theorists have suggested the Basques can understand the fish in the seas, which doesn't seem too far-fetched considering their ability to catch and prepare them.

One tale, acknowledging the impossibility of the language and the sternness of the women, says the devil decided one day he wanted to learn Basque. So he hid himself behind the door in a Basque kitchen to listen. At the end of a whole year he had learned two words in Basque, "yes ma'm."

Language aside, the devil or anyone else might learn fabulous things in a Basque kitchen, for the Basques are reputedly Spain's best cooks. Not stingy with their expertise, these people have spread their talents throughout Spain. There are probably more Basque restaurants in other provinces of Spain than any other one kind. They're also prolific cookbook writers, both in Basque and the more readable Spanish.

Two factors condition life in the Basque country — sea and mountain. Located in the corner of the Bay of Biscay, where Spain curves around to meet France, and straddling the Pyrenees, there are said to be actually seven Basque provinces, four Spanish — Vizcaya, Guipuzcoa, Alava and Navarra — and three French — Laburdi, Zuberoa and Benabar — an enclave protected by sea and mountain which ignores national borders. Culinary boundaries are even less distinct: Alava, not on the sea, seems more akin to the Rioja region, and Navarra, gastronomically, is closer to Aragon.

The Basques take their cooking and eating seriously. A *tripasais* is one who looks after his belly, a gourmand and a gourmet. They are members of cooking societies, open only to men, where kitchen facilities and well-stocked pantry invite fine cooking. This gourmet tradition may explain why it's particularly young Basque chefs who are in the forefront of Spain's "nouvelle" cuisine.

Apalaurreaudiak is lunch and it might include those famous dishes *txangurro,* a crab casserole, or *kokotxas,* a morsel of flesh from the jawbone of the hake, sautéed with onion and garlic, or *txitxardiñak,* baby eels sizzled with garlic. Other great seafood dishes are *marmitako,* a casserole of fresh tuna and potatoes; *bacalao al pil pil,* salt cod cooked with garlic; *merluza a la vasca,* hake in a green sauce; *chipirones en su tinta,* cuttlefish in its own ink sauce; and *besugo a la donostiarra,* bream grilled on a charcoal fire by street vendors on fiesta days. Also clams, mussels, oysters, lobster and even *percebes,* an edible and much appreciated sea barnacle.

Back on the mountain. Meat is excellent and the *chuletas de buey,* beef chops, are famous, each weighing more than a half-kilo! There's good lamb and good game. Quail wrapped in grape leaves is a speciality. *Setas a la kashera* are sautéed wild mushrooms. There are many good egg dishes, including *piparrada,* an omelette with tomatoes and peppers. The Basque *cocido* is cooked in three pots — in one goes beef and chicken; in the second, red beans, ham bone and salt pork, and in the third, cabbage, chorizo and sausages. There are good cheeses in this region, especially the smoky *Idiazábal.* The local wine, *chacolí* is a light, tangy white wine. The flavour is attributed to vineyards seasoned by sea breezes and, indeed, the wine seems to perfectly match the seafood dishes.

Rioja. Hardly a touristic region, it's been off the beaten path since the days of medieval pilgrimages. Yet the names of its towns — Haro, Logroño, Cenicero, Fuenmayor — are hauntingly familiar, as well known as the names of Spain's resort towns. The connoisseur and the inveterate reader of labels know immediately what's so special about the Rioja. It is *the* wine-producing region of Spain, where the country's best table wines are made.

To look at the map, one wouldn't think the Rioja (named for the river Oja) had any claim to being called a region on its own. Tucked in between the Basque country, Navarra and Castile, the Rioja is a swath carved out of other lands by the river Ebro.

Like most good wine-producing areas, the Rioja is famed for its food. It's not delicate food, any more than the wines are delicate wines. Full-bodied is probably the best adjective for both.

The Rioja is famous for beans — red beans, white beans, green beans, they've got them all. And they do marvellous things with them. Also good are potatoes *a la riojana,* with paprika, garlic and slices of pork loin; sweet peppers, both red and green, and hot peppers, *guindillas,* used with discretion for flavouring; good hams and sausages; garlic soup; snails; *pisto,* a vegetable medley that appears in other regions, but here served with lamb or partridge, and several excellent chicken dishes.

Navarra. This historical and varied land is closely associated with the Basque provinces, though its culinary tradition is closest to neighbouring Aragon. It ranges from the deep forests, torrential rivers and green mountain meadows of the Pyrenees, a land of cattle and sheep, to the wide valleys of intensive cultivation to the south and low flatlands crossed by the Ebro and its tributaries. As ever with Spanish food, the culinary customs are determined by the products of the land.

The Navarrese are known for their gigantic appetites and digestive powers. Famous are the chorizos of Pamplona; the quality of the lamb; wild dove, partridge and quail; legumes and vegetables; trout, and the cheeses of the high mountain villages, particularly one called Roncal. Lamb chops *a la navarra* and *cochifrito,* fried lamb, are two excellent dishes. *Garbure,* a dish of pork, ham and sausages, is hardly different from a dish of the same name served in nearby Bearn (France). Other dishes worth trying are partridge in a sauce enriched with chocolate; *huevos al Roncal,* eggs fried with sausages; *trucha a la navarra,* trout wrapped in ham and fried, and *chilindrón,* a lamb dish also a speciality of Aragon.

Aragon. The ancient kingdom of Aragon, comprising the provinces of Huesca, Teruel and Zaragoza, conjures up romantic images of Roman legions, kings and queens, Moors and Christians, convents and castles. More than once it has been a decisive battleground in Spanish history — in the Roman conquest, the Christian reconquest and, more recently, during the Spanish Civil War. It stretches from the French border and the high mountains in the north almost as far south as Valencia.

The region still reminds of its past, with an often desolate landscape hardly changed since Caesar Augustus (corrupted to "Zaragoza") added Spain to the Roman empire. Shepherds in the fields. Medieval towns hung on cliffs. Narrow winding streets and surprising towers that recall the Moorish domination.

Wolves, bears and wild chamoix in the wilderness areas of Ordesa, now a national park.

The food, grave and simple, like the land seems ancient. Lamb, roasted on a wood fire; shepherds' stews whose recipes are Biblical; ham and sausages cured as they have been for centuries, fresh trout from fast-flowing mountain streams. No adornments, no refinements, just quality products, particularly fruits and vegetables, lamb and game.

The most famous dish of Aragon is *chilindrón,* lamb or chicken braised with tomatoes and peppers and garnished with strips of sweet red pepper. It's a holiday dish and no *alifara* or country outing is complete without chilindrón. *Ternasco* is baby lamb roasted on a wood fire with little more than salt, garlic and bacon fat. *Criadillas* are a speciality — lamb's testicles, blanched, soaked, cooked, sliced, batter-dipped and fried. And lamb's head, split and stuffed with pork and roasted. Another Aragon lamb dish is *esparragos montañés,* mountain "asparagus," which are really lambs' tails stewed in tomato.

Where winters can be bitter, good soups are important. Aragonese garlic soup is made with almonds and eggs. Another is flavoured with tomato, pepper and chorizo, to which quantities of bread are added, making a thick porridge which is browned in the oven. Another is *presa de predicador* — "preacher's game" — containing beef, mutton, pork, chicken and sausages.

Aragon is well-watered by rivers, most notably the Ebro and new-born streams plunging down from the Pyrenees. Besides trout, there are crayfish and eels. *Bacalao,* salt cod, is prepared in several ways, *a la baturra* and *al ajo arriero,* mule-driver's style.

Charcuterie is excellent in Aragon, which is known for its *morcilla,* black pudding, here confected with rice and pine nuts. The ham from Teruel is famous, prepared batter-dipped and fried or bathed in a tomato sauce. Hearty, winter dishes include hare and partridge and bean pottages with sausages, such as the well-flavoured *recao de Binefar.*

Sweets are, as in Andalusia, well-spiced with the Moorish flavour. Marzipan and candied fruits are festive offerings. The region also produces fine apples, cherries and peaches.

The Aragonese wines of Cariñena are among Spain's strongest. Almost black in colour, the red wines go nicely with the region's hearty, simple foods.

Cantabria. Verdant meadows, rolling hills, pastures where cows graze and an

extensive coastline make this region, also called La Montaña, not unlike its neighbours, Asturias and the Basque lands. The food is not as sophisticated as the Basque, more subtle than the Asturian, and much more complex than the austere cuisine of Castile.

Inland, deep valleys, rivers and mountains where deer and bear are not uncommon, separate one village from another. A rich and varied agriculture, plus the riches of the sea, make this a land of wonderful eating.

Seafood is exalted. This is real *merluza* country. This fish, the hake, mild of flavour and flaky of texture, is one of the best-loved all over Spain. Here it is featured in many ways. There's also an exquisite variety of other fish, plus trout and salmon, dairy products, chicken, game and pork. An extraordinarily varied cuisine.

Rabas are breaded bits of squid, crisply fried; *sorroputún* is a tuna casserole; *cabracho al ajillo,* scorpion fish or rascasse cooked with garlic; *almejas a la marinera,* clams, fisherman's style; *pollo a la campurriana,* chicken with rice and white wine; *habas a la montañesa,* broad beans flavoured with thyme, and *arroz santanderino,* rice with salmon. Best known of several cheeses is Pasiego, from the valley of Pas, a milder version of Cabrales-type blue cheese.

Galicia. Tucked away in the topmost corner of Spain, the four provinces of Galicia — Lugo, La Coruña, Orense and Pontevedra — seem hardly related to the rest of the country at all, at least not to the picture-postcard image most foreigners have of Spain. Once called Finisterre, the end of the world, beyond which roared the winds of the unknown, Galicia is a region hardly touched by the Moorish influence which flavours much of the peninsula and its cooking.

This is a region of lush green pastures and grey-stone towns, of fat livestock, cold trout rivers, pine-clad hills, witchcraft, bagpipes and lashing Atlantic storms. Deep estuaries, or *rías,* provide sheltered inlets for fishing fleets and small populations. Provincial boundaries are only an administrative convenience; because of the irregular terrain, Galicia actually divides itself into small districts, many very isolated.

The cooking of Galicia, too, is different from that of the rest of Spain. This is not a Mediterranean country. The sombreness of its people and the baroque splendour of some of the dishes as well as the architecture reflect another world. Galicia is, of course, Spain's very first "tourist" centre: way back in the Middle Ages Santiago de Compostela, the shrine of St. James, was a pilgrimage destination almost as important as Rome and Jerusalem. The *vieira,* or sea scallop, to this day a much appreciated dish in Galicia, is also called the *concha peregrina,* or pilgrim's shell. Considered a symbol of St. James, the shells were collected by pilgrims.

Well-watered pastures mean excellent meat and dairy produce. In Galicia, butter and lard are used much more extensively than oil in cooking. Rye flour, cornmeal and wholewheat breads were used extensively in Galicia, though modern agriculture and milling has finally begun to make inroads on what was once a very local cuisine. Cool season vegetables (Galician summers are pleasantly cool) such as carrots, turnips and cabbages appear in many dishes. Game is superb — partridge, pheasant, quail, duck, gamehen, hare, rabbit, roe deer, boar. Specialities are partridge pie, partridge and cabbage, duck with chestnuts, marinated boar steaks.

Seafood of all kinds and shellfish in particular come from Galician coasts and fjords. The oysters of Arcade, dipped in cornmeal and crisply fried, and the scallops of Vigo are famous. Sardines are grilled on iron spikes over grape-vine prunings and served with *cachelos,* jacket potatoes. *Caldeirada* is a fish stew and *sopa de ostras* is oyster soup.

The famous Galician threesome from the land are *lacón con grelos, pote gallego* and *caldo gallego.* Lacon is cured pork hand or shoulder; grelos are a bitter turnip green, said to counteract nicely the fattiness of the pork. To concoct the dish one also needs a pig's ear, potatoes and Galician chorizo. The pote contains white beans, beef or pork bone, chorizo, morcilla, potatoes and greens. The caldo, a thick soup, is similar.

Picnics, fiesta days and hunting expeditions in Galicia call for another speciality, the *empanada,* a pastry which is a cross between a sandwich, a pizza and a pot pie. The pastry is a yeast dough and the filling can be sliced pork loin, chicken or fish in a thick tomato sauce. Cut into wedges, the empanada can be eaten out of hand.

Old Castile and Leon. The ancient kingdoms of Old Castile and Leon have many claims to fame, historically and touristically. This is truly the land of castles in Spain, the birthplace of kings and saints and great warriors, the home of the Castilian — Spanish — language. The provinces of the region — Avila, Segovia, Valladolid, Palencia, Burgos, Soria, Leon, Zamora and Salamanca — share a virtual treasure-trove of Spanish monuments, landmarks and art.

For the casual tourist with limited time, the memory of St. Teresa's birthplace in Avila, El Cid's birthplace in Burgos, the fabulous gardens of La Granja or the wondrous stained glass windows of the Leon cathedral may blur with time. But no one on this cook's tour is likely to forget the experience of eating roast suckling pig, fragrant and crackling from the big ovens, in the shadow of the great Roman aqueduct, at one of the famous *mesones of Segovia.*

Most of the region is a high plain where, contrary to the lines of the song, the rain in Spain doesn't fall. It can be an austere and bleak land, with a severe climate that makes for robust foods. This is also called *tierra de pan,* Spain's breadbasket, for the vast stretches of wheatfields which produce much of the country's grains.

Avila, called the "roof of Castile," is the highest provincial capital in Spain. A sportsmen's paradise, all kinds of game are found here, including the ibex or wild mountain goat. It is a land of severe winters and an almost medieval cuisine that suits its great walled city. Burgos provides a contrast between fertile valleys and high plateaux. *Chacinería,* the curing of meats, is important here as in other cold climates. Palencia, dotted with monasteries on the old pilgrim route, is also known for pork products as well as trout and fresh-water crayfish. Soria, where the River Duero is born, is more pastoral. Valladolid, where Columbus died and where Cervantes' home is preserved as a museum, is a land of excellent wines, game and trout. Segovia, represents the classic Castilian cuisine with the emphasis on roast meats. Leon, once capital of Christian Spain, presents strong contrasts in landscape, from intensely cultivated fields to mining country to pastureland to wheatfields to trout streams to craggy peaks where wild ibex roam. Salamanca, ancient Roman city with Spain's oldest university, is surrounded by ranchland supporting excellent livestock. Zamora, with medieval castles patrolling the Portuguese border, is frontier land — and *garbanzo* country.

These provinces are all known as the *zona de los asados,* the region of roasts. Baby pig, called *cochinillo* or *tostón,* and baby lamb are the specialities. Split in half, they are basted with lard and roasted in huge brick ovens. Tender and succulent, such a meal is a memorable experience and would serve to put Castile on the touristic map even if no castles or cathedrals existed.

Not all pigs of Castile wind up in the oven at the tender age of three weeks. Many are fattened into tasty specimens and grow up to be the hams and sausages for which the region is famous. These pork products find their way into numerous dishes of the region, such as the *hornazo de Salamanca,* a flaky pastry filled with chorizo, roast meat and chopped egg.

Trout, from the Rio Tormes and other fast-flowing cold rivers, may be prepared simply wrapped in ham and grilled. Fresh-water crayfish, *cangrejos de río,* are featured in soups and team up with an unusual partner, lamb, in *sopa burgalesa,* speciality of Burgos. All manner of game is taken in the area and dishes such as *pichones a la abulense,* pigeons Avila style, and partridges stewed with vegetables, herbs and salt pork, are famous.

Other dishes of note are *ajo arriero,* mule drivers' style, which originated in the *posadas,* the "truck stops" of the old world, and is served with eggs, vegetables or codfish; lentils cooked with chorizo; *menestra de cordero a la leonesa,* a lamb stew; chicken in *pepitoria,* a sauce of ground almonds, and *arroz a la zamorana,* a Spanish rice dish without a trace of saffron!

Catalonia. Once a proud kingdom that extended into part of France, Catalonia today is an autonomous region with its own language and dynamic traditions. A seafaring nation, Catalonia has gathered from all over the world an eclectic mix of style. It is, to pardon the culinary pun, the melting pot of Spain. There are pastas from Italy, rice dishes from Valencia, hearty country food from neighbouring Aragon, saffron-hued fish soups straight out of Provence. Catalonia assimilates it all, superimposing the contributions of other cultures on a very ancient culinary tradition. Catalans are extraordinarily proud of their cuisine, claiming it as the best in the country. And, with the sole exception of the Basques, they may well be right.

As far back as 1477, Ruperto de Nola wrote Spain's first cookbook — in Catalan — introducing Italian culinary style to the nobility, for the Italians were the culinary masters of the era. By the 19th century, Barcelona was known for its restaurants and hostelry, some of the best of which were French and Italian. The versatile Catalans adapted these "foreign" dishes to their own inimitable culture and dishes such as *canelones* today are not at all Italian, but truly Catalan.

Five sauces form the basis of many Catalan dishes: the *sofrito, samfaina, picada, alioli* and *romesco*. The "sofrito" is a tomato sauce flavoured with onions and garlic; the "samfaina" calls for aubergine, peppers and zucchini as well; the "picada" is toasted almonds and hazelnuts ground to a paste with garlic and parsley; "alioli" is a garlic sauce, and "romesco," a sweet pepper sauce.

Barcelona is a great and lively city, to which people have migrated from all over, adding individuality and variations on the indigenous genius. It offers an incredible variety of eating. There's pork loin served with white beans; codfish with samfaina; mussel soup spiked with anis; partridges packaged in cabbage leaves; *zarzuela,* a medley of fish and shellfish in a well-seasoned sauce, and *escudella i carn d'olla,* the Catalan version of the cocido.

Gerona, between the heights of the Pyrenees and the ruggedly beautiful Costa Brava, is one of the richest provinces of Spain. Here you find one marvellous seafood dish after another. There is lobster in several preparations, including one combined with chicken in a herb-flavoured sauce that includes wine, anis, almonds, saffron, cinnamon and chocolate! *Suquets* is a seafood soup, not unlike bouillabaisse. Snails *patarralada* are grilled over coals and served with alioli or combined with rabbit. Gerona is famous for its poultry — chicken, ducks, turkeys and geese, many raised free-range and exceptionally flavourful. There is *rostit,* roast chicken basted with lard; duck stuffed with apples; goose stuffed with pears, and truffled turkey, Pyreneese style. Lamb is excellent and a favourite for country outings is *costellada,* lamb chops grilled on an open fire with *butifarra* sausage and served with alioli. There is game from the mountains and many good ways of preparing it.

Neighbouring Lerida, the inland province of Catalonia, is a long province with a diverse geography, stretching from the French and Andorran borders in the Pyrenees, rich with game, to the river lowlands in the south, a very productive region for agriculture and livestock. Much of the food of Lerida is simple, hearty country fare, such as the *cassolada,* a vegetable stew; rice with codfish; broad beans with snails. The region produces fine local cheeses; *xolis,* a kind of sausage, and *confitat,* seasoned pork conserved in lard.

Back to the sea coast. Tarragona, today a small provincial capital, had more than a million inhabitants in Roman days. This province is crossed by the Ebro, which reaches the sea just south of the capital. It's an area famed for its seafood. Many of the dishes are simple fishermen's preparations, such as *pataco,* a stew of tuna, potatoes, zucchini and snails; *arroz negre,* rice tinted black with inkfish; *rossejat,* rice cooked with fish and shellfish. The most famous culinary contribution of Tarragona is romesco sauce, a truly unique concoction, served with fish, chicken, meat and vegetables.

La Mancha. The name La Mancha comes from the Arabic word, Al Manchara, meaning "dry, flat land."

Toledo province most closely exemplifies the regional cooking of La Mancha; Ciudad Real edges off into Andalusia and Extremadura; Cuenca makes an abrupt transition into the Levante; Guadalajara is a throwback to a medieval civilization. Albacete, though historically part of the kingdom of Murcia, is akin to La Mancha in its cooking.

La Mancha is the mother, the source of it all — from Don Quixote's windmills to the cliff-hung houses of Cuenca to the jewel that is Toledo to the lakes and hills of Guadalajara. The regional cooking of La Mancha is, too, the mother of them all, from the country's famous garlic soups to the many variations on the *cocido*.

A land of fierce winters and searing summers, La Mancha is a harsh land, but plentiful. There are great flocks of sheep and goats following the pastures, stretches of waving wheatfields, scrub brush of rosemary and thyme, partridge nesting in arroyos. The cooking is a direct reflection of the countryside, simple, direct, often fierce, the kind of food Spaniards call *fuerte*.

A famous dish of the region is *gazpachos*. The plural distinguishes the dish from the Andalusian cold gazpacho. Also called *galianos,* this is a classic shepherd's and hunter's dish, containing several partridge and rabbits. Lacking game, in the home the dish might be made with chicken and pigeon. An almost Biblical dish, the game is fried with sliced onion, then flavoured with wine, garlic, saffron, cinnamon, rosemary, thyme. The soup is thickened with *torta,* a flat, unleavened bread baked on the hearth stone, very similar to the Hebrew matzoh. Another torta is used as spoon and, in traditional times, everyone ate gazpachos from the pot in which it cooked.

Another country dish, open to wide variation, is *tojunto,* from "*todo junto,* all together,*"* so-called because all the ingredients are put to cook at the same time. This dish is said to be invented by the ladies of Almagro so as not to be interrupted from their lace making to tend the dinner. The dish includes meat or rabbit and vegetables.

Another dish known through Spain is the *pisto manchego,* a vegetable medley of tomatoes, peppers, zucchini and aubergine, derived from the *alboronía* of the Moors, a dish still found in North Africa. Similar to the French ratatouille, the original dish incorporated the tomatoes, peppers and squash after these vegetables found their way to Spain from the New World.

Guisado de trigo, whole-wheat grains stewed with garbanzos and pig's foot and flavoured with onions and tomatoes, is a dish much appreciated in the eastern part of La Mancha and on into the Levante. *Migas* and *gachas* are staple peasant dishes throughout Spain, but most famous in La Mancha. Migas are simply dry breadcrumbs, moistened in water or milk, then fried in lard or oil with garlic, bacon and sausage. They may be served with sardines, with milk, with hot chocolate or with honey and grapes. Gachas are a thick porridge of lentil flour, cornmeal or toasted wheat flour, flavoured with garlic, salt pork, chorizo.

Other dishes of La Mancha are *morteruelo,* a sort of pâté; roast lamb; salt cod cooked with onions, tomatoes and the anis brandy which is made here; *salpicón,* cold salad of chopped, cooked meat, eggs, onion, tomatoes, peppers, parsley dressed with vinaigrette; rice, Toledo style, with chicken, mushrooms and eels; hare stewed with beans; and dozens of different partridge dishes, for La Mancha is the partridge capital of Europe. Aubergine of Almagro is flavoured with fennel; *hornazos* of Zamojón are rolls of ground lamb cooked in cabbage leaves.

Special mention must be made of the cheese, for Manchego cheese is Spain's most famous (see Chapter 2 for lots more about Spanish cheeses). Traditionally a ewes' milk cheese, cured in oil, it comes in all degrees — from fresh, soft and mild, to hard, crumbly and sharp.

La Mancha also might be called the bodega of Spain, so great is its wine production. More than three-quarters of the province of Albacete, adjacent to La Mancha, is planted in vineyards. The wines of Valdepeñas are perhaps the best known of the La Mancha wines. Like the foods, they are simple and direct, sometimes fierce.

Madrid. To talk about the cooking of Madrid is no simple matter. Unlike other regions, the cuisine of the capital is much more than a simple reflection of the produce of fields, mountains, rivers and sea.

The indigenous cooking of Madrid, to the extent that it still exists, is that of La Mancha, an area more pastoral than agricultural, rich in many kinds of game. Also native are the influences of Old Castile, the roast suckling pig and baby lamb, as natural to Madrid as to Segovia.

Had Madrid remained a peasant town on the plains of La Mancha no more need be said of its culinary heritage. But in the early 1600s it became capital of a more or less united country. Kings and queens and wealthy aristocracy lived there and, except for a few religious fanatics in the lot, demanded food fit for kings. Chefs were imported from Italy and later France. Not that the peasants or burghers of Madrid could afford kingly delicacies but, slowly, the influences seeped down. Royalty wanted fresh seafood, so runners brought it in relays from faraway coasts. To this day Madrid is famous for seafood as fresh as that of Bilbao or Cadiz. Before modern transport, Madrid had snow from the high mountains to make ices, luscious fruits from Andalusia, the finest fresh vegetables from the Levante — these were the prerogatives of kings. All roads led to Madrid, opening up the centre of the country to produce from all over. Madrid became the source and the outlet, the supply and the demand.

Another factor contributing to the cuisine of Madrid was the early importance of restaurants. A capital city attracts visitors from everywhere and there had to be services available to them, from the lowliest *fondas* for the traders to the poshest of hotels and dining rooms for wealthy travellers. The cooking of Madrid was affected early by a lively restaurant trade — almost unknown in the rest of the country outside Barcelona.

Yet another influence was the influx of people from all the provinces of Spain, seeking work, culture and trade. They brought their individual cuisines with them and, to this day, in Madrid one can eat a *fabada* as good as Oviedo's, a *gazpacho* as good as Sevilla's or a paella as good as Valencia's.

There are a few dishes famous to the capital itself. Certainly top on that list would be the *cocido madrileño.* Though known throughout Spain with variations, Madrid's version is considered classic. Once a dish of only the wealthy, it later became daily fare of the working people. In these modern days it is fast disappearing, being both too expensive and too time-consuming for every day.

Callos a la madrileña, stewed veal tripe, is a speciality of Madrid's *tascas,* bars where food is served with a *copa* of wine; garlic soup; roast suckling pig; *judias blancas a lo tío Lucas,* white beans; *tortilla capuchina,* an omelette; asparagus from Aranjuez, anis brandy from Chinchón.

Extremadura. Land of the *conquistadores,* this is the "far west" of Spain, on the Portuguese border, an almost forgotten land of rolling plains and wide open spaces, thick forests of cork-oaks and chestnuts, fertile valleys and hillsides planted in olives and vineyards. It is a land of strong contrasts and few resources.

The basic dishes of the land present a similar contrast — simple food of shepherds and peasants contrasted with the resplendent and rich compositions of monasteries with a rich medieval tradition of good eating.

Some of these dishes have been preserved, all with French names — *à la mode d'Alcantara* — by the great French chef, Auguste Escoffier. During the Napoleonic wars, the Benedictine monastery of Alcantara was sacked in 1807 by French troops on their way to Portugal. A cookbook manuscript was salvaged by General Junot, who sent it to his wife. This cookbook contained many extraordinary recipes, today considered *haute cuisine,* such as truffled pheasant and partridge with the breast bone removed, stuffed with duck liver pâté to which are added truffles cooked in Port. After marinating three days in Port wine, the bird is cooked and served with more truffles. Escoffier is said to have pronounced this cookbook the only justification for the Napoleonic wars.

Where, indeed, were those monks getting the truffles? Well, they are a speciality of Extremadura. Called *criadillas de tierra,* "earth balls," they're chopped, sautéed with garlic and finished off with a brown sauce thickened with egg yolk.

Most of the dishes of the region, however, are simple, country pottages based on lamb, kid and pork, game, river fish. The pig reigns supreme here. This is the home of the *cerdo ibérico,* the black Iberian pig. The rough, viper-infested terrain is said to give the hams a special flavour. Feeding on wild acorns and aromatic herbs, they grow rangy and the hams of Montanchez are as esteemed as those of Jabugo.

It's said that one of the best ways to learn the customs of a country is to partake of the local foods and wines. This can lead to some curious culinary experimentations. You've heard of the favoured sheep's eyes of North Africa, or fried beetles and ants. But have you tried lizards?

In Plasencia the *lagarto* is consumed with gusto. I have to admit to never having tried them myself, but a culinary writer of some repute, Luis Antonio de Vega, tells of encountering in Extremadura a local man returning from the fields with a pole from which dangled a dozen or so lizards. The following day in the market he saw various women with tubs of water filled with a skinned, white-fleshed creature, which in no way could be confused with any kind of fish. The inveterate gourmet could hardly resist. He bought them and, on the advice of the lizard-vendor, took them to a nearby *taberna* to have them cooked. Then he invited his friends for lunch. The lizards came in a green sauce, lavish with parsley, and everyone declared the dish excellent. De Vega described the flavour of the lizard as somewhere between that of wild rabbit and frogs' legs. Another writer said lizard is wild and delicate at the same time, with the perfume of thyme and rosemary.

Dishes of more general appeal are *caldereta,* lamb stewed in wine; potatoes, Badajoz style, cooked with pork; roast baby kid; *frite extremeña,* a lamb sauté; and partridge, rabbit and quail dishes. *Tenca,* tench, is one of the freshwater fish to be tried.

Levante. The east of Spain, or the Levante, is actually made up of two kingdoms, the Pais Valenciano, which comprises the provinces of Castellón de la Plana, Valencia and Alicante, and Murcia, which historically includes the inland province of Albacete. (Culinarily, we've placed Albacete with La Mancha.) The Levante may be better known for its holiday coastal names, the Costa Azahar and the Costa Blanca.

It's further known as the land of paella. This fabulous rice dish may be Spain's best-known culinary contribution, but it is, nevertheless, native to the Levante.

On the low, coastal regions where water is abundant, rice has been a staple food for the many centuries since the Moors introduced its cultivation. Water means fecundity, and this area known as the "market basket" of Spain produces an extraordinary range of fine produce. Of course, there are the famous Valencia oranges and also peaches, apricots, melons, grapes, grapefruit, plums, pears, cherries, apples, asparagus, olives, garlic, capers, anise, saffron, onions, mushrooms, peas, broad beans, green beans, tomatoes, lettuce, cucumber, paprika.

The flat coastal strip, almost subtropical and well irrigated, is backed by rough sierra and small valleys which have more affinity for the scrubby inland regions of La Mancha. Though water is the life-blood and consuming passion of the region, with complex irrigation systems dating from the time of the Moors, there are parts of Alicante which have an average annual rainfall lower than some regions of the Sahara desert.

Alicante offers a little of everything, from near desert to irrigated fields, the picturesque coastline of La Marina, the palm groves of Elche, inland scrubland where rabbits, turtle-doves and partridge roam and, where once were small fishing villages, some of Spain's best-known tourist resorts — Benidorm, Javea, Calpe, Denia.

The gastronomy shows the same versatility: *conill i pollastre,* a rabbit and chicken dish; dates from Elche; langostinos of Santa Pola; meat pies of Orihuela; *arroz abanda,* a rice and seafood dish; *gazpachos,* plural, similar to that of La Mancha, with dove and rabbit. And, of course, *turrón,* almond nougat from Jijona and Alicante, a must at fiestas and Christmas time.

In Valencia, besides paella, there's *fideuá,* similar to paella, but made with vermicelli noodles; *arroz rosetxat,* a rice dish with lamb; wild duck of the Albufera, and a wonderful assortment of seafood — *anguila,* freshwater eel; *llisa* or *mujol,* the grey mullet; *dentón,* dentex and *llobarro* or *lubina,* sea bass. Try *mojama,* the "ham of the ocean," salt-cured tuna, thinly sliced and served as aperitive.

Castellón boasts superb langostinos, the *robellons,* a wild mushroom the colour of ochre; *empedrado,* a dish of rice, beans and codfish.

Murcia has a strong Arabic tradition in cooking (even *cous cous* is known here) and a wealth of produce from fertile fields. Salads are a speciality of the region, including one made with wild greens and herbs, lightly blanched and dressed with oil and vinegar. The *mojete murciano* combines sweet green and red peppers, for which the area is famous, with sardines or cod. The mixture is eaten with chunks of bread instead of forks. The *pipirrana* or *rin-ran* is similar, with the addition of tomatoes, garlic and black olives. The *ensalada murciana* combines escarole, tomatoes and watercress.

Snails are as plump and delicious as those of Burgundy and are cooked with thyme, rosemary and fennel and sauced with tomato spiced with paprika, garlic, chili, cumin and mint. The *tortilla murciana* is an omelette with tomatoes, peppers, zucchini, aubergine and ham. *Menestra,* like a miniature vegetable garden, is a stew which includes much of the land's produce in one pot. Another speciality is the *olla gitana,* gypsy pot, which besides vegetables includes fruit. It probably originated on the wayfarer's route as the cook plucked a pumpkin from one field, some tomatoes from another and pears from a nearby orchard, and can be freely varied to suit the available ingredients.

Dorada a la sal, a dish also appreciated on other coastlines, is a whole fish covered with coarse salt and baked. The skin comes off with the hard-baked salt and the flesh is served with a sauce of garlic, parsley and oil or a garlic mayonnaise.

Murcia, is known for excellent wines of Jumilla and Yecla.

Andalusia. At Almeria, Spain turns a corner. This is the south of Spain, fabled Andalusia, the romantic, storybook image of Spain. Dark eyes and flamenco flounces; gypsies and bullfights; dazzling white, jewel-like villages; flowered patios and Moorish palaces; golden beaches, azure water; wide rivers and dusty hillsides. An enormous region, Andalusia includes a lot of Spain. Here are the peninsular's highest mountains, the snow-capped Sierra Nevada above Granada; the golden beaches of the Costa del Sol, where thousands of holidaymakers throng; olive trees, citrus groves and avocado plantations; the bodegas of Jerez, where the world-famous Sherry is made; Roman temples, Arabic mosques and Gothic cathedrals.

Andalusian food, like the culture, can be as subtle and refined as a cool *fino* served in the shade of a grape arbour, as brash and noisy as a *tapa* bar in the evening, as passionate as a red carnation, as simple and direct as the aroma of bread baking in wood-fired ovens. It is a far-ranging cuisine that takes in sardines grilled on spits over a driftwood fire on the beach to hams cured in the high mountains to partridge cooked in Malaga wine to spicy, Moroccan-style *pinchitos* or kebabs to the latest "nouvelle" creation for an international, sophisticated clientele which knows nothing of Spanish food.

Best known to foreigners is the Costa del Sol, which stretches from Almeria through the coasts of Granada, Malaga and into Cadiz as far as Gibraltar.

Almeria is the most arid region of Andalusia. Here some areas are so dry and barren they look like a moonscape. Where there is water, there are lush fields with a year-round growing season which provides Spain and Europe with mid-winter tomatoes and other vegetables. There is good seafood here and wheat dishes similar to those of Murcia and Albacete.

Granada is a lush paradise blessed with just about everything — a beautiful stretch of coastline, the highest mountain peak in mainland Spain, irrigated fields, rolling hills where olive trees thrive, wheatfields and that most special of cities, Granada, with its languorous memory of Moorish kings.

Mountain hams flavour many local dishes, such as *habas con jamón,* broad beans stewed with ham, and *pollo granadina,* chicken cooked with wine and ham. Another famous dish is the *tortilla Sacromonte,* created at the monastery in the Sacromonte gypsy district. *Choto al ajillo* is baby kid braised in wine with lots of garlic.

Málaga, thriving port city of palm-lined avenues, is the gateway to the Costa del Sol. This is also the home of Málaga wines, sweet nectar of the moscatel grape which contains a year of sunshine in a sip. Cooks add it to sweets and to dishes such as partridge and chicken. *Fritura malagueña* is a mixed fish fry, which usually includes fresh anchovies, rings of squid and a slice of a larger fish, all fried to crispy perfection, Excellent seafood soups include *sopa viña AB,* spiked with sherry, and *sopa de rape,* angler-fish soup tinted with saffron.

Cadiz province is Costa del Sol until it rounds the bend of Gibraltar and the Mediterranean becomes the Atlantic. Here is the southernmost point of Europe, the peninsula of Tarifa, that seems closer to North African villages just across the Straits than it does to many places in Spain. Cadiz, the capital, is an ancient seafaring town on the Atlantic. Here and in the environs, seafood is fabulous — prawns, crab, clams, mussels, oysters, lobster and fish of many kinds. Specialities are *abajá de pescado,* a fish stew; *lisa en amarillo,* saffron-tinted mullet; a "dog" soup, *caldillo de perro,* flavoured with bitter oranges, and a "cat" soup, *sopa de gato.* Not far away is the elegant town of Jerez de la Frontera, where sherry is made. The local cuisine is well-flavoured with this flavourful brew: *riñones al Jerez,* kidneys in sherry sauce; *rabo de toro al jerez,* oxtail (or bull's tail, as this is also the region where fighting bulls are raised) braised in sherry.

Huelva is mountains and coast. Famous for its ham of Jabugo, it's also known for excellent seafood. *Atún con tomate* is fresh tuna cooked in tomato; *pez espada* is swordfish, grilled or served in a saffron sauce; *chocos* are tiny squid, which may be cooked with broad beans; *merluza al vino blanco* is hake in a white wine sauce.

Seville, cosmopolitan heart of Andalusia, is magic. From the banks of the Guadalquivir to a tavern in the old barrio to the great cathedral to the promenades of the spring *feria,* where men wearing the handsome *traje corto,* bolero-topped riding breeches, and women in colourful ruffled dresses parade on prancing horses. Seville can somehow bring together the Gothic, the baroque, the rococo and the romantic, the ancient and the modern — and get away with it.

So, too, with the food. The Moorish influence, strong all over Andalusia, is noted here in the sweets and confections, such as *yemas,* candied eggs. Many of these delicacies are made in convents from recipes little changed for centuries. Special mention should be made of the olives of Seville, the plump Manzanillas, so appreciated the world over. They're enjoyed with aperitif wine, in salads, and go into other dishes such as *pato a la sevillana,* duck with olives. Local dishes include *huevas,* fish roe crisply fried; *huevos de codorniz,* quails' eggs, and *huevos a la flamenca,* a very baroque dish of baked eggs garnished with asparagus, peas, pimento and chorizo. *Callos a la andaluza,* savoury veal tripe, is a tapa bar speciality. Other meat dishes are *rollo de ternera,* veal stuffed with ham and braised in wine, and *solomillo de cerdo a la trianera,* pork fillet roasted with sherry.

Cordoba, once seat of the Moorish kingdom which ruled Andalusia, is all that is exquisite about this region. Surrounded by legions of olive trees, it is hot and heavy with jasmine in the summer, cool and airy in the Great Mosque with its candy-striped columns, ponderous with the memory of great philosophers, poets and emirs who once lived here when Cordoba was the cultural centre of the whole western world while the rest of Europe lived in the dark ages.

There are fine wines of Montilla and Moriles, made by the *solera* process, similar to sherry. From the rocky foothills of the Sierra Morena comes an amazing variety of game — venison, partridge, rabbit, boar. Such dishes as *conejo en salmorejo,* rabbit cooked in a marinade, and *pichones con aceitunas,* pigeons cooked with olives, are typical. A grazing region, Cordoba features excellent lamb and kid dishes such as *caldereta de cordero,* a lamb stew. The Cordobeses have a way with vegetables, and artichokes, spinach, asparagus and beans are all treated with imagination.

Jaen, crossroads between Andalusia and Castile, sits with immense solemnity on the slopes of the Sierra Morena. The city has a decidedly Moorish flavour, with narrow streets that wind up to the Castillo de Santa Catalina at the very top. Vast stretches of the province are covered with row upon row of olive trees, ancient, gnarled sculptures against a stark blue sky. Wheatfields and rugged hills, grazing lands, and towns full of renaissance mansions, Jaen is a surprising land. *Ajoharina* is a delicious way of preparing potatoes; *andrajos,* literally "rags," is a game dish with squares of pasta; walnuts are served in a cream sauce in Baeza; *pipirrana* is a concoction between a tomato salad and gazpacho, here garnished with the local ham.

Balearic Islands. Islands are curious. Isolated from the mainstreams of continental culture, yet, as in the case of the Balearics, positioned to receive a confluence of influences, they are unique. The cuisine is all its own, but with flavours reminiscent of other places.

The island of Mallorca lies little more than 100 miles from the Spanish mainland, yet it isn't quite Spanish. It's a blend of ancient myth, fantasy paradise and crazy tourist industry.

The people and language are most akin to Catalonia, and so, too, are most of the dishes. But Italy and France are not so far away and their culinary influences are also apparent. Even before that, the Greeks (Hercules was said to have discovered the Golden Apples in Mallorca), the Romans, the Moors and the Barbary pirates made their way through Mallorcan history and left their imprint on the land and its customs.

The most recent invasion is, of course, by tourists arriving via charter jets. Palma and environs have sprouted with French, Italian and English restaurants to such an extent that the truly local cuisine is being lost.

Two Mallorcan specialities best known all over Spain are *sobrasada* and *ensaimada.* Sobrasada is a soft sausage of pork well-flavoured with sweet and hot peppers. The ensaimada is a sweet bread, traditionally made with *saim,* lard, and baked in spirals from the size of an ordinary bun to wagon-wheel dimensions. Pork has always been the primary meat in Mallorca and the charcuterie is justifiably famous. Baby pigs roasted in big ovens were, in the old style, stuffed with a farce of liver, heart, breadcrumbs, apples and prunes.

Mallorca has a special claim to fame when it comes to soups. Besides the usual liquid kinds, there are "dry" soups. These are basic peasant fare, morning, noon and night and, besides vegetables, contain bread, once made of wholewheat flour. There are also some fine liquid soups, *sopa de pescado,* a sister to bouillabaisse, and *sopa de cangrejos,* a seafood bisque.

Empanadas, pastry with savoury fillings, not unlike pizza, are famous in three areas of Spain: Galicia, Murcia... and Mallorca. The Balearic version is filled with pork or lamb cooked with onions and spices and sobrasada. Though paella is quite at home in Mallorca, the natives prefer their rice dishes soupier and highly flavoured with saffron, as in the typical *arroz con pollo,* a chicken, rice and vegetable casserole. Seafood is excellent on the island. Some curious local specialities are tuna with garbanzos, squid stuffed with raisins and aubergine stuffed with fish. *Tumbet* is a casserole of aubergine and potatoes with either meat or fish.

The islands of the Baleares share similar foods, but Menorca has historical differences which make it unique. For nearly 80 years Menorca was ruled by the

British (and, for a few years, by the French), who left a mark on the island's cuisine. For instance, Menorca still produces excellent English gin, English puddings and jams. Stuffed turkey is very reminiscent of English yuletide feasts and *maccarons con grevi* is macaroni with "gravy." It's made with the excellent local cheese, Mahon.

It's an old culinary quibble, but there are those who maintain that the famous sauce mayonnaise was invented in Mahon on the island of Menorca. It was supposedly discovered there in 1756 by the Duke of Richelieu, chief of the French invading forces, who either first ate it served by a lowly innkeeper or, possibly, by an illustrious Menorca lady who delighted the duke with the sauce as well as other things. He later popularized the sauce in Paris, calling it *sauce mahonnaise.*

Though it probably originated long before the Duke of Richelieu, it doesn't seem at all unlikely that mayonnaise was a Spanish invention, if not Menorcan. To this day it is the one "French" sauce most thoroughly at home in Spain, a basic preparation known even in the simplest of kitchens. Whatever its origin, mayonnaise or mahonnaise is a lovely accompaniment to many foods in Spain.

Ibiza, smallest of the three main islands, has nearly lost its indigenous cuisine in the influx of tourism. *Burrida de ratjada* is ray fish in a sauce of garlic, almonds and egg; *langosta a la ibicenca* is lobster served with stuffed squid and *escupiñas,* a local shellfish; *sofrit pag'es* is a stew of chicken, lamb, salt pork, sobrasada and potatoes.

Canary Islands. The Canary Islands add a very exotic touch to the repertoire of Spanish cuisine. Located more than 500 miles from the European mainland, but only 70 miles from the coast of northwest Africa, the Canaries are said to be part of the lost Atlantis. The seven volcanic islands have a climate so mild that one can bathe in the sea in mid-winter, making them a favourite tourist destination.

Perpetual springtime also means produce unlike that of the rest of Spain. Besides bananas which thrive here, tropical fruits such as mangoes, guavas, papayas, loquats, avocados, melons and yams are also grown.

According to the *conquistadores,* who made these islands a jumping-off point for travels to the New World, the original people of the Canaries, the Guanches, were a simple race, strong people who lived on a mainly vegetarian diet of wild fruits and roots, a native barley which they ground into flour, some fish, milk from goats and, occasionally, goat meat which apparently was consumed raw.

The native barley was ground into a meal, *gofio,* and eaten as a sort of bread. The arrival of the Spaniards, who took over the islands in the 15th century, changed things considerably. The Spaniards brought from Europe everything from wheat to oranges and from the New World, everything from corn to tomatoes. Wheat and corn, first toasted, them ground, became the gofio, which country people carried to the fields in a goatskin and kneaded with water to make a doughy ball of bread. It is also eaten as a porridge, *escaldón;* or fried, *fritangos,* or sweetened as a pudding, *frangollo.*

Seafood is notably good in the Canaries, including some varieties peculiar to the area: *sama,* a type of sea bass, *vieja* and *burro.* A typical dish is *mojo palmero,* boiled fish with sauce. *Mojo colorado* is made with chili and paprika; *mojo verde* is made with coriander.

Frijoles con arroz, black beans and rice, is much like a Cuban dish and *puchero canario,* with beef, squash, corn and yams, might be straight from Argentina. Besides being shipped to Europe, bananas make a creamy sauce for roast chicken or cinnamon-flavoured fried cakes.

CHAPTER 2

At the Market

What impressed me about Spanish food when I first came here to live was the freshness of it — the immediate reality of fish just hours from the sea, eggs still warm from the hen, milk from the neighbour's goat, tomatoes fragrant from the vine, oranges I picked myself. Yes, even the meat — the pork chops that an hour before I watched go squealing and grunting into the butcher's back patio.

There was oil from the trees that grew all around; wine from nearby vineyards; cheese made at a local farm; flour stoneground by a water-powered mill and the bread baked just around the corner. Few village housewives owned a can opener because there were almost no tinned products available. The shopkeeper would open the occasional tin of tuna or sardines for his customers. There were no refrigerated trucks, no freezers, no ice, no preservatives. Food in an Andalusian pueblo was very immediate.

Then, as now, the market is the best place to really appreciate the flavour of Spanish food. Bustling housewives, straw baskets in hand, throng the counters heaped with glittering fish, looking for the day's best buy. Above the butchers' stalls hang freshly killed rabbits, chickens and partridges. There are wire baskets heaped with fresh country eggs and bowls of paprika-flavoured lard to spread on bread. Great slabs of beef share space with miniscule baby lamb chops.

The changing cornucopia of fruit and vegetable stalls is a cook's inspiration — ropes of garlic bulbs, branches of bay leaves, strands of dusky dried chilies, vats of seasoned olives and string bags of nuts and dried fruits form a backdrop for the array of glistening fresh produce. The variety of fruits and vegetables available is astounding. Many markets also have a stall where spices and herbs are sold. From these treasure chests the vendor scoops bits of pepper, cloves, cinnamon, allspice, aniseed, cumin and saffron, and herbs from the mountains, both culinary and medicinal.

In some markets you will also find a knife sharpener, flower sellers, stalls offering dry fruit and nuts, bread dispensary, toy shop, *ultramarinos* (literally, imports; usually means tinned foods), stalls selling nothing but frozen foods and others displaying exclusively cheeses and charcuterie. Near the entrance to the market there may be a wizened old lady selling sprigs of parsley or mint, a country man with bunches of wild asparagus or other wild greens, a vendor with a net bag full of snails, a gypsy selling brass mortars and ornaments and another with bunches of wild camomile and other herbs. The Spanish market is nothing if not lively and varied.

Besides the municipal markets, every town has neighbourhood *tiendas,* small shops where you can purchase staples, some fresh produce, usually milk, yoghurts, cheese, ham and sausages, household cleaning products, a few kinds of wine, and all but the tiniest villages usually have a *supermercado* or an *hipermercado* which will have, besides staples, fresh produce, meat and charcuterie, sometimes seafood as well, frozen foods, wines and liquors, dairy produce and much more. The largest of them, especially in big cities and those catering to the up-market, will have many speciality items as well, everything from imported caviar to English mustard powder to Chinese sesame oil to Scottish kippers to Indian relishes to rice wine with a lizard in the bottle...and more.

Following is a bi-lingual marketing list of many of the foods you can expect to find in markets and shops in Spain.

FRUITS, VEGETABLES AND LEGUMES

Fresh produce is still a seasonal proposition, though modern transport and storage have made more out-of-season vegetables and fruits available to a wider market throughout Spain. In the following list, I've tried to give an idea of seasons, though this will vary throughout the country, with produce maturing much earlier in the south and later in the northern extremes. Produce at the height of its season in your own region will be the least expensive.

Most produce sold in the markets is graded for size and quality, from *extra* to *primera,* first, to *segunda,* second. Price will vary by grade (as well as by region of the country and from one town to the next). Look for labels on packing crates or on price markers indicating grade and variety. Use less expensive grades for fruit *macedonia,* vegetable stews.

FRUITS

Apple *(manzana).* Quite a few varieties, available year round. New crop starts coming in mid-summer through early fall. Store apples in refrigerator crisper or in cool, dark place. Many brands of unsweetened apple juice are available.

Apricot *(albaricoque).* My idea of paradise is to have a prolific apricot tree in the garden. This luscious fruit, of which there are many varieties, provides pop-in-the-mouth eating, wonderful compotes, conserves and jams, purées and elegant desserts. Apricots must be tree-ripened. Once harvested or purchased, keep them refrigerated and consume or conserve promptly — they don't keep well nor travel well. Available early summer through July. Some varieties are especially sweet and are best for eating. Others are tart, best for jam and cooked desserts. Taste before you buy in quantity. Apricots needn't be peeled, but if you wish to, dip them in boiling water briefly and skins will slip off. Dried apricots are *albaricoques secos,* also called *orejones.* Soak them in warm water for two hours. Apricot juice is usually sweetened, in which case it's labelled *nectar de albaricoque.*

Avocado *(aguacate).* Though a native of the New World, the avocado has become naturalized in southern Spain, where great plantations of this fruit are grown. Most varieties mature through the winter months, but there are usually avocados available year round. It is most appreciated for its buttery texture and nutty flavour that combine so well with seafoods and salads. Both the smooth green-skinned and dark rough-skinned avocados are available. Buy them firm and underripe and mature them, wrapped in paper or in a bag, in a slightly warm location. To test for ripeness, squeeze very gently in the palm of the hand — the flesh should feel soft. Store ripe avocados in the refrigerator. To prepare avocados for use, halve them lengthwise, twist gently to separate halves. Whack a sharp knife directly into the large seed and twist to lift it out. Avocados discolour quickly. Sprinkle cut fruit with lemon juice. To keep half an avocado, leave the pit in, sprinkle with lemon juice, cover with plastic wrap and refrigerate.

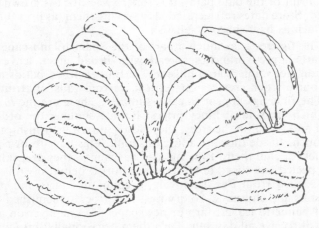

Banana *(plátano).* The bulk of the banana crop comes from the tropical Canary Islands, where this favourite fruit grows very sweet, though some are grown in southern Spain, both for the decorative fronds and the fruit. Ripen them in a bag. Use green ones fried or diced and cooked. Available all year round, so buy only what can be used within a few days of ripening. Refrigeration causes skins to blacken.

Blackberry *(zarzamora)*. Not often found in the markets, these berries grow wild in many parts of Spain, but are best in cold-weather regions where the brambly bushes get plenty of moisture. Good for jam making, tarts.

Blueberry *(arándano)*. Seldom found fresh, jams are available.

Cherimoya *(chirimoya)*. Green, pear-shaped and faceted, this fruit looks a little like an over-sized hand grenade. Inside the flesh is white with shiny, black seeds randomly distributed throughout. It tastes like a creamy, lemon pudding and has become a favourite with creative cooks for mousses, ices and puddings. It is quite delicious just spooned from the shell. Buy it underripe and firm, eat when it's soft to the touch. The cherimoya, also called custard apple, is available in the markets in late fall, early winter.

Cherry *(cereza, guinda, picota)*. Different varieties carry different names. They vary from the deep red, almost black cherries to those that are yellow-orange, and in taste from very sweet to very sharp. Their season is early summer. Buy ripe, unblemished cherries and store them refrigerated. At a *ferretería*, hardware store, you can buy a pitter, useful for cherries, olives and other fruits with small stones. Candied cherries are *cerezas confitadas*, normally available around the Christmas season.

Coconut *(coco)*. Sold with nougat and candied fruits at *feria stalls*. Grated coconut, *coco rallado*, can be purchased in supermarkets. To make coconut milk, pour boiling water onto grated coconut, let set for two hours and strain. The resulting liquid is coconut milk.

Currant *(grosella)*. Used for jams and juice. A delicious juice, the colour of red wine, is *grosella con uva*, currant and grape. Blackcurrants are used to make the appreciated cassis liqueur. Dried white currants — or Corinth raisins — are called *pasas de corinto*.

Date *(dátil)*. Fruit of the date palm, this super-sweet fruit is grown in Spain and also imported. Store dates refrigerated. Try serving them, as hors d'oeuvres, with salty foods such as ham, bacon, salt fish.

Fig *(higo)*. The fig tree is as much a part of the Spanish landscape as the olive. Ancient, gnarled, grey branches spread with broad green leaves, it appears everywhere, on steep unirrigated hillsides, in tiny enclosed patios and growing, impossibly, out of rock crevices on vertical canyon walls. Its fruit is bountiful and sweet. The first figs appear in early summer. These are the *brevas*, plump, black figs which are sold at fancy prices. By late summer the ordinary variety ripens. Hard and green on the trees, they slowly turn a brownish-purple and are soft to the touch. Inside they are a luscious pink. Figs have to be ripened on the tree. Once picked, chill them. Ripe figs can be eaten as they are, skin and all. Or they may be peeled and sliced to be served as hors d'oeuvres (with serrano ham) or dessert. Cooked fresh figs are lovely in compotes, tarts and puddings and make good jams and chutneys. To dry figs, pick ripe, unblemished fruit. Spread on a layer of palmetto leaves, tarp or newspapers in one layer on a flat surface where they will receive all day sun. Turn them occasionally, bringing indoors in case of heavy dew, and discard any rotting or bug-infested ones. When fully dry, the figs are packed into baskets called *serretes*, sewn tightly closed and taken to the fig press. The pressing protects the fruit against bug and worm infestation. Small quantities, to be used within a few months, can simply be stored in tightly sealed containers. Soak dried figs in water to plump them or stew them for compotes.

Grapefruit *(pomelo).* Available fall through spring. Refrigerated, they keep a long time.

Grape *(uva).* The Moors wrote paeans of praise to the Spanish grape, that delectable fruit of the vine. Today's "invaders," the people of many nationalities who flock to this country to live in the sun, also enjoy the sweet nectar of Spanish grapes, sometimes plucked straight from the arbour which shades the terrace. Many varieties of grapes are grown, some specifically for the making of wines, from the sweet dessert wines of both Malaga and Jerez to the dry table wines of La Mancha, Rioja and Catalonia. Of the eating grapes, possibly the most famous is the moscatel, the Malaga grape.

Grapes come into the markets in late summer and last until New Year's Eve, when they are consumed, one at each of the chimes of midnight, to assure twelve months of good fortune in the coming year. Store them in a cool but not cold place. Grapes are sun-dried to make raisins, *uvas pasas,* so appreciated for puddings and other sweets. To plump them for serving as dessert, soak for 10 minutes in warm water and dry well. If seeding them, dust raisins, fingers and knife with flour occasionally. The leaves of the grape-vine, if not treated with pesticides can be used for *dolmades,* Middle-Eastern stuffed vine leaves.

Guava *(guayaba).* A tropical fruit grown in the Canary Islands, it is found in some supermarkets within Spain.

Kiwi. Imported from New Zealand, available in many markets.

Lemon *(limón).* This wonderfully scented fruit is essential in any kitchen, for its zest, verve and flavour, and is a favourite addition to gardens, where, besides providing ready fruit, its flowers perfume the air. Lemons are available year-round and some varieties bear fruit and flower at the same time. There are thick-skinned and thin-skinned types and some varieties come to market quite green. These are usually quite juicy and flavourful in spite of their colour. Store lemons in a cool place. Before juicing, roll the lemon on a board. Lemon juice is a potent anti-oxidant, preventing the darkening of other fruits and vegetables. It can be used in place of vinegar in any salad or sauce and, of course, is indispensable with fish and shellfish.

Lime *(lima)*. Not widely available. Substitute lemons.

Loquat *(níspero)*. A pear-shaped, plum-sized fruit of a deep yellow colour. The flesh is very sweet, slightly grainy, with a central seed. Buy them ripe. Season is late spring, early summer.

Litchis. Available in some supermarkets.

Mango *(mango)*. Another tropical fruit from the Canary Islands.

Melon *(melón)*. Many varieties of superb melons are grown in Spain, from those of pale green flesh to deep orange flesh. Sweet melons contrast nicely with salty ham or smoked salmon, so try them as hors d'oeuvres as well as dessert. Everyone has a favourite method of picking a good melon: thumping, smelling, pressing, scraping. A slight give when pressed with the thumb at the blossom end is a good indication the melon is ripe; too soft, it's overripe. In any case, to be sweet, the fruit must be vine-ripened. Cut up non-sweet melons into salads as for cucumber. Chill the melon before serving. To store melons for eating during the winter, try suspending them by string from the ceiling in a cool pantry. Watermelon is called *sandía* (not *melón de agua,* as one dictionary-toting tourist in the market called it). Some market vendors will be willing to plug the watermelon to verify its ripeness. Chill and eat a plugged or cut watermelon promptly, as once the skin is broken it starts to ferment rapidly. In many places you can buy a half or quarter of a large watermelon. Look for the tiny ones, no bigger than a regular melon.

Nut *(nuez)*. First and foremost in Spain is the almond, *almendra,* widely grown and extensively used in cooking. It's available in the shell, shelled, blanched, toasted, salted. To blanch almonds, put them into boiling water, bring again to a boil and drain. While still warm, slip the skins off them. Almonds still green on the tree are edible and often used. Crack the outer casing, then the immature shell to get at the kernel. The other best-loved nut is not actually a nut, but an underground legume — the peanut or *cacahuete.* This is favourite nibbling food everywhere in Spain and is available roasted in the shells, raw and roasted shelled. Cashews are *anacardos;* Brazil nuts are *nueces de Brasil;* walnuts are *nueces de nogal;* pecans are *nueces americanas;* hazelnuts or filberts are *avellanas;* pistachios are *pistachos.* Chestnuts, *castañas,* come into the markets in the fall and vendors sell them roasted on street corners everywhere in Spain; a warm handful on a nippy evening. *Piñones* are the kernels of pine cones with a subtle, resinous flavour much appreciated in poultry stuffings, sausages, vegetable dishes and sweets. They're very pricey, and once you've gathered your own, you'll understand why. The pine cones must first be heated till they open, then cracked to release the kernels. Then each tiny one must be cracked and the seed extracted. The *chufa,* though not a nut but a tuber, is worth mentioning here. From it is made *horchata* or orgeat, now sold bottled all over Spain. It's a sweet, milky drink (which at home can be made with almonds) with overtones of coconut. The chufa can be eaten raw.

Orange *(naranja)*. The Spanish name comes from the Sanscrit word for this beautiful fruit, *naranga,* which the Moors brought to Spain intact with the fruit. The first orange groves which proliferated in Spain during the rule of Islam (including those in the Great Mosque of Cordoba and the courtyards of the Alhambra) were bitter oranges, appreciated for their ornamental value and the aroma of the peel and blossoms. The juice was used as seasoning for meat and fish, and appears to this day as flavouring in some Spanish dishes. Portuguese travellers in the 15th century brought sweet oranges from China, and today, most eating oranges are called *chinas* in Spain. Curiously, the variety known as Valencia, the world's most popular orange, is little grown in Spain any more. Here, the navel orange, easy to peel and seedless, has become the most popular, both on the domestic market and for export.

Oranges are in season from fall through spring. My children have said oranges are magic, because they always appear in the fall in time for their first snuffly cold. We suddenly consume quantities of oranges, fresh and juiced, and feel immune to the winter's cold germs. The season goes on until spring. Though available through the summer, the quality of the oranges is not usually very good. Oranges have to be fully ripe and sweet when picked — they will never ripen further. Green splotches on the skin do not indicate an underripe orange; skin colour is affected by nighttime temperatures and very warm nights can keep a fully ripe orange green. Store them in a cool place and they will keep for about a month from the time they were picked.

You may encounter another type of orange. Called *dulce,* sweet, it is without the tang and aroma that we expect of an orange. Rather insipid in flavour, the juice is very nice mixed with the sharp juice of *fuertes,* sour oranges.

The bitter orange, *agria* or *cachoreña,* is still grown extensively ornamentally and is used as root stock for other varieties. So the bitter, Seville orange — essential for fine marmalade — is available, though seldom found in the markets.

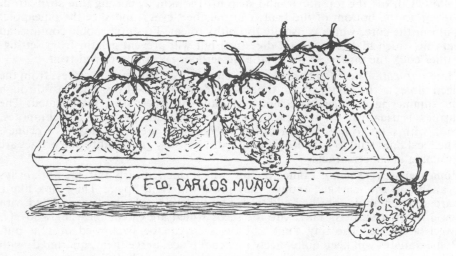

Shops carry fresh, pasteurized orange juice as well as many bottled and tinned juices, both sweetened and unsweetened. There is nothing more flavourful, though, than a tall glass of freshly-squeezed Spanish orange juice, and some quality cafés and restaurants do provide it.

A few recipes, which certainly date from Moorish days, call for orange blossom water, *agua de azahar,* available in some speciality shops.

Peach *(melocotón)*. Peaches are a fruit of full summer. There are both clingstone and freestone varieties and colours range from almost crimson to pale "peaches and cream" colour to fruit that is almost yellow. They must be tree-ripened; underripe ones will simply wither rather than sweeten and mature. Store dead-ripe peaches refrigerated. To peel peaches in quantity, dip them into boiling water and skins slip off easily. Nectarines are a smooth-skinned variety of peach, usually available before peaches come in.

Pear *(pera)*. A summer to early winter fruit which seems to be available year-round. Pears come in an enormous range of colours — green, gold, russet — and sizes, from tiny ones the size of cherries, to some as big as grapefruit. Pears are usually picked when not quite ripe. They will ripen and sweeten at room temperature. Chilling tends to brown them. Some pears store well, other varieties are very perishable.

Persimmon *(caqui)*. Looks like a small tomato when fully ripe. Grown in the south of Spain, this fruit comes into the markets in the fall. It must be allowed to mature, otherwise it's so astringent it puckers the mouth. Very soft to the touch when ripe. Eat with a spoon or use the pulp to confect sorbets, mousses and creams.

Pineapple *(piña)*. The pineapple is the star of the fruit world. Besides flavour, it has presence. Grown in the Canary Islands, pineapples are available in mainland shops particularly at holiday times such as Christmas. A ripe pineapple should have a full, musky aroma. Inside the spiny exterior, the flesh should be pale yellow. Cut off the top-notch, and strip off the skin by cutting thin strips from the top to the bottom of the fruit. Cut out the "eyes" and slice the pineapple. Cut out the core, which is usually too pithy to eat. Fresh pineapple contains an enzyme which makes it a good digestive, but will prevent gelatin from setting. Either cook the pineapple for gelatin desserts or substitute tinned fruit.

Plum *(ciruela)*. These fruit are like precious gems in their market crates, from the deep rubies to the golden topaz, the green jade to the amethyst. They last through the summer in the markets. Choose slightly soft ones; store refrigerated. The tartness is usually in the skins, with sweet flesh beneath. For jams and compotes, cook with skins to preserve flavour. *Ciruelas pasas* are dried plums, or prunes. The local ones tend to be more pit than fruit, but very good California prunes are available in supermarkets.

Pomegranate *(granada)*. Pomegranates, which ripen in early fall, are not always available in the markets, though they grow widely in Spain. They look like a hard-skinned apple, blushed with red, and tufted. Inside the fruit is filled with jewel-like red kernels. These are the seeds which are eaten, releasing a lovely, sweet-tart juice. The tiny "nut" of the seed can be swallowed or spat out. Pomegranates will keep quite nicely in a cool place. Serve them, quartered, with spoons for scooping up the juicy seeds (the juice will stain); use the seeds scattered on salads or other dishes as garnish; crush the seeds to extract the juice. Mix with other fruit juices or enjoy it plain. The juice freezes well.

Prickly pear *(chumbo)*. This prickly cactus was once planted around isolated farms as a fencing, to keep outsiders out and domestic animals in. The fruit is pear-shaped, a rosy-yellow colour, and covered with a spiny skin. It is often sold by street vendors, who peel the fruit and hand you, untouched, the pristine, juicy inside.

Quince *(membrillo)*. The quince looks like an oversized somewhat knobby yellow

apple. It's harder and grainier than an apple and, though can be eaten fresh, is most often cooked. Quince comes into season in the fall. Bake it like apples, stew it or make *dulce de membrillo,* the amber-coloured quince jelly which can be bought in most food shops. For a typical Spanish dessert plate, combine a slice of quince jelly with *queso blanco,* soft, white cheese and a few walnuts or almonds — an inspired combination.

Raspberry *(frambuesa).* This fruit, which ripens in summer, grows best in cold-winter regions, but is now available throughout the country. They are delicate fruit, bruise and spoil easily, so handle them carefully. They must be ripened on the canes and their flavour should be tart-sweet. Buy in quantity when the price is lowest and freeze them, lightly sprinkled with sugar and packaged in plastic bags.

Strawberry *(fresa, fresón).* Strawberries are the first blush of spring, though new varieties and extensive plantings make this fruit available, if extravagant, very nearly the whole year. They should be fully sweetened when picked, for they won't ripen further. However, full red colour is not an indication of sweetness; some varieties are nearly white when fully ripe. Store strawberries, unwashed and unhulled, and loosely wrapped in the refrigerator or prepare them immediately for eating by washing, hulling, slicing, sugaring and chill them, tightly covered, until serving time.

Tangerine *(mandarina).* This dainty member of the citrus family is the first to appear in the markets in the fall and the last to finish the season, with the seedless *clementinas* in the spring. They seem to spoil more readily than oranges, so buy them fresh and use promptly. Chilled tangerine juice is a lovely drink.

VEGETABLES

Artichoke *(alcachofa)*. An edible thistle, the artichoke is ostensibly a spring vegetable. In fact, it's available from early winter until almost summer. A perennial, the plant grows to a stately four feet. The frond-like leaves make it attractive for borders and, if you don't manage to eat all the buds — the artichokes — they will open into spectacular flowers. Buy artichokes with the leaves tightly closed and with no discolouration. Except for the very tiniest ones, only the heart and the fleshy pulp on the inside of the leaves and their bases are edible. Spanish ways with artichokes are, though delicious, less than dainty. The whole or halved vegetable is braised in its sauce, meaning messy fingers for the diner. Artichoke hearts or bottoms can be substituted in such recipes. To prepare them for cooking, remove the first layer of coarse outer leaves. You can trim off the tips, cutting about one-third way down, or leave whole. Rub the artichokes with a cut lemon and drop into acidulated water so they don't darken. If preparing bottoms, continue snapping off leaves, leaving only their base and cut the artichoke top off just above the heart or core. Cook artichokes in enamel, glass or earthenware pots. After cooking, the "choke" or fuzzy centre can be scooped out with a spoon. In case you're a novice at eating them: each leaf is pulled off with the fingers, dipped in sauce, and run between the teeth to extract the fleshy goodness, then the leaf is discarded. When you get to the heart or base of the artichoke, eat it with knife and fork.

Asparagus *(espárrago)*. Harbinger of spring, the first stalks of wild asparagus poke up through damp earth in late winter, though the wonderful cultivated asparagus both white and green doesn't appear until almost Easter. Wild asparagus, called *espárragos trigueros* because it often grows beside fields of wheat, has thin, spindly stalks with a slightly bitter taste, much appreciated in *tortillas,* omelettes. It should be freshly cut or it can be woody and excessively bitter. Fresh green and white asparagus is usually cooked whole, removing the tough butt ends and, if desired, shaving off the thin outer skin right up to the tips.

Aubergine *(berenjena)*. Americans know this gorgeous, deep purple vegetable as "eggplant." A summer vegetable, aubergine is found in sizes from tiny plum-sized ones to big globes. The colours, too, can vary from purple-black to violet striations to white. Aubergine lends itself to numerous delicious dishes — stuffed, fried, stewed and incorporated in omelettes. It can be cooked peeled or unpeeled. The vegetable, after slicing or dicing, is usually sprinkled liberally with salt and left to drain in a colander for about an hour. This removes excess water and any possible bitterness.

Bean, green *(judía verde, habichuela)*. Available year-round, beans are considerably less costly in the summer. There are quite a few varieties — skinny ones, wide and flat ones and plump ones. Beans that are young and tender and freshly picked seldom need stringing. If they do, cut off tops and tails and remove strings.

Bean, broad *(haba)*. Plump, pale green beans inside big pods, they very much resemble the American lima bean, but are actually a relative of the pea. Their season is springtime. Very small and tender ones can be cooked *con calzones,* ("with their breeches on,") unpodded. Otherwise, remove the beans from shells immediately before cooking so they don't darken and harden. Each bean is covered with a thick skin, usually left on. However, if the beans have been sitting around the market or pantry too long, this skin can be tough, in which case the beans may be blanched, the skins slipped off and the beans cooked according to recipe. Cook broad beans in ceramic, enamel or glass pans to prevent their turning dark.

Bean, dry. See PULSES.

Bean sprout *(brote).* Available fresh and bottled in many supermarkets.

Beet *(remolacha).* Red beets, a winter vegetable, are mainly used in Spanish cooking as an ingredient in *entremeses* and salads. Beet greens can be cooked exactly as for spinach and are quite delicious.

Broccoli *(bróculi, brécol).* Winter to spring. Choose broccoli with dark green, compact heads.

Brussels sprout *(col de Bruselas).* Winter to spring.

Cabbage *(col, berza, repollo; lombarda* is red cabbage). Always available, but at its best in the winter, cabbage is a fairly standard ingredient in many Spanish *pucheros* and *cocidos,* the regional variations of boiled dinner. Green cabbage, red cabbage, Chinese celery-cabbage, curly cabbage, are all to be found. Cabbage seems especially good when slowly braised, especially with pork, ham and sausages, as in many Spanish preparations for this vegetable. But it's also good and more nutritious if steamed only about 10 minutes until just barely tender or served raw in slaw salads.

Cardoon *(cardo).* A relative of the artichoke. The stalks are peeled and cooked as for asparagus. It is a typical dish on Christmas Eve.

Carrot *(zanahoria).* A few carrots usually go into the daily *puchero.* They also make a very acceptable marmalade. Carrots are available year-round. Store refrigerated.

Cauliflower *(coliflor)*. A most versatile vegetable, cauliflower turns up raw, cooked in salads, soups and puddings as well as fried, sauced and casseroled. Choose heads with white, compact flowerettes. If the cauliflower is yellowish or has a fuzzy look, it has been stored too long.

Celery *(apio)*. Appreciated for its crunch when served raw and its herbal flavour when cooked. There are several types of celery available: the knobby root, known as celery root, celeriac or celeri-rave, which commands very high prices; the white or pale green type, and a spindly, woody type with an especially aromatic flavour, good for flavouring stews and soups. Celery, available through all the cool months, is usually sold by the bunch, or *manojo*.

Chard *(acelga)*. Also called Swiss chard or white beet this vegetable, which looks like a celery stalk topped with a spinach leaf, is, in fact, a member of the beet family. It's grown extensively in Spain and is worth getting acquainted with. The ribbed, white stalks can be cooked, then sauced or batter-dipped and fried. The broad green leaves can be cooked exactly as for spinach. They taste very much the same, if a little coarser in texture. The smaller stalks are less stringy than the big ones.

Corn *(maíz)*. Sweet corn on the cob has only recently become available in Spain, especially in regions where foreigners live. However, the Canary Islanders have been using corn for centuries as an ingredient in some stews.

Courgette, small marrow *(calabacín)*. Americans call this vegetable by its Italian name, *zucchini*. This member of the squash family, a summer vegetable, looks much like a cucumber, though some specimens grow considerably larger (good for stuffing). Select firm ones with unblemished skin. Wash them well, but they don't need paring. If very mature, it may be necessary to scoop out seeds in the centre.

Cucumber *(pepino)*. Cool cucumbers, though available year-round, are a real summer-time vegetable, a basic ingredient in salads and gazpachos. The skinnier ones usually have less developed seeds than thick ones. If you happen to get a bitter one (due to lack of moisture when it was still on the vine), peel it, slice it and sprinkle liberally with salt. Let drain in a colander for an hour, wash in running water and pat dry. The bitter flavour disappears with the liquid. Cucumbers make an interesting cooked vegetable, lightly sautéed.

Endive *(endibia)*. Called chicory by the English, Belgian endive is shaped like a small, white elongated cabbage, with overlapping leaves tapering to a point. It can be eaten raw in salads or braised and sauced. Endive is available through the winter months. To confuse the issue, curly endive, a frizzy, slightly bitter-tasting "lettuce" is also called chicory and, in Spanish, mistakenly called *escarola*. Powdered chicory for giving coffee a rich taste is called *achicoria,* available in many supermarkets.

Fennel *(hinojo)*. The bulbous root of the cultivated fennel, to be found in many Spanish markets, can be eaten raw or cooked. It has a very subtle anisette flavour and is much appreciated with seafood. Wild fennel grows on hillsides everywhere in Spain. It's used in the curing of olives and flavours some soups and pottages. Try putting a few stalks of fresh fennel on top of the coals when grilling fish.

Garlic *(ajo)*. Read about this favourite seasoning ingredient under the section on spices and herbs.

Leek *(puerro)*. A member of the onion family, these look like fat, overgrown scallions. Favoured for soups and stews, they can also be cooked as a vegetable in their own right. Cut off most of the green tops and discard. Wash very well to get the grit out from between the layers.

Lettuce *(lechuga).* The most common type of lettuce in Spanish markets is the loose-leaf type, dark green leaves branching from a single stalk. Iceberg lettuce *(crispilla),* a compact head lettuce, is also found, as are romaine, *lengua de burro,* long sheaves of leaves; escarole, *escarola,* similar to endive, but not as frizzy; and the above-mentioned curly endive. Lettuce is available year-round, but is most expensive in the winter. Loose-leaf lettuce is often especially gritty. Wash individual leaves under running water or separate the leaves and let them soak briefly in a basin of water.

Mushroom *(champiñón, seta, hongo).* The first of the Spanish names, taken from the French, is used only for the cultivated white mushrooms found in markets everywhere. The second name means every other kind of mushroom, mainly wild ones. The last word, which means "fungus," which is what all mushrooms are, is used for a few varieties. Add to this the dozens of regional names for particular varieties and the names for "mushroom" go on and on. Because the collection of wild mushrooms is a sport with passionate devotees, especially in Galicia, the Basque country and Catalonia, some of the "wild" varieties are often found in the markets and certainly contribute to the culinary spectrum. The most usual are *boleto,* the boletus, also known as cèpe; the chanterelle or *cantharellus cibarius,* known as *seta amarilla, saltxa-perratxiku,* or *rossinyol;* the *russulas cyanoxanta* and *virescens,* called *gibeludiñas* by the Basques or *carbonera;* and the *lactarius deliciosus,* the ochre-coloured *rovellón* or *níscalo,* saffron milkcap, also available tinned. Store unwashed mushrooms in a basket or string bag in a cool, dry place. Discard any which are mushy or soft and discoloured. Rotting mushrooms probably cause more toxic reactions than the consumption of actually poisonous mushrooms. Some mushrooms can be dried. Thread them in a strand and hang in a dry place. Reconstitute by soaking in warm water. A few speciality shops import dried Chinese mushrooms. Truffles, trufas, are available tinned, very rarely fresh.

Olive *(aceituna).* Strictly speaking, these are a fruit, not a vegetable. They are not, by the way, edible straight from the tree, a fact of which I was unaware the first time I saw a real, live olive tree laden with ripe fruit, and popped one in my mouth. Incredibly bitter, the fruit must be soaked, cured and fermented (see Chapter 4 for how to do it). Olives in Spain come in an incredible variety — pitted and stuffed with anchovies, almonds, pimento, onions; green, black and purple; seasoned with garlic and herbs, tangy with vinegar, red with paprika and zingy with chili pepper. They are sold from open stock, dipped from vats, in bottles, tins and plastic envelopes.

Onion *(cebolla).* How could we cook in any language without this pungent member of the lily family? In Spain it's used in many guises. Raw spring onions, washed and topped, are munched with typical soups; chopped onions go into many salads, and sautéed they are essential to many dishes, in particular the *sofrito,* a sauce of fried onion and tomato. The best onions are the sweet, yellow Spanish onions. There also red ones; tiny ones, called *cebollas francesas;* green onions, usually harvested a little bigger and more bulbous than scallions; and, where available, shallots, *chalotas* or *escalonia.* Chives, which can be grown from seed, are *cebollina.* Onions come into the market in early summer, full-sized globes, but with their tops still on. Store them in a cool, dry, dark place. Already dried onions keep for several months unless the pantry is too warm or humid. To remove the odour of onions from hands, rub with salt and lemon juice, then rinse in soapy water.

Palm heart *(cogollo de palmito)*. These are usually only found tinned, an exotic addition to salads. However, they are sometimes sold by street vendors, who gather the wild palmettos, pare them down to the woody heart for consumption raw. The leaves are peeled off, rather as one eats an artichoke, and the fleshy part eaten and the leaf discarded.

Parsnip *(chirivía)*.

Pea *(guisante)*. Available winter through spring. Peas are best when very freshly picked, before the natural sugars turn to starch. Snow peas, mange-touts, are sporadically available.

Pepper *(pimiento)*. Red and green, big and small, sweet and hot, peppers come in an enticing variety. Red peppers, the mature version of the green ones, are sweeter and milder. Bell peppers and the smaller narrower Spanish pepper can be used more or less interchangeably. The first are fleshier with a tougher skin; the second are crisper and thin-skinned. Peppers are commonly roasted to facilitate peeling them. Tinned, peeled red peppers are pimentos *(pimiento marrón)*, much used for garnish. Hot *(picante)* chili peppers are affectionately called *guindillas*. The tiny red ones are the fieriest; thumb-sized and plum-sized ones are medium-hot. They come into the market in the early fall, threaded on strands, still fresh in brilliant reds, oranges and yellows. Once dried, they keep for many months. Also used dried are sweet peppers, *ñoras,* or *pimientos choriceros*. Substitute paprika if unavailable.

Potato *(patata)*. It's a good thing Columbus discovered the Americas, else the other half of the world would never have had this remarkable tuber. Spanish explorers brought the potato from South America around 1540 and it was cultivated in Spain long before it became popular in the rest of Europe. The French, in fact, considered it suspect until Parmentier began his potato rehabilitation campaign in 1771. The nicest thing about the potato is its versatility. It makes a fine foil for any meat, fish or fowl, adds body to soups and stews and can even stand alone when times are lean. Oil and butter enhance it;

garlic doesn't hurt it; spices, herbs, milk, eggs are absorbed by it. The potato probably appears on Spanish dinner tables more frequently than any other food except bread. The favourite preparation is, of course, *patatas fritas* "chips" or, as Americans call them, "French" fries. The most common potato is the white, which has a golden-brown skin. Red potatoes are also grown. New potatoes come into the markets in springtime. They are least starchy, have a higher moisture content and tender skins which needn't be peeled. Store potatoes in cool, dark, dry place. Discard any which are sprouting.

Pumpkin *(calabaza)*. A member of the squash family, this hard-skinned variety is harvested in the summer, but keeps well through the winter. Some of them grow to enormous size and are sold in the markets by the piece. Spanish pumpkins are usually green-skinned (orange skinned ones are sometimes found). The flesh is pale yellow in the immature and recently harvested ones to bright orange in the big ones. Scoop out the seeds and fibrous flesh surrounding them and peel the pumpkin before cooking. The seeds can be dried and toasted for snacking. Store cut pumpkin in the refrigerator. The bland, slightly sweet flesh of pumpkin can go sweet or savoury, though in Spain it is most often used as a vegetable in hearty pottages with beans and sausages.

Radish *(rábano)*. These come in all sizes, from tiny, cherry-sized ones to big, turnip-sized. Conserve in refrigerator crisper with tops removed; crisp in ice water before serving in salads.

Spinach *(espinacas)*. Spinach is a cool season crop, available from fall to spring. Fresh spinach needs thorough washing to remove all grit. Wash it in a basin of water, let it sit five minutes so sand and earth sink, scoop the leaves off the top and wash again in running water. Drain well and store it, loosely wrapped in a plastic bag in crisper, or steam it immediately, then refrigerate for later use. Spinach can be cooked with only the water clinging to the leaves. If very mature and likely to be bitter, blanch in boiling water, drain, then cook in fresh water. Spinach leaves can also be eaten raw as a salad green.

Squash *(calabaza, calabacín)*. These vegetables, summer and winter varieties, have been covered under courgette and pumpkin. Occasionally other types are found in the market. If the skins are soft, like courgette, they are summer squash and can be cooked skin, seeds and all. If hard-skinned like pumpkin, they are winter squash, can be baked, steamed, fried and the skin and seeds are not eaten.

Sweet potato *(batata, boniato)*. This sweet-tasting, orange-fleshed vegetable seems to appear in the market in time for All Souls Day, when it is eaten with chestnuts; lasts through November when, of course, Americans enjoy it for Thanksgiving; and disappears shortly after Christmas. Buy firm ones and use them promptly as they do not store well. They can be boiled, then peeled and puréed, or baked and served like jacket potatoes. People often mistakenly call sweet potatoes, yams. Real yams, *ñames,* a starchy root, are grown and eaten in the Canary Islands, much the same as in West Africa.

Tomato *(tomate)*. It just wouldn't be Spanish cooking without the tomato. This is not to say that there aren't many, many dishes which contain no tomatoes at all, but its use is so pervasive that it's considered a basic ingredient. How in the world did the people of Spain eat before the discovery of America? No gazpacho, as it is known today; no *sofrito,* the basic tomato sauce; no *ensalada mixta* with great chunks of vine-ripened tomato. Tomatoes are absolutely a summer crop. However, in Spain's southern regions and the Canaries they are grown year-round in protected places and in hothouses, both for the domestic market and for export. Curiously, Spanish cooks seem to prefer the slightly green, underripe tomatoes for chunking into salads. The dead-ripe ones are selected for gazpachos and tomato sauces. Green tomatoes will ripen on the kitchen counter in a few days. Once ripe, store them refrigerated, but use promptly. To peel a single tomato, rub across the skin with the edge of a knife, then pull the peel off. To peel several tomatoes, dip them in boiling water for a few seconds and the skins slip off easily.

Turnip *(nabo).* Most often used as a flavouring ingredient in *cocidos,* turnips are also eaten raw and cooked. Try them puréed with carrots for a tasty treat. In Galicia, *grelos,* which are the flowering stalks of the turnip, are stewed with cured pork shoulder and beans for the well-known dish, *lacón con grelos.*

PULSES

Pulses, legumes *(legumbres secas),* include all the dried beans, peas and pulses much used in Spanish cookery. All of them are an excellent source of protein, albeit incomplete. However, combined with small quantities of meat, eggs, dairy products or grains, they form whole protein. This helps explain how some of the heavy pottages of beans or chick peas have sustained peasant people through many years.

Dried beans. These are *alubias secas,* but they have a host of other names — *habichuela, judía seca, lingote, faba, fesol, fréjol, fríjol, frisuelo, pocha, mongete...* and they come in various colours — *pintada,* pinto, which are speckled, brown ones; *negra,* black; *roja,* red and *blanca,* white. The fat white beans for the Asturian *fabada* are called *fabes* (where these are not available, use dry Lima beans or butter beans).

Garbanzo, chick pea *(garbanzo).* The garbanzo is a basic ingredient in Spain's national dish, the *cocido.* With long, slow cooking (or a pressure cooker) it is quite toothsome, though never as tender as most beans. It has a delicious, nutty taste and seems to have a special affinity for some of the strong flavours of Spanish cooking — salt pork, strong garlic sausage, black pudding, tomatoes, cabbages and onions. Garbanzos must be soaked before cooking. However, you can often buy them *en remojo,* soaked, at meat and poultry stalls in the market. Pueblo cooks advise not adding salt to the garbanzos until they are at least half-cooked. Though cooking time varies with quality, I find that three hours produces tender garbanzos.

Lentil *(lenteja).* Most shops carry at least two varieties of lentils, the tiny, dark ones and the larger greenish-brown discs. A few supermarkets might have yellow lentils or peas.

Split pea *(guisante mondada).* Great for soups.

Black-eyed pea *(chícharo, figüelo, judía de careta).* Unlike the other real beans, which are native to the Americas, this one comes from Africa. It looks like a white bean but with a black belly button. Can be substituted in any recipe calling for dried beans. Makes an excellent vegetable side dish to accompany meat dishes, particularly pork and ham.

Lima bean *(alubia de Perú).* Though I've never seen fresh Limas in Spain, the dried variety, also called butter beans, can be found occasionally. They should be briefly soaked to prevent the skin splitting during cooking.

Soy bean *(alubia de soja).* Available in some supermarkets and health food stores. These never get as tender as other beans. Mung peas for making bean sprouts are usually found in the same shops which carry soy.

FISH AND SHELLFISH

A visit to the fish market is one of the most quintessential of Spanish experiences, whether it's the raucous wholesale market, where fish are unloaded at quayside, or the shoppers' market in town. Here the hundreds of fish in their incredible variety attest to the fact that the country's hundreds of miles of coastlines provide much more than a sunbather's paradise.

For many newcomers to Spain this variety is both perplexing and just a little intimidating. When I landed on these sunny shores — direct from midwest America, where seafood came frozen and packaged — I had never bought, cleaned and cooked a fresh fish in my life! My first fish, bought at the village market, was an especially large, ugly and scaly specimen. The maid showed me how to scale it, clean and fillet it. I baked it with butter and lemon and it was delicious. I was impressed by the freshness.

The fishmongers can be more or less helpful and more or less straightforward, depending on how business goes. For instance, if not too pressed, a vendor may well tell you exactly how to prepare a good dish of *almejas a la marinera,* clams fishermen's style; he may be more than pleased to fillet your sole or scrounge around to find some tasty trimmings for the cat. Another day, he'll tell you the *lisa* is *lubina,* when you know better; that the sole is fresh, when it's obviously thawed; that he hasn't time to fillet the John Dory, and that it's not his problem if the price has doubled since last week.

You'll get better value if you know your way around the market, what's a *lubina* and what's not, what it's worth, whether it's fresh and how to clean it yourself.

Select fresh fish. All seafood starts to lose in flavour and goodness as soon as it leaves the water. Careful treatment and storage will keep the fish in top quality for a longer time. Look for bright and bulging eyes. Sunken eyes are a dead give-away for a fish that's been around too long. The skin should be shiny, not dull, and scales tightly adhered to the skin and free of slime. The flesh should feel firm and springy. Poke the fish with a finger; it should leave no indentation. The gills should be moist and red. The sniff test should reveal no offensive odours, just a fresh sea tang. Check that the tail and other fins are intact. Brittle, broken or jagged tails may indicate fish was frozen and thawed. Fillets or fish steaks should show no discoloration or dryness around cut edges which also might indicate defrosted pieces.

It is permitted to sell defrosted frozen fish, but it must be marked accordingly. Most markets have a frozen fish section. Though the varieties are limited, the prices are generally less than for fresh fish. Freezing processes (usually done at sea) and warehousing have greatly improved in recent years, but frozen fish just doesn't taste as good as fresh fish. Never refreeze thawed fish.

Unless you are going directly home with your catch, ask the fishmonger to gut the fish *(quitar las tripas)*. If you also want it scaled *(descamado)* or filleted *(en filetes),* he's usually willing to do this. If possible avoid washing the gutted fish until immediately before cooking. Water just hastens the deterioration of very delicate flesh. Don't stash the fish in a plastic bag, which speeds spoilage. Wrap it in newspaper or put it in a loose string bag. If the day is warm or you've far to go before your finned friend sees a refrigerator, take an insulated ice chest on your market fishing expedition.

Once home, refrigerate the drawn fish immediately. Don't wrap the fish directly. Either place it in a covered refrigerator dish or on a plate and cover the plate with plastic wrap. Store in the coldest part of the refrigerator, but use it promptly while flavour and texture are still intact. Fatty fish, such as mackerel, spoil quickest. In no case should you keep a refrigerated fish longer than three days.

Shellfish are highly perishable. Most molluscs (clams, mussels, oysters, scallops) are sold in the shell and should still be alive to guarantee freshness. Shells should be tightly closed. Pitch any that are cracked or open. Don't store them in the refrigerator but place in sea water or fresh water to which 1/3 cup salt to four litres of water has been added. Besides staying fresh, this gives the shellfish a chance to pump out sand inside the shells. If you have to keep them more than a half-day, cook shellfish and refrigerate, covered, in some of the liquid.

Crustaceans (prawns, lobsters) should smell sea-fresh and show no sign of broken tails, claws or feelers which indicates frozen seafood which has been thawed. Store refrigerated and use within a day, or cook immediately and then refrigerate until needed.

Following is a listing of fish and shellfish most commonly found in Spanish markets, some of which are unknown in other waters. The list is loosely grouped by families of fish.

BLUE FISH

Anchovy *(boquerón, anchoa, bocarte)*. Fresh anchovies are a speciality of Spain's southern coasts. Crisply fried these very small fish can usually be eaten bones and all. This silvery fish has a protruding upper jaw, from whence it gets its Spanish name, "big mouth." The anchovy is easy to fillet: cut off the head and grasp the top of spine between knife blade and fingers and pull it down sharply across the back. Cut it off at the tail, leaving the two fillets attached at tail. They can then be "cured" in vinegar or dipped in batter and fried.

Sardine *(sardina)*. Grilled on a driftwood fire on the beach, fresh sardines are a wonderful treat, with little similarity to the tinned fish of the same name. The silvery-blue sardines, usually about six inches long, have black spots just behind the gills. Grilling is the best treatment for sardines, but they can also be fried or casserole-baked with wine and potatoes. Of the same family as herring, the sardine can be substituted for that fish.

Mackerel *(caballa)*. A beautiful blue fish with dark wavy lines across its back and a silvery-blue belly. This is a very oily fish and weighs in at 177 calories per 100 grams. The high fat content helps keep it moist while cooking. Very good grilled or baked, or Spanish style floured and fried. Any leftovers get marinated *en escabeche,* in vinegar, onion and herbs, for a stunning cold appetizer. A very economical fish. *Estornino,* Spanish mackerel, is interchangeable with *caballa.* The wavy lines are not so pronounced and it is more spotted and mottled.

Bonito. It's name means "pretty," and is used for several members of the tuna family. A big, meaty fish which seems to have less wastage than any other, it's wonderful grilled or baked. A very good buy.

Tunny or **Tuna***(atún).* A real treat when found fresh. Usually sold in steaks, the flesh of the tuna is darkly grained and firm textured like meat, with a flavour that's very good. The best meat comes from the belly section. Grill it, bake it, braise it or pot roast it in wine just like veal. Fresh tuna can be used in any way suitable for tinned tuna — salads, sandwiches, casseroles.

Amberjack *(pez limón).* A really excellent fish, suitable for grilling or baking. Fillets may be poached and sauced. It's a pretty blue fish with a yellow streak from cheek to tail.

Horse mackerel or **scad** *(jurel, chicharro).* A greenish-blue back with a pronounced lateral line, this fish, which is not really a mackerel, is common in pueblo markets where it is usually cheap. It's often fried whole; large ones can be baked.

Pompano *(palometa, palometón).* Very good fish. Can be prepared as for bonito or mackerel.

BREAM OR PORGY

Gilt-head *(dorada).* Probably the best — and most expensive — of a variety of sea breams to be found in Spanish markets. Weighing a kilo or more, the dorada is a pinkish-gold colour and marked with gold spots on the cheeks and between the eyes. The flesh is firm and moist. It's delicious baked whole and is the fish most often cooked *a la sal,* encased in coarse sea salt. Also good grilled. Fillets can be grilled, baked or poached.

Red bream *(besugo).* One of the favourite fish in Spain. It's typically charcoal grilled, but is prepared in numerous other ways. Besugo is a traditional Christmas Eve speciality. It's a pinkish-grey with a large black spot on the shoulder.

Dentex *(dentón).* An excellent bream. Silvery-blue with reddish tints. Good grilled like the previously-mentioned ones. Others of this family also found in markets are *breca, pargo, urta, zapata, sargo, boga, chopa, salema and oblada.* The smaller ones tend to be bony, though are quite suitable for fish soups: add to court-bouillon, then strain and pick the flesh from the bones to return to the soup.

Redfish; blue-mouth; Norway haddock *(gallineta).* This is not a bream — it's related to the rascasse family — but can be treated as one. A ruddy colour with bulging eyes. A firm-fleshed fish very good grilled or baked. Relatives to the redfish are the rascasses, essential to bouillabaisse, but good eating in their own right: *cabracho,* scorpion fish, is armoured in coppery red; and *rascacio* or *cabra,* grey with a pink belly. All of the rascasses can be cooked as bream and are excellent choices for fish soup.

Pomfret, Ray's bream *(palometa negra, japuta)*. Very good. Prepare as for bream or fillet and pan fry.

FLAT-FISH

These are divided into two groups which help to identify them in the market — sinistral and dextral. Sinistral doesn't mean a fish of evil character, it simply means one with eyes on the left side. If you hold a flat fish upright between two hands, in a swimming position, you will notice it has both eyes on one side. If they're on the side of your left hand, it's a sinistral fish; if right-handed, it's dextral. The other side is blind and usually a much paler colour.

Turbot *(rodaballo)*. One of the most expensive fish in the market because it is scarce and so highly esteemed. A sinistral fish, it has dark spotted back with hard protuberances. The flesh is white, delicate and very slightly gelatinous. The fillets are usually poached and sauced.

Whiff, megrim *(gallo)*. Fishmongers regularly hawk this one as sole — though it should cost about half the price of real sole. However, the gallo or similar *llisera* is sinistral and the sole is dextral. This fish is a yellowish-grey and the flavour is very bland and dry. It can be cooked as for sole, whole or in fillets, but is best with sharp seasoning.

Halibut. Not found in Spanish waters. Imported smoked halibut is sold in supermarkets.

Lemon sole *(limanda)*. Not found in the Mediterranean, but occasionally in northern markets. Rough-scaled, brownish colour. Can be cooked as for true sole.

Brill *(rombo, rémol)*. An excellent fish, similar to turbot in appearance, but without the knobby protuberances. Cook as for turbot or sole.

Scaldfish *(peluda, serandell)*. Looks very much like sole, but is left-handed. And not nearly as good.

Plaice *(solla)*. A very good-tasting fish. Dextral, it is a brownish grey with obvious red blotches or spots. It may have a crest on the head of small bony protuberances.

Flounder *(platija)*. This fish, which makes excellent eating, is usually dextral, but often sinistral. It's an olive-drab colour and may have orange spots and a row of spiny protuberances.

Sole *(lenguado)*. Chances are, fish vendors will call any flat-fish that vaguely resembles a sole, *lenguado*. As noted above, some of them are very good indeed, and others definitely are not. The fish which the English call Dover sole, the Spanish, *lenguado,* by no means hangs out exclusively around Dover, but is found from the warm Mediterranean to the far north. It is not, however, found in American waters — a fish called sole there is either another variety or else imported from Europe. The sole is dextral and is usually a smooth brown or greyish-tan colour. The flesh is very delicate, delicious poached, sautéed or grilled. Unless purchased frozen, the vendor will usually skin it and often will fillet the fish as well. Keep the heads, bones and trimmings for making a fumet in which to poach the fillets. Other members of the sole family, also quite good, are the *tambor* or *tigre,* tiger sole, with distinctive dark spots; the *sortija* or French sand sole, which may be lighter in colour and flecked with spots; and the *suela,* which has a black rim on the fins.

Angler or **monkfish** *(rape)*. This is one of the least attractive specimens in Spanish markets, but very, very good eating. A grey colour and without scales, the angler fish has a huge head and slim tail, a little like an enormous tadpole which never got around to turning into a frog. The flesh is firm and sweet-flavoured and can readily be substituted in recipes which call for lobster. Slices from the tail are very good grilled or braised with sauce. Head and trimmings make wonderful soups.

John Dory *(Pez de San Pedro)*. Though not actually a flat-fish, I have included it here because the flesh can be separated easily into four bone-free fillets, much resembling those of sole, which can be prepared as for flat-fish. Called St. Peter's fish in Spanish, French and Italian (for the so-called fingerprints the saint left on either side of the fish) it is a big-headed, spiny-finned creature with very tasty flesh. Head and trimmings make good additions to fish soup or fumet.

MULLET

Red mullet *(salmonete)*. A superb fish. It is very rosy in colour and has a chin barb. Very small ones are usually fried; larger ones are usually grilled whole. The flesh is firm, moist and beautifully flavoured.

Grey mullet *(lisa)*. A pretty, silvery fish with dark striations, the lisa is sometimes sold as *lubina,* sea bass, which its colouring somewhat resembles. However, the grey mullet is not nearly so pricey as the bass. A fairly oily fish, the grey mullet lends itself to grilling and baking, and can also be poached. It has good flavour, is easy to bone. It is quite good smoked as for trout or mackerel. Other grey mullets, all good, are *pardete, galupe, corcón, mújol* and *capitón.*

51

SEA BASS

Sea bass *(lubina)*. One of the finest fish to be found in Spanish markets — and priced accordingly. Firm fleshed, fine flavour, free of bones, it is wonderful grilled, baked, poached, hot or cold. It is a lovely silvery fish with a white belly and darker markings on the back. The *baila* is very similar to the lubina, but with small dark spots on the back and sides and is usually less expensive. Another member of the bass family is the *cherna*, the wreckfish or stone bass. Darkly coloured and with a much thicker body than the bass, it can be prepared in the same manner.

Meagre *(corvina)*. White-fleshed, good eating. Prepare as for sea bass, or cut into slices, flour and pan fry.

Grouper *(mero)*. Sometimes called sea perch, this is a delicious fish, lean and flaky. It has a ruddy colour with darker mottling, but is more frequently encountered in the frozen food section than fresh on the market slab. An excellent fish for grilling, baking, poaching. Two lesser members of this family are the *serrano* and *cabrilla,* comber.

HAKE AND ITS RELATIVES

Hake *(merluza, pijota)*. This must certainly be the favourite fish all over Spain, and for good reason. Its white, fine-flavoured, flaky flesh makes it a good choice for many different preparations. It's delicious floured and fried, poached and sauced, grilled or baked. A beautiful silver fish, it usually weighs in around a kilo, though smaller ones, called *pescadilla,* are very common, often seen in the markets with their tails between their teeth. Hake which is hooked on a long line, *anzuelo,* is pricier — and in better condition — than that caught in a net.

Cod *(bacalao)*. Cod is not found in Spanish waters, but the far-ranging Spanish fishing fleet brings cod to northern ports where it is salted and dried. In this form it is a staple food, basis of many tasty dishes, throughout Spain. Frozen or fresh cod is available in some areas.

Haddock *(eglefino)*. Not generally available fresh, though imported smoked haddock can be found in many supermarkets.

Blue Whiting *(bacaladilla)*.

Whiting *(merlán)*. Very bland, light and digestible. Fish similar to whiting are the forkbeard, *brótola,* which is quite good; the ling, *arbitán, escolano or maruca;* and the excellent rockling or *lota*.

Pollack *(abadejo)*. Lean and flavourful.

Coley, saithe, coalfish *(carbonero)*. Similar to cod.

OTHER FISH

Chanquetes. Tiny, transparent fish of the goby family, somewhat similar to whitebait. Long a Malaga culinary trademark, these fish have nearly disappeared from local waters and their fishing is now prohibited in order to prevent the larvae of other species being sold as chanquetes.

Dogfish *(cazón, galludo, pintarroja)*. These small sharks make excellent eating.

They are usually sold in steaks, except for the very small ones, which are marketed whole. The flesh is white, firm and somewhat dry. *Cazón en adobo,* a favourite tapa bar speciality, are chunks of dogfish marinated in vinegar and herbs, then batter-dipped and deep fried. The *pez angel* or *angelote,* angel fish, is another member of the shark family which is good to eat. Others which are sometimes found are *cailón, alitán, musola, pez martillo* and *mielga.*

Eel *(anguila).* These are usually brought to market alive, then skinned and cut into chunks for sale. The tiny baby eels, sold frozen, *angulas,* are very popular in Spain, sautéed with lots of garlic. *Congrio* is the conger eel and *morena* is the moray. Eel, much appreciated by some connoisseurs, can be used in fish soups or braised with wine and herbs.

Gar, needle fish *(aguja).* Very good eating, in spite of a curious appearance — long and skinny with a needle for a snout and a spine that turns blue-green when cooked. Cut in chunks, batter-dip and fry, or stew it in a tomato-based sauce.

Gurnard *(perlón, rubio).* Quite an ugly fish with an odd-shaped head, of a flamboyant red colour. It is quite tasty at table. Grill or bake, whole or filleted, and baste it well as flaky flesh tends to be dry. Other rosy cousins often found in local markets are the *armado,* with a snout like a tank; the *garneo* or piper; *bejel,* tub gurnard; *borracho,* grey gurnard; and *arete,* red gurnard.

Rosada. Widely served in Spain, this fish is never found fresh, but only frozen. It is ocean catfish or wolf-fish, taken off the coast of South America and frozen at sea.

Skate, ray *(raya).* This is usually found in the market already dressed, as the wing flaps are the edible part. Somewhat strong in flavour, skate responds nicely to well-flavoured sauces or poaching in a vinegar court-bouillon.

Swordfish *(pez espada, emperador).* The giant of the market, the swordfish often comes to market whole, where it is cut into steaks. Though expensive, there is very little wastage. The firm textured, almost meaty flesh is most often grilled, but can be baked or pot roasted. It is only medium fatty and needs basting while cooking to prevent its drying out.

Weever *(escorpión, araña, víbora).* Scorpion, spider and viper — sound like a nasty lot. Weevers have poisonous spines which are removed before they get to market. They are, in spite of name and appearance, good to eat, lean and flavourful. Filleted and fried, braised or added to fish soup. A related but non-poisonous fish of especially ugly demeanor is the *rata,* or star-gazer, so-called because its eyes are set at the top of its head.

Wrasse *(bodio, gayano, maragota, tordo, merlo, doncella).* Some of these are spectacularly coloured with combinations of royal blue, yellow and red. They are all good for fish soups and large specimens may be fried, whole or filleted.

RIVER AND FRESHWATER FISH

Trout *(trucha).* Trout hatcheries in many regions of Spain provide a good supply of this delectable freshwater fish.

Salmon *(salmón).* Fished in the north of Spain and also imported, fresh, frozen and smoked, from Norway and Canada. Salmon trout is *trucha asalmonada, trucha del mar* or *reo.*

Tenca, tench; *carpa,* carp; and *barbo,* barbel, are fished in rivers and lakes throughout Spain, but are seldom seen in markets.

CRUSTACEANS

Prawn *(gamba).* Used generically, the word gamba includes all of what the English call prawns and Americans call *shrimp.* The common prawn might also go by the name of *quisquilla* or *camarón;* the enormous, scarlet-coloured ones are *carabineros.* The big, pinkish tan prawns so appreciated for grilling are in Spanish called *langostinos,* which is not the same thing as that which the French (and often the British, too) call *langoustine* (see *cigala,* below).

Prawns range in size from tiny to jumbo. The tiny ones, a chore to peel, are often added, unshelled, to paella and soups, where they impart flavour. The bigger the prawns, the higher the price. Some prawns at the market are frozen ones which have been defrosted for sale. Fresh ones appear more limpid, transparent and softer than the frozen, which have a slightly "cooked" look. Frozen ones can be excellent as long as they were properly stored at sufficiently low temperatures all along the way. It is safer to buy them still frozen and thaw yourself. Frozen langostinos, most of which are imported, are graded by size. Supermarkets also carry packages of frozen shelled prawns. When buying unshelled prawns, allow approximately a half-kilo for three servings. Store refrigerated and use promptly. Never refreeze those which have been frozen.

Dublin Bay prawn *(cigala).* This is the French *langoustine,* the Italian *scampi,* and what the Americans call sea crayfish. Like miniature lobsters, these creatures have small pincers and a tougher carapace than prawns. They are a lovely coral colour with white tipping and do not change colour when cooked.

Lobster *(langosta, bogavante).* The langosta is the spiny lobster or rock lobster which has no claws, but long antennae appended from the head. The sweet, succulent meat comes from the tail. They are a reddish-brown colour before cooking. The bogavante is the true lobster, the French *homard,* with heavy claws containing good meat. It is a mottled greenish-black. Lobsters should be purchased live. Check to see if the legs are moving and that the tail curls under when picked up. The smell should be fresh. Buy approximately one lobster of a half-kilo or so per person. Frozen lobster tails are sold in some speciality shops.

Crab *(cangrejo, centolla, buey, nécora).* Crab is much-prized for the sweet-tasting flesh inside the armour. Unfortunately, a good-sized crab weighing about a half-kilo doesn't really provide a lot of meat. The *centolla* is the spider crab, whose shell is covered with knobby protuberances; the *nécora* is a tiny crab, often served as a finger-food tapa or cooked in soups. Buy crabs live, picking those which seem heavy for their size. They're alive if the legs are moving. They should have no disagreeable odour. Cook immediately, then store refrigerated.

Crayfish *(cangrejo del río).* Freshwater crayfish are a real delicacy. They look rather like prawns. Buy them live and wiggling; cook immediately.

MOLLUSCS

Bi-valves are the ones with two hinged shells, gastropods have a single shell, cephalopods — which include squid and octopus — have their "shell" on the inside in the form of a cartilage stiffener.

Oyster *(ostra)*. As oyster beds proliferate, this wonderful mollusc has become more widely available — and a little less pricey — in recent times. The Portuguese oyster, *ostión,* longer and flatter than the regular oyster, is a speciality near Cadiz. Oysters, by the way, are safe to eat any time of the year. The old adage about not consuming them during months with no "R" stems from the fact that in some areas oysters spawn during warm months and are thus not so plump and tasty. Buy oysters alive with shells tightly closed. Allow six per person. Store them refrigerated, but consume while still pristine fresh.

Clam *(almeja)*. These range from tiny ones the size of a peseta to those as big as a 50-peseta coin. Their colour varies from grey to tan and they are lightly ridged. They're all quite delicious if great care is taken not to overcook them. Shells should be tightly shut or should close when tapped. Discard broken and open ones. A half-kilo of clams provides two good servings. Don't refrigerate clams. Put them to soak in a pot with sea water or salted water (1/3 cup per 4 litres of water). Change the water every 45 minutes to replenish the oxygen. During this soak, the clams pump water through, eliminating sand inside the shells. If you need to keep them more than a day, steam them and store, refrigerated, covered by their own liquid.

Cockle *(berberecho)*. Rounder and bigger than clams, with deeply ridged shells. Purge them as for clams, then serve them raw or steamed.

Venus shell *(concha fina)*. Beautiful smooth shells, the colour of mahogany. Buy them live. They can be soaked in salt water as for clams. Serve raw with lemon, as cooked they become quite rubbery, though they can be finely minced and added to soup.

Wedge shells *(coquinas)*. Tiny, wedge-shaped shells, brown-yellow-beige. Absolutely delicious. Prepare as for clams.

Razor-shell *(navaja)*. Long gold-brown rectangle, looking like a pen-knife. These can be eaten raw or steamed open. They're very good.

Mussel *(mejillón)*. Sometimes called the poor man's oyster, these black-shelled bi-valves make very good eating. They're highly nutritious and very digestible. Because the shells are so thin, a kilo of mussels provides more food than a kilo of clams or oysters. Mussels sold commercially are harvested from non-polluted waters and are safe to eat all year round — as long as they're alive. Shells should be tightly closed or close upon being tapped. Throw out any cracked or open ones or any that float. Rinse in water and let them soak as for clams. If it's necessary to keep them more than a day, clean them, steam them open, then refrigerate covered in their liquid.

Scallop *(vieira, concha peregrina)*. Also called pilgrim shell and coquille St. Jacques, this shellfish has a beautiful scalloped shell, which makes a serving dish for its contents. It was the symbol for the pilgrims to Santiago de Compostela, the shrine of St. James, patron saint of Spain. The name vieira comes from Galicia, where the scallop is most abundant and appreciated. Scallops are available in southern markets only during the winter months. Because scallop shells don't close as tightly as clams or mussels, this shellfish doesn't stay alive as long after leaving the water. If most of the scallops in the market heap are closed, you can figure the few open ones are also fresh as long as their odour is sweet. If they're alive, you can let them purge sand in salted water. They seem to be especially gritty and, after opening, may need to be rinsed in running water. For

55

a first-course serving, such as the richly sauced coquille St. Jacques, allow at least three scallops per person; for an entrée, fried or sautéed, allow from six to eight. Both the white, marshmallow-shaped muscle or eye and the red coral "foot" are edible.

Sea snail or **whelk** *(caracola, búsano)*. They come from tiny to pretty good-sized. Wash well, soak in salt water, cook in a court-bouillon about 45 minutes and extract the dollop of flesh with a pin or toothpick.

Barnacle *(percebe)*. People do eat the strangest things! These are much enjoyed. Wash in running water. Cook in boiling salted water for five minutes, turn off heat and let them cook in the liquid.

Sea urchin *(erizo de mar)*. These hedgehogs of the sea, whose spines are always getting lodged in children's feet, are not commonly found in the markets. Alive and fresh, cut in half, the coral is extracted to eat raw with lemon, cook in omelettes or make an attractive sauce (very nouvelle) to serve over fish.

Squid *(calamar)*. Not the sort of thing your normal Englishman or North American would even consider eating — until tasted one day, perhaps by accident in a Spanish tapa bar, piping hot and crisply golden. After which, this odd creature can get to be an addiction. They're delicious in many different ways, as Mediterranean peoples and the Japanese have known all along. High in protein and other nutrients, squid are about 98 per cent edible, so a good buy for the money. It's one of the few shellfish that doesn't seem to suffer from freezing. It is available both fresh and frozen. It's the one with a long, slender body pouch from which protrudes a head with short tentacles. Tiny squid are sometimes called *chipirones* or *chopitos,* though these may refer to small cuttlefish as well. Squid is very quick cooking, can be fried, braised or poached.

Cuttlefish *(jibia)*. A related creature, the cuttlefish body is much rounder than the squid. Its ink is the "sepia" of antiquity; its interior cartilage is the canary's cuttlebone. Not as tender as squid, cuttlefish is usually braised or stewed in a sauce.

Octopus *(pulpo)*. The skin-diver's favourite bounty along Spanish coasts, the octopus is quite edible. Freshly caught, it's usually beaten against a stone to tenderize it. Home from the market, Spanish housewives usually resort to the pressure cooker. Otherwise it takes several hours of slow simmering. Once cooked, it can be sauced or diced into salads. The octopus has a bulbous head and eight long tentacles lined with a double row of suction cups.

POULTRY AND GAMEBIRDS

Poultry is usually sold in the same shops and market stalls which sell butcher's meat, though there are some shops which specialize in poultry *(aves)* and eggs.

Chicken *(pollo)*. Spanish chickens are excellent — plump, tender and flavourful. They are battery raised and come to market fresh and well-plucked and at a price that makes chicken a very economical choice. Their weight can vary between one and a half and two and a half kilos, or more or less what would be called a roaster. The butcher will weigh the bird whole — with head and feet still attached — then cut it up for you.

Big supermarkets often offer chicken parts — legs, breasts, wings — weighed and packaged. Generally the price per kilo will be more for part of a chicken than for a whole one. If you have freezer space, it's economical to buy two or three chickens at a time, specially when price goes down, and have them cut into parts for freezing. Usually you must buy at least a quarter of the bird, so, for instance, if you ask for the breast, *pechuga,* you also get the wing; if you want the leg, *pata,* you also get part of the back. The butcher will bone the breast if you wish.

Unless you ask the butcher to remove them, a whole chicken will contain all the giblets and viscera (though the livers are sometimes removed and sold separately). For some dishes, such as paella and chicken fried with garlic, it is customary to hack the chicken into small pieces. Though this makes for quick cooking, it also makes for nasty bone splinters.

Some stores sell already boned chicken breasts *(filetes de pechuga).* These are often frozen ones, defrosted for sale. If you intend to store them in a home freezer, buy them still frozen. Don't refreeze thawed chicken. Store fresh chickens loosely wrapped in the refrigerator. Don't hold more than a couple of days.

Very small spring chickens are called poulets. Capons, large and tender, are available in some markets at Christmas time. Stewing hen, *gallina,* is usually available where chickens are sold.

Turkey *(pavo).* Native of the New World, this flavourful fowl has been naturalized in Spain since the 16th century, when a recipe for its preparation is mentioned in one of the earliest cookbooks. Turkey is favourite holiday fare in Spain and shortly before Christmas it will be found in all the markets — fresh, frozen and "on the hoof." Some few supermarkets carry fresh turkeys year round or can special-order frozen ones. The preferred size seems to be between three and four kilos and it often takes some searching to find a really big turkey. Free-range turkeys, usually sold fresh, should be selected only when they're quite small or they will tend to toughness. The battery-raised turkeys are plumper and more tender. Turkey is the most economical of the fowl, providing more meat to bone than chicken or duck. Allow about 350 to 400 grams per serving.

Duck *(pato).* Frozen duckling is available in most poultry shops. It's not often found fresh. Duck has a much heavier bone structure and higher fat content than chicken, so allow about 500 grams per serving. Wild ducks, taken in marshy regions, are often fish-feeding. Their flavour can be strong and they are usually prepared in pungent sauces such as *pato con aceitunas,* duck with olives.

Goose *(oca, ganso).* Not widely appreciated in Spain, perhaps because on one memorable day in the 16th century, Queen Elizabeth was eating roast goose when news arrived of the sinking of the Spanish Armada. Like duck, it has heavy bone structure and is very fatty. It must be quite young to be good.

Guinea fowl *(pintada).* This fowl, which originates in Africa, is available in some speciality markets and appears on the menus of gourmet restaurants. Its flesh, which is very lean, somewhat resembles pheasant or partridge and can be cooked as for either of those birds.

Quail *(codorniz).* These tiny game birds are now farm-raised and readily available, both fresh and frozen, in poultry markets all year round. They can be spit-roasted, grilled over charcoal or braised in casserole, but need frequent basting as they are quite lean. The beautiful, speckled eggs, which look like beach stones, are also available in many supermarkets. Serve them, poached on a crouton of fried bread, in a steaming bowl of *sopa de ajo,* garlic soup, or hard boiled with aperitif wines.

Partridge *(perdiz).* Spain is known as the partridge capital of Europe and, during the winter hunting season, it's quite usual to see men returning to the village with several of these handsome birds tied to their belts. They must be young, otherwise they need long, slow braising. Partridge are also farm-raised, so they reach the market while still tender. The flesh is very lean, so requires barding or basting to keep it from being dry.

Pheasant *(faisán).* Not nearly so widely found as partridge, pheasant is taken in some areas of Spain and can often be ordered through butchers and poultry dealers who specialize in luxury products. This bird is very lean, should be young to be tender and profits by being hung for a few days.

Squab, pigeon, dove *(pichón, paloma).* Though battery-raised, these are not available everywhere. Young and tender, they are quite tasty.

Small wild birds: neither size nor song matters to the hunter of tasty morsels. Thus *pajaritos,* tiny birds of hardly a mouthful, are a speciality of many tapa bars. These birds are usually netted or trapped. *Zorzales* are thrushes, *alondras* are larks, *becadas* are woodcock, *tórtolas* are turtle doves.

Rabbit *(conejo).* No, it's not bird, but it's frequently found at poultry shops, so is included here. Wild rabbit is taken, by gun and by trap, all over Spain, but most rabbit found in the market is domestic. They are usually young and small, weighing under two kilos. They are skinned, but weighed whole. You can usually buy half a rabbit — split lengthwise. Rabbit can be cooked in many of the ways suitable for chicken, such as *al ajillo* and in paella, or in the many preparations for wild rabbit and hare, *liebre,* which often call for marinades and wild mountain herbs.

MEAT

The Spanish butcher shop and meat section of supermarkets can be a bewildering experience to the uninitiated — chunks of red meat, pink meat, fatty meat, bony meat, often not even labelled as to what animal it derives from, and seldom named by cut. Nor is the method of butchering here comparable to either British or American, so you won't find a piece of meat that looks like, for instance, a silverside or porterhouse. With a little knowledge, however, you can choose meat that comes from roughly the same part of the beast as the familiar cut.

Meat to be sold commercially must be slaughtered in a municipal *matadero,* where it is veterinarian-inspected to ensure it derives from healthy animals. The carcasses will carry a stamp of inspection approval. After slaughtering, carcasses are split lengthwise *(en canal),* cleaned of viscera and organ meats. They are then delivered to butcher shops, where they will be cut up with more or less finesse. It is not unusual to see a whole side of beef or pork displayed, cut to order as the customer wishes. In supermarkets increasingly the meat is cut up and may even be weighed and packaged.

Freshly killed meat does not make good eating — it is hard, dry and flavourless. All meats profit by a period of refrigerated storage which softens tissues before cooking. The larger the carcass, the longer the meat can be held, with two weeks being about maximum for beef. Spanish consumers don't much appreciate aged meat, probably due to the fact that proper hygiene and refrigeration are fairly new to the meat industry. Most meat is sold within 72 hours.

Meat is graded or classified according to its weight for age of animal, colour of meat and fat, water content. The wholesale price depends on this grading. Though the consumer may never know what grade meat she purchases, it is what explains a difference in prices between the same cut of meat in two different butcher shops in the same area.

Meat prices are based on a percentage mark-up over the cost of the animal on-the-hoof, so will fluctuate with supply and demand. Lamb and young veal are the most expensive meats; beef is next and pork the least expensive. Goat meat is cheaper yet, though baby kid commands prices similar to baby lamb.

Prices are also classified by cut — depending on degree of tenderness and the proportion of meat to bone. The ones with the most connective tissue and gristle and bone are the cheapest, though their nutritional value is the same as costlier cuts. The cheapest cuts are not always the most economical — this depends on proportion of edible meat to bone and wastage. In general, allow about 150 grams per serving of boneless meat; 225 grams of meat with some bone (such as chops) and 450 grams for a serving of bony meat (such as spare ribs). Some people, of course, will eat more than one serving.

Most butchers sell one or more minced meat mixtures, *carne picada* or *molida,* as well as ready made *hamburguesas,* which may be all pork, pork and beef, or all beef. Ground meat may contain flavouring or colouring additives and more or less fat. Any butcher will be willing to grind the meat of your choice. You can request that the selected meat, after weighing, be trimmed of all fat, sinew and connective tissue before grinding or, for very lean meat, have it ground with additional fat. Most butchers are happy to make up a mixture for *albondigas,* meatballs, by grinding meat, ham, onion, garlic and parsley, but not all are willing to grind liver, which requires cleaning the machine before the next order. Usually you can have a selected piece of meat boned, rolled, barded and tied for oven roasting.

The art of butchering has improved enormously and most meat vendors really know their meat and can give you sound advice about what to buy.

In general, the younger the animal, the more tender will be the meat — less exercise means less fibrous meat — the older the animal, the more flavourful the meat. In buying meat, beware of any with discolorations, sliminess, slipperiness, or strong odours. Cut meat shouldn't exude more than a little beading of moisture — if it's sweating a puddle it can indicate either meat which was frozen and thawed or which derives from animals which received feed hormones (prohibited in Spain).

Store meat, loosely wrapped, in the refrigerator. Large pieces can be kept longer than small ones (up to four days). Minced meat, cubed meat and organ meats should be consumed within 24 hours of purchase, as they are the most perishable. Meat should not be kept in the freezer longer than eight months as it begins to deteriorate in flavour and texture. Never refreeze meat that has once thawed.

Beef, veal *(carne de vacuno, ternera).* Beef in Spain — today — is excellent. It didn't use to be. New breeds introduced into Spain in recent years and crossed with the indigenous strains have produced cattle adaptable to local conditions, but also better producers of quality meat. The fact remains that cattle raising requires grazing lands and feed crops, something that much of Spain, with fiercely hot and dry summers, cannot provide. Much of the beef comes from the top third of Spain. Beef raised in the central and southern regions is seldom as tender or flavourful.

Let's start with nomenclature — which can be confusing. Asking for a slice of *vacuno* unfortunately won't get you a steak. And asking for *ternera,* veal, won't necessarily get you a scallop of pale pink, milk-fed veal. Generally, beef cattle in Spain are slaughtered at from one to two years, whereas what is called beef in the United States, England or France comes from an animal from three to five years. This is why beef here is often called *ternera,* veal, though it is more correctly labelled *añojo* or yearling. In many regions *carne de buey* is used to mean meat from an animal between two and five, or it may be called *vacuno menor.* The younger the animal, the paler the flesh; the older, the deeper, more scarlet its colour.

Age makes a big difference in the quality of the meat. The younger animal makes tender eating, but the flavour is more insipid than full-grown beef. It will have much less fat layering, so will be less juicy than that from an older animal. Meat from an older animal will have more real-beef flavour, but it's likely to be tougher and of a coarser texture.

Bull meat from animals fought in the *corridas* is called *carne de lidia* and a butcher is not allowed to sell it in the same place as other beef. It is a very deep red-black colour.

If what you want is real veal, not young beef, then look for *ternera lechal* or *ternera de Avila,* named for the province where much of is raised. This is meat from a milk-fed calf between three and 12 months. The flesh should be a rosy-pink, not red.

Each carcass is divided into cuts which are price-categorized depending on degree of tenderness and proportion of meat to bone. The most expensive cuts are *extra,* which includes the *solomillo,* fillet or tenderloin and boneless pieces of the *lomo bajo,* sirloin or loin. The fillet is the most tender part of the whole animal and can be roasted or grilled whole or cut into smaller pieces (châteaubriand, tournedos, filet mignon). In most butcher shops you must specially order the fillet in advance and are usually required to buy the whole piece. In butchering veal the fillet is usually not removed and chops are cut across the loin and fillet, called *chuletas de solomillo.*

The next best cuts, usually boneless, are *lomo alto* the widest part of the loin, and the *lomo bajo,* which narrows to the hip. The contrafilet or eye of sirloin can be grilled or roasted as for the fillet. Entrecotes, "between the ribs," can be cut from the lomo alto or bajo and make excellent steaks. *Chuletas* are bone-in rib steaks from the *lomo alto.* A rack of them makes a standing rib roast.

The remaining part of the hind quarter *primera A,* first category, includes the *cadera* or hip, which corresponds roughly to the rump or U.S. sirloin. It can be grilled or roasted, though will be less juicy and less tender than cuts from the loin. Several cuts of *primera* category are taken from the leg. The *redondo* or round is a long, thin muscle from the back of the leg. From the sides of the leg are cut the *tapa* and *contratapa* and, from the inside, the *babilla.* Any of these pieces can be rolled, barded, tied and labelled *rosbif.* They can be successfully roasted, though should be removed at rare to medium, so the meat does not become too dry. Any of these cuts, which are quite lean and close-grained, can be braised, pot-roasted, stewed or ground for hamburger.

Meat from the fore quarter, above the loin section, is generally coarser and stringier, best for braising and stews. These are classed as *primera B,* cheaper than *primera A.* They include the *espaldilla,* shoulder, good for *cocido* or pot-roasting; the *pez,* a long, narrow piece adjoining the shoulder which is quite juicy and flavourful; the *aguja* or chuck which, adjoining the *lomo alto,* makes medium-quality steaks, and adjoining the neck, for pot-roasting, *culata de contra* and *rabillo de cadera.*

Cuts classed as *segunda,* second category, are *morcillo,* the shin or shank meat, especially flavourful and appreciated for stocks and soups; the *llana,* from behind the shoulder, which is sometimes cut with the grain into *filetes* or steaks, but is better for stew meat or braising; the *aleta,* a strip attached to the brisket, good for pot roasting and mince meat; *brazuelo,* like the shin, excellent for the stock pot, and *morcillo,* below the neck, also good for the cocido.

The *costillas,* ribs; *falda,* skirt or flank; *pecho,* brisket; *pezcuezo,* neck; *jarrete,* shin bone and *rabo,* tail, are sold, with bones, as *tercera,* third category. Often the flank and brisket will be boned, presenting a thin slab of meat quite acceptable for braising or mincing, and priced as *segunda.*

Pork *(cerdo).* Years ago, before there was municipal rubbish collection, refuse was dumped into a nearby *arroyo* or over the back patio wall. Being ecologically minded, I gave table scraps and vegetable peelings to my neighbour for the pig she was fattening. Come butchering day, there were a few links of well-flavoured sausages in return. Though pigs today are fattened on commercial feeds and not hand-raised in village back patios, their meat is still of excellent flavour and quality. With prices approximately a third less than beef, pork is an economical as well as tasty choice.

The pig has long been the monarch of meat in Spain, ever since the reconquest and Inquisition, when Moslem and Jewish converts substituted Christian pork, forbidden in their religions, for the lamb and kid of their traditional dishes. Also, unlike other animals which require good grazing land, the pig is not particular about what it eats, and can be raised on scraps. A fat hog for a poor family was like money in the bank; food for the winter, and the *matanza,* or hog slaughtering, an occasion for an annual pig-out, when several families would get together to feast while making the sausages, hams, blood puddings, salt pork which would see them through many months.

Pork is divided into fewer cuts than beef, but the pricing is similar. *Solomillo,* pork fillet, and *lomo,* boned loin, are extra; bone-in loin chops, *chuletas,* and cuts from the leg or ham, *pierna* or *jamón,* are *primera* (here the *babilla* and *tapa* are especially good cuts for pork roasts); *segunda* is from the shoulder section, the *paletilla* or *brazuelo;* and *tercera* includes the spare ribs, *costillas* (allow about a half-kilo per person) and hocks, *manos.* Some typical Spanish dishes call for the ear *(oreja),* tail *(rabo)* and everything but the squeal. Because pork is fattier than beef, it is virtually self-basting and almost any cut can be successfully roasted or grilled. Choose meat which is pink — the redder the pork, the stronger its flavour. Suckling pig, *cochinillo,* is found in many meat markets around Christmas. It is a year-round speciality in Madrid and Castile.

Lamb *(cordero).* Spain raises excellent lamb. Rocky uplands, unsuitable for crops or cattle pastorage, provide fine grazing for huge flocks of sheep, from which come wool for clothing, skins for rugs, milk (especially esteemed for cheese-making, from the Spanish Manchego to French Roquefort) and very fine meat. Aragon, Navarre, Castile, Extremadura and Murcia are the prime sheep-raising regions, though the meat is generally available in markets throughout the country.

Most familiar to English and American consumers is spring lamb, *cordero pascual,* butchered between three months and a year, after the animal has begun grazing. It is flavourful and succulent meat, rosy-coloured with a thin layer of white fat. The lamb is cut into sections and sold, bone-in. The leg *(pierna)* and chops *(chuletas)* are the most expensive cuts. The shoulder *(espaldilla* or *paletilla)* is considerably cheaper, but has a large proportion of bone to meat. The breast of lamb *(pecho)* and ribs *(costillas)* are least costly. These can be cut into riblets and cooked much like pork spare ribs. With any of these bony cuts, allow about a half-kilo per person. For trimmed, boneless meat, about 150 grams per serving.

Considered a delicacy in Spain and available in most butcher shops is tiny, baby lamb, *cordero lechal.* They are butchered between one and three months, before they have been sent to pasture. The meat, almost white in colour, has very little fat and is very delicate in flavour. It's sold either whole or split lengthwise. Country-style, the meat would be hacked into evenly-sized pieces for evenness of cooking. However, to avoid bone splinters, it's best to have the meat cut into joints. The chops can be cut separately, allowing about six per person, as each one provides only a tiny morsel of meat.

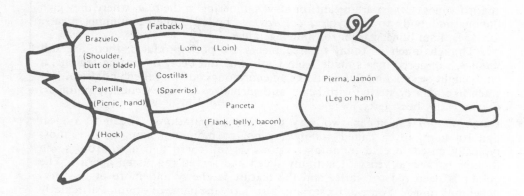

Mutton, *carnero,* is meat from sheep older than a year. The flavour is stronger, the meat coarser and its colour darker. Mutton is butchered similarly to lamb, or may be sold in smaller pieces.

Kid *(choto, cabrito).* Kid is much appreciated. It's flesh is pale and without fat, very similar to baby lamb. Older goat meat *(carne de cabra)* is seldom found in butcher shops any more. It is coarse, and can be cooked like mutton.

Offal, organ meats and other edible parts *(despojos).* Many, if not all, of these variety meats can be found in the butcher shop. Liver is *hígado,* and can be of veal, beef, pork or lamb. Pork liver is much appreciated in Spanish dishes, often flavoured with pungent sauces and herbs. Kidneys, *riñones,* are most delicate from veal and lamb, but pork and young beef kidneys are also consumed. *Mollejas* are sweetbreads, the thymus gland from young animals, usually veal or lamb. Brains are *sesos;* tongue is *lengua;* cheeks are *carrillos;* heart is *corazón.* *Criadillas,* is kitchen terminology for the testicles of beef, lamb, veal or pork. *Callos* is tripe, a tapa bar speciality in many regions of Spain. Rennet, a substance taken from the stomachs of suckling animals, used for cheese making, is also sold at the butcher shop. It's called *cuajo para queso.* A tiny piece, about 30 grams, is sufficient for a small cheese.

Not widely used for human consumption, but available in meat markets for pet food are lung, *pulmón,* and blood, *sangre.* Fresh pork fat is *tocino;* lard is *manteca;* beef suet is *sebo.* Bones are *huesos;* marrow is *tuétano.*

Game *(caza).* Quite a few types of game are taken in Spanish hunting preserves. *Jabalí* is boar; *rebeco* is chamois; *corzo* is a roe deer and *ciervo* is deer. Only venison, *venado,* and boar are likely to be found in speciality butcher shops.

Cured meats *(chacinería, charcutería).* Salting, smoking, drying and curing are ancient ways of preserving meats, without the benefit of refrigeration, from one season to the next. Today the many varieties of cured meats are enjoyed as much for their flavour as for keeping qualities. In Spain there are many types of hams, sausages and *fiambres,* or pressed meats, some of them common everywhere and others which are particularly regional. Many are still made on a very small scale by local butchers or by country folk on the occasion of a *matanza,* or pig butchering. Others have been industrialized and are available by brand-name all over the country. The finest of Spanish hams and sausages, which are very costly, are best served on a platter of *entremeses,* hors d'oeuvres, or as *tapas* with aperitif wines. Others are meant for slow simmering in the *olla,* where they give flavour and body to the typical *cocidos,* or boiled dinner containing meats, sausages, ham bone, garbanzos and vegetables.

Though much of today's cured meats are pork products, there are still *salones,* salt-cured meats made from lamb, kid and beef. In grazing regions, a lamb might be split and flattened like an enormous codfish, salted and dried. It is eaten like ham or stewed with beans and garbanzos in hearty country pottages. *Cecina* is dry beef jerky.

Ham *(jamón)* can mean two very different preparations. The most typical Spanish ham, often called *jamón serrano,* or mountain ham, as it is most typically cured in cold mountain regions, is salt-cured and aged from seven months to several years. It is thinly sliced and served raw as an aperitif. The colour is deep red to scarlet and the texture is chewy and more or less dry, depending on age. Some of these hams also carry the name of origin. Particularly appreciated are those of Trevelez (Granada), Jabugo (Huelva), made from the black Iberian pig, Montanchez (Caceres), Lerida and Teruel. These will all be considerably more expensive than ordinary *jamón serrano.*

These hams are traditionally hand-sliced lengthwise, with the grain of the meat. However, most supermarkets and charcuterias today also sell boned ham, which can be machine sliced across the grain. If you are buying a whole ham, look for the metal stamp, the producer's guarantee.

If, instead of the hind leg or ham, the front leg hand or shoulder of the pig is cured, it is called *paletilla, paleta* or *lacón.* These pieces are cheaper than ham, are coarser in texture and contain more bone.

In addition to salt-cured, air-dried *jamón serrano,* there are several types and qualities of cooked ham, *jamón cocido,* and hand or shoulder *paleta cocida.* Colour of the label indicates quality (based on proportion of lean to fat, gelatin, water, etc.), with red indicating *extra;* green, *primera;* yellow, *segunda* and white, *tercera.* With ham and shoulder, the yellow label usually indicates *fiambre de jamón,* pressed ham, which can contain fillers and thickeners. *Magro de cerdo cocido* is similar to ham, but made of a piece of meat of undefined cut; *fiambre de lomo* is the pork loin, salted, seasoned and cooked. Any of these pieces can additionally be smoked, *ahumado,* for flavour.

Spanish sausages *(embutidos)* come in many shapes, sizes and colours. Probably the best known everywhere is *chorizo,* a semi-hard sausage of pork and pork fat tinctured with paprika. More or less garlic, black pepper and chile pepper flavour the mixture, which, once packed into sausage casing, can be tied into short segments or long ones. Chorizo de Pamplona is similar in flavouring, but the mixture is more finely chopped and homogenous in texture. Best quality chorizo (coloured labels indicate quality, as for ham) is sliced and served with bread and on sandwiches. The soft ones which have not cured for a long time and which usually have a high proportion of fat are excellent for cooking. Try a few links of it added to a pot of lentils during the last 30 minutes of cooking.

Dried beans, vegetables, sausages... some of the basics of Spanish cuisine.

Morcilla is black pudding or blood sausage. Its confection varies from one region to another, but may contain rice, pine nuts, cloves, anise and cinnamon. In Asturias, where it is indispensable for a real *fabada,* the morcilla is hung in huge chimneys to smoke, which gives it an especially rich and robust flavour. *Butifarra* is the famous Catalan sausage. The white ones confected of pork, are plump links, especially appreciated for grilling and frying. *Butifarra negra* is black pudding. In the Balearic islands where the pig reigns supreme, a soft sausage flavoured with paprika called *sobrasada* is favoured. It can now be bought all over continental Spain.

Salchichas are fresh pork sausages, usually in short links. Their seasoning varies from quite bland to very spicy. They are not cured, must be refrigerated and eaten fresh. *Salchichón* is cured sausage, quite hard, the Spanish equivalent of salami (which is also widely available, of a finer grind than salchichón). It is usually speckled with peppercorns and may be smoked. Long skinny ones are called *longaniza. Lomo embuchado* is whole pork loin which has been seasoned and cured in sausage casing. *Lomo adobado* is loin which has been marinated with garlic, paprika, oregano and vinegar and may also be smoked. It is, however, fresh meat, not cured, and must be thoroughly cooked. Any of these speciality items can also be made with meat from the black Iberian pig, *cerdo ibérico,* especially appreciated for its flavour.

Bacon is variously called *bacón* or *beicon* and may be smoked, *ahumado.* It is machine sliced to order and also comes sliced and packaged. *Panceta* is pork fat streaked with lean and it, as well as pork fat, *tocino,* can be fresh or salt cured. In regions where they are appreciated, salt-cured ribs, ears, tails may also be available at butcher shops, as are the powerfully scented old ham bones, called *añejo* or *rancio.* If you've wondered about those tins of red coloured stuff, it's *manteca colorada,* rendered pork fat seaoned with paprika. It's used as a spread for bread.

A wide selection of prepared luncheon meats, *fiambres,* and pâtés are also found at the supermarket's charcuteria. Some of these, such as *mortadela,* are also sold in packets. In a cafeteria, a hot dog is called, literally, a *perrito caliente,* but at the supermarket, you'll find the package labelled *salchicha de frankfurt.*

DAIRY PRODUCTS

Except in the lush pasture lands of Galicia and Asturias, dairy cattle has never been extensively raised in Spain. Nor are dairy products part of the gastronomic heritage. Oil and lard are more extensively used in cooking than butter; cream is only recently used in confecting or garnishing desserts. Much of the regional

Fresh shellfish in Spain includes **cigalas** *(Dublin Bay prawns, top left),* **búsanos** *(whelks, bottom left),* **buey de mar** *(crab, bottom right) and* **centollo** *(spider crab, top right).*

cheeses, including the best-known Manchego, are made from goats' milk or ewes' milk.

Milk (leche). Pasteurized, homogenized cows' milk is sold in supermarkets everywhere. It is dated. Store refrigerated and use before date indicated. Also widely sold and especially useful because it requires no refrigeration is sterilized milk, *leche esterilizada* or UHT. It is treated at higher temperatures than pasteurized milk, which effectively destroys all bacteria, allowing the milk to be stored without refrigeration for many months. Once opened, keep it in the refrigerator. This milk is available whole, *con toda su nata;* skimmed, *desnatado* or *descremado,* and partially skimmed, *semidesnatado.* Powdered milk, *leche en polvo,* also comes whole and skimmed. Evaporated milk, *leche evaporada* and sweetened condensed milk, *condensada con azúcar,* are available everywhere.

Fresh raw milk, whether from cow, goat or sheep, is always boiled before using in order to destroy bacteria.

Cream *(nata).* Available in many supermarkets fresh, pasteurized or sterilized. This is heavy whipping cream. If a lighter cream is desired, it can be thinned with milk. There is also tinned, sterilized cream, which will not whip. Frozen food sections may have cartons of already-whipped cream. These contain stabilizers.

Yoghurt *(yogur).* Many brands, many flavours, also made with skimmed milk. A different kind of cultured milk, kefir, is sold in some health food stores.

Butter and margarine *(mantequilla, margarina).* Butter comes unsalted, *sin sal,* and salted, *con sal* and so do margarines. Most margarines are made with vegetable fats, though several brands contain animal fats, so it's wise to read the label. There are now "light" margarines, which have more liquid, less fat.

Cheese *(queso).* Manchego cheeses, hard, crumbly and mildly pungent, are somehow reminiscent of rocky hillsides and strong sunshine. They make you think of crusty bread, tangy olives, dark red ham and strong wine. What few people realize is how many different cheeses are produced in Spain — a catalogue of Spanish cheeses published by the Ministry of Agriculture lists 36 different ones, 17 of ewes' milk, 12 of cows' milk and seven of goats' milk. If the local supermarket only stocks three or four of these many cheeses, it's because most of them are still products of *artesanía,* hand crafted on such a small scale that they seldom reach markets beyond the immediate region. Like other local crafts, the cheeses are worth seeking out when you travel through these regions. Some of them are available in speciality stores and can be ordered through gourmet selection clubs.

Most commercially produced cheese nowadays is made from pasteurized milk. The heating process destroys any possibly dangerous bacteria, such as that from milk infected with Malta fever or tuberculosis, but it also does away with natural bacteria which produce natural fermentation. In many cases ferments must be reintroduced. Fresh cheeses (unaged) must be made from pasteurized milk (though country people still make cheese from surplus milk, fresh and unboiled). Cheese made from unpasteurized milk is required to be aged more than two months. The fermentation process eliminates bacteria.

Supermarkets here have a range of cheeses as international as their clientele, with imported types as well as copies of other types which are manufactured in Spain.

Besides moulded cheeses, some of which are consumed fresh and some of which are aged, there are several types of soft cheeses, usually marketed in cartons or small pots. *Cuajada,* which just means curd, is mild-flavoured and of custard consistency. Sweetened, it is the same as junket or rennet pudding. *Requesón* or *queso fresco* is like a smooth cottage cheese. It can be made with skimmed milk, but may have cream added to it for richness.

Following is a listing of Spanish cheeses:

Afuega el pitu: The name means "choke a rooster," supposedly because to test the cheese's readiness, a piece was fed to the barnyard cock: if he gagged, the cheese was declared *en su punto*. Small, cone-shaped cheese, very dry in texture, pungent in aroma and flavour. Not available outside the Asturian region of Montaña de Morcin, Oviedo, where it is made.

Anso: Named for the valley of Huesca where it is produced, from milk of the Pyrenean sheep. White and creamy, good with white wine.

Alicante: A soft, white goats' cheese, not aged.

Armada: A unique cheese made from cow's colostrum in the province of Leon. Semi-hard, sharp and lightly bitter in flavour. Keeps two or three years.

Beyusco: Made in Beyos de Ponga, Asturias, of a mixture of ewes' milk and goats' milk. Hard, amber skin if aged or soft and creamy if fresh. Pleasant aroma, sharp flavour, lightly smoked.

Burgos: Widely available and much appreciated. A soft, but compact cheese of ewes' milk, round and completely white, with no rind. It is not fermented, but after forming in moulds, the cheeses are submerged in a brine for 24 hours. Good dessert cheese with honey, nuts, fruit. A Spanish expression says, *"miel y queso saben a beso"* — honey and cheese taste like a kiss.

Cabrales: Spain's indigenous Roquefort, a real gourmet cheese. Made from cows' milk, sometimes mixed with small quantities of sheep's and goats' milk, produced at Cabrales (Asturias), also called *picón, tresviso* or *cabraliego*. The skin is dark grey, but the cheese is encased in leaves. The flesh is off-white veined with blue-green. The flavour is strong, more acidic than Roquefort, with a lovely creamy consistency. These cheeses are aged in natural mountain caves where certain bacteria cause the veining. This is one of the cheeses now being produced industrially on a large scale and available all over Spain.

Cadiz: Fresh, white goat cheese, full of *ojos,* tiny holes. Made in a number of localities of Cadiz province. Strong in flavour but pleasant, good with sherry wines, which are also produced in this region.

Camerano: Fresh goat cheese from the area around Logroño (Rioja). Ball-shaped and marked by the wicker basket in which it is moulded. Flavour is pleasant, lightly acidic.

Cebrero: An excellent, tangy cheese made in the mountains of Cebrero (Lugo) from cows' milk. It is mushroom-shaped, with a semi-hard skin and smooth, white flesh.

Cervera: A fresh, unaged cheese made in Cervera (Valencia) from sheep's milk with a little cows' milk. White and mild, doesn't keep.

Gallego: Also called Ulloa, this cheese is made in Galicia, of cows' milk. It has a mild flavour, is pale yellow inside with yellow skin in the shape of a slightly flattened ball. Keeps well.

Gamonedo: Made in Cangas de Onis (Asturias) of a mixture of cows', ewes' and goats' milks. The cheese is smoked for 10 to 12 days before being placed in natural caves to mature for about two months. The rind is yellow, but the cheeses are wrapped in fern leaves. The flesh is white with blue veins, with tiny, oval "eyes." The flavour is rather more *picante* than Cabrales or Roquefort.

Gorbea: From the Gorbea mountains in Vizcaya. A ewes' milk cheese with large *ojos,* holes. Strong aroma and flavour. Dark yellow rind, creamy yellow flesh, flat bottom, rounded top.

Grazalema: From the mountains of Cadiz. A ewes' milk cheese very similar to Manchego. It is marketed fresh, semi-cured and well aged. Pleasant flavour, hard rind, pale yellow flesh with tiny holes throughout.

Idiazabal: Made in the provinces of Guipuzcoa and Navarre of ewes' milk, and sold fresh, semi-cured and hard. It has a dark, hard rind and light yellow flesh with an excellent flavour. The cheese is smoked during initial curing, then conserved in olive oil which adds an extra taste dimension.

Leon. Cows' milk cheeses from mountain regions. Well-aged ones are crumbly and strong, keep well. Brown rind, yellow flesh.

Mahón: Made in the Balearic Islands, particularly Menorca, usually of cows' milk, though may include sheep's milk. It is consumed both fresh and aged, in which case it becomes a very hard cheese of strong aroma and flavour. Shape is usually a rounded square. It has amber, oily skin and pale yellow flesh. Interestingly, this cheese is produced in greater quantity than any other in Spain, but a great part of it is used in the production of the many types of *queso fundido,* processed cheese.

Málaga: White goat cheese moulded in esparto forms, traditionally preserved in earthenware vats of oil.

Manchego: Native of La Mancha, the high central plateau of Spain, where sheep have long been raised for wool, meat and milk. Originally a cheese handmade by shepherds, usually in small quantities, it is now produced industrially, not only in La Mancha and not only of ewes' milk. The cheese is a pale yellow colour with a hard, straw-coloured rind, or sometimes black if the cheeses aren't cleaned of mould after the fermentation. The rind shows the striations of the braided fibre basket used to mould the curds. When still fresh, these cheeses are of a creamy, mild consistency. Semi-cured ones have a little bite, are quite well-rounded and smooth. Manchego cheese, aged more than three months, is dry and should splinter when cut. It has a tantalizing sharpness, needs a good red wine to set it off nicely.

Morella: Small goat cheeses from Castellón, mild in flavour.

Orduña: sheep's milk cheese from Alava, very strong, with a bite to it. Hard skin of dark yellow, pale yellow inside. Keeps well for two years.

Oropesa: Sheep's milk cheese similar to Manchego, made in Puente del Arzobispo and Talavera de la Reina (Toledo). The cheese is yellow, full of tiny holes and strong in flavour.

Pasiego: Made from cows' milk, occasionally with addition of ewes', in the southwest of Santander. The curd is white, firm with a creamy consistency and a pleasant bite. Also made *sin prensar,* without pressing, in which manifestation it is the main ingredient of the *quesada,* a Santander cheesecake.

Pedroches. A sheep's milk cheese made in the province of Cordoba. Light yellow outside and in, with a strong aroma and a salty, tangy flavour. Keeps well for months, longer if conserved in oil.

Puzol: An unfermented ewes' milk cheese from the Valencia area, similar to Burgos cheese. A white, fresh cheese, very mild, meant to be eaten fresh, with a conical indentation left from the mould.

Quesucos: Also called Lebeña, this is a smoked cheese made from a mixture of cows', ewes' and goats' milk in Santander. Smoky yellow rind, pale yellow inside with "eyes." Mild in flavour.

Roncal: One of the most highly regarded cheeses of Spain, but made in limited quantities. Made with ewes' milk or mixture of ewes' and cows', in the Roncal valley of Navarre. Hard rind the colour of leather; inside hard and full of tiny holes. Aroma and flavour are sharp but mellow.

San Simón: Made in San Simon de la Cuesta (Lugo) of cows' milk. Looks like a plump, amber-coloured pear, shiny on the outside from exuded oil. The cheese is smoked over herbs and oak wood and keeps well up to two years. The creamy inside has a mild, smoky flavour with a pleasant tang.

Serena: Sheep's milk cheese from Badajoz. One of the few cheeses made with a vegetable coagulent, the pistil of the wild cardoon flower, instead of the more usual animal rennet. Both semi-cured and cured, it is mild with a slight bite; golden skinned, pale curd.

Soria: Goats' milk cheese made in the province of Soria. White skin and curd. Aroma of fresh milk, lightly salty flavour.

Tetilla: Named for its shape, a rounded cone which reminds of a breast. Made of cows' milk in the province of Pontevedra. Yellow on the outside, paler on the inside, smooth consistency, salty, tangy flavour.

Tronchón: Ewes' milk cheese made in Teruel and Castellón de la Plana. Yellow skin, whitish-yellow inside. Domed shape with an indentation. Very mild flavour.

Villalón: Also called *pata de mulo,* mule's foot, for its shape, a long cylinder. A very bland, white cheese, made from sheep's milk, often recommended for delicate stomachs. It is sold *con sal* and *sin sal,* with or without salt. Made in Tierra de Campos (Valladolid). Like Burgos cheese, it is good with honey and fruits.

SPICES, HERBS, SEASONINGS AND CONDIMENTS

There's something tantalizingly exotic about the spice sellers in Spanish markets with their bags of spices and herbs, sweet and pungent, dull and bright, so reminiscent of more Eastern markets and Oriental cuisines.

Though the use of spices and herbs in Spanish cookery is subtle — there are few dishes which could be described as "spicy" — it is a constant. Saffron to colour rice dishes, aromatic wild thyme in the rabbit stew, nutmeg in the meatballs, a sprig of fresh mint in the consommé — the touch of flavouring is what makes a dish special. Generally, spices and herbs are purchased whole and freshly ground in the mortar as needed for use in a dish. Ground spices are sold in supermarkets. Their flavour diminishes rapidly and should be replaced within a year. Wild herbs are free for the picking all over Spain and many people enjoy growing them on patios.

Allspice *(pimienta de Jamaica).* A spice which combines the flavours of cinnamon, nutmeg and cloves.

Aniseed *(matalahuva).* Extensively used in Spanish sweets and fried pastries, often in combination with cinnamon and lemon peel. Seeds are usually used whole or may be ground in the mortar. They are sometimes toasted or fried in oil which is then incorporated. Aniseed also flavours a clear brandy, *aguardiente,* both sweet and dry, which is used in cooking. Try a dash of it with fish and shellfish.

Basil *(albahaca).* Pots of sweet basil adorn many Spanish kitchens, where it is said to freshen the air, and young girls might pluck a sprig for wearing in the hair, as young men are said to be attracted by the sweet fragrance. In spite of such popularity, the lovely herb is never used in traditional Spanish dishes. It can be bought dried and, in the spring, pots of it are to be found in flower markets. Fresh basil can be frozen.

Bay leaf *(laurel).* Essential to many stews and pottages. Bay is usually added whole to the pot, but is sometimes fried crisp, then pulverized in the mortar.

Cardamom *(cardamomo).* Remove the black seeds from the hull. Good in breads, fruit compotes, curry mixtures. If the spice vendor doesn't have it, try the *herboristería,* herbalist or health food store.

Chili pepper, cayenne *(pimiento chile, cayena).* The chili is used with great moderation in Spanish cuisine. Whole hot peppers come fresh or dried, usually strung in *ristras.* They are a colourful adornment in a kitchen, though few families could consume so many fiery peppers. Generally, the larger the pepper, the milder the flavour. The tiny ones, called *guindilla,* are the hottest. There are also dried sweet peppers, *ñoras* or *pimientos choriceros.* These can be rehydrated by soaking in water or ground to a powder and used like paprika. Ground chili pepper is called cayenne. Chili powder, the Mexican-type seasoning, is a blend of ground chili, cumin, coriander, oregano, paprika and garlic.

Caraway seed *(alcaravea).* Not widely used in Spanish cooking. Try caraway with breads, potted cheese, cabbage and cauliflower.

Celery *(apio).* A leafy stalk of bitter celery is used in a bouquet garni to flavour soups. Both the seed *(semilla de apio)* and celery salt *(sal de apio)* can be purchased from spice vendors or in jars.

Chervil *(perifollo).*

Chives *(cebollina).* Grow this member of the onion family from seed.

Cinnamon *(canela).* This sweet spice comes ground and in sticks. It is much loved in sweets and puddings, but is also used in some meat and poultry dishes.

Cloves *(clavos).* The word in Spanish means a nail, which the whole spice resembles. It goes into everything — soups, stews and sauces — usually crushed in the mortar with whole peppercorns. Use it sparingly, as the flavour is strong.

Coriander *(cilantro).* One of the ingredients in *pinchito* spice and curry powder. The seeds can be bought whole or ground. Sprout them to grow the herb for its leaves, which resemble parsley. Sometimes called Chinese parsley or Mexican parsley, it is widely used in these cuisines as well as in nearby Morocco. Freshly cut, the herb has a sharp, acrid smell, which diminishes after addition to food. It is appreciated in salads and seafood cocktails, with beans, lentils and garbanzos, and as a garnish for purée soups.

Cumin *(comino).* This is one of the exotic spices brought to Spain by the Moors which really caught on here. Cumin is often used in tomato sauces and even in gazpacho, though always in very small quantities. Like coriander, it is one of the basic spices of North African cookery. Buy the seeds whole and grind in the mortar or purchase the spice ground.

Curry powder *(cari).* This is a blend of spices and can be bought in Spain, both imported and mixed here.

Dill *(eneldo).* Not an ingredient in Spanish food, but the seeds can be purchased. Plant them to grow the fresh dill, so necessary for pickles and many Scandinavian dishes.

Fennel *(hinojo).* Grows wild throughout the countryside, a tall, rangy plant with ferny leaves. The young sprouts are added to soup and are good with fish. The seeds which form after the yellow flower, can be used in any way dill is used, with vegetables, fish and breads. Fennel is added to home-cured olives. Cultivated fennel, grown for the root bulb, can be found in markets.

Garlic *(ajo).* The spice of Spanish life. Garlic is sold in the markets by the head, *cabeza,* or plaited into strands, *ristras.* A single clove of garlic is a *diente* or "tooth" of garlic. Select bulbs which feels firm and store in a cool, dry place. They will keep for months, slowly desiccating rather than rotting. Besides garlic salt, spice vendors sell dry garlic flakes.

Ginger *(jengibre).* Ginger root is available dried, in bulb form and powdered, and in tins. Can be grown from rhizome starters.

Juniper berry *(enebro).* A few of these dried berries impart a nice flavour to marinades for game.

Marjoram *(mejorana).* Similar but slightly sweeter than the much more common oregano.

Mint *(hierba buena).* In Spanish it's called "the good weed." Next to parsley, this is probably the favourite home-grown herb in Spanish kitchens and is usually available fresh in vegetable markets. It turns up in the most unexpected places — in a fish soup, in a saffron-flavoured noodle casserole, even in gazpacho.

Mustard *(mostaza).* Available in seeds *(en grano),* both black and yellow; powdered, and prepared.

Nutmeg *(nuez moscada).* A very versatile spice, it goes in custards and a number of meat and chicken dishes. Whole nutmeg best preserves the flavour, is quickly grated fresh. Also available ground. Mace, *macis,* found ground, is the thin outer shell of the nutmeg.

Oregano *(orégano).* The Mediterranean herb. Used in meat stews and in most marinades with vinegar.

Paprika *(pimentón).* As with chili pepper, this is a type of capsicum pepper, this one sweet rather than hot, which is dried and ground. Comes both strong, *fuerte,* and sweet, *dulce.* Beloved for its strong red colour as much as for its flavour, in Spanish cookery it is an integral ingredient — not a sprinkle or garnish — in many dishes, from sausage to paella.

Parsley *(perejil).* Ubiquitous, it goes into just about everything but sweets. The Spanish housewife grows it on her patio, a mild, flat-leafed variety. Sold fresh at vegetable stalls. Handfuls, finely chopped, go into salads and marinades; crushed in the mortar with spices, it flavours sauces; a few stems and leaves in a bouquet garni for soups and stocks; combined with chopped garlic and lemon in an *aliño* for grilled fish.

Pepper *(pimienta).* Pepper is most fragrant when freshly ground. Spanish style, it is crushed in the mortar. Buy whole peppercorns, *en grano,* and crush in mortar or in pepper mill. White pepper is *pimienta blanca.* Tinned green peppercorns are *pimienta verde de Madagascar.*

Pinchito spice *(especia para pinchitos).* Pinchitos are skewered meat, very similar to the brochettes of Morocco. A blend of spices, with cumin and coriander predominating, is used to marinate the meat before charcoal grilling. Where the spice is not available, substitute a curry powder, and add cumin and coriander.

Rosemary *(romero).* Grows wild on the mountainsides, an attactive shrub with violet flowers. Its powerful, resinous aroma and flavour is milder when the herb is dried. Still used to fuel wood-burning stoves and bread ovens, rosemary is little used in Spanish cookery.

Saffron *(azafrán).* The queen of spices in Spain, legacy of the Moors. The word comes from the Arabic, *zafran,* meaning yellow. Though grown in Spain, this precious spice is expensive. It takes the stigmas of 75,000 crocus sativus to make a single pound of the dried herb. Besides paella, it colours and flavours many typical Spanish dishes. In fact, *la comida amarilla,* the yellow meal, is so loved that powdered yellow colouring, *azafrán de color,* or *colorante* is often used instead of or in addition to pure saffron. Real saffron is sold in "threads" or *hebras,* the whole stigma. A wonderful souvenir of Spain.

Sage *(salvia).* Grows wild in many parts of Spain, though not widely used in Spanish cooking. Try it with pork, poultry, rice and vegetables.

Sesame seed *(ajonjolí).* Used in holiday pastries such as *mantecados* and *polvorones.* When not available where spices are sold, try the pastry shop.

Tarragon *(estragón).* Used to flavour vinegar, this lively herb lends an interesting piquancy to everything from chicken to beans to eggs. Best when fresh, so worth growing from seed.

Thyme *(tomillo).* Several varieties of this aromatic herb grow wild on rocky hillsides. A wonderful flavour with poultry, rabbit, meat stews, stuffings, pâté. It is a standard ingredient in the home curing of olives, lending a wild taste of the countryside and sierra.

Turmeric *(cúrcuma).* A basic ingredient in curry powders, turmeric imparts a bright yellow colour and a pungent flavour. Also used in Moroccan spice blends. Available in powdered form, it can be used — with discretion — in place of saffron.

Vanilla *(vainilla).* Available in pods, the vanilla "bean," which can be steeped in milk to flavour puddings and also bottled vanilla extract.

Herbal teas *(infusiones).* These are very popular in Spain, for their flavour and medicinal properties. Hundreds of different ones are found at the health food stores and herbalists. Some are packaged in tea bags for easy preparation. The most usual ones are camomile, *manzanilla,* both bitter and sweet; mint, *poleomenta;* linden flower, *tila;* lemon verbena, *hierba luisa;* and hibiscus flower, *malva.*

Condiments *(condimentos).* Most of the usual condiments and bottled sauces are to be found on the shelves of supermarkets — catsup, Worcestershire, steak sauce, bottled dressings, prepared mustards, Tabasco and soy. Capers are *alcaparras;* pickles are *pepinillos en vinagre;* horseradish is *rábano blanco picante.*

Vinegar *(vinagre).* Most used is wine vinegar. Its colour varies between amber and pink. Gourmet vinegar produced from sherry wine can be found in speciality food shops and is worth looking for when visiting Jerez. There are also herb-flavoured vinegars and cider vinegar. Bottled lemon juice used to dress salads, *limón para aderezo,* is found with the vinegars. Pickled foods or those in a vinegar marinade are *en escabeche,* a favourite preparation for tinned tuna and sardines.

Salt *(sal).* Not all table salts are free-flowing type. Check the label. Sea salt, available in health food shops, is *sal marina;* iodized salt is *con yodo.* Rock salt for ice cream makers can be found in many supermarkets and at ice factories in ports where seafood is packed for shipping.

Sugar *(azúcar).* Sugar cane is grown in many areas of southern Spain and sugar refineries and rum distilleries are quite common. Confectioners' or icing sugar, *azúcar tamizado,* can be found in some supermarkets and in bakeries which make pastries. It should be sifted before using, as it tends to be lumpy. Brown sugar, *azúcar moreno,* is a light brown sugar. Demerara sugar is not widely available. Health food shops carry other sugars — dextrose, fructose, lactose. Sugar substitutes are sold in pharmacies. Molasses, called *miel de caña* or *melaza,* a favourite baking sweetener, can be found in supermarkets and health food shops.

Spain is a paradise for the honey connoisseur, with different regions specializing in single-flower honeys. Especially appreciated are those from bees kept in the sierra where they feed on wild thyme flowers *(miel de tomillo)* and from orange groves where orange blossoms flavour the honey *(miel de azahar).* The traveller in Spain can find wonderful selections of natural honey at roadside stands — a very special souvenir. Store honey, tightly covered, at room temperature. Natural honey will crystalize — set the jar in a pan of hot water to restore its fluidity.

Jarabes are fruit-flavoured sugar syrups which can be used for making drinks or ices. There are strawberry, blackberry, lemon and pineapple, but probably the most widely known is *granadina,* grenadine, made with pomegranate juice.

Leavening ingredients *(levadura).* Baking powder is *levadura en polvo.* Baking soda is *bicarbonato sódico.* Both are the same as those to be found in English or American shops. Yeast is *levadura* and it is not often found in supermarkets, but must be purchased from a bread bakery. Most widely available is *levadura prensada,* fresh, pressed yeast. Store it refrigerated for a week or keep it in the freezer. Some bakeries carry dry yeast, *levadura en polvo.* It can be stored in a tightly covered jar without refrigeration. You can also purchase bread starter dough, *masa de levadura,* from a *panadería.*

Chocolate *(chocolate).* This is chocolate as a cooking ingredient. There is, of course, a big assortment of bon bons, filled chocolates and chocolate bars for eating, to which the chocoholic needs no guidance. Unsweetened baking chocolate is not to be found in Spanish shops — substitute semi-sweet chocolate and decrease sugar in recipe. Some bar chocolate is meant for making a thick chocolate drink, *chocolate a la taza,* and contains a thickening ingredient. This is not suitable for baking, so read labels carefully. *Cacao* is cocoa powder, and there are some unsweetened, non-instant ones, very useful for baking and desserts.

Gelatin *(gelatina).* Gelatin for making sweet and savoury moulds comes in two forms — imported, powdered gelatin and leaf gelatin, *cola de pescado.*

GRAINS, CEREAL AND FLOUR

Wheat is the grain of Spain, but rice, which is grown in several regions, runs a close second. Almost every cereal can be bought here in some form — if not available in supermarkets, check in a health food store.

Wheat *(trigo).* As in many western countries, highly refined, white wheat flour is much appreciated in Spain for breads. That, unfortunately, it sacrifices much of the nutrient value of the whole grain wheat is seldom considered. Stone ground, whole wheat flour *(harina integral)* is available directly from mills where it is freshly ground, and from health food stores. More and more bread bakeries also provide whole grain breads. Some few produce bread from unbleached white flour. Whole grains should be stored in a cool place (preferably refrigerated) to guard against rancidity and tightly covered against insect infestation.

Available at health food shops and some supermarkets are wheatgerm, *germen de trigo;* bran, *salvado;* wheat flakes, *copos de trigo,* and whole-wheat pastas. Cous cous, Moroccan cracked wheat, can be found in many supermarkets, as can semolina for making porridge. Durum wheat is not widely available, except from manufacturers of pasta products. Buckwheat, *trigo sarraceno,* can be found in health food shops.

Wheat flour, *harina de trigo,* is good, all-purpose flour. *Harina para repostería,* cake flour, is finer milled and *harina para rebozar,* for breading fish to be fried, is coarser.

Rice *(arroz).* Spanish rice, which is extensively grown in the lowland coastal regions of the Levante, is plump, short-grained rice with a slightly sticky consistency once cooked. A proper paella cannot be made with any other type rice. Rice dishes are often slightly undercooked and left to set for 15 minutes before serving in order to prevent their being gummy. Long-grained rice or pilaf style grain is *grano largo* or *variedad americana.* Brown rice, which preserves the bran and germ, is *arroz integral,* available in health food shops and some supermarkets. It is also a short-grained variety, but takes considerably longer cooking time to become tender. Converted rice, quick cooking, is costlier than regular rice.

Corn *(maíz).* Corn meal, *maíz molido,* is used for breads, porridge and polenta. Finely ground cornstarch for thickening sauces and breading is *harina fina de maíz, almidón de maíz,* or, named for one if its brand names, Maizena. Popcorn is *maíz de flor* or *palomitas. Gofio canario* is a corn meal made from the toasted grain.

Oats *(avena).* Packaged porridge oats are *copos de avena,* oat flakes, some of which are quick cooking.

Rye *(centeno).* Grown in cooler regions of Spain, rye breads are appreciated in some parts of the country.

Barley *(cebada).* Sold in polished grain and in flakes.

Millet *(mijo).*

Alfalfa *(alfalfa).* These tiny seeds make wonderful sprouts.

Soy *(soja).* Soy flour, beans and other products, available at health food shops, make high-protein additions to many dishes.

Breadcrumbs *(pan rallado).* Packaged fine breadcrumbs for breading foods to be friend.

COOKING OILS, FATS AND SHORTENING

When I bought a plot of land in Spain I acquired a small olive grove of 20 trees and built my house in their midst. Each fall a family comes to pick the ripening fruit and I receive an owner's percentage, which, depending on the harvest, is between 10 and 25 litres of pure olive oil. I love it for salads, tomato sauces, stews, pasta, soups, frying and for any dish I want to give an authentic Mediterranean flavour.

For those who didn't grow up on the Mediterranean, olive oil probably wasn't a staple in the pantry. Bland vegetable oils, hydrogenated vegetable fats, butter, margarine and lard have always been the preferred fats in lands where the olive doesn't grow. Only in recent years has olive oil acquired gourmet status.

For much of Spain, where lack of grazing land meant no animal fats, the use of olive oil has flavoured cooking ever since Roman times. The Spanish word for oil, *aceite,* comes from the Arabic which means "juice of the olive."

Olive oil is the only oil which, extracted by mechanical and physical processes, can be consumed without any further refining. This is known as virgin oil or *aceite de oliva virgen,* a completely natural product containing all the flavour, aroma, vitamins and other nutritional attributes of the fruit from which it derives. Virgin oil can vary enormously, in colour and flavour depending on variety of olive, region, time of picking, transport and processing times. Olives picked too green, for instance, produce a bitter oil; those over-ripe give a rancid taste.

The oil is classified by degree of acidity (percentage of oleic acid). The higher the degree of acidity, the stronger the oil's flavour. *Extra-virgen* is allowed an acidity of not more than 1°; *fino,* between 1° and 1.5°. Virgin oils with greater acidity are generally considered too strong tasting and are treated with refining procedures.

In order to raise the standards of Spanish olive oil, the government is now allowing *denominación de origen* labels for extra-virgin oils of consistently high quality. So far, there are only four of these: Borjas Blancas of Lérida; Siurana of Tarragona; Sierra de Segura of Jaen and Baena of Cordoba.

Curiously enough in this land of the olive, virgin oil is not easy to find on supermarket shelves — most of it is exported to a more appreciative public willing to pay the high prices. What is called *aceite de oliva puro* — pure olive oil — is a mixture of virgin oil and refined olive oil. These may range from an acidity of 0.4° to 1 per cent. They still have the real olive flavour, but without the fruitiness so prized in virgin oil. The higher the acidity, the lower the price and the stronger the flavour.

There is yet a third type of olive oil, *aceite de orujo,* extracted from the pulp left after previous pressings. It has to be refined like other vegetable oils to make it edible.

All other vegetable oils are extracted by means of chemical dissolvents, followed by a distillation process to remove the dissolvents. None are edible at this point and must undergo refining. This consists of neutralization, bleaching, deodorization and winterization. Each step, especially the ones involving heat, changes the composition of the oil and destroys natural vitamins and antioxidants, which must be replaced as additives. Most other vegetable oils are cheaper than olive oil, which, because of labour-intensive cultivation and picking, will never be price-competitive.

All oils, by the way, are equally "light." They all contain the same number of calories, nine per gram, and none of them contains cholesterol (which animal fats do). Most vegetable oils are polyunsaturates which lower blood cholesterol levels. Olive oil is a mono-unsaturate and does not affect blood cholesterol one way or the other. Chemical analysis has further shown that olive oil is more stable at higher temperatures, making it the best frying medium.

After olive oil, the most extensively produced oil in Spain is sunflower, *aceite de girasol,* a New World plant which was introduced into Europe by Spaniards, just as it was Spanish explorers who carried the olive tree to the New World. The sight of vast fields of them, great yellow heads nodding towards the sun, is as beautiful in its way as the hillsides dotted with silvery olive trees. Today's consumer, even a Spanish one who grew up smearing his breakfast toast with olive oil, more and more chooses this low-priced oil.

Safflower oil *(aceite de cártamo),* so widely used in other countries, is little found in local markets. Buy it in health food shops. Peanut oil, *aceite de cacahuete,* and soy oil, *aceite de soja,* are sporadically available. Corn oil, *aceite de maíz,* has become very prevalent, but is by no means cheap. Rapeseed oil, *aceite de colza,* is little used as a cooking oil, but has many industrial uses. *Aceite de semillas* is an authorized mixture of any of these oils except soy and olive.

Though cooking oils today are marketed in plastic containers, for storage it is advisable to keep them in either glass or metal tins, tightly covered and always protected from heat and light.

Hydrogenated vegetable shortening is not made in Spain — substitute butter, margarine, lard or a combination in pastry recipes calling for shortening.

WINES AND LIQUORS

Spain is one of the greatest wine producing countries of the world and has been since Roman times. Even the Moors, whose religion forbade alcoholic beverages, were known to let their grape juice ferment during their centuries-long sojourn on Spanish soil. Wine is produced in almost every region of Spain and is consumed before meals, during meals, after eating and between meals. It is probably, along with olive oil, the most distinguishing flavour of Spanish cooking, in the casserole as well as at the table.

One of the pleasures of travelling in Spain is trying out the local dishes accompanied by the wines of the region — many of which are not commercially available further afield. My travel memories are well-flavoured with such brews — a slightly fruity Jumilla red with a roast lamb in Murcia; an amber brew that warmed one from the inside consumed in the mountains of the Sierra Nevada with slices of the local ham; a superb Rioja *reserva* served with fillet of beef — utter simplicity; a Montilla fino the colour of sun-baked earth with a plate of thyme-scented olives; rabbit stew at a country *venta* paired with a straight-forward Valdepeñas, served in an earthenware jug; a perfumed and fruity Penedes white, light as air, with seafood on the beach near Barcelona; dry sherry with the world's freshest shellfish at Puerto Santa Maria, where the bodegas flank one side of the port and the fishing wharves the other; fountains of sparkling *cava* in the village plaza at midnight on New Year's Eve, bottles passed from hand to hand to accompany the twelve grapes of good luck; and sweet nectar of Malaga sipped to the dulcet tones of baroque music played by a classical guitarist.

Following is a resumé of the principal wines of Spain. These carry *denominación de origen* labels, meaning grape varieties and region of production are controlled — a wine with a D.O. map on it can't use grapes from another area. However, most Spanish wines are a blend of several grape varieties. There are lots of Spanish wines which don't carry the dominación de origen label. Some, in fact, are produced in such small quantities that they don't carry any label at all, and are consumed from one *cosecha,* harvest, to another in a small locality. D.O. wines can specify vintage only if the wine is from a single year's harvest. Some wines are aged, *con crianza,* in oak barrels; others are consumed fresh. *Reservas* are wines which profit by ageing, have been kept in wood and bottles for several years before marketing.

Sherry *(vino de Jerez)*. Possibly the best known of Spanish wines and exported all over the world. The English word, sherry, is a corruption of the name Jerez, a beautiful town in Andalusia where this wine is made. Sherry, which varies from dry aperitif wines to velvety-smooth dessert wines, is made by a very special process, the *solera* method of blending. New wines are added to the top barrels and, after a proper rest, are introduced into casks of slightly older wine. Fully matured wine, after several such blendings, is drawn off from the end of the line. Sherries have a higher alcoholic content than most table wines (between 15° and 20°). The dry ones, *fino, manzanilla* and *amontillado,* vary from the colour of pale straw to topaz, their flavour is nutty without a trace of sweetness and their aroma is golden. Enjoy them with aperitif foods — olives, nuts, shellfish, some soups. With a hint of sweetness on the edge of their rich palate are the *olorosos* and *palos cortados,* old gold in colour and velvety in texture. These are also appreciated as aperitif wines. The sweet sherries are mahogany in colour with a pleasant sweetness, good with biscuits for afternoon tea or with coffee after a meal. Most of Spanish brandy is also produced by the Jerez bodegas. It is, in general, not as dry as a French brandy, but a very pleasing after-dinner drink.

Montilla-Moriles. Produced in the province of Cordoba, like sherry, by the *solera* method. Montilla *finos* are a little sharper than sherry, with a pleasantly bitter background. They are also considerably less expensive.

Málaga wine. This is produced primarily from the Pedro Jimenez and muscatel grapes which give a wine with a high sugar content and a high alcoholic content (as much as 23°). The colour varies from a rich, burnished gold to deepest amber, and the flavour from sunny fruit to intense raisin. Why the wine with the highest alcohol should be considered a ladies' wine, I'm not sure, but it is! Lovely with a selection of pastries or, after dinner, with fresh fruits and cheeses.

La Mancha. A vast area which produces the greatest quantity of Spanish wines — much is destined for quick consumption as *vino común,* some is transported to other regions for blending with other wines and a great quantity is exported.

The best known wines of this region are Mancha, Manchuela, Méntrida and Valdepeñas. The Mancha and Valdepeñas wines, clarete, red and white, are not heavy, low alcohol, very soft wines. They're very pleasant served chilled, including the reds, and are a good base for making *sangría,* the wine punch spiked with fruit. The Méntrida wine is the *vino de la casa* everywhere in Spain. If a little rough, it goes just fine with many Spanish dishes not ashamed of their peasant roots. These wines, in general, lack the tannin and body which make them improve with age. Drink them young and enjoy their simplicity and low cost. (There are, of course, exceptions, a few *reservas.)*

Cariñena. The wine of Aragon, dark and solid as ancient castles. This is strong wine, the perfect accompaniment to the region's *chilindrones,* lamb and chicken stewed with peppers.

Catalonia. The wines of this region are as diverse as the people and the landscape. Though there are some very fine red table wines, the region's climate and varieties seem to favour white wines, which may well be the finest in Spain. At San Sadurní de Noya are made most of the *cavas,* the Spanish word for sparkling wines made by the champagne method, fermented in the bottle. *Granvas* wines are fermented in tanks, then bottled. *Vino gasificado* is "soda pop" wine, made bubbly by the addition of carbon dioxide. Choose cavas from *brut* and *seco,* dry, to *semi-seco* and *semi-dulce,* sweet and fruity.

Alella wines, white and rosé *(rosado),* tend to be slightly sweet and spicy. From Ampurdan come excellent rosés, dry and delicate. The wines of Priorato and Tarragona include tart, fruity reds and delicate whites. From Penedés come wonderful crisp white wines, light and dry with a delicate perfume.

Levante. Wines with denominacion de origen labels are made in Alicante, Cheste, Utiel-Requeña, Valencia, Almansa, Jumilla, Yecla. The red wines are the best, with pronounced aroma and soft flavour.

Galicia. The wines of Ribeiro, Valdeorras and Albariño. The whites are fruity, fairly acidic, with a slight fizz. The reds are a deep, blood-red, quite strong with a flavour of grapes.

Rioja. This region brings together excellent growing conditions with a long tradition of dedication to wine making. The result is Spain's finest table wines, both red and white. Divided into three distinct regions, Rioja Alta, Rioja Baja and Rioja Alavesa, the region produces some fairly diverse wines, from the aromatic and acid to the thick and fruity. Many are especially suited for ageing, reaching a peak of smoothness and maturity after several years. Whites are dry and pleasant. There are also rosés, and lighter red wines, *claretes.* Prices for Rioja wines vary enormously. No matter where they fall on the price range, they are excellent value for money. In choosing wines, an easy rule of thumb is to match wine price to meal price. So if you're serving an inexpensive dish of *macarrones con chorizo,* the brash flavour of a low-priced Rioja will probably suit the meal just right. To accompany the fillet of beef, opt for a well-aged reserva which will carry a high price.

Navarra. Contiguous to the Rioja, this region shares many of the characteristics of its wines that fall in the middle category.

Other regional wines. There are many more wines on the supermarket shelf which don't carry the denominación de origen label. Some of them may be made in a particular locale, but from grapes of a variety not specified or in other proportions. Other wineries may actually import grapes or *mosto,* fermented grape juice, from other regions. Some are experimenting with varietal wines. Other wines are made in such small quantities that there isn't enough to market outside the region. They are worth trying while visiting the region. *Extremadura:* Badajoz and Cáceres. Try a Montanchez wine with the ham of the same town. *Castilla-León:* strong table wines, both red and white, from all the provinces, particularly the area along the River Duero. In Valladolid, the wines of Tudela de Duero, Peñafiel, Cigales, Nava del Rey and Quintanilla are well known. *Cantabria:* A local "green" wine. *Asturias:* Almost no wine is produced, but here the drink for local imbibing is *sidra,* apple cider. It's made both naturally fermented or *gasificado,* dosed with fizz. Bottled cider can be bought everywhere in Spain, and makes a good summer drink when well chilled. *Basque provinces:* Cider is also made here and a light and tangy wine called *chacolí.* Red and white table wines are produced in the *Baleares* and also in the Canary Islands, where *malvasía* is still made. This is the much-appreciated malmsey, with a rich musky flavour.

Buying wine. How wine is transported and stored from bodega to supermarket to your home affects its quality and flavour when uncorked at table. Buy from reputable stores and, if you should ever get an "off" bottle, return it courteously. In the home, store wines on their sides (so the cork stays moistened) in a cool place away from direct light. Some wines, by the way, really don't travel well, so the wine that so enchanted you at a little village in the mountains, might be a terrible disappointment after you've brought a whole case of it 200 kilometres in the boot of your car.

You can also order wines direct from bodegas, sometimes saving money. There are also "wine of the month" clubs which turn up some very interesting wines not to be found in supermarkets, and at very good prices.

If you live outside of Spain, a visit to your favourite wine shop will show you that many excellent Spanish wines are being exported, and at very competitive prices. Though the enormous variety won't be available, Spanish wines abroad do make a fine introduction.

Liquors. The word *aguardiente* means any distilled liquor — as in *aguardiente de caña,* rum. However, in much of Spain, aguardiente means specifically an anise-flavoured brandy, both dry and sweet. In Galicia, *aguardiente de orujo,* is a potent brew that packs the punch of molten lava, distilled from the last pressings of grapes. It is a little like French *marc,* clear, dry and with a grape taste. The word *licor* usually means liqueur, a sweetened and flavoured after-dinner drink. Spanish brandy, much of which is produced by the makers of sherry wines, is excellent — but different. It has a rich, mellow taste, but is never as dry as a true French cognac. If today whisky has become the preferred drink in middle class society, not so many years ago the properly accoutred bar would have a silver tray with decanters of good brandy, dry anise aguardiente and Malaga wine for the ladies, and tiny crystal *copitas* in which to serve them.

All of the world's best-known liquors can be found in Spain — whisky, gin, vodka, rum, tequila, aquavit, saki, bourbon, rye, Irish. Some of these are produced inside Spain as well as imported. So "whisky español" is Scotch-type whisky, made in Spain. It's considerably cheaper than imported whisky. Most of the best-known liqueurs are also found here, many produced inside Spain.

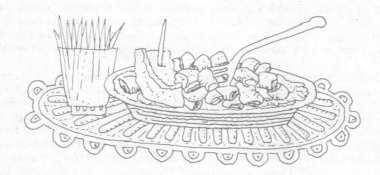

CHAPTER 3

In the Kitchen

The music of the brass mortar and pestle, the *almirez,* has been a call to good food since time was in Spain. Such love is there for the sound of the almirez that it is used as a musical instrument in some festivities. Whole, unground spices and herbs are crushed and ground in the mortar, then dissolved in a little liquid before addition to the pot. This is especially important with saffron, for its taste and colour will be spotty if simply sprinkled into the pan. When producing a blend in the mortar, begin with the small, hard ingredients, such as cloves and peppercorns. Then add saffron and garlic, next such items as almonds, and last, bulkier items such as bread. Dissolve the paste in a little water, wine or stock before adding it to the pot.

The mortar is still the most convenient utensil for preparing a small quantity of spices and garlic. However, when a quantity of almonds or vegetables for gazpacho or other purées is to be made, the electric blender or food processor saves time and energy. Machines are used today for many of the chores once done manually in the mortar and for making mayonnaise, chopping vegetables or fruits, mixing of batters, whipping of egg whites.

The cook who wants to produce paella at home, whether in Spain or abroad, needs a proper *paellera* — paella pan — big enough to serve the assembled guests (46 cm. to serve 12). Curiously enough, this is not a standardized utensil. There are those who swear by the earthenware paellera, which holds the heat and finishes the cooking after removal from the fire. Others prefer the two-handled, high sided pan, blackened from many uses on a fast-burning wood fire. Then there is the shallow two-handled pan, in which all the ingredients cook in a single layer. Brought beautifully garnished to table, it makes a stunning presentation. Though usually made of hammered metal, these can also be purchased with non-stick surfaces. The metal ones should be well-scoured, then stored with a thin film of oil to prevent rusting. A Chinese wok makes an excellent stand-in for a paellera.

Earthenware bowls, crocks and casseroles are indispensable in the kitchen. Many foods which are discoloured by metal cookware can be safely cooked in earthenware which holds heat wonderfully. Clay casseroles for cooking should be either unglazed, in which case the porous surface becomes "seasoned" with flavours, or glazed only on the inside. They can be used on direct heat as well as in the oven. Bring them up to temperature very gently or use an asbestos pad beneath. Treat new earthenware by soaking overnight in water before the first use.

In this book, the word "casserole" refers to an earthenware cooking vessel. If not available, any heat-proof casserole or ordinary cooking pot can be used.

The most commonly used pots and pans in Spanish kitchens are enamelware, a porcelain, glass-like finish bonded to metal pans, though all types of cookware are to be found in stores. In addition to the basic saucepans in graduated sizes, every household needs an *olla,* the characteristic tall Spanish pot with a narrow bottom, thick middle and narrow top, perfect for long-cooking meals like the *cocido.* Deep, long-handled frying skillets of rolled steel and high sides are useful for turning out Spanish *tortillas,* omelettes, and for frying foods. They do rust, however, and must be kept seasoned with a film of oil after scouring. Other pots, pans and utensils can be added as needed — custard cups for *flan* making; apparatus for *churro* making; olive pitters; a *plancha,* griddle for grilling fish; ham slicing board, and other speciality items.

KITCHEN HOW-TO

The recipes in this book are written for people who already know how to cook, know what to do if the recipe says sauté, blanch, poach or simmer. However, there may be some few techniques peculiar to Spanish cooking which need explaining.

For instance, there are quite a few different ways of cooking with garlic — none of which calls for a shake of garlic salt — ranging from the subtle to the sublime. In its raw state, garlic is at its most powerful. Chopped, raw garlic might be used in marinades or sprinkled liberally over some salads. The quantity can be adjusted to personal tastes. Cooking diminishes the bite of garlic, but infuses other foods with its flavour. It might be included in a bouquet garni to flavour soups, stews and stocks, wrapped in cloth and later removed; slivers of it can be inserted in meats to be roasted; it can be sautéed or poached. A typical Spanish preparation calls for whole, peeled garlic cloves to be fried in oil until golden (don't let them burn) then crushed in the mortar with spices, dissolved in water or stock, then added to the food to be cooked.

Yet another method is roasting, usually done with a whole bulb of garlic, which takes on a mild, nutty flavour. To roast garlic, grasp the head of garlic with kitchen tongs or spear it on a fork and hold it over the gas flame or place under broiler. Turn it slowly until well charred and blackened. Separate the cloves and either add them whole to the cook pot or peel them.

Raw garlic cloves are easy to peel if given a light blow with a wooden mallet or pestle, not enough to crush them, but sufficient to break the skin, which then peels off in one piece.

Garbanzos and dry legumes, pulses. These should be soaked overnight in water to cover before cooking. Only lentils, *lentejas,* and black-eyed peas, *chicharitos,* can be cooked without previous soaking. Garbanzos, or chickpeas as they are called in English, need almost three hours to cook, and never get as soft as other legumes. (Spanish cooks like the pressure cooker for reducing cooking time.) Do not add salt to garbanzos until they are about half-cooked, as salt tends to toughen them. Legumes cooked in hard water don't get as tender. Left-over cooked garbanzos and beans, drained, make wonderful salad ingredients and can also be puréed for thickening soups.

Cooking oil. The golden crisp *fritos,* fried foods, so typical of Spanish food depend on the right oil heated to the right temperature. Though olive oil is absolutely the best for fried foods — including sweets — many people prefer other vegetable oils, both for blander flavour and lower cost. Do not mix two kinds of oil in cooking, for heat can cause release of possibly toxic material, though mixing for salad dressing and mayonnaise is fine. Discard oil after about four or five uses. Keep separate jars of oil for frying fish, and oil for frying potatoes and other foods. After use, let the oil cool, then strain it through a dampened cloth. For oil in which fish was fried, dampen the cloth with diluted vinegar or lemon juice or gently heat the oil with a thick slice of lemon until all but the rind disintegrates, then strain and store.

If using a thermostatically controlled deep-fryer, heat oil to about 190° C or just below the "smoking" level (varies with the kind of oil used). If you're not using an electric fryer, heat the oil until hot enough to brown a bread cube in less than 30 seconds. The idea with crisply fried foods is to immerse them in oil hot enough to seal the outside so no fat is absorbed, but without browning too quickly while the interior cooks. Don't crowd food and let oil reheat between each batch. The exception to this rule in Spanish cookery is *patatas fritas*. Fried potatoes in Spain are not equivalent to British chips, American "French" fries or French *pommes frites*. They're not supposed to be crisp, and in fact are often added to a sauce after they have been fried. There are many who are addicted to Spanish *patatas fritas*. For frying potatoes Spanish style, you just break all the usual rules — not enough oil for the quantity of food to be fried; not quite hot enough.

Sauces. There are really very few authentic sauces in Spansh cuisine, though there are lots of foods *con salsa,* saucy. All this means is that foods are usually cooked in their sauce. The sauce is not a separate preparation. For example, chicken *en pepitoria* or *en samfaina* is chicken cooked in its sauce — which occasionally is made separately and served separately. Any of these sauces can be made on its own and added to other foods.

A basic sauce in much of Spanish cooking is the *sofrito* or fried tomato mixture (see recipe in Chapter 12). Though it is sometimes served separately as a sauce, for instance to accompany a *tortilla* or the meats from the *cocido,* it would more likely be added to a food while it is cooking. The sofrito can be sieved for a perfectly smooth texture or left roughly chopped. *Tomate frito* is a tinned tomato sauce which can be used for the *sofrito*.

Thickening ingredients. There are not very many flour-thickened sauces in Spanish cuisine. Occasionally, a gratin dish is coated with a bechamel or cream sauce, and a thick bechamel is the basis of the beloved *croqueta*. Sauces are more usually thickened either by slow cooking and reduction or by the addition of bread or ground nuts (almonds, hazelnuts and walnuts being the most common). The usual procedure is to fry a slice or more of crustless bread until crisply golden on both sides, then crush it in the mortar (or processor) with spices and garlic, then dilute in water, wine or stock before adding to the cooking pot. For some dishes, such as gazpacho, the bread is not fried, but soaked in water and then squeezed out. Use only "real" bread (Spanish, French or Italian loaves); packaged, sliced bread contains texturizing additives which prevent it from turning into a doughy mass for dissolving in a sauce. Some recipes call for *galletas,* plain biscuits, finely ground, to thicken a sauce.

Stock and consommé. Typical Spanish home cooking is not based on fortified stocks, though, of course, restaurant chefs do use this flavour-adding basis for many dishes. The Spanish housewife, if she wanted to enrich a sauce or stew, would use the *caldo,* broth, from the *cocido,* which is usually highly flavoured with chicken, meat bones and ham bone. This broth, which is not the same as a clear, de-fatted consommé, is the starting point for several soup variations. Packaged soups and stock cubes are also used for their quick flavour boosts. When a recipe calls for stock, use any home-made broth or stock cube, or water which has been boiled with a little wine, carrot, onion and bouquet garni.

Pimento. A favourite garnish for paella and other dishes and basis for several salads are sweet red peppers, roasted and skinned. Tinned red pimento can be used, but the flavour is better if freshly made. To roast peppers, spear them on a fork or hold with tongs over gas flame or place under broiler, turning the peppers until the the skin is charred. While still warm, peel off the blackened skin. Remove stem and seeds and cut the peppers into strips.

Wine in cooking. One the nicest things about cooking in Spain is that you can afford to experiment with wine-based dishes that in other countries would be an expensive luxury — fillets of sole in champagne sauce, beef in a red wine marinade, sherry-laced soups, wine-spiked fruit cup — can be added to the culinary repertoire for a few hundred pesetas and the twist of a corkscrew.

Sweet wines, such as Malaga moscatel and cream sherries, are mainly used for puddings and sweets but, in discreet quantities, are an interesting addition to savoury foods as well. Avoid sweet wines with fish, however, as they tend to emphasize the fishiness rather than point up the delicacy. Sparkling wines are good with delicate sauces. As the bubbles get dissipated in cooking, this is a good way to use up the tag ends of a bottle of *cava*.

Aperitif wines, sherry and Montilla in particular, are good cooking wines. Another one to try is dry vermouth. With a herb-based flavour, it can be substituted for white wine in cooking.

Spanish recipes often call for *vino rancio,* aged, mellow wine. If not available use an amontillado Sherry. The tried and true guidelines — red wine with red meat and white wine with light meat and fish — are not so definite in the kitchen as at the table. For instance, a white wine which could never stand up to a hearty beef dish might, in the cooking pot, add just a hint of piquancy. Or a strongly-flavoured fish stew, which has already been coloured by onions and tomatoes, might get just the oomph it needs with a good splash of red wine. Rosé wine, less used in cooking, can add interesting colour contrasts to otherwise bland dishes.

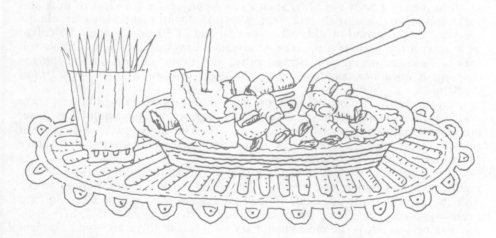

What wines to choose? The alcohol content in wine is completely evaporated within a few minutes of cooking, leaving only the flavour. The better the wine, the better the finished dish. Don't pick the cheapest *vino común* for cooking, but neither do you need to select the finest *reserva* vintages. Of the red wines, the moderately priced ones are excellent for cooking. The equivalent white wines don't stand up to cooking as well. They tend to be a bit thin and can give a finished dish a sort of tinny taste instead of mellow silver. With whites, a higher priced wine or a more full-bodied one is best. An insignificant wine, red or white, can be given a boost in the cooking stages by the addition of a tablespoon or two of brandy.

Don't cook with wine in aluminium pots and pans. The acidity can cause discoloration and off-tastes. When marinating food in wine — a most flavourful and tenderizing procedure — use glass, enamel or crockery utensils. Under-salt dishes cooked with wine and taste before serving. Natural salts and minerals in wine, especially when reduced, can make for excessive saltiness.

MENUS AND MEAL SERVICE

Not so many years ago, before many village people owned cars, at midday women would carry food to their menfolk working in the fields or on construction sites several kilometres from town. No simple sandwich, but an *olla* of hot food. Though the pace of life has changed incredibly everywhere in Spain, the midday dinner is still an important part of life. Even in cities, where fast-food restaurants proliferate, many working people will return to their homes for a proper meal and, in hot weather, enjoy the leisure of a siesta before returning to work in the late afternoon.

The day starts with *desayuno,* breakfast, which at first glance seems too small to sustain a body until lunch: *café con leche,* coffee with lots of milk and sugar and bread, toast or *churros,* fritters sprinkled with sugar. However, almost everyone eats a second breakfast between 10 and 11.30, which might be coffee with a sweet roll such as a *suizo* or *ensaimada;* a *tostada,* which is a whole roll split and toasted on the grill, served either with butter or with oil and salt for dipping; a *bocadillo,* sandwich with sausage, tuna; or a chunk of *tortilla,* omelette.

To further fortify oneself until the main meal between two and three, there is always the tapa bar, from which, around 1 p.m. when shops and offices close, are wafting tantalizing smells. Here, a crisply fried anchovy or croquette, a small pile of prawns, perhaps a few slices of ham with a *copita* of sherry help to stave off hunger until the main meal.

The *comida,* or midday dinner, consists of at least three courses — a starter, main course and *postre,* dessert. The first course might be soup, *potaje,* an egg dish, a vegetable dish or salad, followed by a main course of meat or fish, probably accompanied by potatoes. Fresh fruit, in a country where it is astonishingly good, is the most customary dessert, but there are some excellent puddings to be had as well.

Late afternoon — any time from 5 until 7 p.m. — is the hour of the *merienda,* a light lunch or snack. *Pasteles, bizcochos, tartas* and *galletas,* pastries, cakes, tarts and biscuits, with coffee or tea are typical. In the evening, the tapa bars fill up again as shops close around 8 p.m. Supper, *cena,* comes any time from then on, though tends to be somewhat earlier in winter than summer. In Madrid and other major cities, supper might be as late as 11 p.m. Unless dining out, most people would make this a lighter meal than the midday one, as for example, soup followed by an omelette and fruit for dessert.

Many holidays and local fiestas feature special foods or menus. For instance, *bacalao,* salt cod, is consumed everywhere during Semana Santa, Holy

Week. Christmas customs vary. Usually the feast is served on Christmas Eve. Almond soup, grilled fish and stuffed turkey are Christmas favourites. Of course, no holiday meal is complete without the typical *turrón,* nougat candy, marzipan confections and other sweets.

Of course, you needn't plan a whole Spanish meal in order to enjoy the dishes in this book. Any of them could fit quite comfortably into your regular menu planning — gazpacho is a wonderful prelude to fish and chips, paella can become a side dish to accompany grilled fish or chicken, and tortilla is every bit as good for breakfast, even if that's not traditional breakfast food in Spain.

Putting together a typical Spanish menu should be an easy matter from the selection of recipes that follows.

Here are some menu suggestions featuring Spanish dishes. Check the recipe index for page numbers.

A Tapa Party. An easy party to put together because most of the food can be prepared in advance and a welcome change from the canapé circuit and the chip-dip route. Serve wine, sherry, Montilla and beer and as many different *tapas,* or appetizer foods, as you like. You can provide *conchas,* the tiny, oval dishes used in tapa bars, or use regular plates. Cocktail forks are needed, but no knives. In addition to the prepared foods, serve olives, sliced *serrano* ham and cubes of cheese. Chunks of bread should accompany the food. Chapter 4 has lots more tapa foods. Additionally, many other dishes, from beef stew to chicken with garlic, are also served as *tapas.* It is only the size of the portions which makes them appetizers.

Huevos Rellenos	(Stuffed eggs)
Boquerones al natural	(Marinated fresh anchovies)
Mojete	(Roasted pepper and onion salad)
Pipirrana	(Fresh tomato relish)
Ensaladilla de patatas	(Potato salad)
Gambas rebozadas	(Batter-dipped prawns)
Calamares a la romana	(Crisp-fried Squid Rings)
Cazón en adobo	(Marinated fried fish)
Mejillones a la marinera	(Mussels, Fisherman's Style)
Tortilla Española	(Spanish Potato Omelette)
Champiñones al ajillo	(Garlicky Mushrooms)
Callos a la madrileña	(Tripe Stew, Madrid Style)
Albóndigas en salsa de almendras	(Meatballs in Almond Sauce)
Riñones al jerez	(Kidneys in Sherry Sauce)
Magro con tomate	(Pork in Tomato Sauce)

A Cocktail Party. These are finger nibbles. Serve crudités — carrots, celery, mushrooms, cauliflower, cucumber sticks and sweet red peppers cut in strips, etc. — for dipping the two sauces.

Porra antequerana	(Vegetable dip)
Salsa de Cabrales	(Cabrales blue-cheese dip)
Panadons amb espinacs	(Spinach turnovers)
Tortillitas de camarones	(Shrimp fritters)
Coques en llanda	(Spanish "pizza")
Huevos de codorniz	(Quail eggs)
Almendras tostadas	(Toasted almonds)
Bollos preñados	("Pregnant" buns)

A Buffet Supper

Remojón	(Orange salad)
Xato	(Tarragona salad)
Empanada de espinacas y queso	(Spinach and cheese tart)
Escabeche de pescado	(Marinated fish)
Fiambre de bonito	(Fish pâté)
Flan de tomate con langostinos	(Tomato custards with prawns)
Alcachofas Aliñadas	(Marinated artichokes)
Pavo trufado	(Boned, stuffed turkey)
Lomo en adobo	(Marinated pork loin)
Peras al horno	(Pears baked in wine)
Brazo gitano	("Gypsy's arm" cake roll)
Tocino de cielo	("Heavenly bacon" custard squares)

Brunch

Vino jerez con zumo de naranja	(Sherry "screwdrivers")
Pomelos en almibar	(Grapefruit in syrup)
Buñuelos de higos	(Fig fritters)
Huevos a la flamenca	(Flamenco baked eggs)
Higadillos de pollo salteados	(Sautéed chicken livers)
Ensaimadas	(Sweet rolls)
Carne de membrillo	(Quince jelly)
Queso blanco	(White cheese)
Mermelada de naranjas	(Orange marmalade)
Café con leche	(Coffee with milk)

Luncheon on the Terrace

Ardaugogatza	(Basque lemonade wine cooler)
Ajo blanco con uvas	(Cold garlic soup with grapes)
Pimientos rellenos	(Stuffed peppers)
Ensalada de judías verdes	(Green bean salad)
Pastel de berenjena	(Aubergine mousse)
Sorbete de chumbos u higos	(Sorbet of prickly pears or figs)
Mostachones	(Pine nut biscuits)

Picnic

Naranjada	(Orangeade)
Gazpacho	(Cold gazpacho)
Amanida	(Catalan salad)
Tortilla de Murcia	(Aubergine omelette, Murcia style)
Empanada de lomo	(Pork pie)
Fruta del tiempo	(Fruit in season)
Soplillos granadinos	(Meringue puffs, Granada style)

Patio Barbecue

Sangría	(Red wine punch)
Pinchitos	(Moroccan-style kebabs)
Calçotada con romesco y alioli	(Grilled spring onions with sauces)
Berenjenas en escabeche	(Pickled aubergine)
Parrillada de patatas	(Grilled potatoes)
Pez limón al hinojo	(Fennel-grilled fish)
Costillas a la parrilla	(Grilled spare ribs)
Melón al vino tinto	(Melon in red wine)

Spring Dinner

Esparragos con dos salsas	(Asparagus with two sauces)
Cordero al chilindrón	(Baby lamb with peppers)
Patatas bravas	(Bold potatoes)
Menestra de verduras	(Spring vegetable medley)
Natillas	(Creamy custards with meringue)

Fall Dinner

Albóndigas de bacalao	(Codfish balls)
Perdiz a la navarra	(Partridge, Navarra style)
Cebollas guisadas	(Braised onions)
Coliflor al ajo arriero	(Cauliflower, mule-driver's style)
Castañas con leche	(Chestnut pudding)

Seafood Dinner

Txangurro	(Basque crab casserole)
Arroz Abanda	(Poached fish, rice and garlic sauce)
Pisto	(Stewed summer vegetables)
Cuajada	(Cheese custard tart)

More Dinner Menus

Sopa viña AB	(Sherried seafood soup)
Pollo granadina	(Chicken with ham, Granada style)
Patatas fritas	(Fried potatoes)
Acelgas a la malagueña	(Chard with Malaga raisins)
Leche frita	("Fried milk")

Sopa de col	(Cabbage soup)
Empanada de cerdo	(Breaded pork cutlet)
Patatas a lo pobre	(Poor man's potatoes)
Calabaza frita	("Fried" pumpkin)
Manzanas rellenas	(Baked apples stuffed with dates)

Salpicón de mariscos	(Shellfish cocktail)
Ternera mechada	(Veal pot roast)
Patatas cerdeña	(Mashed potatoes)
Judías verdes salteadas	(Sautéed green beans)
Macedonia de frutas	(Fruit cup)
Empanadillas	(Fruit turnovers)

Family supper

Ensalada de verduras	(Mixed vegetable salad)
Moros y cristianos	(Black beans and rice)
Flan de caramelo	(Caramel custard)

Christmas Dinner

Sopa de almendras	(Almond soup)
Besugo asado	(Grilled bream)
Pavo relleno	(Stuffed turkey)
Lombarda a la castellana	(Lombard cabbage, Castilian style)
Cardos	(Cardoons)
Intxausalsa	(Walnut cream soup)
Helado de turrón	(Nougat ice cream)
Mazapanes	(Marzipan)
Roscos	(Doughnuts)
Mantecados	(Almond lard cakes)
Pan de higos	(Fig roll)
Copa navidad	(Christmas cup — anise with raisins)

SUBSTITUTIONS, ADAPTATIONS AND VARIATIONS

The recipes in this book are intended to be an introduction to "classic" Spanish cooking: the traditional, authentic and typical dishes, many of which are still to be found today. But they're also a starting point, the inspiration, for ways of combining foods, of spicing and seasoning, which are quite out of the ordinary.

In my own kitchen I often make substitutions, adaptations or variations, either for reasons of practicality or for those of inventive cookery. Though the pueblo *abuela* would never dream of putting chopped basil in a typical vegetable *pisto* (a delicious addition) or a dollop of cream with the stewed chard or a bit of chili pepper in the *escabeche* of marinated fish, it doesn't mean *you* can't. There is always a fresh way of looking at the typical. You'll enjoy Spanish cooking most if you adapt these dishes to your own menus.

For those of us who come to live here, cooking in Spain is a two-way proposition, adapting familiar dishes from our home lands to produce available here as well as learning the cuisine of our adopted country. For those who live abroad, Spanish cooking sometimes presents the problem of finding necessary ingredients. Again, don't be afraid to change and adapt recipes to suit yourself. For example, if you can't find squid to go in the *paella,* try substituting frozen scallops — it won't change the nature of the dish. However, if you substitute corn oil for olive and long grain rice for short, then it's really no longer paella. Likewise, if you don't like so much oil in the *gambas al pil pil,* sizzled prawns, it's quite all right to decrease the quantity of oil and even sprinkle the prawns with a favourite herb. But if you use butter instead of oil and omit the garlic, don't call it *pil pil.*

CONVERSIONS

"First you beat a few eggs together with some sugar. Then you add your wine, a little oil and the cinnamon. Then you work in as much flour as it will admit. Form the *roscos* and fry them in plenty of oil."

This is a translation of one of my authentic village recipes. How many eggs? How much wine and oil? How much flour will it admit? These recipes are like cryptograms — if your mother and grandmother before you hadn't been making that recipe for ever and ever, you wouldn't have the slightest idea how to proceed. It wasn't until I had helped my village friend make *roscos* and weighed and measured the ingredients that her recipe meant anything.

An experienced cook works more by taste, smell and feel than by measuring. Few cooks will slavishly follow the dictates of a recipe — a little more wine here, a little less garlic there, three tomatoes instead of four, omit the aniseed... It's such creativeness that makes cooking and eating fun. Most cooks can get by with very rough conversions. For example, a recipe that calls for a chicken of 1½ kilos to be cooked in ½ litre of wine would be equally successful with a 3-pound chicken cooked in 1 pint of wine. We can even ignore the fact that the U.S. pint and the British pint are not the same.

But with some goods, especially baked goods, quantities are important and, for the novice cook or even the experienced one working with a new cuisine, a fairly precise formula is a necessary starting point.

In Spain, foods are bought and measured in grams and litres, so that is how these recipes are written. Whether you are British and still accustomed to pre-metric recipes in ounces and pints, or a North American who's never weighed a cup of flour, I suggest you immediately buy an inexpensive one-kilo set of scales and a one-litre measuring cup. It's much simpler than trying to convert these recipes back to familiar measures.

Americans measure volume as well as liquid in standardized measures, so flour, sugar, rice and butter are all measured in cups, not on the scales. As all the rest of the world measures dry ingredients on scales — which, by the way, gives more accurate results than the cup-volume method — that is how these recipes are written.

British readers sometimes ask me: "How do you Americans measure butter by cups?" It's easy: by displacement. Say you want ½ cup butter. Fill a 1-cup measure with water to the ½-cup mark, then add butter until the water reaches the 1-cup mark. Drain off the water and you have ½ cup of butter.

The American quart, pint or cup is 5/6 the quantity of the British Imperial quart, pint or cup. The American tablespoon equals 14.2 millilitres; the British tablespoon equals 17.7 millilitres. Where the measure "cup" is used in this book it means a Spanish breakfast cup, 250 ml. or about 9 fluid ounces. A tablespoon means a Spanish tablespoon or 15 millilitres.

Following is a table of *approximate* equivalents of commonly used foods (based on ingredients in Spain).

	American Standard Measure	Avdp. Weight	Metric Weight
Butter, margarine	1 tbsp.	1/3 oz.	13 gm.
	7 1/2 tbsp.	3 1/2 oz.	100 gm.
	1/2 cup	3 2/3 oz.	105 gm.
Cheese, grated	3/4 cup	3 1/2 oz.	100 gm.
Cornstarch	1 tsp.		3 gm. (5 ml.)
	1 tbsp.	1/3 oz.	10 gm. (15 ml.)
Flour (all purpose)	3/4 cup	3 1/2 oz.	100 gm.
	1/4 cup	1 1/4 oz.	35 gm.
	1/2 cup	2 1/4 oz.	65 gm.
	1 cup	4 1/2 oz.	130 gm.
	3 3/4 cups	1 lb. 2 oz.	500 gm.
Gelatin	1 tbsp.	1/4 oz.	7 gm.
Rice	1 cup	7 oz.	200 gm.
Salt	1 tbsp.	1/2 oz.	15 gm.
Sugar (granulated)	1 tbsp.	1/2 oz.	15 gm.
	1/4 cup	2 oz.	55 gm.
	9 tbsp.	3 1/2 oz.	100 gm.
	1 cup	6 oz.	175 gm.

For those who use Spanish cookbooks, here are some common measuring terms. The cups are filled to 1 centimetre of container rim; the spoons are level.

Copa (sherry glass or brandy snifter)	100 ml.
Vaso (wine glass)	150 ml. or 1 1/2 decilitres
Taza (breakfast cup) or *vaso* (water glass)	250 ml. or 1/4 litre
Cucharadita (teaspoon)	5 ml.
Cucharada (tablespoon)	15 ml.
Cucharón (soup ladle)	100 ml.
Un dedo de grueso (one finger thick)	1 centimetre
Un dedo de largo (one finger long)	6 centimetres
Arroba	11.3 kilos (25 lbs.)

The calculator in the kitchen. On the inside back cover of this book you will find a conversion table, giving metric, British, and American measures. For weights and measures beyond those on the chart, here is an easy-to-follow rule for converting: get out the calculator — sometimes the decimals make a difference. When calculating grams, centimetres or millilitres, you can round off decimals to the nearest whole number, but with kilos, metres or litres, don't round them off. For instance, 50.4 millilitres is close enough to 50 millilitres, but 1.4 kilos is 1 kilo 400 grams. Where a second decimal appears, round it off. Thus 1.48 kilos becomes 1.5 or 1 ½ kilos.

FLUID MEASURE

To convert from	To	Multiply by
Millilitres	Fluid ounces British	0.035
Litres	Fluid ounces British	35.0
Millilitres	Fluid ounces U.S.	0.034
Litres	Fluid ounces U.S.	33.8
Litres	Pints British	1.75
Litres	Pints U.S.	2.1
Ounces, U.S. fluid	Litres	0.03
Ounces, U.S. fluid	Millilitres	29.6
Ounces, U.S. fluid	Ounces, British fluid	1.04
Ounces, British fluid	Ounces, U.S. fluid	0.96
Ounces, British fluid	Litres	0.028
Ounces, British fluid	Millilitres	28.4
Pints, U.S. fluid	Litres	0.47
Pints, British fluid	Litres	0.57
Pints, U.S. fluid	Pints, British fluid	0.83
Pints, British fluid	Pints, U.S. fluid	1.2
Quarts, U.S. fluid	Litres	0.95
Quarts, British fluid	Litres	1.14

LINEAR MEASURES

To convert from	To	Multiply by
Centimetres	Inches	0.39
Inches	Centimetres	2.5

WEIGHTS

To convert from	To	Multiply by
Ounces (Avdp. British and American)	Grams	28.3
Grams	Ounces	0.035
Kilograms	Ounces	35.2
Kilograms	Pounds	2.2
Pounds	Kilograms	0.45
Pounds	Grams	453.6

TEMPERATURE

To convert from	To
Fahrenheit	Celsius: Subtract 32; multiply by 5; divide by 9.
Celsius	Fahrenheit: Multiply by 9; divide by 5; add 32.

METRIC EQUIVALENTS

Weight

250 grams (gm.) = 1/4 kilogram (kg.)
500 grams = 1/2 kilo
750 grams = 3/4 kilo
1000 grams = 1 kilo

Fluid

100 millilitres (ml.) = 1 decilitre (dl.) = 1/10 litre = 100 cubic centimetres (c.c.)
250 millilitres = 2 1/2 decilitres = 1/4 litre
500 millilitres = 5 decilitres = 1/2 litre
750 millilitres = 7 1/2 decilitres = 3/4 litre
1000 millilitres = 10 decilitres = 1 litre = 1000 c.c.

FLUID EQUIVALENTS

U. S. (also used for volume)	British
3 teaspoons = 1 tablespoon = 1/2 fluid ounce	5 fluid ounces = 1/4 pint
4 tablespoons = 1/4 cup = 2 fluid ounces	10 fluid ounces = 1/2 pint = 1 cup
4 fluid ounces = 1/2 cup	20 fluid ounces = 1 pint
8 fluid ounces = 1 cup	40 fluid ounces = 2 pints = 1 quart
16 fluid ounces = 2 cups = 1 pint	4 quarts = 1 gallon
4 cups = 2 pints = 1 quart	
4 quarts = 1 gallon	

WEIGHT EQUIVALENTS

Avoirdupois — U.S. and British

4 ounces (oz.) = 1/4 pound (lb.)
8 ounces = 1/2 pound
16 ounces = 1 pound

The following chart lists some (very approximate) equivalents.

Food	Quantity	Weight
Almonds, other nuts	40	50 grams
Breadcrumbs	8 tbsp. (1/2 cup)	50 grams
Capers	4 tbsp.	50 grams
Mussels	2 1/2 dozen	1 kilo
Olives	20 (pitted or stuffed)	50 grams
Onion	1 medium	150 grams
Peas	1/2 kilo	1 1/2 cups shelled
Potatoes	7-8 medium	1 kilo
Tomatoes	4 large	1 kilo
Tomato sauce	2 tbsp.	30 ml.

Jamón serrano — *mountain-cured ham* — *is served as a* **tapa** *and is used as an ingredient in many Spanish dishes.*

Following page, pickled olives — a tasty appetiser (recipe, page 106).

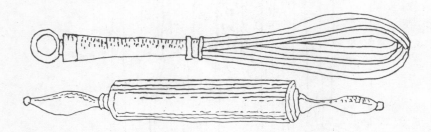

CHAPTER 4

Appetisers: Tapas, Entremeses & Salads

The *tapa* bar or *tasca* is a very special part of Spanish life. Here wine, sometimes from the barrel, is dispensed along with a huge variety of foods, both hot and cold, which are usually consumed standing up. After enjoying several small portions of food lots of people go on to eat a whole meal. Others make a meal out of tapa foods. They are a great introduction to Spanish cooking.

Besides the usual finger foods — olives, nuts, crisps — one can order plates of sliced cheese, ham and sausages, croquettes and fried foods, as well as many more substantial dishes — tiny, breaded pork cutlets, prawns sizzled in garlic, rabbit stew, chicken in tomato sauce — and a variety of cold salads, plus fish and shellfish. A *tapa* portion, usually served on a tiny plate with a chunk of bread, really is just a nibble. A larger serving is a *ración*.

Many of these appetizer foods make great selections for parties. Except for the *fritos* — fried foods which must be served piping hot from the oil — most can be made in advance and reheated to serve.

Entremeses, the Spanish equivalent of an hors d'oeuvre or antipasto plate, are also appetizer foods, but served at table as a first course. A typical *entremeses* serving might contain a mound of potato salad garnished with pimento and olives, asparagus dressed with mayonnaise, pickled beets, sliced *serrano* ham and sausages, fried sardines, a slice of omelette, a few prawns and olives. A platter of *entremeses* makes an agreeable luncheon dish all on its own.

Under the heading of "salads" falls a wide variety of cold dishes, many of which are commonly served as a *tapa,* others which make very elegant starters and yet others which might serve as garnish or accompaniment to the main dish.

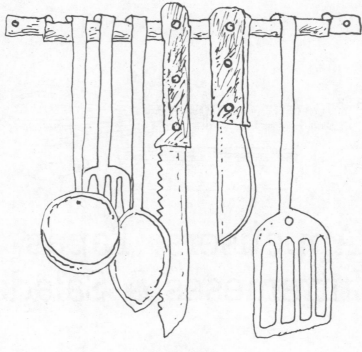

FRITOS

Fritos. These are fried foods which include croquettes, fritters, pastry puffs and batter-dipped foods, all wonderful with aperitifs, but also nice supper dishes. Use any vegetable oil for deep frying, never butter or margarine, which burns. The oil should be deep enough to completely cover the pieces of food. Use a heavy pan with high sides or an electric deep fryer which has a basket for lowering food into the oil. Heat the oil until just short of smoking. If not hot enough, the food will soak up the oil before it cooks; if too hot, the surface will brown before the food is cooked. Don't crowd the pieces of food. Remove when golden and drain on absorbent paper. Serve sizzling hot and crispy. Salad garnishes are good with fried foods or you can invent a zippy dipping sauce.

GAMBAS REBOZADAS
Batter-dipped Prawns

1/2	kilo fresh or frozen prawns	1/2	teaspoon salt
	wooden toothpicks	1/4	teaspoon baking soda
1	egg	65	grams flour
80	ml. water		deep oil for frying

Shell the prawns, wash and de-vein them. Spear each one on a toothpick and set aside. In a mixing bowl, beat the egg with the water. Add the salt and baking soda, then gradually beat in the flour, making a thick batter. Let it set for an hour. Heat oil in deep fryer. Dip the prawns, toothpicks and all, into the batter, and fry them until golden. Serve hot with lemon.

CROQUETAS
Croquettes

3 tablespoons oil	400 grams finely chopped cooked chick-
1/2 small onion, minced	en, ham, tuna or fish
4 tablespoons flour	2 eggs, beaten with a little water
1/4 litre milk	200 grams fine breadcrumbs
1/8 teaspoon grated nutmeg	oil for frying
1/2 teaspoon salt	

Heat the oil in a saucepan and sauté the minced onions until they are transparent. Do not let them brown. Stir in the flour and let it cook briefly, then whisk in the milk. Cook, stirring constantly until this sauce thickens. Season it with nutmeg, salt and pepper. Stir in the cooked and chopped filling — any choice of cooked meat, fish or vegetables can be used, as long as they are very well drained of all liquid. Spread the mixture in a dish and refrigerate it until solid. Place the beaten eggs in a dish, the breadcrumbs in another. With moistened hands, form the croquette mixture into balls, cylinders or cones. Dip each croquette first in breadcrumbs (or flour), then in beaten egg, then again in breadcrumbs, taking care that they are well covered. Allow to dry in a cool place for 30 minutes. Heat oil in deep fryer and fry the croquettes, a few at a time, until they are golden — about 3 minutes.

REBOZADAS
Fritters

These delectable tidbits are also called *buñuelos*. All kinds of foods can be prepared in this manner — small bits of chorizo sausage, dry salt cod which has been soaked overnight, pieces of cooked cauliflower, artichoke hearts or aubergine and shellfish such as mussels, scallops and oysters.

1/2 small onion, minced	1/2 teaspoon salt
1 clove garlic, minced	1/2 teaspoon baking soda
1 tablespoon chopped parsley	140 grams flour
1/4 teaspoon crumbled saffron	300 grams salt cod, chorizo, etc.
1 egg, separated	oil for frying
160 ml. water (approximately)	

If using salt cod, soak it overnight in water to cover, changing the water at least once. Then remove all bones and skin and cut it in small chunks. In a bowl mix the minced onion, minced garlic, parsley and crushed saffron with the egg yolk. Beat in the water, salt and baking soda. Beat in the flour and enough water to make a thick batter which will adhere to the food. Let the batter rest for an hour.

Before frying, beat the egg white until stiff and fold it into the batter. Dip the food into the batter and fry it in deep hot oil, a few pieces at a time. Drain and serve hot.

FLAMENQUINES
Ham Roll-Ups

Top slices of cooked ham with slices of cheese. Roll them up and secure with a toothpick. Dredge the rolls in flour, then beaten egg, then fine breadcrumbs and fry them in deep, hot oil until golden and crisp. Serve with salad garnish.

EMPANADILLAS
Fried Pies

For the dough:

270 grams flour	1/2 teaspoon salt
100 grams butter, margarine or lard	100 ml. white wine

Place the flour and salt in a bowl and cut the butter or margarine into it until crumbly. Add the wine, mix quickly into a ball and turn out onto a floured board. Knead very briefly, adding only enough additional flour to make a dough which doesn't stick to the hands. Form into a ball, cover with plastic wrap and refrigerate for at least two hours.

For the filling:

200	gm. tuna or any cooked meat, chicken fish, prawns or ham, finely chopped	1	tablespoon brandy salt and pepper
3	tablespoons tomato sauce	20	pimento-stuffed olives, chopped
1	hard-cooked egg, chopped	1	tablespoon chopped onion
1	tablespoon parsley, chopped		

Mix all the ingredients together. Roll out the chilled dough on a floured board and cut it into rounds about 10 cm. in diameter. Place a spoonful of filling on each round and fold over the dough to make half-circles. Crimp the edges together with the tines of a fork. Fry the pies, a few at a time, in deep hot oil. Drain and serve hot or cold. The pastries may also be baked in a medium-hot oven. Makes about 2 dozen.

TORTILLITAS DE CAMARONES A LA GADITANA
Shrimp Fritters, Cadiz style

1/2	onion, minced		
2	tablespoons parsley (or seaweed)	1/2	litre water
1/4	kilo shrimp or tiny prawns (125 grams shelled)	50	ml. white wine
		1	teaspoon salt
1/4	kilo flour		dash of cayenne
1/4	teaspoon baking powder		oil for frying

Mix the minced onion and chopped parsley with the shrimp (regular prawns, chopped, can be used). Add the flour and baking powder, then stir in the water and wine to make a heavy batter. Season with salt and a dash of cayenne. Cover and let the batter set for 3 hours, refrigerated. Heat oil about 2 cm. deep in a frying pan. Drop spoonfuls of the batter into the oil and fry until golden-brown, turning to fry the other side. Remove and drain on paper towelling and serve hot. Makes about 3 dozen.

BUÑUELOS DE QUESO
Cheese Puffs

200 ml. water	4 eggs
80 ml. oil	150 grams Manchego cheese, grated
1/2 teaspoon salt	oil for frying
130 grams flour	

Put the water, oil and salt in a saucepan and bring it to a boil. Remove from fire and add all the flour, beating hard with a wooden spoon. Return to a low heat and beat the dough until it forms a ball. Remove from heat and beat in the eggs, one at a time, beating hard after each addition. Then mix in the grated cheese. Drop the dough by spoonfuls, a very few at a time, into deep, hot oil. They should rise to the surface and puff up quite a bit. Turn them over once in the oil and remove with a skimmer when they are golden-brown. Drain and serve hot. Makes about two dozen.

QUESO FRITO
Fried Cheese

Cut slices of semi-cured Manchego cheese into triangular slices about 1 cm. thick. Dredge in flour, dip in beaten egg, then in breadcrumbs and fry in a little oil, turning to brown both sides.

ENTREMESES

In Spain, much appreciated are *entremeses con apellido* — hors d'oeuvres with surnames — meaning you don't serve just any old *jamón serrano* or sliced sausage, but a particular one from a particular place.

JAMON CON MELON O HIGOS
Ham with Melon or Figs

Salt-cured *serrano* or mountain ham is served either very thinly sliced or cut into small cubes and accompanied by chunks of bread. Another delicious presentation contrasts the salty ham with fruit.

Remove the seeds from well-chilled Spanish melon and cut into slices. With a sharp knife cut the flesh from the skin, leaving it in place. Then cut crosswise slices. Push pieces alternately to one side and the other. Drape thinly sliced ham over the top of the melon slices and serve.

Arrange sliced ham on salad plates. Peel well-chilled ripe figs and cut them in quarters. Arrange decoratively around the ham.

Variation: use slices of smoked salmon in place of ham.

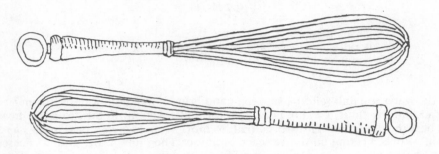

HUEVOS DE CODORNIZ
Quail Eggs

Serve hard-boiled (about 5 minutes) quail eggs in a bowl accompanied by a mixture of salt, ground pepper and ground cumin to sprinkle on them after peeling.

ALMENDRAS TOSTADAS
Toasted Almonds

Blanch almonds in boiling water very briefly, drain and slip off skins while they are still warm. Dry them well on paper towels. Spread the almonds on a baking tin. Drizzle them with olive oil, sprinkle with salt and a little paprika and toast in a hot oven, stirring frequently, just until they are slightly coloured. They may also be toasted in a little oil in a frying pan.

ACEITUNAS
Olives

Many types of olives are to be found in Spain and always accompany hors d'oeuvres. Some of the best don't come bottled but are the home-cured ones. Because so many people living in Spain have their own olive crop, two recipes for their preparation are included here.

Method 1: This is similar to the process used for commercial olives. Pick through the olives and remove any bruised or blemished ones. Wash them thoroughly and place in an earthenware, glass or plastic jug. Add water to cover, *measuring it as you fill the container.* In a separate container, dissolve 100 grams of soda-lye *(sosa cáustica,* sold in *droguerías)* for every 5 litres of water which you have added to the olives. Be careful with the lye, as it can burn the hands. Add the solution to the jug of olives, mix well and leave them for 24 hours. Then pour off the lye solution and wash the olives in running water. Cover them with clear water. The following day, wash and change the water again. Repeat this procedure for eight days. Then prepare a strong brine — about 7 tablespoons of salt for every litre of water. Place the drained and washed olives in the brine, cover the vat and leave them for two weeks. They are now ready to eat. They can be additionally flavoured as in the following recipe.

Method 2: Remove any bruised or blemished olives. Using a stone or mallet, crack the olives lightly, just to split open the fruit (wear old clothes, as you'll be spattered with olive juice). Wash them and place in an earthenware, glass or plastic jug. Cover them completely with water. Change the water every few days for several weeks, or until the olives, when tasted, are no longer bitter. This will take about a month. Then prepare a brine (see preceding recipe) and place the olives in it along with cloves of garlic, quartered lemons, and sprigs of thyme and fennel. The lemons (oranges can also be used, giving an interesting flavour) keep the olives from darkening, but tend to make them mushy. Other herbs can be used, or the olives can be spiced with paprika or hot chili peppers. Cover the olives and let them set for at least a week. They are then ready to eat. Replenish the brine as necessary and the olives should keep for several months. (If mould forms on top, skim it off. It will not hurt the olives.)

BOQUERONES AL NATURAL
Marinated Fresh Anchovies

1/2	kilo fresh anchovies *(boquerones)*	50	ml. oil
250	ml. vinegar	4	cloves garlic
1	teaspoon salt	2	tablespoons chopped parsley lemon

Remove heads of the fish. Grasp top of the backbone, give it a sharp jerk down across the back and the bone will come free. Cut it off, leaving the two fillets attached at the tails. Wash them and place in a single layer in a shallow dish. Add enough vinegar to cover and the salt. Marinate from 6 to 24 hours, or until the fillets are white and solid — they are "cooked" by the vinegar. Drain them, rinse in cold water and arrange on a bed of shredded lettuce on a serving plate. Sprinkle with the oil, minced garlic and parsley. Chopped onion and lemon juice can be added.

ESCABECHE DE PESCADO
Marinated Fish

This recipe originated as a way of preserving fish without refrigeration. However, it is such a good hors d'oeuvre it's worth making for its own sake. Mackerel, *caballa,* is most commonly used, but *escabeche* can also be made with tunny, bonito, sardines or herring.

2	kilos mackerel	2	cloves
	flour	10	peppercorns
	oil	2	teaspoons paprika
1	head garlic	1/2	litre vinegar
100	ml. oil	1/4	litre water
4	bay leaves	1/4	litre white wine
1	sprig thyme or 1 teaspoon	2	teaspoons salt
1	sprig oregano (or 1 teaspoon)	1	chili pepper (optional)

Clean the fish and cut it into crosswise slices (or it can be filleted). Dust the pieces with flour and fry in just enough oil to cover the bottom of the pan. Remove them as they are cooked and let them cool, then place the fish in glass or earthenware jars, bowls or jugs. Add the remaining oil to the pan and in it heat the peeled cloves of garlic with the bay leaf, thyme, oregano, cloves and peppercorns. Remove from the heat and stir in the paprika. Heat the vinegar, wine, salt and chili to the boiling point, add the oil mixture to it and cook briefly. Let it cool slightly and pour over the fish. Cover and marinate for at least 24 hours. Store refrigerated. Serve at room temperature, garnished with sliced onions, tomatoes and peppers.

PORRA ANTEQUERANA
Vegetable Dip

This dish, which comes from the town of Antequera (Malaga), is traditionally made in a wooden bowl and served as a starter, eaten as a thick soup with a spoon. However, it makes a wonderful party dip or a cold sauce for grilled fish, poultry or meat.

1/2	kilo bread, crusts removed	50	ml. vinegar
200	ml. olive oil	1	teaspoon salt
3	large, ripe tomatoes, peeled and chopped	1	large tin tuna
		300	grams serrano ham
3	green peppers, seeded	4	hard-cooked eggs
6	cloves garlic		

Cut the bread into chunks and sprinkle it with water or a little juice of bitter orange and set aside. In blender, processor or wooden bowl with a pestle, purée the tomatoes, peppers and garlic. Add the pieces of bread and process until you have a smooth paste. Add the oil to the mixture, pouring it in slowly with the processor running. Then add vinegar and salt to taste. Serve the *porra* either garnished with chunks of tuna, julienne pieces of ham and sliced egg, or serve them separately as accompaniments, along with chopped tomatoes and onions, for each person to add to his serving.

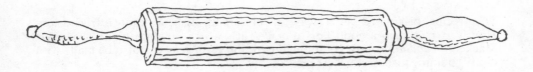

HUEVOS RELLENOS
Stuffed Eggs

8	eggs		1	small tin pimento
200	grams tinned tuna or cooked and peeled prawns		1	teaspoon lemon juice
				salt and pepper
8	green olives, chopped		100	ml. mayonnaise

Hard cook the eggs, plunge them in cold water and peel them. Cut them in half lengthwise, remove the yolks and set aside. In a small bowl mix the flaked tuna or chopped prawns with the chopped olives, part of the red pimento, chopped finely, the salt and pepper and lemon juice. Fill the egg whites with this mixture. Arrange the eggs on lettuce leaves on a serving dish. Top each egg with a dab of mayonnaise and garnish with a strip of remaining pimento. Sieve the egg yolks and sprinkle over the eggs.

ESPARRAGOS CON DOS SALSAS
Asparagus with Two Sauces

This starter can be prepared with tinned white asparagus, rinsed in water and drained, or cooked fresh asparagus, white or green. The asparagus should be served cool. Place 6 spears each on individual plates and garnish with lettuce and tomato. Accompany with sauce bowls of mayonnaise to which lemon juice has been added. For the second sauce, mix finely minced green pepper, red pimento, onion, parsley, garlic and hard-cooked egg. Season with salt and pepper and a few drops of oil and vinegar.

AGUACATE CON GAMBAS
Prawn and Avocado Cocktail

Allow half an avocado and 6 cooked and peeled prawns per person. There are several ways of serving this delectable dish. The prawns may be heaped onto the halved avocado and topped with the dressing, or the dressing can be spread on a dish and the slices of avocado and prawns arranged on it, or the two can be mixed on a bed of shredded lettuce in a traditional cocktail cup set in ice and the sauce spooned over. Garnish with tomatoes, olives and strips of red and green peppers. For the dressing, mix 200 ml. mayonnaise with 4 tablespoons bottled catsup, 4 tablespoons lemon juice, 1 tablespoon minced onion, dash of brandy, pinch of cayenne.

TOMATES RELLENOS CON ENSALADILLA RUSA
Tomatoes Stuffed with Russian Salad

2	medium potatoes		1/2	teaspoon salt
1	large carrot		75	ml. mayonnaise
60	grams shelled peas		1	teaspoon vinegar
1	red pimento, chopped		4	large tomatoes
1	tablespoon chopped parsley			lettuce

Cook the whole, unpeeled potatoes with the carrot, peeled and cut in pieces, in water to cover until they are just tender. Cook the peas until tender. Peel the potatoes and cut into small dice. Add the diced carrots, peas, chopped pimento, parsley and salt. Stir the vinegar into the mayonnaise and blend into the potato mixture. Cut the tops off the tomatoes and scoop out the seeds and pulp. Drain the shells and fill them with the potato mixture. Place on lettuce leaves to serve. Serves 4.

PIPIRRANA
Fresh Tomato Relish

6	medium tomatoes	1	teaspoon salt
1/2	onion	6	tablespoons olive oil
4	green peppers	50	ml. vinegar
1	clove garlic		tinned tuna
2	hard-cooked eggs		diced *serrano* ham

Chop the tomatoes, onions and green peppers and mix together in a bowl. Finely mince the garlic and add it with the salt. Separate the yolks and set aside. Chop the whites into the salad. Mash the yolks in a bowl and beat in the oil, drop by drop, then beat in the vinegar. Add the dressing to the salad and toss lightly. Serve garnished with chunks of tuna or ham, or both. Finely diced cucumber may also be added. This salad-relish, which in North Africa is further seasoned with cumin and chopped coriander, is a wonderful accompaniment to fried fish.

SALPICON DE MARISCOS
Shellfish Cocktail

Add cooked prawns and pieces of lobster, scallops and mussels to the above salad. Serve on lettuce.

REMOJON
Orange Salad

One of the most colourful and exotic salads, this is a legacy of the Moors, who brought the bitter orange to Spain and appreciated its juice in many different dishes. Though this would typically be served as a *tapa* or *entremeses,* it makes a very special accompaniment to fish dishes.

1/4	kilo dry salt cod (or 1 tin tuna fish)	1	clove garlic
1	medium tomato, peeled, seeded and chopped	3/4	kilo sour oranges
6	scallions or 1 onion, chopped	2	tablespoons oil
50	grams pitted olives	1	tablespoon vinegar
			chili pepper (optional)

Toast the salt cod by holding it, skin side up, over the flame for a few minutes until it has an evenly browned surface and is softened. Leave it in a bowl of water while preparing the other ingredients. Chop the peeled tomato and combine with the chopped onion, olives and minced garlic. Peel the oranges, separate into sections and chop them into the bowl. Drain the codfish and remove all skin and bones. Shred it and add to the salad. Drizzle with oil and vinegar and toss the salad. Mince the chili pepper and add it, if desired. Serves 4.

ENSALADILLA DE PATATAS
Potato Salad

1	kilo potatoes	2	tablespoons chopped parsley
4	scallions or 1 small onion	100	ml. mayonnaise
1	large tomato, peeled and chopped	2	hard-cooked eggs, sliced
1	lemon	1	small tin pimentos
50	ml. olive oil	12	pitted olives

Cook potatoes in their skins in water until tender. Drain well, peel and dice them into a bowl. Clean the onions and chop into the potatoes. Chop the tomato finely and add to potatoes. Sprinkle with parsley. Squeeze juice of lemon (to taste) over the potatoes and drizzle with oil. Toss lightly. Shape the potato salad into a loaf on a serving plate and coat it with a thin layer of mayonnaise. Garnish with egg slices, strips of pimento and green olives. Serves 6.

ENSALADA DE VERDURAS
Vegetable Salad

1/2	head cauliflower	3	tablespoons chopped parsley
1/4	kilo green beans	1/2	teaspoon salt
4	carrots	1	lemon
3	medium potatoes	100	ml. olive oil
3	beets	3	hard-cooked eggs
	lettuce		olives
4	cloves garlic		

Wash cauliflower and cook in salted water until just tender. Drain and cut into flowerettes. Snap ends off beans, remove strings and cook until tender. Pare the carrots, cook them and cut into thin strips. Cook unpeeled potatoes, then peel and slice them. Cook beets, slip off skins and slice. Cover a platter with a bed of lettuce. Arrange each vegetable in groups on the lettuce. Cover and chill. In a bowl mix the minced garlic with the parsley, salt and pepper. Add the juice of the lemon, then whisk in the oil. Drizzle the vegetables with this dressing and serve garnished with quartered eggs and olives. Other vegetables — artichokes, asparagus, broccoli — can be added to this salad. Serves 6.

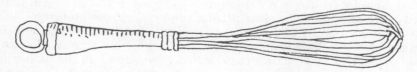

ENSALADA DE PULPO
Octopus Salad

2	medium octopuses, cooked and diced	1	tablespoon chopped parsley
2	small green peppers	2	cloves garlic, minced
3	scallions or 1 small onion	50	ml. oil
1	small tomato	1/2	lemon
			salt

See Chapter 9 for how to cook octopus. Use kitchen scissors to snip the cooked octopus into small dice. In a bowl mix it with chopped green peppers, chopped onion and chopped tomato. Add the chopped parsley and minced garlic. Drizzle with oil and lemon juice and salt to taste. Toss the salad. Serves 6.

AMANIDA
Catalan Salad

1	escarole	100	ml. mayonnaise
3	stalks celery, diced	1	clove garlic
6	scallions, chopped	1	tablespoon vinegar
100	grams ham, diced		salt
1	small tin anchovies, rinsed and drained	2	hard-cooked eggs
		150	grams butifarra

Wash and drain the escarole and place the cut-up leaves in a salad bowl. Add the diced celery, chopped scallions and diced ham. Cut the anchovies into small pieces and add to the salad. In a bowl mix the mayonnaise with a clove of crushed garlic, the vinegar and salt. Toss the dressing with the escarole and garnish with sliced egg and pieces of butifarra sausage. (Where the Catalan sausage is not available, pieces of bratwurst or frankfurters might be substituted.)

XATO
Tarragona Salad

2	lettuces	1	piece chili pepper (optional)
2	stalks celery	1	bunch parsley
4	artichoke hearts cooked and quartered (optional)	50	grams almonds, blanched
		10	hazelnuts
1	ripe tomato	50	ml. olive oil
4	cloves garlic	2	tablespoons vinegar
1	dried pepper		salt

Wash and drain the lettuce, tear it into pieces and place in a salad bowl with the chopped celery and artichokes. Roast tomato and garlic under broiler grill until tomato is softened and garlic somewhat charred. Peel them. Soak the dried pepper and chili in a little water. (If sweet dry pepper is not available, use a spoonful of paprika made into a paste with a little water.) In the mortar (or processor or blender) crush the peeled tomato and garlic with the drained peppers, the parsley, the blanched and skinned almonds and the hazelnuts. When this is a smooth sauce, beat in the olive oil, then the vinegar and salt. Pour the dressing over the salad and let it macerate for an hour before serving. Serves 6.

ENSALADA DE PIMIENTOS ASADOS
Roasted Pepper Salad

1	kilo sweet peppers, red and/or green	3	tablespoons vinegar or lemon juice
2	cloves garlic, minced	2	tablespoons chopped parsley
50	ml. olive oil		salt and pepper

Wash and dry the peppers. Roast them in the broiler grill, turning frequently until they are charred on all sides. Remove and wrap them in a towel, just until they are cool enough to handle. (Peppers can also be speared on a fork and roasted over gas flame, or laid on charcoal grill, which gives a wonderful flavour.) Peel the skin from the peppers, cut out stems and remove seeds. Tear the peppers into strips and put them on a serving plate. Mix the minced garlic, olive oil, vinegar, chopped parsley, salt and pepper. Drizzle the peppers with this and toss lightly. Serve at room temperature as an appetizer or as an accompaniment to grilled meat or poultry. Serves 6.

Variations: If an equal quantity of onions are roasted with the peppers, then cut into strips, the dish becomes *mojete,* a Murcia salad. If aubergine and peppers are roasted, the dish is *escalibada,* a Catalan speciality.

ENSALADA DE JUDIAS VERDES
Bean Salad

1/2	kilo green beans	2	tablespoons vinegar
1	medium potato	1	clove garlic
1	tablespoon minced onion	1	sprig fresh fennel leaves
6	tablespoons olive oil		(or parsley)
	salt and pepper	2	hard-cooked eggs
1/2	teaspoon cumin		

Remove strings from beans if necessary, but leave them whole. Cook the beans and the unpeeled potato in boiling salted water until just tender. Rinse in cold water and drain. Peel the potato and slice it. Arrange the beans on a serving platter with layers of sliced potatoes between. Sprinkle the minced onion over the top. Whisk together the oil, vinegar, minced garlic, salt and pepper and cumin and drizzle this over the salad. Sprinkle with finely chopped fennel and garnish with quartered eggs. Serves 6.

Variations: This salad can also be made with leftover cooked broad beans, garbanzos, black-eyed peas or white beans.

ENSALADILLA DE ARROZ
Rice Salad

400-500 ml. cooked, chilled rice
1   small onion, minced
1   green pepper, minced
1   clove garlic, minced
2   tablespoons chopped parsley
20 black or green olives, pitted and chopped.

salt and pepper
6   tablespoons oil
3   tablespoons vinegar
    red pimento
    lettuce
    tomatoes
    anchovy fillets (optional)

Fluff the rice with a fork. Add to it the minced onion, pepper, garlic, parsley and olives. Season to taste with salt and pepper. Drizzle with oil and vinegar and toss with a fork to blend. Arrange mounds of the salad on lettuce leaves. Garnish with strips of red pimento and arrange quartered tomatoes around the edge. This salad also makes a good filling for stuffed tomatoes. Cooked prawns can be added to the mixture. Serves 4 to 6.

CHAPTER 5

Soups, Gazpacho, One- pot Meals & Pottages

Soup is a big category in any language, but in Spanish it's enormous. And it's as basic to life as is bread. In fact, quite a few Spanish soups are little more than bread and water gruel which, besides sustaining people through poor times, are surprisingly tasty. Of these, *sopa de ajo,* garlic soup, in its myriad variations, even turns up on restaurant menus, a peasant dish in sophisticated surroundings.

Though visitors to Spain immediately think of gazpacho when they think of soup, this concoction, a sort of liquid salad, is a genre all by itself.

Naturally enough in a country surrounded by the sea, fish soups are among the best. Some are rich medleys containing four or five kinds of fish, clams, prawns and squid, not unlike the French bouillabaisse. Others are smooth bisques.

The basic soup in Spain is the broth from the *puchero* or *cocido,* interchangeable words for the Spanish boiled dinner of chicken, beef, sausages, garbanzos and vegetables. On the first serving it would contain rice or thin vermicelli noodles *(fideos).* For a second meal, perhaps supper the same day, the broth forms the basis of a new soup.

Then there are the *potajes* and *cazuelas.* Potaje just means pottage and is a thick soup, usually containing garbanzos or pulses, vegetables and small bits of meat or sausage. Though it is often served as a first course for the main meal, it is certainly substantial enough to stand alone. A cazuela is an earthenware cooking dish and these meals are, quite simply, casseroles, similar to the potajes.

Within these various categories there is a soup for every taste and every season. The gazpachos are light summer fare; the potajes are sturdy winter eating; the seafood soups are delicious any time, the garlic soups make satisfying family meals.

GAZPACHO

Gazpacho, in one form or another, is nearly as old as these hills. Some say it derives from the *alboronía* of the Moors, which certainly didn't include tomatoes until after the discovery of the New World. The name probably derives from the Latin *caspa,* meaning fragment or little piece, and refers to the breadcrumbs which are such an essential ingredient. Gazpacho was and still is basic fare of the Andalusian peasant.

It was little appreciated by the upper classes until not so long ago when both vitamins and tourism were "discovered." Then we learned that this poor man's soup was extraordinarily nourishing and the tourists decided that, furthermore, it tasted good. Between that and the invention of the electric blender, gazpacho was soon out of the fields and onto the restaurant tables.

Here's my tried and true recipe for Andalusian gazpacho: Take a hot August afternoon at a little finca deep in the countryside. Pick the reddest, ripest tomatoes, sweet-smelling off the vine, a few green peppers, a cucumber, and dip them all in the cool water of a spring to rinse off the sun's heat. In the deep shade of a carob tree, start mashing all these ingredients in a big wooden bowl, adding a bit of garlic and onion stored under the straw in the shed. Pick a lemon from a nearby tree and add its tang to the gazpacho. Oil, bread and salt — brought from home in a cloth bag — complete the gazpacho. From the earthenware jug add cold water. Serve immediately and follow with a siesta!

GAZPACHO
Andalusian Liquid Salad

2	slices bread, crusts removed (50 gm)	70	ml. olive oil
4	large ripe tomatoes, peeled (1 kilo)	2	teaspoons salt
2	small green peppers	1/4	teaspoon ground cumin
1/2	cucumber	5	tablespoons vinegar or lemon juice
1/2	onion	1/4	litre water (approximately)
2	cloves garlic		

Put the bread to soak in water to cover. Cut the peeled tomatoes into chunks and put them in blender or processor with the seeded peppers, cucumber and onion, all cut in pieces, and the garlic. (If blender container is too small, process in two batches if necessary.) Whirl until the vegetables are puréed and strain them into a large bowl or tureen. Squeeze the water from the bread and purée it in processor. With the motor running, add the oil in a slow stream until it is incorporated into the bread. Then add the salt, cumin and vinegar. Ladle some of the tomato back

into the processor, then mix it with the tureen of tomato purée. Stir in the water (more may be added for a thinner gazpacho) and correct the seasoning, adding more salt and vinegar to taste. Chill the gazpacho until serving time. Serves 6.

Garnishes: Typically, gazpacho is accompanied by small bowls of chopped tomatoes, chopped onions, chopped peppers, small croutons of toasted bread, diced chopped hard-cooked eggs, chopped cucumbers. Not so typical but quite acceptable garnishes: chopped mint, chopped olives, strips of red pimento, diced apples, pears, melon or peeled grapes.

Serving suggestions: As a "soup" course, serve gazpacho in wooden or ceramic bowls. Glasses or mugs might be used for serving as an aperitif. A chilled thermos of gazpacho is wonderful picnic fare — serve into paper cups. Store it in the refrigerator in a glass jar or pitcher with a lid and have a gazpacho "pick-up" any time of the day (try it for breakfast!). Leftover gazpacho can be used as dressing for lettuce salads, made into aspics with the addition of gelatin, or turned into a sauce for rice or pasta. Concoct a *maría sangría* by thinning gazpacho with vodka; serve over ice with a cucumber stick.

Adaptations: If you don't have a blender or processor and don't fancy the effort it takes to make gazpacho in the mortar, use a food mill, or a sieve, or finely chop the vegetables, add the bread and oil mixture, then water. This is really quite authentic.

Variations: Try green tomatoes instead of red ones with cucumber and a little onion, finished with dill and a dollop of sour cream or yoghurt; experiment with other seasonings — paprika, oregano, parsley, basil, chili powder, chopped chili peppers, coriander leaves.

GAZPACHO DE AGUACATES
Avocado Gazpacho

Omit the tomatoes and substitute 3 ripe avocados in the previous recipe. Thin to taste with water or chicken broth which has been chilled and de-fatted.

GAZPACHO BLANCO CON HUEVOS
White Gazpacho with Eggs

1	thick slice bread	2	teaspoons salt
1	egg	3/4	litre water
2	cloves garlic		apples
150	ml. olive oil		peanuts
6	tablespoons lemon juice		

Soak the bread in water to cover. Put the egg and garlic in blender or processor and whirl them. With the motor running, add the oil in a slow stream until the sauce is amalgamated. Squeeze the water out of the bread and add it to the processor with the lemon juice and salt. Then add, slowly, as much water as the container will hold. Pour the contents into a bowl and thin with more water. Chill the gazpacho and serve with chopped apples and chopped peanuts in each bowl. Serves 4.

AJO BLANCO CON UVAS
White Garlic Soup with Grapes

This sensational summer soup is better than the sum of its ingredients might indicate. Try it.

3	thick slices bread (about 100 gm.), crusts removed	150	ml. olive oil
		50	ml. vinegar
100	grams almonds, blanched and skinned	2	teaspoons salt
		1 1/2	litres water
3	cloves garlic	200	grams muscatel grapes

Soak the bread in water until softened, squeeze it out and put in blender or processor with the almonds and peeled garlic. Blend to a smooth sauce (adding a little water if necessary). Then, with the motor running, add the oil in a slow stream, then the vinegar and salt. Beat in some of the water, then pour the contents of the container into a pitcher, wooden bowl or tureen and add the remaining water. Taste for seasoning, adding more salt or vinegar if necessary. Serve garnished with peeled and seeded grapes. Serves 6.

GAZPACHO CALIENTE
Hot Gazpacho (Tomato Soup)

1	medium onion, chopped	1/4	teaspoon saffron or paprika
1	green pepper, chopped	1/4	teaspoon cumin
2	large tomatoes, peeled, seeded and chopped	1/4	teaspoon ground pepper
		1	teaspoon salt
1	clove garlic, minced	1	litre water or stock
50	ml. oil	4	slices bread, toasted and cubed

In a soup pot combine the onion, pepper, tomatoes, garlic and oil and let them stew for 10 minutes. In a mortar crush the saffron and mix with the cumin, pepper and salt. Add to the pot with the water or stock. Bring to a boil and cook for 10 minutes more. Serve garnished with croutons of toasted bread. (Clams, prawns and pieces of fish can be added to this soup.) Garnish with mint and serve with figs and pieces of green pepper and raw onions.

GAZPACHUELO
Quick Soup

This is another hot soup, not really like gazpacho in spite of its name. It is made like *sopa Viña AB,* in the seafood soups, without the seafood and with diced potatoes instead of fish and prawns.

SEAFOOD SOUPS

From the elegant to the homely, seafood soups are wonderful. Take advantage of the lower-priced fish at the daily market for these soups, which are usually subtly flavoured with saffron, garlic and other spices. Choose firm-fleshed fish that won't disintegrate in cooking — *rape,* angler; *lubina,* bass; *corvina,* meagre; *mero,* grouper; *congrio,* eel; *breca* and *besugo,* bream; *palometa,* pompano; *lisa,* grey mullet; *rubio,* gurnard; *gallineta,* redfish; *cabracho* or *rascacio,* scorpion-fish; and any of the tiny fish, from which the bones can be easily picked after the fish has cooked. Seafood soups also make tasty use of inexpensive frozen fish.

Try several kinds of fish and shellfish in the same soup, but allow different cooking times depending on their texture. For instance, *merluza,* hake, will disintegrate if left to simmer too long, and prawns need little more than two minutes. Clams and mussels to be added to soup are best prepared by steaming them in a saucepan with a little water just until the shells open. Strain the liquid and add to the soup then add the clams or mussels at the very last instant. A very Spanish touch is to leave them unshucked, though it's certainly easier to have them shelled.

Enrich any fish soup by first preparing a good stock (fumet) as a basis for the soup. Simmer head and trimmings of the fish, prawn shells, etc., with a quarter of an onion, a bouquet-garni of herbs, a carrot, stalk of celery and a good swallow of white wine or sherry. Cover with 1½ litres of water; boil, skim, and simmer for 45 minutes. Strain the stock through a fine sieve. Keep stock in the freezer handy for making quick soups with bits of leftover fish and shellfish.

SOPA VIÑA AB
Sherried Fish Soup

1 1/2	litres water or fish stock	1	tinned pimento, diced
100	grams peas, shelled	220	ml. mayonnaise

1/2	kilo cleaned fish (angler or hake)	1	tablespoon lemon juice
1/4	kilo prawns, shelled	50	ml. dry sherry
50	grams serrano ham, diced		salt and pepper

Heat the water or stock in a soup pot, reduce to a simmer and add the cleaned fish. Cook for five minutes, then add the prawns and cook just until they are pink. Remove from fire and strain the soup through a colander into another pot. Pick skin and bones from the fish and set the cleaned pieces aside with the prawns. Add the peas, ham and pimento to the soup. Cook until they are tender. Meanwhile, beat the mayonnaise (preferably home-made) in a bowl with the lemon juice until it is smooth and creamy. Then beat the sherry (Viña AB is a type of sherry) into the mayonnaise. Add the cooked pieces of fish and prawns to the soup and keep it at a low simmer. Ladle a cupful of hot soup into the mayonnaise, beating constantly, then whisk this mixture into the soup. Heat very briefly, but do not boil. Serve hot, accompanied by lemon wedges. Serves 6 to 8.

CACHORREÑAS
Fish Soup with Orange Peel

This soup is named for the bitter orange (the real marmalade orange) grown everywhere in Andalusia. It can also be made without fish, a winter-time gazpacho. A similar soup in Cadiz is called *caldo de perro,* dog soup. (Cadiz also has a "cat soup" — see *Sopa de Ajo.)*

1 1/2	litres water or stock	2	cloves garlic
1	medium tomato	1	teaspoon paprika
1	green pepper	4	tablespoons oil
1/2	onion	3	teaspoons salt
1	bitter orange	300	grams clams
2	slices bread	1/2	kilo *pescadilla* (small hake, or
6	peppercorns		other white fish)
1/4	teaspoon cumin	1	orange for garnish
1	tablespoon chopped parsley		

Bring the water or stock to a boil in a soup pot with the tomato, pepper and onion. Peel the orange in a spiral and add the skin and its juice (if bitter orange is not available, use orange peel and vinegar). Boil the broth for 15 minutes, then strain into another pot. Soak the bread in water, squeeze it out and add to blender or processor with the cooked tomato, pepper, onion, peppercorns, cumin, parsley, garlic, paprika and oil and salt. Whirl until smooth, then beat in some of the hot broth. Add this mixture to the soup pot with the cleaned clams and sliced or filleted fish. Cook just until fish is done, about 8 minutes. Skim out the fish into soup bowls. Top with a thin slice of orange and fill the bowls with the broth.

SOPA AL CUARTO DE HORA
Fifteen-minute Soup

50	ml. oil	150	grams rice
1	small onion, chopped finely	100	grams shelled peas
1	tomato, peeled and chopped	1/4	kilo clams, cleaned
1 1/2	litres water or fish stock	1/4	kilo prawns, shelled
1/2	teaspoon crushed saffron or paprika		salt and pepper
			chopped parsley
100	grams diced ham	2	hard-cooked eggs, chopped
50	ml. dry sherry		

Heat the oil in a soup pot and in it sauté the chopped onion. Add the peeled and chopped tomato, the fish stock, crushed saffron, diced ham, sherry, rice and peas and bring to a boil. Cook on a lively fire for 10 minutes, then lower heat and add the clams and prawns. Season with salt and pepper and cook five minutes more. Serve with a sprinkling of chopped parsley and the chopped egg. Serves 6.

SOPA DE PESCADO
Seafood Soup

This five-star soup changes somewhat from one region to another and is freely varied depending on the day's catch. It starts with an aromatic fish stock to which tomato sauce or *sofrito* (Chapter 12) is added. It's flavoured with a touch of saffron and is usually slightly thickened with bread. I like to use at least two different kinds of fish: one, like angler, which keeps its firm texture in cooking and one more delicate, like hake, which disintegrates in the soup, giving it more body.

2	kilos fish		herbs — bay, thyme, parsley and fennel
1	kilo crustaceans — lobster for a luxury version, prawns, langostinos, crab		
		4	tablespoons oil
1	kilo clams, mussels, scallops or other bi-valves	1/4	onion, finely chopped
		1	clove garlic, minced
1	squid, cleaned and diced (optional)	50	ml. brandy
2	litres water	100	grams bread, toasted or fried
100	ml. white wine	1/2	teaspoon saffron
	salt and pepper	10	peppercorns
1/4	onion		cayenne
1	carrot	300	ml. tomato sauce
1	stalk celery		parsley

There are several ways to prepare the fish. Sometimes it is cut in slices and cooked in the stock and each person removes the bones at table. An easier method is to have the fish vendor fillet the fish, saving all the heads, bones and trimmings. Cut the fillets into chunks, removing any remaining bones, and set aside. Shell the prawns or slice the halved lobster, remove from shell and hack the shell and head into pieces. Scrub the clams, mussels, etc., and steam them open over a high heat in a covered pan. Remove from shells and discard these.

Strain the liquid and reserve it.

Put all the fish trimmings and crustacean shells into a large pot with the water, white wine, salt and pepper, onion, carrot, celery and herbs. Bring to a boil, skim the froth and simmer, partially covered, for an hour. Meanwhile, in another pot or deep casserole heat the oil and in it sauté the minced onion and garlic. Add the pieces of fish and sauté them, then add the peeled prawns or pieces of lobster and the reserved clams or mussels (they may be chopped). Pour over the brandy (it can be flamed if desired). Crush the toasted bread in mortar or blender with the saffron, pepper and cayenne. Dissolve in some of the fish stock and add to the fish with the tomato sauce. Strain the prepared stock and add about 1½ litres of it to the fish. Simmer the soup for 10 minutes. Serve with chopped parsley and triangles of fried bread. Makes 6 servings.

SOPA DE RAPE
Angler Fish Soup

1	angler fish, about 1 kilo	3	slices bread
2	litres water	1	sprig parsley
	herbs — bay leaf, oregano, thyme	1/2	onion, chopped
	and celery	2	tomatoes, peeled and chopped
	salt and pepper	1/4	teaspoon saffron
1/2	onion		grating of nutmeg
4	tablespoons oil	1/8	teaspoon cinnamon
20	almonds, blanched and skinned	1/4	teaspoon pepper
10	hazelnuts	2	teaspoons salt
3	cloves garlic		

Have the angler fish cleaned and the head separated. Put the water to boil in a pot with the herbs, onion and salt and pepper. Add the head and any trimmings

of the fish and cook for 30 minutes on a hot fire. Reduce to a simmer and add the rest of the fish. Poach it for 10 minutes and remove from heat. Strain the stock and reserve. Cut the cooked fish from the bone into small pieces and reserve it. (Discard head and bones.) Heat the oil in a soup pot or deep casserole and in it fry the almonds, hazelnuts, peeled garlic, sliced bread and sprig of parsley, just until almonds, garlic and bread are toasted. With a skimmer, remove them to mortar or blender. In the same oil, fry the chopped onion just until translucent. Add the tomatoes and fry for 15 minutes. (This *sofrito* can be used as is or puréed in a blender or passed through a sieve.) In the mortar or blender, purée the toasted almonds, etc., with the saffron, nutmeg, cinnamon, pepper and salt, adding a little of the reserved stock to make a smooth paste. Stir this into the tomato mixture, add the stock and bring to a boil. Simmer for 10 minutes, then add the pieces of cooked angler fish and simmer another minute or two to reheat. Makes 6 servings.

SOPA DE MEJILLONES
Mussel Soup

3	dozen mussels	2	cloves garlic
1/2	litre water	1	tablespoon chopped parsley
3	tablespoons oil	1/4	teaspoon cinnamon
1	small onion, finely chopped	2	tablespoons *aguardiente* (dry anise brandy)
4	tomatoes, peeled seeded and puréed (or use tomato paste)		salt and pepper
50	grams bread, toasted or fried		fennel or parsley

Clean the mussels very well and steam them open in the water, covered, over a very hot fire, shaking the pan while they cook. Remove from heat the instant they open. Shuck the mussels, discarding the shells. Chop the mussels coarsely and reserve. Strain and reserve their cooking liquid. Heat the oil in a soup pot or earthenware casserole. In it sauté the onion. Then add the puréed tomatoes. Fry for 15 minutes until the tomatoes are reduced to a sauce. Add the crushed garlic, parsley and cinnamon, then the anise brandy (if unavailable use anise-flavoured drink such as Pernod). Add the strained liquid to the tomato mixture. Bring to a boil, then reduce to a simmer and add the chopped mussels. Cook 5 minutes and serve. Garnish with toasted croutons and chopped parsley or fennel. Makes 4 servings.

SOPA DE CANGREJOS DE RIO
Crayfish Bisque

1	kilo freshwater crayfish	2	tablespoons brandy
2	carrots	1	teaspoon paprika
1	onion		dash cayenne
	parsley, bay leaf and thyme	2	hard-cooked egg yolks or 1 small cooked potato or toasted bread
100	ml. white wine		
2	tablespoons oil, butter or lard		salt and pepper
2	tomatoes, peeled and chopped		chopped parsley

The crayfish must be purchased live. Wash them in running water. To de-vein them, grasp the middle tail fin and give it a sharp twist. It should break off, bringing with it the dark viscera. Put the crayfish to cook in water to cover, adding the carrots, half onion, herbs, white wine and salt and pepper. Bring to a boil and simmer for 10 minutes. Drain, reserving the broth. Divide half of the cooked crayfish among four soup bowls and keep warm. In a saucepan heat the oil, butter or lard and in it sauté the remaining chopped onion. When softened, add the peeled and chopped tomatoes, the brandy, paprika and cayenne. Simmer this mixture for 15 minutes. Meanwhile finely chop the remaining half of the crayfish in a processor, adding a little of the liquid if necessary. Rub through a sieve, pressing hard on the solids to extract all the flavourful pulp. Put the sieved pulp in a saucepan and add the remaining broth. Then purée the tomato mixture with the egg yolks, potato or toasted bread and add it to the soup. Bring to a boil and season with salt and pepper. Pour over the cooked crayfish and garnish with parsley. At table each person shells his own crayfish, so provide paper towels and finger bowls. Serves 4.

CONSOMMES, GARLIC SOUPS, VEGETABLE SOUPS AND PUREES

Authentic consommé — a thin, clarified broth — is rare in Spanish cookery, though it certainly appears in formal dinners or *alta cocina,* haute cuisine. The *caldo* or broth from the *puchero* is usually served, unclarified, with the fat from a stewing hen floating on the top, embellished with rice, pasta or bread and a garnish of chopped herbs. The consommé madrilène *(caldo madrileño)* of classic cookery calls for sieved tomato pulp or juice to be added to a clarified and reduced chicken broth and fortified with a dash of dry sherry. It can be served hot or cold, garnished with chopped parsley and very finely diced sweet red pimentos.

SOPA DE PICADILLO
Garnished Broth

This is what happens to the leftover broth from the *puchero* or *cocido,* which is a very rich brew of chicken, beef and ham bone. It would appear as a light evening meal or a first course for a different dinner the following day. When real *puchero* broth is not available, substitute any good chicken broth or tinned consommé, boiled briefly with a piece of ham, ham bone or even bacon.

In the bottom of a soup tureen put croutons of fried bread, chopped and fried ham and chopped, hard-cooked eggs. Add the hot, strained broth, a dash of sherry and serve the soup garnished with a sprig of mint. Rice, thin noodles or chopped potatoes can be used instead of the croutons.

SOPA DE AJO
Garlic Soup

Here is the perfect example of a poor man's soup — nothing more than bread, oil, garlic and water — which is now to be found on sophisticated restaurant menus everywhere in Spain. Garlic soup, like gazpacho, is better than the sum of its parts, a category to itself, a unique contribution to the world's culinary delights. Every province has a variation on garlic soup — in some places it is called *oliaigua* (garlic water), and might, additionally contain onion, tomato and peppers; or *sopa de gato,* "cat soup" typical of Cadiz, with the addition of grated cheese. You can use an aromatic stock for this soup, but plain water is just fine.

6	tablespoons olive oil	1 1/4 litres boiling water or stock
4	cloves (or more) garlic, chopped	2	teaspoons salt
6	slices bread, cut in cubes (300 gm.)	4	eggs
1	teaspoon paprika		chopped parsley

Heat the oil in a soup pot or heat-proof casserole and add the chopped garlic and bread cubes. Fry until lightly golden, then stir in the paprika. Immediately add the boiling water and salt. Cover and simmer slowly for 20 minutes. The bread should almost dissolve in the broth. Place the soup in four individual earthenware bowls and add one egg per bowl. Poach the eggs in the soup (in oven or on top of stove) and serve with a garnish of chopped parsley. Alternatively, the eggs can be beaten together and stirred into the pot of hot soup, letting it cook just until the eggs have set, thickening the soup. Serves 4.

SOPA DE COL MALLORQUINA
Mallorcan Cabbage Soup

This is one of the "dry" soups of Mallorca, so called because a quantity of bread is added to soak up the broth. Instead of the cabbage, you can substitute broccoli, cauliflower, spinach, chard, asparagus or other vegetables.

400	grams wholewheat bread	1	medium cabbage, chopped
100	ml. oil	2	tablespoons chopped parsley
2	onions, chopped	1	teaspoon paprika
2	tomatoes, peeled and chopped		salt and pepper
3	cloves garlic, minced		boiling water or stock, about 1 litre
2	small peppers, chopped		

Cut the bread into thin strips. In a casserole or soup pot heat the oil and in it fry the strips of bread. Remove them when browned and set aside. In the same oil, sauté the chopped onions until they are softened, then add the peeled and chopped tomatoes, the minced garlic, chopped peppers and chopped cabbage. Sauté the vegetables on a high heat for a few minutes, then add the chopped parsley, paprika, and salt and pepper. Add the boiling water or stock to just cover the vegetables. Bring to a boil and simmer for 10 minutes. Then add the fried bread. Cover the casserole and simmer until the liquid is absorbed, another 10 minutes. Serve with a sprinkling of chopped parsley. Makes 4 to 6 servings. This "soup" can also be served at room temperature.

CREMA DE ARANJUEZ
Cream of Asparagus Soup

1/2	kilo fresh asparagus	1	litre chicken stock
1	leek or small onion		salt and pepper
1	carrot	2	egg yolks
4	tablespoons butter, lard or oil	50	ml. fresh cream
4	tablespoons flour		

Wash the asparagus well, cut off the tips and cook them in boiling water just until tender. Drain and set aside. Chop the stalks into small pieces. Heat the butter in a soup pot and in it sauté the leek or onion, minced, and the carrot, chopped, with the pieces of asparagus. Stir in the flour, then add the stock and season with salt and pepper. Bring to a boil and simmer the vegetables for an hour. Purée them in a processor or blender, then strain through a sieve. Reheat the strained soup. In a bowl, beat the egg yolks with the cream. Very slowly beat a ladleful of the hot soup into the yolks, then whisk the yolk mixture into the soup. Heat, but do not boil. Season with a grating of nutmeg and add the cooked asparagus tips to the soup. Makes 4 servings, though the soup can be thinned with additional stock. Other vegetables — courgettes, spinach, cauliflower, peas — can be prepared in the same manner. The soup is very good sprinkled with grated cheese.

GARBURE NAVARRO
Pork and Vegetable Soup

150	grams pork loin	150	grams green beans
1	piece ham bone	2	large potatoes
150	grams salt pork or bacon	1	small cabbage
150	grams broad beans, shelled	150	grams pork sausage links
1 1/2 litres water			salt and pepper
150	grams peas, shelled		

Cut the pork loin into cubes and put in a soup pot with the piece of ham bone and the salt pork or bacon, cut in dice. Add the broad beans and peas. Cover with water and bring to a boil. Skim the froth, then simmer, covered, until the broad beans are tender, about 40 minutes. Remove strings from green beans and cut them into short lengths. Peel and dice the potatoes. Wash the cabbage and chop it. Add these three vegetables and the pork sausage links, diced, to the soup with salt and pepper to taste. Simmer another 40 minutes, or until all the vegetables are very tender. Remove the ham bone and serve the soup. Makes 4 servings. Other vegetables — cauliflower, leeks, spinach, carrots, lettuce — can be added instead of, or in addition to, the ones given.

SOPA DE ALMENDRAS
Almond Soup

This savoury brew hints at its Moorish ancestry. It is typically served for Christmas dinner, and a delightful starter it makes, light, yet so full of flavour.

In this dish the flavour of real olive oil is essential. There are numerous versions of this soup. This one, typical of Granada, is flavoured with saffron and cumin, whereas in Castile it might contain cinnamon, mint and lemon juice.

50	ml. olive oil	1/4	teaspoon cumin
400	grams blanched almonds		salt
1/4	teaspoon saffron	1 1/2	litres chicken broth
2	cloves garlic	1	teaspoon vinegar
100	grams bread (4 slices), diced		chopped parsley
10	peppercorns		

Heat the oil in a soup pot and in it toast the almonds, saffron, garlic and bread. Remove them when just golden and place in blender, processor or mortar with the peppercorns, cumin and salt, reserving a few of the croutons of fried bread for garnish. Purée these ingredients, adding a little of the broth and the vinegar. Heat the broth in the same soup pot, stir the puréed almond mixture into it and bring to a boil. Simmer for 15 minutes and serve hot, garnished with chopped parsley and the reserved bread cubes. Serves 6.

SOPA CON COSTRON
Crusty Soup

50	ml. oil	1 1/4	litres water or stock
150	grams chopped ham	1	teaspoon salt
2	onions, chopped	1/2	teaspoon ground cumin
2	cloves garlic, chopped		pepper
2	medium tomatoes, peeled and chopped	2	eggs, beaten
1/4	kilo bread, crusts removed	2	tablespoons grated cheese
			paprika

Heat the oil in an oven-proof casserole and sauté the chopped ham with the chopped onions and garlic. Add the peeled and chopped tomatoes and cook on a high heat for a few minutes. Then add the bread, cut in strips and crusts removed, and the water or stock. Season with salt, cumin and pepper. Bring to a boil and cook the soup, stirring, until the bread is completely dissolved. Pour the beaten eggs over the top of the soup, sprinkle with the grated cheese and dust with paprika. Put the casserole in a hot oven just until the eggs are set and the top very lightly browned, about 8 minutes.

PURE DE VIGILIA
Lenten Purée

1/4	kilo garbanzos	2	potatoes, peeled and cut up
1/4	kilo salt cod		pepper
1 1/2	litres water	1/2	teaspoon paprika
5	leeks, chopped		dash of cayenne
1	onion, chopped	3	tablespoons oil
1	sprig parsley, chopped		croutons
2	carrots, cut up	1	clove garlic minced
2	cloves garlic		

In separate containers put the garbanzos and the salt cod to soak in plenty of water to cover the night before. On the following day, clean the salt cod of all skin and bones and put it to cook in the fresh water with the garbanzos, leeks, onion, parsley, carrots and garlic. Cook the soup, covered, for one hour, then add the potatoes, pepper, paprika and cayenne and cook until garbanzos are quite tender, about another hour. Purée this soup in blender, processor or food mill and keep it simmering. Heat the oil in a frying pan and toast the croutons of bread with the minced garlic. Remove the croutons as they are browned. Pour the oil and garlic into the purée and serve garnished with the croutons. The purée can be thinned with additional water, if desired.

PURE DE SAN JUAN
Kidney bean Soup

1/4	kilo kidney beans	1	sprig thyme
1 1/2	litres water	1	piece ham bone
1	onion, quartered		salt and pepper

1	carrot	50	grams olives, pitted and chopped
6	cloves garlic	2	hard-cooked eggs
1	bay leaf		chopped parsley

Soak the beans in water to cover overnight. Put them to cook in fresh water with the quartered onion, carrot, garlic, bay leaf, thyme, ham bone and salt and pepper. Bring to a boil, then simmer until the beans are tender. Purée in blender, processor or food mill and return to the pot and keep simmering. Serve, garnished with the chopped olives, chopped eggs and chopped parsley.

COCIDO

The usual English translation of this meal-in-a-pot — boiled dinner — hardly does justice to this fantastic dish. It's more like an elaborate theatre production in three acts, with plenty of drama, fabulous costumes and saucy interludes. Though you seldom find *cocido* on restaurant menus, it is the real national dish of Spain. It's hardly a set piece, however, as each region stages it a little differently. It is variously called — besides *cocido* — *puchero, pote, olla, escudella*. Mostly they are named for the pot in which they cook.

The original cocido in Spain was the *adafina* of the Spanish Jews, a dish nearly identical to today's. It was left to cook very slowly all during the Sabbath — when it was forbidden by Mosaic law to work — to be ready to eat at sundown. After the reconquest, Jews who chose to be baptized added pork and sausage. *Olla podrida,* much appreciated centuries ago by Don Quijote and his sidekick Sancho Panza, was a similar dish. Literally translated as the "rotten pot," it might have been so-called because the ingredients were allowed to cook to nearly a mush. At first it was a dish of the upper classes and might have contained chicken, beef, mutton, bacon, doves, partridge, pork loin, sausages, hare, beef and pork tongues, cabbages, turnips and other vegetables. The garbanzo was added early on and remains today a standard ingredient. In the 18th century, the potato arrived from the New World and got thrown into the pot too.

With the accession of the Bourbons to the Spanish throne, the olla podrida disappeared from aristocratic tables and passed on to the bourgeois and lower classes. It was much simplified in the process. The cocido today is still standard fare in pueblo homes, where the housewife puts the *olla* to cook while going about household chores. In fast-moving cities, however, the cocido is becoming nostalgia food. For one thing, the ingredients, once locally produced and cheap, have become increasingly expensive. And fewer people have the time and patience to tend the slow cooking of the cocido. Packaged soups, ready in minutes, and quick-cooking *filetes* of pork and beef are replacing the traditional cocido.

The *cocido madrileño* is certainly the most representative of all. It is made with beef, ham, salt pork, stewing hen, sausages, black pudding, garbanzos, potatoes, cabbage, carrots. The broth is strained out and cooked with fine soup noodles to provide the first course, then the vegetables and garbanzos are served on one platter and all the meats, cut up, on another.

The Catalan *escudella i carn d'olla,* "soup with meat of the pot," includes the *pelota,* a huge dumpling of minced pork seasoned with garlic, cinnamon and parsley, and *butifarra* sausages, both white and black. The first-course soup is cooked with rice or noodles or, for special occasions, might be *de galets,* with huge tubes of pasta. The *puchero* or Andalusian cocido usually contains a wider range of vegetables — pumpkin, courgette, green beans and other seasonal vegetables are allowed to make an appearance. The whole might be flavoured with garlic, paprika and saffron or a *sofrito,* tomato sauce. The *cocido vasco,* Basque version, adds red kidney beans, cooked separately with the chorizo and black pudding. The soup is made up of the broth from both pots. Then follow four platters: garbanzos and potatoes, red beans, cabbage and other vegetables and the meats, served with sauces of tomato and peppers. The *pote gallego,* Galician pot, includes *grelos* and *nabizas,* turnip leaves and flowers. *Sopa y bullit mallorquín,* the Mallorcan version, adds lamb and *sobrasada,* the local soft sausage. In the Canaries, both corn and sweet potatoes are included. The *puchero de las tres abocas* of Valencia substitutes lamb for the beef.

I like to make cocido as a full-scale production for at least six guests with good appetites (whereas the *potajes* which follow I consider more as homely, family meals), using the finest ingredients and serving the platters heaped with the different foods, each cooked to perfection. It's a most impressive meal.

COCIDO
Soup, Meat and Vegetables in a Pot

3	litres water	2	cloves
500	grams stewing beef	1/2	large stewing hen (about 2 kilos)
1	beef marrow bone	2	teaspoons salt
1	salted pig trotter (optional)	6	medium potatoes
100	grams salt pork	1	small cabbage
200	grams ham (or ham bone)	150	grams chorizo
1/2	kilo garbanzos, soaked overnight	150	grams morcilla
2	carrots	2	tablespoons oil
1	turnip	1	clove garlic
2	leeks	200	grams fine noodles, rice or bread
1	stalk celery		parsley or mint
1	onion, halved		tomato sauce

Put the water to boil in a very large *olla* or pot. When it is boiling, add the beef, beef bone, trotter, salt pork and ham. Keep the water boiling and skim off the froth as it rises to the surface. When no more froth boils up, reduce the liquid to a simmer and add the garbanzos which have been soaked overnight. Add the carrots, peeled and halved lengthwise, the turnip cut in quarters, the leeks and the celery cut in half. Cut the onion in half and stick a clove in each and add to the pot with the chicken. Keep the liquid at a good simmer and cover the pot and let it cook for an hour. Then add the salt. Cook another 30 minutes.

In a separate pot, using some of the broth from the *cocido* or with additional water, cook the cabbage, coarsely chopped, with the two kinds of sausage. This operation is done separately to avoid flavouring the soup broth with the cabbage and colouring it with the red chorizo. Those who enjoy this flavour and colour can add these ingredients directly to the cooking pot. When they have cooked for 30 minutes, drain, reserving the liquid if desired. Heat the oil in a frying pan, sauté the garlic and add the cooked cabbage to it.

Meanwhile, add the potatoes, peeled and cut in half, to the main cooking pot and simmer another 30 minutes, or until all the ingredients are tender and garbanzos are cooked.

Now strain some of the broth into another pot, bring it to a boil and cook in it the thin noodles or the rice. If bread is to be used instead, remove crusts and cut it into strips and place in six soup plates. Ladle the broth into the soup plates, garnish with a little chopped parsley or mint and serve as the meal's first course. The broth from the cabbage and chorizo can be combined with this broth if desired.

Drain the garbanzos and place them on a serving platter accompanied by the carrots, turnip, leeks, celery, onion, potatoes and cabbage. Cut all the meats, sausages, salt pork and ham into serving pieces and serve them on a second platter. Serve separately a tomato sauce which can be mixed with the meats and vegetables in any combination. Serves 6 to 8.

The flavourful broth can be used for making other soups (see *sopa de picadillo*). Leftover meats and sausages can be finely minced, bound with egg and breadcrumbs and made into dumplings for the soup. The leftover vegetables can be puréed with some of the broth, seasoned with nutmeg and served garnished with chopped ham and hard-cooked eggs.

PUCHERO CANARIO
Soup and Vegetables, Canary Islands' Style

3	litres water	2	potatoes, peeled
1/4	kilo white beans, soaked overnight	3	tablespoons oil
1/2	kilo pork	1	small onion, chopped
150	grams salt pork	2	tomatoes, peeled and chopped
4	stalks chard	2	cloves garlic, chopped
1	bunch watercress	4	tablespoons *gofio* (toasted maize
1	courgette, diced		flour, or cornmeal)
	salt and pepper		parsley or coriander leaves
3	ears corn (or 1 tin sweetcorn)		

Put the water to boil in a large pot with the soaked beans, the pork and salt pork. Cook until beans are partially cooked, about 30 minutes. Then add the washed and chopped chard, watercress and courgette. Season with salt and pepper. Cut the corn kernels from the cobs and add them to the pot with the potatoes, peeled and cut in chunks. Continue cooking the soup until everything is quite tender. In another pot heat the oil and sauté the chopped onion until it is softened. Add the peeled and chopped tomatoes and the garlic, and fry until tomatoes are reduced to a sauce. Stir in the *gofio* or cornmeal, then add the strained broth from the soup pot. Cook this soup for five minutes and serve it first, garnished with chopped parsley or coriander. Then serve a platter of the beans, vegetables and meat, cut into individual portions. Serves 4. Where available *morcilla dulce*, black pudding sweetened with sugar and almonds, would be added to this dish.

POTAJES & CAZUELAS

These are among my very favourite Spanish dishes — such rich and satisfying flavours for a small expenditure of money and effort. Most contain legumes or pulses — beans, garbanzos or lentils — and, though not exactly soups, they're somewhat soupy. Typically, these pottages and casseroles would be served as a first course, but many are substantial enough to make an informal supper accompanied by salad and good bread. They are different from the cocidos in that the broth is not strained to make a first course soup.

FABADA
Asturian Ham and Beans

This is Spain's most famous bean dish, wonderfully flavoured, robust food from the northern regions. The *fabes* are big, fat white beans which cook up soft without disintegrating. Where unavailable, substitute the bigger dry Lima beans or butter beans, or any large white bean. The *morcilla* and *chorizo* should be, if possible, from Asturias, where they are oak smoked. *Lacón* is cured pork hand. If not available, use ham. Salt beef, salt-cured pig trotters and hard *longaniza* sausage are also used.

1/2 kilo *fabes* (dry, white beans)	100 grams ham
2 *morcillas* (black pudding), smoked	100 grams streaky salt pork
2 *chorizos* (red sausage), smoked	1/2 teaspoon saffron
400 grams cured hand or ham	1 bay leaf

The day before: put the beans to soak in plenty of water. Put the *lacón* or ham to soak overnight in hot water. Blanch the salt pork in boiling water for five minutes. The following day: wash the sausages to eliminate excess smokiness. Put the beans in an earthenware casserole or large cooking pot and add water to a depth of two fingers. On a hot fire, bring to a boil and skim off the froth. Toast the saffron in a frying pan, crush it in the mortar and dissolve in a little water and add to the beans. Add the lacón, ham and salt pork to the casserole, pushing them to the bottom of the beans. Cover and cook five minutes and skim again. Now add the chorizo and morcilla, boil five minutes and skim. Add bay leaf,

***Gazpacho**, the famous Andalusian vegetable soup (recipe, page 116).*

cover and cook very slowly, two to three hours. Add cold water occasionally just to keep the beans barely covered so they don't dry out and split. Do not stir, but shake the casserole from time to time. When beans are quite tender, let them set for 20 minutes to blend and mellow the flavours. If too much liquid remains, purée some of the cooked beans in the blender and add them to the casserole to thicken the sauce. Serves 4.

CALDO GALLEGO
Galician Soup

1/4 kilo white beans, soaked overnight	50 grams lard or salt pork
300 grams salt-cured spare ribs, soaked overnight	1/4 kilo *grelos* (or use chard or collards)
200 grams stewing beef	3 medium potatoes
2 litres water	salt and pepper

Put the soaked beans, de-salted pork ribs (or substitute any meaty pork bone) and the stewing beef to boil in the water. Skim the froth, then add the pork fat. Cover partially and simmer for two hours. Wash and chop the *grelos* or other vegetable and add them to the pot with the potatoes, peeled and cut in small pieces, and salt and pepper to taste. Cook another hour, or until the contents are all very tender. Remove some of the potatoes, beans and pork fat to the blender and purée them. Stir into the soup to thicken it. Cut the beef into small pieces. Serve in soup bowls. Serves 6.

BERZA DE ACELGA
Andalusian Vegetable Pot

Of the hundreds of Spanish recipes I have collected over the years, this one is the most stained, the most used. It is straightforward pueblo food and its earthiness and simplicity appeal to me on a gut level. In my own home I would serve it with a whole-grain bread or an American-style cornbread — though certainly neither is typically Spanish. I love the contrasts of flavour and texture and, besides, the proteins in whole grains complement those in the garbanzos or beans and small quantities of meat. In village homes, chard would be used in winter months, green beans in their place in the summer. Other more unusual vegetables, such as cardoons, carrots, artichokes, lettuce, broad beans, might be added in addition or in their place. Though the chard is trimmed to include only the stalks — the deep-green leaves being saved to cook as spinach — I prefer to add the leafy part as well as the stalk to the *berza*. This pottage is sometimes made with both garbanzos and white beans. Black-eyed peas can be used in place of either.

Simple and delicious, the Spanish potato omelette (recipe, page 140).

400 grams *garbanzos* and/or white beans, soaked (separately) overnight	2 cloves
100 grams salt pork or bacon	8 peppercorns
200 grams pork or meaty pork bone	3 cloves garlic
2 litres water	2 teaspoons salt
1/2 kilo chard and/or green beans	2 teaspoons paprika
1 chorizo	4 medium potatoes
1 morcilla	1/4 kilo pumpkin

If using both the garbanzos and beans, put the garbanzos to cook first with the salt pork, piece of fresh pork and water. After 30 minutes, add the soaked beans. Let all simmer for about one and a half hours, then add the chard, or green beans, which have been cleaned and chopped, and the chorizo and morcilla. In the mortar crush cloves and peppercorns with the garlic, salt and paprika and add to the berza. When meat and garbanzos are nearly tender — about two hours total — add the potatoes and pumpkin, both peeled and cut in small chunks. Cook another 30 minutes. Cut the pork and sausages into small pieces (kitchen scissors work well for this) and serve into soup bowls. Serves 6. This can also be cooked, more like a cocido, with a large piece of boiling beef, and served with a first-course broth followed by drained meats and vegetables on a platter. Add quartered pears or other fruits to the berza and you can call it *olla gitana,* gypsy pot.

MOROS Y CRISTIANOS
Moors and Christians (Black Beans with White Rice)

400 grams black beans, soaked overnight	2 teaspoons salt
2 litres water	pepper
1 onion	dash cayenne
1 carrot	1 orange
1 stalk celery	300 grams rice
1 head garlic, peeled	parsley
1 bay leaf	sliced onion
1 teaspoon paprika	sliced orange
3 tablespoons oil	sliced hard-cooked eggs

Put the beans to cook in the water with the quartered onion, sliced carrot and celery, crushed garlic and bay leaf. Bring to a boil, skim, then simmer, partially covered, until the beans are nearly tender, about one hour. Mix together the paprika, oil, salt, pepper and cayenne and stir into the beans with the juice of one orange and finish cooking. Let the beans set for 15 minutes. Ladle them with a skimmer into a serving bowl. Meanwhile cook the rice with salt just until done. Pack it into a buttered bowl or ring mould, let it rest 10 minutes, then unmould onto the black beans. Garnish with parsley, sliced onion, sliced orange and sliced eggs.

CAZUELA DE LENTEJAS
Lentil Pot

1/2	kilo lentils	1	tablespoon salt
2	litres water	2	cloves
50	ml. oil	2	large potatoes, chopped
1	medium tomato	1/4	teaspoon cumin
1	medium onion, quartered	1/2	teaspoon paprika
1	green pepper	1/4	teaspoon ground pepper
1	bay leaf		dash cayenne
1	head garlic, roasted	200	grams spicy pork sausage links

Bring the lentils to a boil in the water, turn off the heat and let them soak for two hours. Then add the oil, the whole tomato, quartered onion stuck with cloves, whole pepper cleaned of seeds, bay leaf, roasted garlic cloves, salt. Bring to a boil, then simmer slowly for one hour. Meanwhile in the mortar crush the cumin, paprika and pepper together with the cayenne. Add to the pot with the potatoes, peeled and chopped, and the sausage, scissor-cut into short pieces. Cook the lentils another 30 minutes until they and the potatoes are quite tender. Makes 6 servings. Rice instead of or in addition to the potatoes can be cooked with the lentils. Pumpkin, peeled and cut in chunks can also be added. Chorizo can be added during the last 30 minutes, instead of or in addition to the pork sausage.

JUDIAS A LO TIO LUCAS
Uncle Lucas' Bean Pot

50	ml. oil	1	bay leaf
200	grams salt pork or bacon	1	teaspoon paprika
1/2	kilo dry white beans, soaked over-night	1/4	teaspoon ground cumin
1	onion, quartered	1	sprig parsley
1	head garlic, roasted		salt and pepper

Heat the oil in a soup pot and in it fry the salt pork or bacon, cut in small dice. Add the soaked beans, the onion, roasted garlic, bay leaf, paprika, cumin and parsley. Cover with approximately two litres of water, bring to a boil and simmer for an hour. Season with salt and pepper and continue cooking until beans are quite tender, about 30 minutes more. Ladle into soup bowls and serve hot. Makes 6 servings.

POTAJE A LA CATALANA
Catalan Bean Pot

1/2	kilo garbanzos, soaked overnight	4	tomatoes, peeled and chopped
2	litres water	50	grams pine nuts
1 1/2	onions	150	grams *butifarra*, white sausage
1	bay leaf		salt and pepper
50	grams lard	2	hard-cooked eggs

Put the garbanzos to cook in the water with the half onion and bay leaf. After 30 minutes, add 2 teaspoons salt and continue cooking until garbanzos are tender, about two hours total. Meanwhile, heat the lard in a frying pan and in it sauté the whole, chopped onion. When softened, add the peeled and chopped tomatoes, the pine nuts and sausage, cut in chunks. Cook this mixture on a medium heat until reduced, about 15 minutes. Season with salt and pepper and place the *sofrito* in an earthenware casserole. Add the cooked garbanzos and enough of their cooking liquid to make a thick soup. Cook another 20 minutes and serve garnished with the chopped, hard-cooked eggs. Serves 6.

POTAJE DE GARBANZOS CON ESPINACAS
Garbanzos and Spinach Pottage

1/2	kilo garbanzos, soaked overnight	1/2	kilo spinach
2	litres water	80	ml. oil
1	carrot	2	cloves garlic, chopped
2	onions	1	tomato, peeled and chopped
1	sprig parsley		salt and pepper
1	bay leaf		hard-cooked eggs

Put the garbanzos to cook in the water with the carrot, 1 onion, parsley and bay leaf. Bring to a boil and simmer, partially covered, for one hour. Then add 2 teaspoons salt and 2 tablespoons oil and continue to cook the garbanzos until they are tender. Meanwhile, clean the spinach and chop it. Add it to the garbanzos to cook. In a frying pan heat remaining oil and in it sauté the other onion chopped and garlic. Add the peeled and chopped tomato and continue frying until reduced, about 15 minutes. Season with salt and pepper. Skim the garbanzos and spinach into a casserole and add the tomato sauce and enough of the cooking liquid to make it just saucy. Cook another 10 minutes and serve garnished with chopped hard-cooked eggs. This dish, especially typical during Lent, might have salt cod, soaked overnight, cooked with the garbanzos. For non-Lenten dishes, lard, salt pork and ham might be included.

CHAPTER 6

Tortillas & Egg Dishes

In the pueblo where I once lived, the most familiar sound on a sleepy afternoon was the cackling of hens and the chorusing of cocks as they perched on high patio walls. I would put the butter to melt in the frying pan and go next door where my neighbour reached under the chattering hens and handed me two, three or four eggs. They were so fresh and delicious that I liked making them the starring dish for lunch — scrambled with mushrooms; baked flamenco style, with bright strips of pepper and peas; bound with potatoes in a fat omelette.

Today I buy fresh eggs at the supermarket, but I continue to enjoy them prepared, Spanish style, for luncheon and supper. Though a Spaniard might eat a boiled or fried egg for "elevenses," the mid-morning snack, eggs are seldom consumed for breakfast. They're most likely to appear as starter for the main meal or main course for a light supper, and a good deal of imaginative flavourings are combined with the simple egg.

Certainly the most popular egg dish on Spanish tables is the *tortilla española*. A Spanish *tortilla* is a kind of omelette — not related to the Mexican tortilla (which is a pancake made out of cornmeal), and only a distant cousin of the French omelette. Omelette, Spanish style, is served round and flat, not folded, and contains potatoes or bits of meats, vegetables, seafood, mushrooms or herbs. It may be cooked in a huge disc, which is sliced like a pie, or in small, individual portions. For *tapa* servings, the tortilla is cut into small squares, a perfect nibble. No train journey or excursion is complete without a hamper of ample provisions, always including a tortilla or two.

Tortilla-making is not as simple as it looks. My first ones were disasters — sort of potato scrambled eggs — though they tasted just fine, washed down with the local wine. I advise not to invite guests to sample your first attempt. But don't be scared off, either. The tortilla is a quick and easy meal from ingredients almost always to hand.

The type of frying pan contributes much to the success of the tortilla. You need a lightweight pan to facilitate the tricky flipping of the omelette. I still use an old-fashioned rolled steel pan with a long handle and high sloping sides. It has to be kept well-seasoned and free of rust or the omelette tends to stick. Plenty of Spanish housewives today use frying pans with non-stick surfaces. A four-egg tortilla should be cooked in a pan with a bottom diameter of 20 cm. (8 in.) or smaller so that it comes out quite thick, about 4 or 5 cm. (2 in.). The outside should be golden-brown, the inside, still juicy.

Olive oil makes the best frying medium and you're going to need quite a bit of it to keep potatoes and other ingredients from sticking (less, if you use a non-stick pan). The following instructions for the classic potato omelette can be adapted for any type of tortilla.

TORTILLA ESPAÑOLA
Spanish Omelette

1	kilo potatoes	4-5	eggs
3	tablespoons chopped onion (optional)	1/2	teaspoon salt
50	ml. olive oil		

Peel the potatoes and either cut them in dice or into very thin slices. Heat the oil in the frying pan until very hot and add the potatoes, and onions if desired. Stir them into the oil to completely coat and seal them, then reduce the heat slightly and continue frying without letting the potatoes brown, stirring them frequently. With the edge of a metal spatula or skimmer, keep cutting into the potatoes, dicing them as they cook. When they are quite tender (about 15 minutes) place a plate over the frying pan and drain off the oil into a heatproof container. Place the potatoes in a bowl. Beat together the eggs and salt until very well combined and stir the eggs into the potatoes and mix well.

Return the oil to the frying pan and let it reheat. Now pour in the egg and potato mixture. Let it set on the bottom, regulating the heat so it doesn't brown too fast. Use the spatula to firm the edges of the tortilla all around its circumference. Shake the pan frequently to keep it loose on the bottom. Place the plate over the pan, drain off the oil and turn the tortilla out onto the plate. Return the oil to the pan, adding a little more if necessary and slide the tortilla back in to cook on the reverse side. Remove the tortilla when it is golden by sliding out onto serving plate. Serves two as a main dish or four to six as an appetizer or first course.

Serve with a garnish of salad or vegetables such as *pisto,* fried chorizo or ham and a tomato sauce, or ketchup.

All sorts of other ingredients may be incorporated in the tortilla, either instead of or in addition to the potatoes. It's a good catchall for leftover bits of meat, ham, sausage, seafood and vegetables. Try green beans, peas, mushrooms, spinach, prawns, chicken livers, sweet peppers, asparagus, etc. One of my favourites is made with *habas*, broad beans, which look like pretty green gems when the tortilla is sliced. Allow 2 to 3 cups diced, cooked vegetables, meats, etc. Favourite additions to the omelette are chopped onion, ham, parsley and garlic, though you can certainly experiment with other seasonings.

TORTILLA DE ESPINACAS
Spinach Omelette

6	tablespoons cooked spinach (about 80 grams)	2	eggs, beaten
2	teaspoons minced onion	1	tablespoon oil
	salt and pepper		grated cheese

Drain the spinach well, chop it finely and mix with the minced onion, salt and pepper and beaten eggs. Heat the oil in a small frying pan and pour in the spinach-egg mixture. Let it cook on the bottom without browning, then, with a spatula, flip it over to cook the other side. Serve sprinkled with the cheese. This omelette is thinner than the classic tortilla. It can be served individually or several of them stacked, a tomato sauce poured over, and sliced to make individual servings.

TORTILLA CAPUCHINA
Capuchine Omelette

400	grams potatoes (2 large)	100	grams asparagus tips, cooked
1	onion, sliced thinly	1	tablespoon chopped parsley
50	ml. oil	1/2	teaspoon salt
100	grams fine breadcrumbs	6	eggs, beaten

Cut the potatoes into dice and fry them with the onions in 2 tablespoons of the oil. When potatoes are tender, stir in the breadcrumbs and asparagus. Fry all for a few minutes. In a bowl mix with the chopped parsley, salt and beaten eggs. Add remaining oil and pour in the mixture. Cook on both sides. Serves 6 as a starter.

TORTILLA MURCIANA
Murcia Omelette

3	tomatoes, peeled, seeded and chopped	1	small aubergine, peeled and diced
4	sweet peppers	1/2	teaspoon salt
50	ml. oil	6	eggs

Prepare the peppers by cleaning them of seeds and cutting in strips. Heat part of the oil in a frying pan and fry the prepared tomatoes, peppers and aubergine together for 10 minutes. Meanwhile beat the eggs and salt together in a bowl. Mix the fried tomato mixture into the eggs, add remaining oil to the pan and pour in the egg mixture. Cook on both sides. Cut into six slices.

TORTILLA SACROMONTE
Granada Omelette

This omelette is named for an abbey in the gypsy cave district of Granada, where it is served every year on San Cecilio's day. The authentic version is made with lamb's brains and *criadillas* (testicles), but if you order the omelette in a Granada restaurant it will probably be made with chopped ham and kidneys instead.

One year the monastery's chief cook was ill on San Cecilio's day and the abbot hired the chef of the Alhambra Palace Hotel to fill in. The chef ordered ham, peas, kidneys for the famous omelette. When the abbot questioned him he was told, "Don't give me cooking lessons, I've made thousands of Sacromonte omelettes in my career!" The abbot gently suggested that, though the hotel's version might be a most excellent interpretation, it wasn't the true *tortilla Sacromonte.*

You can try it both ways, for they are both delicious. For the restaurant version, combine minced ham, cooked peas, and cooked and chopped kidneys with beaten eggs and fry as a tortilla.

For the abbey's version: Cook the brains and criadillas together in salted water. Drain, and brown them slightly in oil. Then mash them together in the mortar or blender to make a paste. Beat together four eggs. Add a little oil to the frying pan and pour in a layer of beaten egg and a layer of the paste. When it is slightly set, pour in another layer of egg and let it set slightly, then turn the omelette and cook the other side. The omelette should be about a finger and a half thick.

TORTILLA DE GAMBAS
Prawn Omelette

6 prawns, cooked, peeled and chopped	salt and pepper
2 eggs	2 tablespoons oil
1 tablespoon finely chopped parsley	

Chop the cooked and peeled prawns and add them to the well-beaten eggs. Season with the parsley and salt and pepper. Heat the oil in a small frying pan and pour in the mixture. Let it set on the bottom, then flip it like a pancake. These omelettes can also be made folded, like a French omelette.

PIPERRADA
Basque Pepper Omelette

2 bell peppers, red and/or green	2 large tomatoes, peeled, seeded
6 tablespoons oil	and chopped
4 cloves garlic	8 eggs, beaten
1 small onion, shredded	salt and pepper
50 grams cooked ham, cut in strips	

Roast the peppers under the broiler grill until charred, wrap them in a cloth for a few minutes, then peel them. Discard the seeds and stem, then cut the peppers into strips. Heat the oil in a frying pan and in it sauté the chopped garlic and shredded onion. Add the strips of ham, then the peeled and chopped tomatoes with the strips of pepper and fry about 15 minutes, until some of the liquid has evaporated. Turn into a bowl and set aside. Beat the eggs with the salt and pepper. Add a little oil to the pan and pour in the eggs. Stir them, cooking very gently, until they are just barely set, as for scrambled eggs. Pour into a well-buttered oven casserole and top with the pepper mixture, mixing it very slightly into the eggs. Bake in a medium oven for about 8 minutes or cover and let the omelette set on a low flame. Serves 4.

REVOLTILLOS DE HUEVOS

Scrambled eggs are just shapeless omelettes. Any of the previous combinations of foods can be used for scrambled eggs, and any of the following can be just as well turned into omelettes. Scrambled eggs should be cooked on a very low heat and removed from the fire before the eggs are set. Serve them very soft and creamy.

REVUELTO DE SETAS
Scrambled Eggs with Chanterelles

This Basque combination — so simple — makes a wonderful supper dish. If chanterelles are not available, use any other wild or cultivated mushroom.

150	grams chanterelles	1	tablespoons chopped parsley
2	tablespoons oil	1	tablespoon water
1	clove garlic		salt and pepper
4	eggs		

Clean the mushrooms carefully of all grit; wash and dry them. Cut them into small pieces. Sauté them in a frying pan in the oil with the minced garlic. Beat the eggs with the chopped parsley, water and salt and pepper, and stir into the mushrooms. Continue stirring the egg mixture until it is just set. Serve hot with strips of fried bread and a garnish of parsley. Serves 2.

REVOLTILLO DE HUEVO CON TOMATE
Tomato Scrambled Eggs

3	tablespoons oil	1 teaspoon salt
1	medium onion, chopped	pepper
2	large tomatoes, peeled, seeded and chopped	4 eggs

Heat the oil and fry the chopped onions until they are soft. Add the tomatoes and salt. Fry until the tomatoes are reduced to a smooth sauce, about 15 minutes. Beat the eggs with another pinch of salt and pepper and stir them into the tomato mixture. Stir constantly on a low fire until the eggs are just set. Serve on triangles of fried bread. Serves 4. This makes a very nice brunch dish, especially when topped with *riñones al jerez,* sautéed kidneys.

HUEVOS REVUELTOS CON ESPARRAGOS
Scrambled Eggs with Asparagus

100	grams asparagus tips	4	eggs, well beaten
100	grams ham		salt and pepper
2	tablespoons lard		

Blanch the asparagus tips in boiling water (or, if using tinned ones, rinse them and drain). Cut the ham into fine dice. Heat the lard in a frying pan and sauté the asparagus and ham for several minutes. Then add the eggs, beaten with salt and pepper, and stir them over a low heat until the eggs are just set. Serves 2.

HUEVO FRITO

The fried egg. In Spanish, it really *is* a fried egg, using a cooking technique quite unlike a typical English or American fried egg. The egg should emerge from its immersion in oil with the white a little crackly around the edges, *estrellada,* and the yolk still unset. The procedure is more like poaching, only the medium is oil, not water. The eggs must be very fresh and at room temperature. In a small frying pan heat more than enough oil to cover the egg until it shimmers, just short of smoking. Break the egg onto a saucer and slip it into the hot oil. Use the skimmer to baste the top of the egg with the oil. Remove it to drain and continue frying eggs, one at a time.

The eggs may be served with pieces of ham or chorizo, slices of bread and chopped garlic, all fried in the same oil. One of the best ways to serve Spanish fried eggs is atop garlic-flavoured croutons (see *migas)*. A very heartwarming meal, whether you call it breakfast or supper.

HUEVOS AL MODO DE SOLLER
Mallorca Fried Eggs

2	tablespoons lard or oil		salt and pepper
2	carrots	8	fried eggs
2	leeks	8	slices sobrasada (soft, red Mallorcan sausage)
200	grams shelled peas		
50	ml. milk		

Melt the lard in a saucepan and in it sauté the carrots and leeks, finely chopped, and the peas. Add water (or fish stock, if available) to cover and simmer the vegetables until they are quite tender. Purée them in a blender, add the milk and salt and pepper and return to the saucepan to cook another 15 minutes. The purée should be the consistency of thick cream. Fry the eggs (as in preceding recipe) and fry the slices of sobrasada. Place an egg on each slice of sausage and top each with a spoonful of the sauce. Serves 4.

HUEVOS SERRANOS
Eggs, Mountain Style

3	large tomatoes	6	fried eggs
100	grams ham	100	grams grated cheese
	salt and pepper		paprika

Cut the tomatoes in half crosswise and scoop out the seeds. Finely chop the ham and divide it amongst the six tomato halves. Season with salt and pepper and put them in the oven for five minutes, just until hot. Place a fried egg in each tomato half, sprinkle with grated cheese and dust with paprika. Serve hot.

HUEVOS A LA CORDOBESA
Fried Eggs, Cordoba Style

750	grams potatoes (4 large)	1	small chili pepper (optional)
50	ml. oil	6	eggs
1	small onion, sliced		salt and pepper
2	sweet red peppers	150	grams chorizo

Peel the potatoes and cut them in thin slices. Heat the oil and fry the potatoes, adding the sliced onions. When they are tender, remove to a serving platter. Adding more oil if necessary, fry the peppers, seeded and cut in thin strips, in the same pan. Place them on top of the potatoes. Then fry the eggs, season with salt and pepper and place them around the potatoes. Cut the chorizo in six slices and fry it very briefly. Add to the platter and serve immediately.

HUEVOS AL PLATO

This means eggs served in the same plate in which they're cooked, most often baked, though sometimes cooked on top of the stove. Some terrific dishes come in this category — such as Flamenco Eggs, a flouncy flourish of garnishes, and Basque-style casserole eggs. Any of them might do nicely as breakfast or brunch, but I like them best for supper, when they seem quite special, but light.

HUEVOS A LA FLAMENCA
Flamenco Eggs

50	ml. olive oil	100	grams cooked green beans or peas
1	small onion, chopped	1	small tin red pimento
1	clove garlic, minced	12	asparagus tips
100	grams ham, diced	100	grams chorizo
600	grams tomatoes (3 large)	4	artichoke hearts
1/2	teaspoon paprika		salt and pepper
8	eggs		chopped parsley

Heat the oil in a frying pan and sauté the chopped onion and garlic and half of the diced ham. When onion is soft, add the tomatoes, peeled, seeded and chopped. Season with salt and pepper and cook on a medium fire until reduced to a sauce, about 15 minutes. Oil four individual earthenware ramekins. Divide the sauce between them. With the pestle or back of a spoon make two indentations in the sauce and carefully break an egg into them. Sprinkle each ramekin with some of the cooked beans or peas. Cut the pimento into strips and arrange it decoratively over the eggs. Surround with the asparagus tips. Slice the chorizo and arrange around the eggs. Cut the artichoke hearts in half and put them on also. Sprinkle with salt and pepper and chopped parsley. Put in a medium hot oven just until the whites are set, the yolks still liquid, 10 to 12 minutes. Serve immediately with triangles of fried bread.

HUEVOS A LA VASCA
Basque Eggs

4	tablespoons oil	200	grams chopped, cooked asparagus
4	cloves garlic	100	grams cooked peas
3	scallions	8	eggs
4	teaspoons flour	2	tablespoons chopped parsley
24	tablespoons water or stock		salt and pepper

Put one spoonful of oil in each of four individual ramekins. Place them on the fire. Chop the garlic and scallions and divide between the four dishes. Sauté until softened, then stir a teaspoon of flour into each. Add 6 tablespoons of stock to each and stir while the sauce thickens. Season with salt and pepper and divide the cooked, chopped asparagus and cooked peas between the four casseroles. Break two eggs into each and sprinkle with some of the chopped parsley. Cook just until the whites are set and yolks still liquid. Serve immediately with pieces of fried bread.

HUEVOS EN NIDO DE PATATAS
Eggs in Potato Nests

1/2	kilo potatoes (4 medium)	4	eggs
3	tablespoons butter	50	grams grated cheese
1	egg yolk		chopped parsley
	salt and pepper		paprika
	grating of nutmeg		

Peel the potatoes, cook them in boiling salted water until tender, and drain them well. Purée the potatoes, adding 1 tablespoon of the butter, the egg yolk, salt and pepper and nutmeg. Butter an oven dish and either spread the potatoes in it or pipe them in with a pastry gun. Make four indentations — nests — in the potatoes. Dot the potatoes with butter and put them in a hot oven or under the broiler and let the potatoes brown very lightly. Remove and break an egg into each nest. Sprinkle with grated cheese, dot with butter, sprinkle with salt and pepper and return to the oven. Bake just until the whites are set. Sprinkle with chopped parsley and paprika. Good served with pork sausage links or with sautéed chicken livers.

HUEVOS EN NIDO DE ESPINACAS
Eggs Baked in Spinach Nests

400	grams cooked spinach		butter
	salt and pepper	4	eggs
	grating of nutmeg	100	ml. bechamel sauce
1	tablespoon grated onion	50	grams grated cheese

Finely chop the cooked spinach and season it with salt and pepper, nutmeg and grated onion. It should be hot, so if not freshly cooked, reheat it. Then spread it in a buttered baking dish. Make four indentations in the spinach and break an egg into each. Cover the eggs with the bechamel sauce and top with grated cheese. Dot with butter and bake in a medium oven until the whites are set and yolks still liquid.

HUEVOS DUROS

The main use for hard-cooked eggs is for stuffing (see *huevos rellenos* in Chapter 4). But there are a number of hot preparations as well which make nice luncheon dishes. Place room temperature eggs into cold water, bring to a boil, then reduce heat and simmer for 10 minutes. Drain them, then cover immediately with cold water and let them sit until ready to use.

HUEVOS EN SALSA DE ALMENDRAS
Eggs in Almond Sauce

8	hard-cooked eggs	1/4	teaspoon saffron
3	tablespoons oil	1/8	teaspoon cinnamon
20	almonds, blanched	1	clove
2	cloves garlic	1	teaspoon salt
2	slices bread	300	ml. water or stock
1	tablespoon dry sherry		chopped parsley
10	peppercorns		

In a frying pan heat the oil and in it fry the almonds, peeled garlic and bread slices until the almonds are golden and the bread crisp. Remove them and crush in mortar or blender with the sherry, peppercorns, saffron, cinnamon, clove and salt. Dissolve this paste in a little of the liquid. Stir it into the oil in the pan and add the remaining water or stock. Simmer for five minutes. Peel the eggs and cut them into quarters and add to the sauce. Heat them thoroughly, sprinkle with chopped parsley and serve. Good accompanied by cooked rice or toast. Serves 4 or 5.

HUEVOS A LA VIZCAINA
Biscay Eggs

3	tablespoons oil	100	grams cooked peas
1	onion, chopped	200	ml. water or stock
2	red peppers, chopped		salt and pepper
2	tablespoons flour	2	cloves garlic
1	teaspoon paprika	1/4	teaspoon saffron

| 500 grams sieved tomatoes | 1 | tablespoon parsley |
| *(tomate triturado)* | 8 | hard-cooked eggs |

Heat the oil in a saucepan and sauté the chopped onions and chopped peppers until they are soft. Stir in the flour and the paprika, then add the tomato purée, the cooked peas, the water or stock and salt and pepper. Let this sauce simmer for 20 minutes, stirring occasionally. Meanwhile, in the mortar crush the garlic with the saffron and parsley. Add to the sauce. Peel the cooked eggs, halve them and add to the sauce. Simmer very gently for another 10 minutes and serve hot with a garnish of parsley.

FLAN CON TOMATE
Tomato Custards

This savoury custard makes an interesting starter. Once unmoulded, surround it with one of the following: asparagus tips, cooked crayfish or prawns, artichoke bottoms, sliced ham, sweetbreads or chicken livers.

6	eggs	grating of nutmeg
1/4	litre milk	dash of cayenne
250	ml. tomato sauce	butter
salt and pepper		

Beat the eggs in a bowl until frothy. Beat in the milk and the tomato sauce. Season with salt and pepper, nutmeg and cayenne. Butter 4 custard cups and divide the egg mixture between them. Set them in an oven dish, add boiling water to half their depths and place in a medium oven until the custards are set. Test them by inserting a tooth pick — when it comes out clean, they are done, about 30 minutes. Let them set a few minutes, then unmould onto individual plates and garnish. Or chill the custards, then unmould.

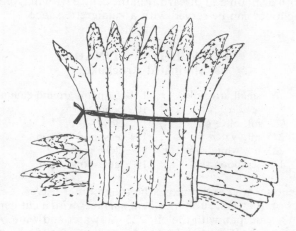

CHAPTER 7

Vegetables

Vegetable dishes in Spain get preferential treatment, often enhanced with inspired sauces. Many are designed to stand on their own, being quite substantial. Though they can certainly be served as an accompaniment to a meat, poultry or fish dish, try them as starters or as light luncheon entrées.

Though Spaniards traditionally prefer their vegetables very well cooked, they almost always incorporate the cooking liquid (with all the vitamins and minerals) into the accompanying sauce. For instance, the real way to make any of the vegetables *salteadas,* sautéed, is to fry the chopped, raw vegetable in oil with garlic, then add just enough water to keep from scorching and cook until tender. Modern cooking techniques have given us a taste for crisp, lightly cooked vegetables. Certainly these recipes can be adapted if so desired. (In addition, see Chapter 2 on marketing, for many tips on selecting, storing and preparing vegetables.)

The recipes selected for this section emphasize those vegetables and ways of cooking them which are not so likely to be found in ordinary British or American cookbooks.

ALCACHOFAS CON MAYONESA
Artichokes with Mayonnaise

One of the simplest possible preparations, and my very favourite. Cut off stalks and remove outer leaves from artichokes (one large one per person). Rub each with a cut lemon and drop into water to which the juice of a lemon has been added. When all are prepared, add salt, bring to a boil and simmer until the artichokes are tender (when a leaf pulls of easily), from 20 to 40 minutes, depending on size. Drain them well upside down. Place upright on salad plates and gently pull open the leaves. When the choke (the fuzzy centre) is exposed, scoop it out with a spoon and discard. Fill the centre with mayonnaise and serve. Similarly, artichokes can be served with a vinaigrette sauce.

ALCACHOFAS ALIÑADAS
Marinated Artichokes

16	small artichokes	1/4	teaspoon ground cumin
1	lemon	10	peppercorns
75	ml. olive oil	1	clove
275	ml. water	1/4	teaspoon saffron
225	ml. white wine	1	clove garlic
1	teaspoon salt	1	tablespoon flour

Wash the artichokes well and remove the tough outer leaves. Leave them whole or cut in halves or quarters, rubbing all cut surfaces with a cut lemon. Place them immediately in a saucepan with the oil, 225 ml. water and wine. Add the juice of the lemon and the salt. Bring to a boil and simmer about 15 minutes. Meanwhile, in the mortar crush the cumin, peppers, clove, saffron and garlic. Blend in the flour, then add remaining water to form a smooth paste. Add this to the

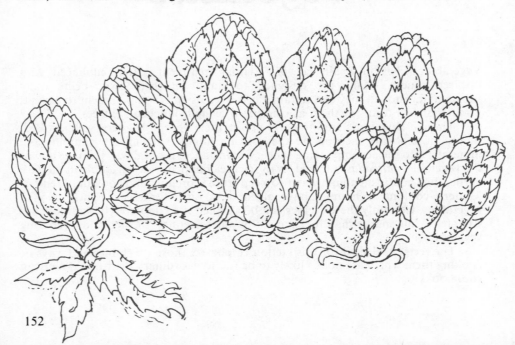

artichokes, stirring until the liquid is slightly thickened. Cook until artichokes are completely tender, then remove from heat and let them cool in the sauce. Serve at room temperature as an hors d'oeuvre or reheat to serve as a vegetable dish. Very nice as a garnish with cold cuts, smoked meats and sausages.

ALCACHOFAS SALTEADAS CON JAMON
Sautéed Artichokes with Ham

12	artichokes or 1 package frozen arti-choke bottoms	100	grams serrano ham, diced
2	teaspoons lemon juice	2	cloves garlic
1	teaspoon salt	2	tablespoons red wine
3	tablespoons olive oil		salt and pepper

Trim the artichokes of outer leaves and cut them about 3 or 4 cm. (1 1/2 in.) from the bottom. Cut these pieces in half and rub all the surfaces with a cut lemon. Cook in boiling water to cover to which the lemon juice and salt have been added. When tender, drain well. In a frying pan or shallow casserole heat the oil and sauté the diced ham and garlic. Add the drained artichokes and sauté on a medium heat without letting them actually brown. Add the wine, the salt and pepper, and cook just until wine has evaporated. Serve immediately.

ALCACHOFAS AL LIMON
Artichokes with Lemon Sauce

8-10	artichokes	1	tablespoon oil
	lemon juice	100	ml. water
2	tablespoons fine breadcrumbs	1	bay leaf
2	cloves garlic, minced		salt and pepper
3	tablespoons lemon juice		

Trim the artichokes, but leave them whole and put to cook in boiling salted water to which lemon juice has been added. In a saucepan combine the breadcrumbs, lemon juice and oil and cook until the liquid has evaporated. Then add the water, bay leaf and salt and pepper. Cook for several minutes until the sauce is thickened. Arrange the cooked and drained artichokes on a serving dish and pour a little of the sauce into and over each. Serves 4 to 8.

ALCACHOFAS REBOZADAS
Deep-fried Artichokes

16	tiny artichokes	75	grams flour
2	tablespoons chopped cooked ham	1	egg, beaten
3	tablespoons bechamel sauce	75	grams breadcrumbs
	salt and pepper		oil
	dash of cayenne		parsley

Trim the artichokes and blanch them for 5 minutes in boiling salted water to which a little lemon juice has been added. Drain them very well and pat dry. Mix the finely chopped ham with the bechamel sauce and season with salt and pepper and cayenne. With the fingers, open the leaves of the artichokes very slightly and spoon in a little of the filling. Pat the leaves back into shape (they can also be tied with thread). Dredge them in flour, dip in beaten egg, then roll in breadcrumbs. Fry the artichokes a few at a time, in hot, deep oil until they are golden. Remove, drain and serve hot with parsley sprigs.

ALCACHOFAS A LA CORDOBESA
Artichoke and Potato Casserole, Cordoba Style

12	artichokes (or 1 package frozen artichoke hearts)	1/4	teaspoon saffron, toasted
	lemon	1	teaspoon salt
50	ml. oil	1	tablespoon vinegar
2	cloves garlic	100	ml. stock or water
500	grams small new potatoes	1	tablespoon flour
			mint sprigs

Trim the artichokes to bottoms or hearts, rubbing them with lemon. Leave them in a bowl of acidulated water. Heat the oil in a casserole. Fry the garlic until it is toasted and remove. Crush in a mortar with the saffron (toasted lightly in a dry pan or in the oven). Dissolve in the vinegar and stock. Drain the artichokes and add them to the oil with the potatoes which have been peeled and left whole if they are small. Sauté them for five minutes, then stir in the flour. Let cook another few minutes, then add the stock and mortar mixture. Cover and let cook until the artichokes and potatoes are tender. Garnish with sprigs of mint.

ALCACHOFAS RELLENAS
Stuffed Artichokes

18	artichokes	3	tablespoons oil
	lemon	2	tablespoons finely chopped onion
200	grams minced meat (pork or beef)	50	ml. white wine
50	grams ham, finely chopped	1	egg, beaten
1	clove garlic	250	ml. tomato sauce
1	tablespoon chopped parsley		oil
	salt and pepper		breadcrumbs

Remove tough outer leaves from the artichokes, rub them with lemon and put to cook in boiling salted water. Cook them only about 10 minutes — they will not be quite tender. Drain well. Open the leaves carefully. Cut out the cone of leaves at the centre, scoop out and discard the fuzzy choke. Set the artichokes aside. Season the minced meat with the garlic, parsley and salt and pepper and let it set for 15 minutes. Heat the oil in a frying pan and sauté the chopped onion. Then add the meat and ham. Let it brown, then add the wine and cook until the wine is reduced. Remove from the heat and add the egg. Stuff the artichokes with this mixture, topping each with a spoonful of the prepared tomato sauce. Place the artichokes in an oiled oven dish. Drizzle them with oil, sprinkle with bread-crumbs, cover the dish and put in a medium oven for about 10 minutes. Remove the cover and cook another 5 minutes.

ESPARRAGOS A LA ANDALUZA
Asparagus, Andalusian Style

This is usually made with the thin, slightly bitter, wild asparagus, but it's quite good with cultivated asparagus as well. Choose thin stalks.

500	grams asparagus	1	tablespoon vinegar
50	ml. oil	150	ml. water
2	cloves garlic		salt and pepper
1	slice bread, crusts removed	2	eggs
1	teaspoon paprika (or 1/2 teaspoon saffron)	1	tablespoon water
			pinch of paprika
1/2	teaspoon cumin		

Cut off and discard the woody ends of the asparagus. Chop the stalks into short lengths and blanch them in boiling water for two minutes and drain well. Heat the oil in a heat-proof casserole and fry the garlic and the bread until they are toasted. Remove them to mortar or blender and crush with the paprika, cumin, vinegar, a little of the water and salt and pepper. Add the drained asparagus to the oil and sauté it for five minutes, tossing with a fork. Add the mortar mixture and more water and cover and simmer the asparagus until tender, about 15 minutes, adding more water as necessary. The sauce should be thick, but should not cook dry. The asparagus can be served as it is. Or beat two eggs with the spoonful of water, salt and pepper and paprika. Pour them into the casserole and cover. Cook on a low heat just until the eggs are set. Serve the casserole with pieces of fried bread. Alternatively, one egg per person can be placed on top of the cooked asparagus and the casserole placed in the oven until the eggs are set. Serves 4 as a starter or side dish.

ESPARRAGOS GRATINADOS
Asparagus au Gratin

1	kilo white and/or green asparagus	2	tablespoons flour
3	tablespoons butter	220	ml. milk
1	tablespoon chopped onion		salt and pepper
50	grams chopped ham	50	grams grated cheese

Snap off the butt ends of the asparagus spears. With a vegetable peeler or sharp knife shave off the thin outer skin of the stalks almost to the tips. Tie them in bundles and cook in plenty of salted water until they are tender, about 10 minutes. Remove and drain well. Place them in a buttered oven dish.

In a saucepan melt the butter, and sauté the chopped onion and ham for a few minutes. Stir in the flour, then the milk and let it cook, stirring, until thickened. Season with salt and pepper. Spoon the sauce over the asparagus and top with grated cheese. Put in a hot oven or under broiler just until top is browned and cheese bubbly. Serves 6.

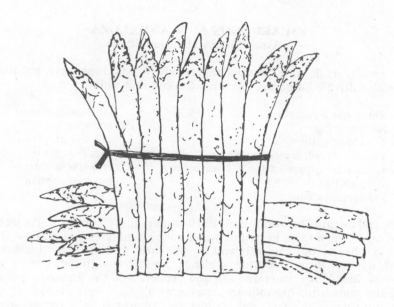

PASTEL DE BERENJENAS
Aubergine Mousse

3	aubergines	1	teaspoon salt
1	onion		grated nutmeg
1	red pepper		dash of cayenne
1	clove garlic	2	egg whites
3	tablespoons lemon juice	1/4	litre cream

Roast the aubergines, onion and pepper under the broiler grill until aubergines are soft when pierced with a knife and peppers are charred. Scoop the aubergine pulp from the skins and chop it with the onion fairly finely (can be done in processor). You should have about 700-750 ml. of vegetable pulp. Season it with minced garlic, lemon juice, salt, nutmeg and cayenne. Peel the peppers, cut them in strips and set aside. When the vegetable mixture is completely cool put it in processor with the egg whites and whip the mixture. With the motor running, pour the cream into it in a slow stream. Pour half this mixture into a well-oiled loaf pan. Lay the strips of red pepper on top of it and fill the pan with the rest of the vegetable mixture. Set the pan in a larger receptacle and add boiling water to half the depth of the pan. Cover the mould with foil and bake in a medium oven until a knife inserted in the centre comes out clean, about 1½ hours. Let the mousse cool for a few minutes in the pan, then unmould it onto a serving platter. It may be served hot or cold. After setting, pour off accumulated liquid on the dish, cover the loaf and chill it. Serve with a tomato or garlic sauce. Serves 8 to 10 as a starter. The mousse can be made with other vegetables — carrots, leeks, spinach, broccoli, asparagus. The vegetable pulp can be combined, or baked in three layers, using 1 egg white and 80 ml. of cream for each 230 ml. of vegetable pulp.

BERENJENAS FRITAS
Fried Aubergine

Peel and slice the aubergines. Layer the slices in a colander, sprinkling them liberally with salt and let them drain for an hour. Rinse in running water, drain, then pat the slices dry. Dredge them in flour, then sauté them in a frying pan in a small quantity of oil (enough to cover the bottom of the pan), adding more oil as needed. Drain on absorbent paper, sprinkle with salt and serve hot.

ESCABECHE DE BERENJENA
Pickled Aubergine

8	small aubergines	3	tablespoons chopped parsley
	salt	1	teaspoon chopped fennel leaves
150	ml. oil		freshly ground pepper
50	ml. lemon juice or vinegar	1	teaspoon paprika

Peel the aubergines, cut them in half lengthwise and salt them. Set aside. In a bowl mix the oil, lemon or vinegar, parsley, fennel and pepper. Pat the aubergines dry and grill them over hot charcoal, adding a few stalks of fennel to the fire, if available. (The aubergines can also be cooked under a broiler). When they are fork-tender, place them in the marinade. They can be served hot or left to marinate and served cold as an hours d'oeuvre. Alternatively, put the marinade in a saucepan and simmer whole, tiny aubergines in it, piercing them with a knife. When tender let cool in the marinade.

BERENJENAS A LA CATALANA
Aubergines, Catalan Style

3	medium aubergines	2	medium tomatoes, peeled, seeded and chopped
6	walnuts (or 15 hazelnuts)		
50	ml. oil	50	ml. stock or water
1	onion, chopped		salt and pepper
2	cloves garlic, chopped		parsley

Peel the aubergines and cut them into cubes. Put them in a colander, salt them and let them set for an hour. Rinse, drain and pat dry. Heat the oil in a heat-proof casserole and fry the walnuts or hazelnuts and remove them with a skimmer. Add the aubergine to the casserole and sauté it a few minutes. Add the chopped onion and garlic and continue frying. Then add the prepared tomatoes. Crush the toasted nuts in the mortar or blender to a smooth paste and dissolve it in the stock. Add this to the casserole with salt and pepper and continue cooking until the aubergines are tender. Serve in the same casserole sprinkled with chopped parsley. Good with grilled and roast meats and a delicious accompaniment to fried eggs.

BERENJENAS AL HORNO
Baked Aubergines

3	aubergines	400 ml. tomato sauce
	salt	100 grams grated cheese
	flour	30 grams fine breadcrumbs
	oil	15 grams butter

Peel the aubergines, cut them in slices, salt them and let them drain for an hour. Rinse, drain and pat dry. Dredge them in flour and fry the slices in oil, turning once to brown both sides. Oil an oven casserole and arrange a layer of the fried aubergines in it. Cover with a layer of tomato sauce and grated cheese, then repeat with another layer of aubergines, sauce and cheese. Top with breadcrumbs and dot with butter. Put in a medium hot oven until bubbly and lightly browned on top, about 20 minutes. Serves 6 as a side dish. If you use tinned tomato sauce, be sure to flavour it well with crushed garlic, a pinch of cumin and paprika and a dash of cayenne, and chopped parsley or another herb, such as oregano.

BERENJENAS RELLENAS A LA MALLORQUINA
Stuffed Aubergines, Mallorcan Style

4	aubergines	50	ml. white wine or water
4	tablespoons oil	1	tablespoon flour
200	grams minced beef or pork	100	ml. milk
50	grams chopped ham		grating of nutmeg
1	onion, finely chopped		salt and pepper
1	tomato, peeled, seeded and chopped	2	eggs
		50	grams fine breadcrumbs
1/4	teaspoon cinnamon		

Cut the aubergines in half lengthwise. With a sharp knife cut out the pulp, leaving the shells about a centimetre thick. Either stew the shells in oil until they are soft or place them in a baking tin, brush with oil and bake until soft or boil in water until soft. Chop the pulp and reserve it. (Processor does it quickly.) Heat 3 tablespoons oil in a frying pan and sauté the minced meat and chopped ham. Add the chopped onion and aubergine pulp and continue frying a few minutes. Then add the tomato, cinnamon and wine. Cook until liquid has evaporated and the mixture is dry. In a saucepan heat the tablespoon of oil, stir in the flour, then whisk in the milk. Stir this sauce until it is thickened. Season with a grating of nutmeg and salt and pepper. Add the meat mixture to the sauce and then add one of the eggs, well beaten. Arrange the aubergine shells on a baking tin. Spoon the stuffing mixture into them. Beat the remaining egg and spoon a little of it over each, top with breadcrumbs and drizzle with oil. Put in a medium hot oven for 15 minutes. Makes 4 main course servings or 8 starters.

BERENJENA A LA MORISCA
Moorish Aubergines

4	small aubergines	1	teaspoon salt
3	tablespoons lemon juice	1	clove garlic, minced
1	small onion, finely chopped		freshly ground pepper
1	tablespoon chopped parsley		minced chili or dash cayenne
1/2	teaspoon oregano	4	tablespoons olive oil
1/2	teaspoon cumin	1	tablespoon vinegar or lemon juice

Bake or grill the whole aubergines until they are fork-tender. When they are cool enough to handle, peel them and cut in dice. Place in a bowl and toss with the lemon juice. Add the chopped onion, chopped parsley, oregano, cumin, salt, minced garlic, pepper, minced chili. Drizzle with the oil and lemon juice. Serve at room temperature. Serves 8.

JUDIAS VERDES A LA CASTELLANA
Castilian Green Beans

500	grams green beans	3	cloves garlic
3	sweet red peppers	1	tablespoon chopped parsley
3	tablespoons oil	1/2	teaspoon salt
50	grams salt pork or bacon (optional)		freshly ground pepper

Snap the ends off the beans and remove strings if necessary. Put them to cook in boiling water until tender. Drain them and keep warm. While they are cooking, roast the peppers under the broiler grill until they are charred on all sides. Remove, wrap in a towel until cool enough to handle, then peel them. Remove seeds and cut the flesh into strips. Heat the oil in a frying pan and in it sauté the diced salt pork or bacon, and then add chopped garlic. Add the beans, the strips of peppers, the parsley, salt and pepper. Toss for a minute or two and serve. Makes 6 servings.

CAZUELA DE JUDIAS VERDES CON CHORIZO
Green Bean and Sausage Casserole

500	grams green beans	1	medium onion, chopped
1	bay leaf	2	cloves garlic, chopped
5	medium potatoes	1	tablespoon flour
50	ml. oil	3	tablespoons tomato sauce
1/2	teaspoon salt		salt and pepper
3	chorizo sausages		

Snap the beans into regular size pieces, remove any strings and cook them in boiling water with the bay leaf. When tender, drain, saving the liquid. Meanwhile peel the potatoes and cut them in thin slices. Heat the oil in a heat-proof casserole and fry the potatoes slowly, sprinkling them with the salt. When they are nearly tender, add the chorizo, cut in slices. Fry for a few minutes more then remove them to another plate. In the same oil fry the chopped onion until softened and add the minced garlic. Stir in the flour, tomato sauce and about 50 ml. of the reserved bean liquid. Stir until thickened and return the potatoes, chorizo and green beans to the casserole. Season with salt and pepper and simmer another 10 minutes, adding a little more liquid if necessary. Makes 6 servings.

JUDIAS VERDES SALTEADAS
Sautéed Green Beans

500	grams green beans	4	tablespoons oil
1	slice bread	50	grams chopped ham
2	tablespoons vinegar	1/2	teaspoon salt
1	clove garlic	2	hard-cooked eggs
8	peppercorns	1	tablespoon chopped parsley
1/2	teaspoon paprika		

Snap the beans into pieces, remove any strings and cook them in boiling water until tender. Drain, saving some of the liquid. Put the slice of bread in a bowl, drizzle it with the vinegar, then add enough water to cover and let it soak until softened. Then squeeze out and discard the liquid. Mash the bread in the mortar or blender, with the garlic, peppercorns and paprika. Dissolve in a little of the reserved bean liquid. Heat the oil in a frying pan or heatproof casserole and sauté the beans with the ham for 5 minutes. Stir in the mortar mixture, salt and a little more liquid if necessary. Cook for 5 minutes more and garnish with quartered eggs and chopped parsley. Makes 6 servings.

POCHAS A LA RIOJANA
Shelled Beans, Rioja Style

These are freshly-shelled beans, harvested when the shells are too dry to be edible, but before the beans have been spread to dry. Dry beans — white, pinto or black — could be substituted, but they must be soaked before cooking. (For other recipes for dry beans, see the section on *potajes* in Chapter 5.)

1	kilo shelled beans	1	teaspoon paprika or 1/2 teaspoon saffron
350	grams lambs tails or lamb riblets, cut in very small pieces	3	tablespoons chopped parsley freshly ground pepper
100	grams lard	1	teaspoon salt
1	large onion, chopped	1	chorizo (optional)
2	chopped cloves garlic		

Heat half of the lard in a frying pan and sauté the chopped onion and garlic until they are softened. Stir in the paprika or saffron, which has been crushed, and the parsley. Melt the rest of the lard in a heat-proof casserole and in it brown the pieces of lamb. When very well browned add about 50 ml. of water and part of the fried onion mixture. Cover and cook until the meat is tender. Meanwhile, put the shelled beans in a pot, add the rest of the fried onion mixture, the salt and pepper, the chorizo if desired and cold water to cover. Bring to a boil and simmer until they are nearly tender. Using a skimmer, add the beans to the meat in the casserole with a little of the liquid and cook them together another 15 minutes. Cut the cooked chorizo into pieces and use it to garnish the top of the casserole. Six servings.

HABAS CON JAMON
Broad Beans and Ham

2	kilos broad beans	4	cloves garlic, chopped
100	ml. olive oil		salt and pepper
150	grams serrano ham, diced		chopped parsley or fennel or mint

Shell the beans. Heat the oil in a heat-proof casserole and add the beans, ham and garlic. Fry them on a high heat very briefly, then reduce the flame and let the beans stew in the oil until they are quite tender, about 20 minutes. A little water can be added if needed. Season with salt and pepper to taste and serve with a sprinkling of one of the chopped herbs. This dish can also be made omitting the ham and using a chopped onion.

HABAS A LA CATALANA
Broad Beans, Catalan Style

4	kilos broad beans		salt and pepper
2	tablespoons lard		bouquet garni of thyme, bay, rosemary, mint and cinnamon stick
150	grams streaky salt pork		
6	scallions or 1 onion, chopped	60	ml. medium-dry sherry or a *vino rancio,* if available
3	cloves garlic		
200	grams *butifarra* (white Catalan sausage)	2	tablespoons dry anise brandy
			chopped parsley
200	grams *butifarra negra* (Catalan black pudding)		

Shell the beans. Heat the lard in a soup pot or heat-proof casserole. Cut the piece of salt pork into 6 or 8 pieces and brown in the lard. Then add the chopped scallions or onion and the chopped garlic. Let them brown, then add the shelled beans and the two kinds of *butifarra* sausage. Season with salt and pepper and add the herbs tied with a thread. Add the sherry or *vino rancio,* the anise brandy and enough water or stock to just cover the beans. Cook them, covered tightly, until they are very tender, about 35 minutes. Discard the bouquet garni. Cut the sausages into pieces and arrange them on top of the beans. Sprinkle with chopped parsley. Six to 8 servings.

FAVES AL TOMBET
Broad Beans, Alicante Style

800	grams shelled broad beans	50	ml. water
2	lettuces	1	tablespoon vinegar
4	tablespoons oil	1	teaspoon paprika
1	slice bread		salt and pepper
3	cloves garlic		

Wash the lettuce and chop it. Mix with the shelled beans. Heat the oil in a flameproof casserole and fry the bread and the garlic. When they are toasted, remove to mortar or blender and mash with the water, vinegar and paprika. Add the beans and chopped lettuce to the same oil and sauté them for several minutes. Then add the bread paste and salt and pepper and a small quantity of water. Cover the casserole and cook the beans very slowly until they are tender, about 25 minutes. Serves 4.

HABAS A LA RONDEÑA
Broad Beans, Ronda Style

1	kilo shelled broad beans	150	grams diced ham
4	tablespoons oil	1	teaspoon paprika
1	onion, chopped		salt and freshly ground pepper
1	clove garlic, chopped	2	tablespoons fine breadcrumbs
1	tomato, peeled, seeded, chopped	2	hard-cooked eggs

Heat the oil in a casserole and sauté the chopped onion and garlic. When they are softened, add the tomato, ham, shelled beans, paprika, salt and pepper. Add just enough water to barely cover the beans. Cover the casserole and cook until they are tender, 25 to 30 minutes. Stir in the breadcrumbs to thicken the sauce, cook a few minutes more and serve garnished with the quartered eggs. Serves 6.

CAZUELA DE HABAS A LA GRANADINA
Casserole of Broad Beans, Granada Style

12	artichokes	1/4	teaspoon saffron
3	kilos broad beans	1/2	teaspoon cumin
60	ml. oil	6	peppercorns
1	slice bread		salt
3	cloves garlic	6	eggs
6	scallions or 1 onion, chopped		
2	tomatoes, peeled, seeded, chopped		
	bouquet garni of bay, parsley and mint		

Trim the artichokes (they are easier to manage in the finished dish if cut down to the hearts only, or substitute frozen artichoke hearts). Blanch them in boiling water for 5 minutes. Shell the beans and blanch them for 5 minutes. Drain and reserve. Heat the oil in a heat-proof casserole and in it fry the bread and garlic until they are toasted. Remove them and set aside. Add the chopped scallions to the same oil and fry until slightly browned. Add the blanched beans and artichokes and sauté a few minutes more, then add the prepared tomatoes and the bouquet garni. Add enough water to barely cover. Cover the casserole and simmer. Meanwhile, in mortar or blender crush the saffron, cumin and peppercorns with the fried bread and garlic. Dilute with a little of the liquid from the vegetables and add this mixture to the casserole. Season to taste with salt and cook until beans are quite tender. Break eggs on top of the vegetables and put the casserole in a hot oven just until the whites are set. (Can also be spooned into individual casseroles.) Garnish with a little chopped parsley or chopped mint. Serves 6.

HABAS CON CALZON
Beans in Their Breeches

1	kilo small broad beans	2	cloves garlic
3	medium potatoes		salt and pepper
1	onion, quartered		chopped parsley or mint
11	tablespoons oil	100	grams ham (optional)
1	piece ham bone		

Use very young, tender beans for this dish, which is prepared without shelling the beans. Snap off the ends, remove any strings and break the beans in half. Put them to cook in water to cover with the potatoes, quartered onion, 3 spoons of oil and ham bone. Cook until beans are tender. Drain and place them in a serving bowl, discarding the bone. Heat the oil in a small frying pan and fry the chopped garlic with the diced ham. Toss with the beans, season with salt and pepper and served garnished with chopped parsley or mint. Serves 4 to 6.

PURE DE HABAS
Purée of Broad Beans

Cook the shelled broad beans in boiling salted water to cover until they are tender. Drain and purée in blender or processor, then sieve the purée to remove the skins. Season with salt and pepper and butter or with chopped garlic fried in oil. Serve as a side dish. Also good topped with grated cheese and gratinéed. Makes a good pasta sauce with the addition of chopped ham or bacon, and can be turned into a soup by reheating the purée with stock. The broad beans can be combined with spinach, chard, carrots, cabbage or potatoes.

REMOLACHAS A LA VINAGRETA
Beets Vinaigrette

Scrub the beets, cut off the tops and cook them whole in water to cover until they are fork-tender, about 45 minutes. Drain and cool. The skins will slip off easily. Slice the beets thinly or cut them into dice and put in a serving bowl. Season with salt and pepper, drizzle with oil and vinegar, or vinaigrette dressing (Chapter 12), and mix gently. Garnish with chopped hard-cooked egg and chopped parsley. Serve as garnish for salads or as an hors d'oeuvre.

COLES A LA CATALANA
Cabbage, Catalan Style

Wash and chop the cabbages and cook in salted water until tender. Drain. Return the cabbage to the pan with romesco sauce (see Chapter 12). Cook for a few minutes, then remove from heat and let the cabbage marinate for an hour or more. Reheat before serving.

COL BLANCA CON AJOACEITE
White Cabbage with Garlic Sauce

Cut white cabbages into wedges and boil in salted water to which 2 tablespoons of vinegar have been added. When tender, drain, saving some of the liquid, and place in a serving bowl. Meanwhile, crush 2 cloves garlic and mix them into 125 ml. mayonnaise (or make alioli). Beating constantly, add a little of the hot reserved cabbage liquid to the sauce to thin it. Pour over the cabbage and serve. Potatoes can be cooked with the cabbage if desired.

REPOLLO A LA VALENCIANA
Cabbage, Valencia Style

Chop the cabbage and cook in boiling salted water until tender. Drain. In a casserole, heat oil and in it sauté 2 chopped cloves of garlic. Add the cabbage and sauté for a few minutes. Then add pitted and chopped olives and capers. Toss the cabbage and serve.

LIADILLOS SEVILLANOS
Cabbage Rolls, Sevilla Style

12	large cabbage leaves	1	tablespoon chopped parsley
2	tablespoons oil	1	clove garlic, minced
200	grams minced meat	15	black olives, pitted and chopped
50	grams salt pork or bacon		flour
50	grams ham	2	eggs
	salt and pepper		breadcrumbs
	grating of nutmeg		oil or lard

To remove the leaves from the cabbage, cut all around the core with a sharp knife, then put the whole cabbage into a pot of boiling water for 1 minute. Remove it and drain. The leaves should easily separate from the head. (Save inner leaves for another dish.) Return the leaves to the boiling water and blanch them for about 3 minutes. Drain and set aside. In a frying pan sauté the minced meat in the oil until it is browned. Add the salt pork or bacon, chopped, and the ham, diced. Season with salt and pepper, and nutmeg. Remove from heat and add the chopped parsley, minced garlic and chopped olives. Add 1 beaten egg to the mixture. Spread out a cabbage leaf, place a spoonful of the filling on it and roll it up, securing with a pick or string. When all the leaves are rolled, dredge them in flour, dip in beaten egg, then breadcrumbs, and sauté them until browned in oil or lard. Serves 4.

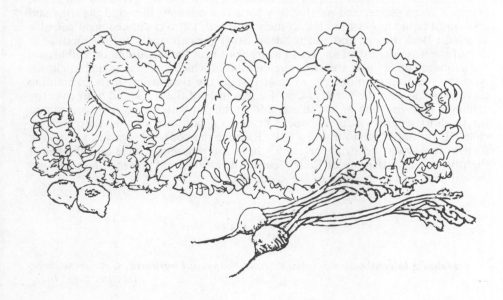

COL RELLENA
Stuffed Cabbage

This is one of my favourite supper dishes, so satisfying on a chilly winter's night. There are several ways to stuff a cabbage. The one I like best is to remove all the leaves from the head of cabbage (as in preceding recipe). Place them on a clean dampened cloth or towel in layers with the filling, keeping the "construction" as round as possible. Then tie the corners of the cloth together, making a round ball. Cook, and remove the cloth to serve. The second way is to cut out the core and some of the inner leaves, leaving a hollow in the cabbage (works best with tight-leafed head of cabbage). Fill the hollow with stuffing and cover with one or two large leaves. The third way, which is nice with the loose-leafed curly cabbage, is to stuff each leaf. First blanch the whole head of cabbage briefly and drain well. Gently spread apart the leaves. Starting in the centre, spread a little stuffing mixture on each leaf and press it closed. Continue until all the leaves have been stuffed. Tie with string to keep the stuffing in place.

1	large cabbage	1	small green pepper
300	grams minced meat	2	tablespoons chopped parsley
3	cloves garlic	50	ml. white wine
1	teaspoon salt	1	egg
75	ml. oil	150	grams ham or bacon
2	onions	3	carrots
2	tomatoes, peeled, seeded and chopped	1/2	litre stock
			salt and pepper

Prepare the cabbage for stuffing as described above. Season the minced meat with 1 clove of garlic, finely minced, and the salt and let it sit for 15 minutes. In a frying pan heat 3 tablespoons oil. Chop 1 of the onions and sauté it with 1 clove of minced garlic. Then add the meat and brown it. Add the prepared tomatoes, chopped green pepper and parsley. Fry for a few minutes, then add the wine and cook until liquid has evaporated. (Finely chopped, leftover cooked meat can also be used.) Beat the egg and add to meat. Stuff the cabbage with this mixture in one of the ways described above. In a large pot heat the remaining oil and brown the cabbage (unless you are using the method in which cabbage is tied in cloth). Add the remaining onion, cut in quarters. In the mortar crush the remaining clove of garlic with the parsley. Dissolve in a little of the stock and pour over the cabbage. Dice the ham or bacon and add to the pot with the carrots, peeled and cut in short lengths. Add the stock, bring to a boil and simmer the cabbage, covered, for about an hour and a half. Remove the cooked cabbage to a serving platter, removing the string or cloth. Sieve the remaining juice and thicken it slightly with 1 tablespoon of flour. Scatter the carrots and pieces of ham around the cabbage and pour some of the sauce over it.

Habas a la catalana, made with broad beans and **butifarra,** Catalan sausage (recipe, page 161).

LOMBARDA A LA CASTELLANA
Red Cabbage, Castilian Style

This dish is served in many parts of Spain on *Noche Buena,* Christmas Eve. In some regions the Christmas Eve dinner, before taking communion at midnight mass, is a "fasting" meal. In other places it is definitely a "feast" and the red cabbage would accompany stuffed turkey or other meats.

Shred a large red cabbage and put it to cook in salted water with a few spoonfuls of oil, an onion stuck with 2 cloves and a bay leaf. Cook for 10 minutes and drain. In a casserole heat 3 tablespoons of oil, add 1 chopped clove of garlic, 1 apple, peeled and diced, 2 tablespoons chopped parsley and the cooked cabbage. Sauté for several minutes, seasoning with salt and white pepper. Add 50 ml. white wine and cook until liquid is absorbed and serve hot.

CARDOS
Cardoons

If you were to cross an artichoke with celery, you would have a cardoon. *Cardo,* a thistle, is related to the artichoke and can be prepared as for artichokes or asparagus. The outer leaves are stripped off, the stalk is peeled and rubbed with lemon juice to prevent its darkening. Cook in acidulated water for an hour. Drain and serve with a bechamel sauce or the following garlic-almond sauce.

3	tablespoons oil	100	grams almonds, blanched and peeled
2	cloves garlic, chopped	5	peppercorns
1	tablespoon flour		salt
50	ml. white wine		

Heat the oil in a saucepan and sauté the chopped garlic. Stir in the flour, let it cook until lightly coloured, then add the white wine and about 150 ml. of the liquid in which the cardoons cooked. Cook, stirring constantly, until the sauce is thickened. Crush the almonds in mortar or blender with the peppercorns. Season with salt and dissolve in a little liquid. Add to the sauce. Return the cooked cardoons to the sauce and heat thoroughly.

ZANAHORIAS CON VINO DE MALAGA
Carrots Braised in Malaga Wine

1	kilo carrots	100	ml. Malaga wine
4	tablespoons oil		salt and pepper
2	tablespoons stock		

Peel the carrots, slice them and cook in boiling salted water until almost tender, about 10 minutes. Drain. Heat the oil in a frying pan and sauté the carrots very

Seafood **paella,** *one of many Spanish preparations for rice (see pages 187-194).*

gently, turning them with a fork so they brown very lightly. Add the stock, wine and salt and pepper and cook until the liquid is partly evaporated and carrots are very tender, about 20 minutes. Serves 6 to 8.

COLIFLOR AL AJIACEITE
Cauliflower with Garlic Sauce

1	large cauliflower	1	slice bread, crusts removed
2	cloves garlic	2	tablespoons vinegar
1	sprig parsley	100	ml. oil
1	sprig celery leaves		salt and pepper

Cut the cauliflower into flowerets. Where stalks are especially thick, slice into them almost to the flower head so they will cook quicker. Bring salted water to a boil and add the cauliflower. Cook without covering until it is just tender, about 12 minutes. Drain and rinse with cold water. In the mortar or blender crush the garlic with the parsley and celery leaves. Drizzle the bread with the vinegar, then add enough water to cover it. Soak briefly, then squeeze out and discard the liquid. Add the bread to the garlic and crush to a paste. Add the oil, drop by drop, beating hard until it is all incorporated. Season with salt and pepper and thin, as desired, with a little water. Place the cooked cauliflower in a serving bowl and pour the sauce over. Garnish with parsley and strips of red pepper.

COLIFLOR EMPANADA
Breaded Cauliflower

Cook cauliflower as in preceding recipe. Drain it well, then drizzle with a little vinegar and sprinkle with salt, minced garlic and chopped parsley. Let it marinate for 30 minutes. Then dredge the flowerets in flour, dip in beaten egg, and roll in fine breadcrumbs. Fry the pieces in hot oil until they are crisp and golden. Serve garnished with lemon wedges and sprigs of parsley. A good use for leftover cooked cauliflower.

COLIFLOR AL AJO ARRIERO
Cauliflower, Mule Driver's Style

Cook the cauliflower as in the recipe for cauliflower with garlic sauce. Drain, reserving a little of the cooking liquid, and place the cauliflower in a serving bowl. In a frying pan heat 75 ml. oil and in it sauté 4 cloves of chopped garlic. Remove from heat and stir in 1 teaspoon paprika, 1 tablespoon vinegar, 2 tablespoons chopped parsley and 2 tablespoons liquid. Pour this sauce over the cooked cauliflower.

CHARD

Chard, *acelga,* is a wonderfully versatile vegetable because it can go white or green or both. The stalks can be prepared in any way suitable for cooked celery, leeks or asparagus (very nice au gratin) and the leaves in any way in which spinach is cooked.

ACELGA FRITA
Fried Chard Stalks

1 dozen chard stalks	breadcrumbs
flour	oil
1 egg, beaten	salt

Cut off the green leaves and save them for another use (cook as for spinach). Remove strings from chard stalks and cut them into short lengths, about 5 cm. Cook in boiling salted water until they are just tender, but not limp. Drain and pat dry. Dredge the pieces in flour, dip them in beaten egg, then coat in breadcrumbs. Fry in hot oil, turning the pieces once, until they are crisply golden. Remove and sprinkle with salt. Fried chard makes a good garnish for meat dishes and is also good as an appetizer, served with lemon wedges or a dipping sauce. Serves 6.

ACELGAS A LA MALAGUEÑA
Chard, Malaga Style

1 1/2 kilos chard	100	grams Malaga raisins, seeded
3 tablespoons oil		salt and pepper
3 cloves garlic, chopped		

Chop the chard, both stalks and leaves, removing strings. Cook the chard in boiling salted water until it is tender, about 25 minutes. Drain it well and set aside. Meanwhile, in a frying pan sauté the chopped garlics in the oil. When they are golden, add the raisins and cook briefly, then add the cooked chard. Toss it and season with salt and pepper and serve hot. Serves 6. Spinach can be prepared in the same manner.

LOCRO DE MAIZ
Stewed Corn

In Galicia where this dish comes from the corn (maize) would be the dry grains, first soaked overnight and cooked slowly until soft. However, it's a quick dish substituting fresh corn, off the cob, or tinned, well drained.

1/2 kilo corn, cooked	4	cloves garlic
2 tablespoons lard		salt and pepper
1 kilo tomatoes (4 large)	1/2	teaspoon paprika

Place the cooked corn in a serving bowl and keep it warm. In a frying pan melt the lard and in it fry the tomatoes, peeled, seeded and chopped, and the garlic, chopped. Season with salt and pepper and paprika and cook until sauce is reduced, about 15 minutes. Pour over the corn and serve. Six servings.

CALABACINES RELLENOS
Stuffed Courgettes

This version of stuffed courgette, which contains no meat, makes an admirable accompaniment to a simple main course such as roast chicken, or might serve as a light luncheon dish. For a more substantial preparation, prepare as for stuffed aubergine. The usual manner of stuffing a courgette is to split it lengthwise and scoop out the pulp. However, a very attractive way is to split the courgettes crosswise into pieces of about 8 cm. Serve them upright on a plate.

2	large courgettes (zucchini)	1	tablespoon parsley
3	tablespoons oil	1/4	teaspoon paprika
1	onion, chopped	2	tablespoons brandy
1	green pepper, chopped	1/2	teaspoon salt
3	medium tomatoes, peeled, seeded and chopped	1	hard-cooked egg
2	cloves garlic	50	grams grated cheese

Wash the courgettes and cook them whole in boiling water just until they can be easily pierced with a fork, about 10 minutes. Drain and cut them in half lengthwise. With a spoon hollow out the pulp. Heat the oil in a frying pan and sauté the chopped onion and chopped green pepper until onion is soft. Add the tomatoes and the pulp of the courgettes, finely chopped. Crush the garlic in a mortar with the parsley and add to the pan with the paprika, brandy, salt and chopped egg. Cook the mixture until liquid has evaporated, about 10 minutes. Spoon the mixture into the courgette shells and place them in an oiled oven dish. Sprinkle with grated cheese and bake in a hot oven until the cheese is melted, about 10 minutes. Serves 6 to 8.

CALABACINES AL HORNO
Baked Courgettes

	3 or 4 small courgettes	2	large tomatoes, peeled, seeded and chopped
50	ml. oil		
	flour	2	tablespoons chopped parsley
1	onion, finely chopped		salt and pepper
2	cloves garlic, chopped	75	grams grated cheese

Cut the courgettes into crosswise slices. Dredge them in flour and fry in oil, turning to brown both sides. As they are cooked, arrange them in layers in an oven dish. In the remaining oil fry the chopped onion and garlic until soft. Add the prepared tomatoes, parsley and salt and pepper. Cook for about 15 minutes, until reduced to a sauce. Purée this mixture in a blender or sieve and pour it over the courgettes. Top with the grated cheese and bake in a medium oven until the cheese is melted, 10 to 15 minutes. Serves 6 to 8.

PURRUSALDA
Stewed Leeks

This Basque dish is usually made with *bacalao,* salt cod. However, it's a delicious preparation on its own, as an accompaniment to any other fish or poultry dish. It can be served "soupy" or "dry."

3/4	kilo leeks (about 8)	1	bay leaf
50	ml. oil		salt and pepper
2	cloves garlic	1/2	teaspoon paprika
1/2	kilo potatoes	1/4	litre water or stock

Clean the leeks very well and slice them, including a little of the green part. Heat the oil in a saucepan and fry the garlic just until toasted, and remove. Add the sliced leeks to the oil and sauté them very gently. Peel the potatoes and cut into pieces similar in size to the leeks. Add to the oil with the bay leaf, and salt and pepper. Then add the water or stock (it can be poultry or fish stock or, if using *bacalao,* the liquid in which the codfish cooked). In the mortar crush the fried garlic with the paprika and add to the vegetables. Cook slowly for about 35 minutes, or until the leeks are very tender and the potatoes almost disintegrated. Serves 4 to 6.

ROBELLONS A LA BRASA
Grilled Mushrooms

This simple preparation can be used for any kind of mushroom, wild or cultivated. Wipe the *rovellons* clean, but do not wash them unless they seem very dry. Put them whole onto a hot griddle and drizzle with oil. Turn them after five minutes and grill the reverse side. Sprinkle with more oil, a few drops of water and chopped parsley and garlic if desired.

CHAMPIÑONES AL AJILLO
Garlic-sizzled Mushrooms

1/2	kilo mushrooms	1/2	teaspoon salt
100	ml. oil		freshly ground pepper
1	head garlic	2	tablespoons chopped parsley
1	chili pepper (optional)		

Clean the mushrooms. Slice them if they are large or quarter them if small. Heat the oil in a frying pan or earthenware casserole and sauté the mushrooms, adding the chopped cloves of garlic after a few minutes and the chili pepper if desired. When mushrooms are cooked, about 10 minutes, season with salt and pepper and sprinkle with parsley. Serve hot. Serves 4 as a starter or side dish.

SETAS AL JEREZ
Mushrooms with Sherry

500 grams mushrooms	125 ml. dry sherry
50 ml. oil	salt and pepper
1/2 onion, chopped	1 hard-cooked egg
2 cloves garlic, chopped	chopped parsley

Clean the mushrooms well and cut them into regular-sized pieces. Heat the oil in a frying pan or casserole and put in the mushrooms. Fry them until they stop sweating out liquid (some wild mushrooms, such as the boletus, will need about 20 minutes or more of cooking). Then add the chopped onion and garlic. When it is browned, add the sherry, salt and pepper and simmer for 10 minutes. Serve sprinkled with chopped egg and parsley. Serves 6.

CRIADILLAS DE LA TIERRA A LA EXTREMEÑA
Earth Balls (Truffles), Extremadura Style

Truffles are found in both Extremadura and Cataluña.

Brush the truffles clean of grit, wash and dry them. Chop very finely. Heat lard in a frying pan and sauté in it some finely sliced onion and minced garlic. Add the chopped truffles and sauté for a few minutes. Then add meat stock to cover and simmer for a few minutes. Skim them out and reserve. Beat 2 egg yolks with 1 tablespoon vinegar for each 1/4 litre of stock. Stir this into the stock and cook, stirring, until the sauce is thickened. Pour over the truffles and serve.

CALCOTADA DE VALLS
Grilled Spring Onions

A Catalan speciality, this is a fine addition to a charcoal grilled meal. The grilled onions would traditionally be served with grilled pork chops and *butifarra* sausage.

The onions should be 2 or 3 cm. thick and 15 to 20 cm. long. Lay them on the grill over hot coals and cook them until charred. To eat, peel back the charred skin with the fingers, dip the roasted onion into sauce and eat. Serve with a *romesco* sauce and alioli (Chapter 12).

CEBOLLAS GUISADAS
Braised Onions

1/2 kilo tiny onions (about 2 dozen)	1 clove
3 cloves garlic	1/2 teaspoon paprika
3 tablespoons oil	1/2 teaspoon salt
1 bay leaf	50 ml. white wine
5 peppercorns	

Peel outer skins from the onions. If they are small, leave them whole, otherwise cut in halves or quarters. Put them in a saucepan with the whole garlic cloves, oil, bay leaf, peppercorns and clove. Put on a medium heat and toss them in the oil, without letting the onions brown. Then add the paprika, salt and wine and cover the pan and cook slowly until the onions are quite tender, about 25 minutes, shaking the pan from time to time to prevent the onions from scorching. Serves 4.

GUISANTES EN SALSA
Saucy Peas

1	kilo peas (about 3 cups shelled)	1	tablespoon flour
3	tablespoons oil	1	teaspoon salt
1	medium onion, chopped	1/4	teaspoon saffron
2	cloves garlic, minced	1	hard-cooked egg

Cook the peas in salted water to cover until just tender (5 minutes for small, freshly picked peas, up to 25 minutes for bigger, drier ones). Drain, reserving some of the liquid. Heat the oil in a frying pan or casserole and sauté the chopped onion until softened. Add the minced garlic, drained peas and fry a few minutes longer. Then stir in the flour, salt and saffron. Stir in about 100 ml. of the reserved cooking liquid. Simmer, stirring, until the sauce thickens, about 5 minutes. Pour into a serving dish and garnish with chopped egg. Serves 6.

GUISANTES A LA VALENCIANA
Peas, Valencia Style

1	kilo peas	bay, thyme and parsley
3	tablespoons oil	1/4 teaspoon saffron
1	onion, chopped	1/4 teaspoon cumin
2	cloves garlic	salt and pepper
100	ml. white wine	strips of red pepper
3	tablespoons anise brandy	

Shell the peas. Heat the oil in a saucepan and add the peas and the chopped onion and 1 clove of garlic. Sauté briefly, then add the wine, anise and herbs. Cover and simmer until the peas are nearly tender. Meanwhile crush the other clove of garlic in the mortar with the saffron and cumin. Dissolve in a little water and add to the peas with the salt and pepper. Simmer until peas are tender. Serve garnished with strips of red pepper and chopped parsley. Serves 6.

PIMIENTOS FRITOS
Fried Peppers

16	small green peppers
	salt
100	ml. oil

Wash and dry the peppers. Cut slits in the bottom ends of each and rub a pinch of salt inside each one. Fry them slowly in the oil, turning to ensure both sides are cooked. Serve when very tender. The peppers are picked up by the stems and eaten whole, discarding the stem and seeds. They are usually served as a *tapa,* but make a nice side dish with meat or poultry.

PIMIENTOS A LA MALAGUEÑA
Peppers, Málaga Style

6	large peppers, green and/or red	1/2	onion, chopped
2	tablespoons oil	50	grams raisins, seeded

Roast the peppers over gas flame or under broiler grill, turning them to char all sides. Remove and cover with a cloth and let set until cool enough to handle. Then peel off the skins and discard seeds. Tear or cut the peppers into strips. In a frying pan heat the oil and sauté the chopped onions. Add the raisins and cook for a few minutes, then stir in the pepper strips. Heat and serve. Also good room temperature as an hors d'oeuvre. Serves 6 to 8.

PIMIENTOS RELLENOS
Stuffed Peppers

6	medium bell peppers	80	ml. white wine
1/2	kilo minced meat (pork and/or beef)	2	slices bread (75 grams) crusts
1	clove garlic		removed
5	tablespoons oil		salt and pepper
1	onion, chopped		grated nutmeg
3	tomatoes, peeled, seeded and chopped	2	eggs
			flour
3	tablespoons chopped parsley		oil

Roast the peppers under the broiler grill until skins are charred, and remove. Cover them with a cloth and let set until cool enough to handle. Then carefully peel the skins off and cut out stems and seeds. Season the minced meat with finely minced garlic and let it rest 15 minutes. Heat 3 tablespoons of the oil in a saucepan and sauté in it all but 1 tablespoon of the chopped onion until soft. Then add the prepared tomatoes and fry for 5 minutes. Add 2 tablespoons chopped parsley, 50 ml. white wine and salt and pepper and cook until the sauce is reduced, about 15 minutes. Sieve it or purée in the blender. Heat the remaining 2 tablespoons oil in a frying pan and add the meat and spoonful of chopped onion. Fry until the meat is browned. Meanwhile, soak the bread slices in water or milk until spongy. Squeeze out and add the bread to the meat, mashing it with the back of a fork. Season with salt and pepper and nutmeg. Stir in remainder of the wine and cook the mixture, stirring, to prevent its sticking, for several minutes. Remove from the heat and stir in 1 beaten egg and the rest of the parsley. (A more homogenous stuffing is made by chopping the mixture in the processor.) Spoon the mixture into the prepared peppers, taking care not to split them. Dip the stuffed peppers in beaten egg, then in flour and fry in hot oil until browned. Place them in an oven dish and pour over the sieved sauce. Bake the peppers for 20 minutes in a medium oven. Makes 6 servings.

POTATOES

The visitor to Spain dining only in restaurants might surmise that the ubiquitous *patatas fritas,* chips, and an occasional boiled potato were the only way potatoes were ever cooked here. These two preparations are the most usual garnishes for main course dishes. However, there are dozens of delicious potato dishes in the Spanish repertoire which seldom turn up on restaurant menus. Many of them are meant to stand on their own two feet — as first course in place of a soup or vegetable dish, or a main course for a light meal. These are among my favourites.

PATATAS A LA RIOJANA
Potatoes, Rioja Style

1	kilo potatoes (7 medium)	1	teaspoon paprika
100	ml. oil	2	teaspoons salt
1/4	kilo pork loin	150	ml. water
2	cloves garlic		chorizo (optional)
10	peppercorns		hard-cooked eggs
1	small chili pepper		

Peel the potatoes and cut them in chunks or thick strips. Heat the oil in a pan and fry the potatoes slowly, without letting them brown. Cut the pork loin in pieces and add to the potatoes and continue frying. In the mortar or blender crush the garlic, peppercorns, chili pepper, paprika and salt. Dissolve in the water and add to the potatoes. Chorizo, cut in slices, may also be added. Cover and cook until potatoes are tender, about 30 minutes. Let set 10 minutes before serving, garnished with chopped egg. Serves 4. Try this dish, without the pork, served alongside grilled pork chops.

CAZUELA DE PAPAS A LA ABUELA
Granny's Potato Casserole

This pueblo dish often has pieces of fish and shellfish added to it, in which case it makes a main course. *Papas* are an endearing term for potatoes. This dish is also called *ajo pollo.*

50	ml. oil	6	peppercorns
40	grams almonds, blanched (about 25)	2	cloves
3	cloves garlic	1/4	teaspoon saffron
1	slice bread, crusts removed	1/2	litre water
1	small onion, chopped	1	teaspoon salt
1	small green pepper, chopped	1	bay leaf
1	tomato, peeled, seeded and chopped	1/2	teaspoon paprika
		1 1/2	kilos potatoes

Heat the oil in a pot and fry the almonds, 2 cloves garlic and bread until they are golden and toasted. Remove and set aside. In the same oil fry the chopped onion and green pepper until they are softened. Add the chopped tomato and fry until reduced to a sauce, about 15 minutes. Meanwhile, in mortar or blender crush the peppercorns, cloves, saffron, fried garlic and 1 clove raw garlic, almonds and fried bread. Dilute in some of the water and add it to the pot with the remaining water, salt, bay leaf and paprika. Peel the potatoes and cut them in chunks and add to the pot. Simmer until the potatoes are tender, but not mushy, about 30 minutes. Let them set for 10 minutes before serving. Liquid should remain. If fish and shellfish are to be used, add the pieces of fish during the last 10 minutes of cooking. Garnish with sprigs of parsley. Serves 4 to 6.

BRAZO DE GITANO DE PATATAS
"Gipsy's Arm" Potato Roll

1	kilo potatoes	1	small onion, chopped
1	tablespoon flour	1	green pepper, chopped
2	eggs, separated	5	medium tomatoes, peeled, seeded
2	tablespoons chopped parsley		and chopped
50	grams pimento-stuffed olives (about 20)		salt and pepper
3	tablespoons oil	1/4	teaspoon cumin
1/4	kilo minced pork or pork sausage		

Cook the scrubbed, unpeeled potatoes in boiling water to cover until tender when pierced with a fork. Drain well. Peel the potatoes and sieve or mash them. Beat in the flour and 1 egg yolk. Beat the whites until stiff and fold them into the potato purée with salt and pepper, chopped parsley and the olives, finely chopped. Meanwhile make the filling. Heat the oil in a frying pan and in it sauté the minced pork or pork sausage, broken into pieces, until browned. Add the chopped onion, chopped pepper and fry for several minutes. Then add the prepared tomatoes. Season with salt and pepper and cumin and simmer for 15 minutes until reduced. Oil an oven dish and spread a layer of half the potato purée. Spoon the meat filling into the centre and cover with the remaining potato. With the hands, shape the potatoes into a long, rounded roll. Beat the remaining egg yolk with a few drops of water and brush the top of the roll with it. Put in a medium-hot oven until golden on top, about 25 minutes. Serves 6 to 8.

PATATAS A LA CERDEÑA
Potato Purée, Catalan Style

1	kilo potatoes	4	cloves garlic
100	grams bacon or salt pork cut in dice		salt and white pepper
2	tablespoons oil		

Peel the potatoes, cut in pieces and cook in water to cover until tender. Drain, saving some of the liquid. Mash the potatoes or put them through a ricer, adding a little of the reserved liquid. Heat the oil in a frying pan and fry the diced bacon until browned. Add the garlic, finely chopped. Beat the contents of the frying pan into the prepared potatoes, season with salt and pepper and turn into a serving bowl. Serves 6.

PATATAS EN SALSA VERDE
Potatoes in Green Sauce

1 kilo potatoes	200 ml. water or stock
100 ml. oil	50 ml. white wine
6 cloves garlic, chopped	salt and pepper
2 tablespoons chopped onion	hard-cooked egg
1 tablespoon flour	
chopped parsley	

Peel the potatoes and cut them in thin slices. In a pot or casserole, heat the oil and add the sliced potatoes, turning them so they don't brown. Add the chopped garlic and chopped onion and continue frying. Stir in the flour, mixing it well. Then add 2 tablespoons parsley and the water or stock and wine. Bring to a boil, then reduce to a simmer. Season with salt and pepper and cook until the potatoes are tender. Do not stir the potatoes, for they will break up, but shake the pot occasionally to prevent their sticking. Garnish with lots of chopped parsley and a little chopped egg. Serves 6.

PATATAS CON MEJILLONES
Potatoes with Mussels

3 tablespoons oil	salt and pepper
1 onion, finely chopped	1 bay leaf
1 kilo potatoes	2 dozen mussels
50 ml. white wine	chopped parsley
150 ml. water	

179

Heat the oil in a pot or casserole and sauté the onions. Peel the potatoes and cut them into chunks and add to the onions, frying for several minutes. Add the wine, water, salt and pepper and bay leaf and simmer until potatoes are nearly tender. Meanwhile, scrub the mussels well, put them in a pot and cover them. Place over high heat, shaking the pan, until the shells open. Remove from heat. Discard the shells, adding the mussels to the potatoes. Strain their cooking liquid through a fine sieve onto the potatoes. Cook for a few minutes more and serve, lavishly sprinkled with parsley. Serves 4 to 6.

PATATAS ARRUGADAS
Wrinkled Potatoes

Cook small, unpeeled potatoes in very little water with coarse salt until they are tender. Cut the potatoes in half and serve with *mojo verde* or with alioli (Chapter 12).

PARRILLADA DE PATATAS
Grilled Potatoes

The perfect accompaniment to barbecued foods. Cook medium sized, unpeeled potatoes in salted water until just barely tender. Drain well and cut them in half lengthwise. Brush with oil and lay them on the charcoal grill until browned. Turn and brown the skin side. Place on a serving dish and drizzle with a sauce made of oil, lemon juice, minced garlic and chopped parsley. Serve hot. The potatoes can be par-boiled in advance and grilled at serving time.

PATATAS BRAVAS
Bold Potatoes

Cook cubed potatoes in oil until they are tender and browned. Place on a serving dish and sprinkle with salt. Prepare tomato sauce, adding paprika, cumin and chopped chili pepper or cayenne. Serve the sauce spooned over the fried potatoes or served separately. The sauce should be quite *picante,* spicy-hot.

PATATAS A LA PANADERA
Baker's Potatoes

2	kilos potatoes	2	bay leaves
2	onions	100	ml. white wine
150	ml. oil	1/2	teaspoon paprika
3	cloves garlic	100	ml. water
3	tablespoons chopped parsley		salt and pepper

Peel the potatoes and slice them fairly thinly. Peel and slice the onions. Pour a little of the oil into the bottom of a flame-proof casserole and arrange the potatoes and onions in layers in it. Sprinkle with the garlic, finely chopped, the chopped parsley and the bay leaves, broken into pieces and sprinkle with paprika. Pour over the rest of the oil. Place on a medium flame until the potatoes start to sizzle. Add the wine and the water. Season with salt and pepper. When the liquids come to a boil, cover the casserole with foil and put in a medium oven until the potatoes are tender, about 30 minutes. Let the casserole rest for a few minutes before serving. Serves 6 to 8.

PATATAS A LO POBRE
Poor Man's Potatoes

1	kilo potatoes	1/2	teaspoon paprika
100	ml. oil	50	ml. water
10	peppercorns	1	teaspoon salt
2	cloves garlic	1	tablespoon vinegar
1/4	teaspoon cumin		

Peel the potatoes and cut them in slices. Heat the oil in a frying pan and fry them slowly, turning frequently, until they are tender and slightly browned. In the mortar, mash the peppercorns, garlic, cumin and paprika. Dissolve in the water and add to the potatoes with the salt and vinegar. Cook a few minutes more and serve hot. Serves 4.

PATATAS VIUDAS
Widowed Potatoes

Cook peeled and cut-up potatoes in salted water until tender. Drain and place in a serving bowl. Fry chopped garlic and onion in a few spoonfuls of oil until softened. Remove from heat and stir in a little paprika. Pour the oil over the potatoes and mix well. Sprinkle with chopped parsley or other fresh herb. (I like this dish with thyme or rosemary, as an accompaniment to roast pork or roast lamb.)

AJOHARINA DE JAEN
Potatoes Stewed in Garlic Sauce, Jaen Style

1	dried pepper *(ñora, choricero)*	1/4	litre water
50	ml. oil	2	cloves garlic
1	kilo potatoes (7 medium)	8	peppercorns
1	teaspoon paprika	1	tablespoon flour
	salt		

Soak the dried pepper in boiling water to cover. Either mash it well in the mortar or scrape the flesh from the skin. (If not available, use a little paprika.) Heat the oil in a pan and fry the potatoes, peeled and sliced, very slowly without browning. Add the paprika, salt and the water. In the mortar, crush the garlic with the peppercorns and flour. Dissolve in some of the liquid from the pan. Stir this mixture into the potatoes and continue cooking until they are tender. Let set a few minutes before serving. Serves 4 to 6. Serve the *ajoharina* also with spinach.

CALABAZA FRITA
"Fried" Pumpkin

1	kilo pumpkin	1	tablespoon vinegar
50	ml. oil	1	tablespoon oregano
2	slices bread, crusts removed		salt and pepper
3	cloves garlic		

Peel the pumpkin and cut it into large dice. Heat the oil in a pot and fry the slices of bread and the garlic until they are golden and crisped. Remove them. Add the prepared pumpkin to the same oil and sauté it for a few minutes. Then cover the pot and let the pumpkin "stew" in the oil. In the mortar mash the fried garlic and bread with the vinegar and oregano, salt and pepper. Add to the pumpkin and continue cooking until tender, adding just a little water if necessary. Very good served with pork. Serves 4.

CALABAZA GUISADA
Stewed Pumpkin

1	kilo pumpkin	1/2	teaspoon cumin
2	red or green peppers	1	teaspoon salt
1	onion	1	bay leaf
2	tomatoes	4	tablespoons oil
2	chopped cloves garlic	1/4	litre water

Peel the pumpkin and cut it in thin slices. Layer it in a pot or casserole with the peppers, cut in strips, sliced onions, sliced tomatoes. Sprinkle with the chopped garlic, cumin, salt. Add the bay leaf, broken into a few pieces and drizzle the oil over all. Add the water. Bring the vegetables to a simmer, cover the pot and stew until they are very tender. Serve as a vegetable dish, or add stock and serve as a soup or purée the mixture and use as a sauce (good with stuffed aubergines, meatballs, fritters). Serves 6 to 8.

ESPINACAS A LA CORDOBESA
Spinach, Cordoba Style

1 1/2	kilos spinach	1	teaspoon paprika
50	ml. oil	2	teaspoons vinegar
1/2	onion, finely chopped	1/4	teaspoon cinnamon
2	cloves garlic, chopped	1/2	teaspoon salt

Wash the spinach well, trim off stems and cook it in just a little water until it is limp. Drain very well. In a frying pan heat the oil and fry the chopped onion and garlic. Remove from heat when they are soft and stir in the paprika, vinegar, cinnamon and salt. Add the spinach to the sauce and reheat it very briefly, mixing well. Serves 4.

PANADONS AMB ESPINACS
Catalan Spinach Pasties

250	grams frozen spinach		salt
100	oil	175	grams sifted flour
2	cloves garlic		water (about 2 tablespoons)
25	grams Malaga raisins, seeded	1	beaten egg
25	grams pine nuts		

Cook the spinach in just a little water until wilted. Drain it well and chop finely. In a frying pan heat 2 tablespoons oil and add the chopped garlic. Toss the chopped spinach in the oil, adding the seeded and chopped raisins and the pine nuts. Season with salt and set aside. Place the sifted flour in a bowl and mix with ½ teaspoon salt. Drizzle in remainder of the oil and mix with the flour. Then add just enough water to make a pliable dough. Knead it very briefly to mix and chill the dough. Roll out on a floured board. Cut into rounds of about 10 cm. Place a spoonful of the spinach on each round. Fold over and twist the edges together to seal. Brush the pasties with beaten egg and bake in a medium oven until they are browned.

FRITOS DE ESPINACAS
Spinach Fritters

1	kilo spinach	salt and freshly ground pepper
	oil	4 eggs
2	tablespoons chopped onion	flour
2	cloves garlic	

Wash and trim the spinach and cook it in a very little water until limp. Drain it well and chop finely. Heat 2 tablespoons oil in a frying pan and sauté the chopped onion and garlic until softened. Add the spinach and fry it until heated. Beat three of the eggs and mix into the spinach, cooking as a tortilla until set. Season with salt and pepper and let cool. Cut into squares and dip them in beaten egg and flour. Fry in hot oil, turning to brown both sides. Serve hot with lemon wedges.

BUÑUELOS DE BATATA
Sweet Potato Fritters

1	kilo sweet potatoes	grated orange peel
2	tablespoons sugar	salt and pepper
3	tablespoons orange juice	grated nutmeg
50	ml. milk	3 eggs, separated
1	tablespoon flour	oil

Cook the unpeeled sweet potatoes in boiling water until tender. Drain and peel. Force them through a sieve or purée in a blender. Beat in the sugar, orange juice, milk, flour and orange peel. Season with salt, pepper and nutmeg. Add the beaten egg yolks. Beat the egg whites until stiff with a drop of lemon juice. Fold them into the sweet potato mixture until blended. Heat the oil in a large frying pan. With a tablespoon drop small rounds of the batter into the hot oil. Fry them until golden and remove to drain on paper for a minute before serving. Serves 8.

Though these fritters are considered a *dulce* or sweet, and would be typically bathed in a honeyed syrup, I've included them in the vegetable section because they make a splendid garnish for roast turkey, chicken and duck.

MENESTRA DE VERDURAS
Mixed Vegetable Medley

Typically, this casserole is made with vegetables in season at the same time — artichokes, broad beans and peas... In the summer it might include green beans, potatoes, courgettes and pumpkin. It's also a good way to prepare frozen vegetables.

1/4 kilo shelled peas	1 red pimento
1/4 kilo artichoke hearts	1 tablespoon flour
1/4 kilo shelled broad beans	salt and pepper
50 ml. oil	1/2 teaspoon paprika
1/2 onion, chopped	3 tablespoons tomato sauce
2 cloves garlic, chopped	100 ml. water
200 grams serrano ham, diced	parsley or mint

Cook each of the vegetables separately until they are tender, and reserve. Heat the oil in a casserole and in it fry the chopped onion and garlic. Add the diced ham and the chopped pimento and fry a few minutes more. Then add the cooked and drained vegetables and sauté them briefly. Sprinkle with the flour, season with salt and pepper and paprika and stir in the tomato sauce and water. Cook on a medium heat for 10 minutes and serve garnished with a sprig of parsley or mint. Serves 4 to 6.

PISTO
Stewed Summer Vegetables

This is the French *ratatouille,* the Catalan *samfaina,* the *tumbet* of the Balearics and the La Mancha *alboronia,* which is what the Moors called it some centuries ago before there were tomatoes and peppers to make it so piquant. In Spain, it might be served on its own, cool as an hors d'oeuvre or salad, or hot as a vegetable, or accompanied by eggs for a light supper dish. It's also a flavourful cooking medium for fish, meat and poultry. Try fresh tuna with *pisto,* lamb stewed in pisto, and chicken. I particularly like pisto with the addition of chopped fresh herbs — oregano, thyme or basil — and served with simple grilled foods.

50 ml. oil	1 teaspoon salt
1 large onion chopped or sliced	pepper
2 green peppers, chopped or cut in strips	6 tomatoes, peeled, seeded and chopped
1 clove garlic, chopped	2 courgettes, sliced or diced
1 large aubergine	eggs (optional)

The vegetables can be prepared very coarsley — large chunks, or slices — or quite finely diced. Whichever way they are cut, take care not to overcook so the vegetables become mushy. Heat the oil in a pan or heat-proof casserole. In it sauté the onions, green peppers and garlic. Add the aubergine, peeled and cut in dice, and continue frying until much of the oil has been absorbed. Then season with salt and pepper and add the prepared tomatoes and courgettes. Cook, covered, on a medium heat until vegetables are tender, about 15 minutes. Remove cover and cook to evaporate liquid. One or two beaten eggs can be added to the vegetables and cooked on a very low heat until they are set. Or, break one egg per person on top of the vegetables and put in a medium oven until set. Or serve as an accompaniment to fried eggs.

Variations: potatoes, pumpkin can be added to the pisto. Diced ham, bacon or salt pork are other frequent additions. In Albacete, a version which includes tuna is garnished with pine nuts.

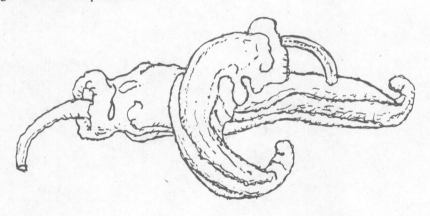

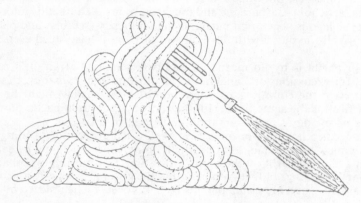

CHAPTER 8

Rice, Pasta and Bread Dishes

I sometimes wonder how many paellas are served up along the sunny coasts of Spain on a single summer's day. It must be thousands, as tourists, residents and Spaniards alike dig into Spain's favourite food.

Paella is native to the area around Valencia, where rice is grown extensively. But it's equally at home in Madrid, Mallorca, Murcia and Malaga. Each region has made adaptations on the original — a fairly simple dish of rice, eels, snails and beans — so today there are dozens of versions, some of them quite luxurious.

Like pasta in Italy, paella rice is typically served as a first course, to be followed by a main dish. For this reason it usually contains only small bits of meat, chicken and seafood. However, super versions containing chicken breasts and lobster can be found both in Spain and in restaurants abroad, where the dish is featured as a main course.

The basic ingredients of paella are rice, oil and saffron. Beyond that a wide variety of meat, poultry, fish, shellfish and vegetables can be included. Some paellas are truly baroque extravaganzas, with a wild assortment of everything from sea, land and sky. Others show an almost Zen-like simplicity — flavourful yellow rice and a few clams strewn with strips of red pepper.

An all-seafood paella, sometimes called *arroz a la marinera,* might include prawns, clams or mussels, squid and chunks or slices of fish or eel. Snails are typical in Levante paellas. The Catalans invented one with no bones, the *parellada*. Rabbit frequently is substituted for chicken. Though a combination of pork, chicken and seafood is the most typical, pork sausage links or slices of chorizo sausage might be used as well. Chicken livers are another favourite addition, instead of or in addition to poultry. The usual vegetables are peas, peppers and tomatoes, but others in season can be used as well — broad beans, green beans, artichokes, asparagus and mushrooms are all authentic additions. (I make a very delicious vegetarian paella, using all these vegetables and par-boiled brown rice. Well-flavoured with olive oil and saffron, it has fooled even Spanish friends.)

Spanish paella is by no means an exclusively indoor affair. It's favourite picnic fare, for excursions on San Juan's Day in June or at *romerías,* fiestas held at sanctuaries in the countryside, where hundreds of paellas might be sizzling over wood fires at the same time. Hunting parties cook up a paella on the spot using some of the day's catch — rabbit and small birds.

Paella needs a hot, fast-burning fire. Well-dried grape vine prunings, twigs of wild rosemary and thyme, almond shells, pine cones and boughs can all be used. Even a charcoal grill on the patio, with some fast-burning wood added, is great for paella making. In fact, you may find the grill far more effective than the kitchen cookstove, as a big paella pan never cooks evenly when placed on a single gas flame.

The *paellera* is a shallow, two-handled pan of rolled steel. A similar, but deeper pan is favoured for large quantities. Then there are those cooks who swear by earthenware casseroles for their paellas. These have the advantage of holding the heat for a long time, meaning the paella keeps cooking even after it is removed from the fire. You can also buy paella pans in Spanish stores with non-stick finishes. Choose a paella pan (of the shallow type) 50 cm. in diameter (about 18 inches) to serve six people. If you don't have a paellera, try making paella in two or three frying pans or in a Chinese wok. Though it's permissable to use more than one pan in the preparation, the paella rice is always served in the same pan in which it cooks.

Paella is seldom oven-cooked (until recently, few Spanish homes had ovens), though it can be put in a low oven for its 10-minute settling time, essential for the rice to finish cooking and flavour to develop. It is cooked uncovered.

Paella really has to be made with short grain rice, which is ''gummier'' than long-grain rice and absorbs the flavours of the food in which it cooks so much better. Because it is so easy to overcook into a sticky mess, paella is usually removed from the heat before the rice is completely cooked and left to finish cooking from the heat of the pan. Good olive oil is essential to a real paella and you really can't decrease the quantity very much. Besides flavour, the oil provides an ''insulation'' to each grain of rice, keeping it from getting sticky. For diet cookery, you can produce an ersatz paella with little or no oil, but it will taste ''steamed.''

Curiously enough, saffron is not always used in paella. Because of its cost, powdered yellow colouring is substituted in many of the paellas which are served up in beachside *chiringuitos*. Paprika is also used, to augment the colour, or in place of saffron for those who don't appreciate its particular flavour. By the way, if you brown large quantities of chicken or meat in the oil in which the paella is to cook, you'll wind up with a muddy-yellow paella. Brown these ingredients in a separate pan.

Though not a difficult dish to make, your first paella is likely to be a hectic experience. Mine was. With all the chopping, mincing, mashing, frying, stirring and heart thumping, I completely forgot to add the salt. Prepare all the ingredients beforehand. Clean the squid, steam the mussels, peel the prawns, peel and chop the tomatoes, cut up the chicken and assemble everything in the order you're going to need them. Once this is done the total cooking time is only about 40 minutes — 20 minutes to sauté all the ingredients and another 20 minutes to cook the rice once the liquid has been added.

Cut up all ingredients so they cook in the time it takes the rice to cook. Chicken, for instance, is usually hacked into very small pieces, which unfortunately, makes for bone splinters. If you're using whole chicken pieces, partially cook them in a separate frying pan. A good alternative is to use boned chicken breasts, each cut into thirds. Add the liquid — which can be chicken broth mixed with fish and shellfish stock or water — very hot or boiling. You need approximately twice the volume of liquid to rice, but the liquid from fish and tomatoes counts towards total. Many cooks add a few drops of lemon juice, declaring this keeps the rice from getting sticky. Stir all the ingredients well with a wooden spoon at this point, then never stir the rice again. Shake the pan to redistribute the rice and keep it from sticking.

Remove the rice from the heat before it is quite tender. It should still have a little kernel of hardness in the centre. Let it rest for ten minutes before serving.

To reheat leftover paella, remove from refrigerator and let it come to room temperature. Place it in an oiled oven dish and sprinkle with water. Cover with foil and bake in a medium oven just until heated through, about 15 minutes.

PAELLA
Spanish Rice

1	dozen clams and/or mussels	2	large tomatoes, peeled, seeded and chopped
1/2	kilo prawns	500	grams rice
1	small chicken (1 1/2 kilos) or rabbit	1	litre liquid, very hot or boiling
200	grams pork loin, cut in cubes	1/2	teaspoon saffron
75	ml. olive oil	10	peppercorns
3	cloves garlic	1/2	teaspoon paprika
1	bay leaf	2	teaspoons salt
1	small onion, minced	1	small tin red pimento
2	green peppers, cut in strips	100	grams cooked peas
1/4	kilo squid, cut in rings		

1.) Clean the clams or mussels and steam them open. Remove a half shell and discard, setting aside the clams on one shell. Strain and reserve the liquid in which they cooked. 2.) Peel the prawns, saving several of them unpeeled for garnish. Cook them in a little water, adding the other shells. Strain and reserve the liquid. 3.) Cut the chicken into serving pieces. (The bony pieces can be cooked in water to make a stock for cooking the paella.) 4.) In the paella pan heat half the oil and in it toast 2 cloves of garlic and the bay leaf. Remove them and set aside. 5.) In the same oil, slowly brown the chicken pieces with the cubes of pork, turning them often. Remove them to a dish when nicely browned. 6.) Now add the minced onion and chopped peppers to the oil. Let sauté a few minutes, then add, 7.) the rings of squid and sauté. 8.) Add the tomatoes and raise the heat to high so that they "fry" in the oil. Add remaining oil at this point so that mixture doesn't stick. 9.) Add the rice and cook it briefly, stirring, so that the grains become slightly opaque. 10.) Combine the reserved cooking liquids and heat them. Add to the rice with the chicken and pork and continue cooking on a high heat. 11.) In the mortar or blender crush the fried garlic and bay leaf with the saffron, peppercorns, paprika, 1 clove raw garlic and salt. Dilute in a little of the liquid from the pan or in a little white wine and add to the paella. Stir it in well to mix. 12.) Now turn down the heat and let the paella continue cooking. 13.) Decorate the top with the reserved clams and mussels, cooked prawns, strips of tinned pimento and cooked peas. 14.) Shake the pan to prevent the rice from sticking on the bottom. 15.) Remove from heat and let the paella sit for 10 minutes before serving. Serve with quartered lemons which are squeezed over rice, chicken and shellfish. Makes 6 servings.

ARROZ A LA MARINERA
Sailor's Rice

Fish head and trimmings	2 cloves garlic
prawn shells	1 sprig parsley
1/4 kilo conger eel, sliced	1 litre water
1/4 kilo angler fish, sliced	salt and pepper
1/4 kilo prawns, shelled	50 ml. oil
1/4 kilo Dublin bay prawns or large prawns or lobster	1/2 teaspoon saffron
	2 teaspoons salt
400 grams squid, cleaned and cut in rings	400 grams rice
	parsley
1/4 kilo clams	lemon wedges
1/2 onion	

Put the fish head and trimmings in a pot with prawn shells, onion, 1 clove garlic, sprig parsley and water. Season with salt and pepper and bring to a boil. Simmer for an hour and strain the stock. Scrub the clams, steam them open, discard empty shells and strain and reserve their liquid. In a paella pan or large casserole heat the oil and in it sauté the sliced eel. Turn to brown the other side and add the slices of angler fish. Add the shelled prawns and the squid, and sauté. Then add the peeled large prawns or chunks of lobster. Meanwhile, cook the Dublin bay prawns in a little water and set aside. In the mortar crush the saffron with the other garlic, 1 tablespoon parsley and salt. Dissolve in a little liquid and add to the pan with the rice. Combine the strained fish stock and clam juice to make about 3/4 litre of liquid. Add it hot to the rice. Cook on a high heat for 5 minutes, then reduce heat and cook until rice is just tender. Place the cooked Dublin bay prawns on top of the rice during the last few minutes of cooking. Let set several minutes before serving garnished with parsley and lemon wedges. Serves 6.

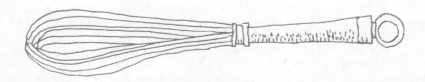

PAELLA PARELLADA
Barcelona's Boneless Paella

3 tablespoons oil	1 tablespoon minced onion
3 tablespoons lard	4 red peppers, roasted and peeled
1 small chicken, cut up and boned	(or tinned)
1/4 kilo pork sausage links, cut up	400 grams rice
1/4 kilo pork loin, cut in cubes	300 grams shelled prawns
200 grams angler fish, boned and cubed	3/4 litre water or stock
1/4 kilo squid, cleaned and cut in rings	1/4 teaspoon saffron
6 artichoke hearts, cooked and halved	2 teaspoons salt
100 grams shelled peas	pepper
50 grams sliced mushrooms	parsley

Heat the oil and lard in a paella pan or earthenware casserole and in it brown the pieces of boned chicken with the pieces of pork sausage and cubed pork. When they are nicely browned, push to the side of the pan and add the pieces of angler fish and squid. Fry them on a high heat, then add the parboiled artichokes, the peas, mushrooms, minced onion and skinned peppers cut in strips (save a few pieces to garnish the finished dish). Stir in the rice and the prawns, then add water or stock. Crush the saffron in the mortar with the salt and pepper and dissolve in a little liquid. Add to the casserole and cook until rice is done. Garnish with strips of pepper and a sprinkling of chopped parsley. Serves 6.

ARROZ ABANDA
Rice and Fish, Fisherman's Style

2-3 kilos fish, preferably 2 or 3 kinds (such as bass, grouper, meagre, rascasse, redfish, scorpion fish, gurnard, mullet, pompano, bream, angler fish)	salt and pepper
	50 ml. oil
	1/2 small onion, minced
	2 tomatoes, peeled and chopped
	2 cloves garlic, minced
fish heads, trimmings	1 green pepper
1/2 onion	500 grams rice
2 tomatoes	1/2 teaspoon saffron
thyme, bay leaf, parsley	10 peppercorns
2 litres water	1 teaspoon salt
250 ml. white wine	1/2 cup mayonnaise
1/2 kilo large prawns	2 cloves garlic, whole
1 dozen clams or mussels, scrubbed	

Clean the fish and either fillet it or cut it into slices. Put all the heads, bones and trimmings into a pot with the onion, tomatoes, thyme, bay leaf, some parsley, salt and pepper. Cover with the water and 200 ml. white wine. Bring to a boil, skim and simmer, covered for an hour. Strain the fish stock into another pot and bring it to a simmer. In it poach the prepared fillets or slices of fish, removing them with a skimmer as they are done and placing on a platter. Continue with the prawns and the clams or mussels, placing each on the platter as it is cooked. In a casserole or paella pan heat the oil nd in it sauté the minced onion. Add the chopped tomatoes, minced garlic and pepper cut in strips. On a high heat stir in the rice. Then measure out about 1 litre of the stock in which the fish was cooked and add to the rice. Crush the saffron and the peppercorns with the teaspoon salt. Dissolve in the remaining wine and add to the rice. Cook over a high heat for 5 minutes, then cook slowly or put in a medium oven, uncovered, until it is done, about 20 minutes. Meanwhile, crush the 2 cloves of garlic and mix with the mayonnaise, preferably home-made and flavoured with lemon juice. Serve the rice in its casserole, accompanied by the platter of cooked fish and shellfish and the garlic mayonnaise. Serves 6.

ARROS NEGRE AMB ALL I OLI
Catalan Black Rice with Garlic Sauce

1	kilo small squid or cuttlefish	1	litre water or stock
6	tablespoons oil	1	teaspoon salt
1	onion, chopped		cayenne
2	peppers, red and green, chopped	50	ml. sherry
1/4	kilo drained tinned tomatoes		cooked prawns and mussels
400	grams rice (2 1/2 cups)		

For the sauce:

3   cloves garlic   100 ml. oil   1/2 teaspoon salt

Clean the squid or cuttlefish, saving the ink sacs. If the fish are tiny, leave them whole, otherwise cut in pieces. Heat the oil in a pot and sauté chopped onions and peppers. Add the squid and fry for another few minutes. Then add the tomatoes, cut into small pieces. Cook for a few minutes, then add 100 ml. water

or stock and cook until quite reduced, about 20 minutes. Then add the rice and about 3/4 litre of the water. Season with salt and a dash of cayenne. Let the rice simmer. In a small bowl crush the ink sacs and dissolve them in the sherry. Stir this into the rice and continue cooking until the rice is done (can be finished in the oven). Let it set for several minutes before serving. Garnish with the cooked prawns and mussels — a bright contrast to the blackened rice. Spoon a little of the sauce over and serve the rest in a small bowl. Serves 6. To make the sauce, crush the garlic in mortar or blender with the salt. Beat in the oil very slowly. Variation: add the sauce to cooked spaghetti with the ink, cook briefly and serve.

ARROS AMB CROSTA
Crusty Rice, Alicante Style

This rice dish, served on special occasions, can be cooked to order, making a rich stock (similar to the following recipe) with chicken, lamb, beef, sausages and salt pork. Or the stock, garbanzos and leftover meats from the previous day's cocido can be used.

50	ml. oil	1/2	teaspoon saffron
200	grams *butifarra* or other sausage		salt and pepper
2	tomatoes, peeled, seeded and chopped	150	grams garbanzos, cooked
100	grams pork, diced		pieces of cooked chicken, meat, sausage, rabbit, meatballs, etc.
500	grams rice	6	eggs, well beaten
1 1/2	litres stock		

Heat the oil in shallow earthenware casserole. Cut the sausage in slices, fry it and remove. In the same oil fry the prepared tomatoes with the diced pork. (Other uncooked meats can be added.) Stir in the rice, then add the hot stock. Crush the saffron with the salt and pepper and stir into the rice. Bring to a boil, then reduce the heat and add the fried sausage, the cooked garbanzos and cooked chicken or meats. Simmer until the rice is cooked. Beat the eggs with a few drops of water and a pinch of salt. Pour it over the rice and put the casserole in the top part of the oven until the eggs have set and browned slightly on the top. Serves 6.

ARROZ ROSETXAT
Rice and Lamb Casserole, Valencian Style

3	litres water	200	grams minced pork
400	grams boneless lamb	1	egg, beaten
150	grams garbanzos, soaked overnight		salt and pepper
1	carrot		pinch cinnamon
1	turnip	1	tablespoon chopped parsley
1	stalk celery	75	ml. oil or lard
2	teaspoons salt	2	cloves garlic, chopped
1	Valencian onion *butifarra negra*	400	grams rice
2	white *butifarra*	1	tomato
50	grams salt pork	1/2	teaspoon saffron, crushed chopped parsley
2	slices toasted bread		

Put the water in a large pot to heat with the lamb. (Bones can be added too.) When it boils, add the soaked garbanzos, the carrot, turnip and celery, peeled and cut in pieces. Skim the froth and simmer until everything is half-cooked, about 1 hour. Then add the salt, *butifarra* sausages and salt pork. Meanwhile, make the *pelota* or sausage ball. Crumb bread in processor, add the minced pork, beaten egg, salt and pepper, cinnamon and chopped parsley. Form it into a ball and add to the pot. Cook until everything is quite tender, about another hour. Then strain out the broth and reserve it. Cut the butifarra sausages and the meatball into slices and set them aside. Heat the oil or lard in an earthenware casserole and sauté the chopped garlic. Stir in the rice and let it fry in the oil briefly, crush saffron, dissolve in a little broth and add to rice with the meat, garbanzos and vegetables from the pot and approximately 1/4 litre of the hot broth. Cook over a hot fire for a few minutes, then place the pieces of butifarra and meatball on top of the rice and put in a medium oven to finish cooking, about 20 minutes. Garnish with chopped parsley and serve after letting the casserole rest for several minutes. Serves 6 to 8.

ARROZ EN PERDIU
Rice with "Partridge"

A Lenten dish in Valencia, this is made similarly to the previous casserole, but adding a whole head of garlic — the "partridge" — to cook with the garbanzos and eliminating all the meats. Add the vegetables and garbanzos to the rice and put the cooked head of garlic in the centre of the casserole.

ARROZ A LA ZAMORANA
Rice, Zamora Style

1	pig's trotter, split	6	cloves garlic, chopped
1	pig's ear	4	turnips
2	litres water	200	grams ham
	thyme, oregano, parsley, bay	400	grams rice
2	tablespoons lard		salt and pepper
1	onion, chopped	150	grams sliced salt pork or bacon

Put the cleaned and split trotter and ear (muzzle can also be used) into a pot with the water, herbs and salt and pepper. Bring to a boil and simmer slowly until the trotter is cooked, about 2 hours. Remove the trotter and ear. Cut them up into very small pieces, discarding all the bone. In a casserole melt the lard and sauté the chopped onion. Add the garlic. Peel the turnips, dice them and add to the casserole with the ham, also cut in dice. Add the cut up trotter and the rice. Fry for a few minutes, then add about 1 litre of the reserved liquid in which the trotter cooked. Season with salt and pepper and cook until most of the liquid is absorbed, about 10 minutes. Cover the top of the rice with thin strips of salt pork or bacon and put in the top of the oven to finish cooking or until the bacon is crisped. Pueblo style, the rice would be finished by covering the casserole with a tin in which were placed hot coals from the cooking fire.

PASTA

Close behind the paella and other rice dishes on many menus are the listings for *macarrones, espaguetis* and *canelones*. Can this be typical Spanish food? Absolutely, especially Catalan. Whether pasta got to Spain via Italy is beside the point — most of the Spanish ways with pasta are unique to this cuisine.

Pasta is, basically, a flour and water paste, either hand-rolled and cut or forced through a die to shape it. Commercial pastas are made from durum wheat semolina, the best for a chewy consistency. They may or may not contain eggs, or may be coloured green with spinach or pink with tomato paste. Making pasta at home is easy and rewarding. But, using all-purpose flour, beware of overcooking it to mush.

Spanish supermarkets offer more than 25 varieties of pasta, from the tiny ones for soups to chunky shells and tubes to big squares of lasagne noodles. However, they're seldom named in Spanish — or Italian — so the shopper has to choose by sight.

Fideos may be the most typically Spanish pasta. These can be as thin as capellini or as fat as spaghetti and are often sold packaged wound into nests. The thin varieties are used in soups and every region has its version of *sopa de fideos*. The thicker ones are preferred for casserole-type dishes. Pasta squares for *canelones* and lasagne come packaged in small boxes. They are like slabs of cardboard until boiled.

Allow 80 grams of pasta per serving for a main course, about 40 grams for a starter or side dish, and about 20 grams per serving for addition to a soup. So a quarter-kilo of pasta should make six servings as a side dish. (This is not per person, but per serving — some persons eat more than one serving.)

To cook pasta: allow three litres of water for each quarter-kilo of pasta. Bring the water to a full, rolling boil and add a tablespoon of salt and a tablespoon of oil. Add pasta gradually so water never stops boiling. Boil, uncovered, stirring occasionally with a fork to separate the pieces. Pasta takes from six to twelve minutes, depending on size and type. The only way to know if it's done is to taste it: it should be tender but still firm. Drain in a colander and mix immediately with prepared sauce or coat with oil. Don't rinse the pasta unless it's to be used in a cold salad.

MACARRONES A LA ESPAÑOLA
Macaroni, Spanish Style

1	package (1/4 kilo) macaroni *(penne)*		salt and pepper
3	tablespoons oil	100	grams serrano ham
1	medium onion, chopped	2	soft chorizo sausages
2	green peppers, chopped	100	grams grated cheese
1	clove garlic, chopped		
4	large tomatoes, peeled, seeded and chopped		

Cook the macaroni in salted water until tender and drain well. Meanwhile heat the oil in a saucepan and sauté the onions and green peppers until they are tender. Add the minced garlic and fry a minute. Then add the prepared tomatoes.

Continue frying and season with salt and pepper. Add the ham, cut in dice, and the sliced chorizo. Cook another 10 minutes until tomatoes are reduced. Season with salt and pepper to taste (not too much salt, with ham and sausage). Either toss the sauce with the cooked macaroni and serve immediately with grated cheese or layer the macaroni and sauce in an oiled oven dish and top with the cheese and bake until cheese is melted. Serves 4.

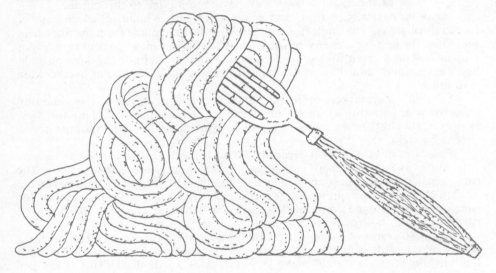

CANELONES A LA CATALANA
Cannelloni, Catalan Style

This is a festival dish, a must on Boxing Day — or, as it is called in Spain, San Esteban, St. Stephen's Day.

1 package cannelloni shells (or pasta dough cut in rectangles)	50 ml. sherry
2 tablespoons lard or butter	50 grams butter
1 small onion, very finely chopped	50 grams flour
200 grams minced pork or veal	450 ml. milk
1 chicken breast, boned and minced	salt and pepper
2 chicken livers, chopped	100 ml. tomato sauce
1 set lamb's brains, blanched and chopped	100 grams ham, cut in strips
	150 grams grated cheese
	butter

Cook the cannelloni squares in boiling water. Place them on clean towels to drain (or leave in cold water until needed, then dry and fill). Melt the lard in a frying pan and sauté the chopped onion. Add the minced meat and chicken breast and the chopped livers. Then add brains, blanched and chopped, and sauté briefly. Add the sherry and cook gently until the meats are cooked through and the liquid evaporated, about 10 minutes. Remove and mash with a fork or grind the mixture in a processor. Add salt and pepper to taste. Let it cool slightly while making the white sauce. In a saucepan melt the 50 grams butter and stir in the flour, letting it cook for a few minutes without browning. Then whisk in the milk and cook, stirring constantly, until the sauce is thickened. Season with salt and pepper and a grating of nutmeg. Butter an oven dish. Place a layer of the white sauce in it. Place a spoonful of the filling on each cooked cannelloni square and roll it up, placing it, seam side down, on the oven dish. When all are filled, cover them with remaining white sauce. Decorate with dollops or piped strips of the tomato sauce and strips of ham. Cover with grated cheese and dot with small knobs of butter. Put in the top of a medium oven until cheese is melted and very lightly coloured (do not let it brown). Serves 4.

CAZUELA DE FIDEOS
Seafood Spaghetti Casserole

This dish is also called *paella de fideos,* a paella made with spaghetti instead of rice, or *fideua.* I also like it cooked in fish stock without the addition of seafood to be served as a side dish with a fillet of any fish.

500	grams angler fish slices	1/4	teaspoon cumin
50	ml. oil	1/4	teaspoon saffron
1	small onion, chopped	1/4	teaspoon paprika
2	green peppers, chopped		salt and pepper
2	cloves garlic	200	grams prawns, peeled
2	large tomatoes, peeled, seeded and chopped	1/4	kilo clams, well scrubbed
		500	grams *fideos* or spaghetti
100	grams shelled peas or broad beans		sprigs of mint
1 1/2 litres fish stock or water			

Heat the oil in a casserole or pot and fry the pieces of fish, which can be left in whole slices or cut into smaller, boneless strips. When browned on both sides, remove to a plate. In the same oil sauté the chopped onion and peppers. Add the chopped garlic, then the prepared tomatoes and fry until reduced to a sauce. Add the shelled peas then the stock. Bring to a boil. Meanwhile, crush in a mortar the cumin, saffron, paprika, salt and pepper. Dissolve in some of the liquid from the casserole and stir into the casserole. When the liquid is boiling, add the prawns, clams, pieces of fried fish and the *fideos.* Lower heat and cook until the spaghetti is just tender, about 10 minutes. Remove from heat, cover the casserole and let it rest for several minutes. Garnish with the sprigs of mint. Serves 6. This dish should be juicy, but not soupy.

GREIXERA DE MACARRONES
Macaroni Casserole

400	grams macaroni		cinnamon
1/4	litre milk, warmed		salt
150	grams grated cheese (aged Mahon if available, otherwise aged Manchego or Parmesan)	4	hard-cooked eggs
		150	grams butter

Cook the macaroni in water until it is almost tender. Drain and return to the pan with the milk. Cook very slowly until macaroni is done. Most of the milk should be absorbed. Then add half the grated cheese and a pinch of cinnamon. Salt to taste and place the macaroni in a buttered oven dish. Cut the eggs in half and embed them in the macaroni. Dot with the butter, sprinkle lightly with cinnamon and place in oven or broiler to very lightly brown the top. Serves 4.

FIDEOS A LA CATALANA
Catalan Style Spaghetti

4	tablespoons oil or lard		500	grams *fideos* or spaghetti
1/4	kilo pork spare ribs, cut in short pieces		40	grams hazelnuts and/or almonds and/or pinenuts
100	grams spicy pork sausage links		1	clove garlic
100	grams white sausage *(butifarra)*		1/2	teaspoon saffron
1	onion, chopped		1	tablespoon parsley
3	tomatoes, peeled, seeded and chopped		1/4	teaspoon cinnamon
1/2	teaspoon paprika		1	slice bread, toasted
1 1/2	litres meat stock		100	grams grated cheese

Heat the oil or lard in a casserole or pot and in it fry the pieces of ribs until they are nicely browned. Then add the chopped onions and sauté until softened. Add the prepared tomatoes and the paprika and cook a few minutes more. Add the link sausage, cut into pieces, and the sliced butifarra. Pour in the stock and bring it to a boil. Add the pasta, lower heat and cook. In the mortar or blender crush the nuts with the garlic, saffron, parsley, cinnamon and toasted bread, adding some of the stock to make a paste. Stir this into the casserole and cook until meat is tender, about 20 minutes. Serve in the same casserole, sprinkled with grated cheese. Serves 4.

ANDRAJOS
"Tatters and Rags"

This dish, typical of Jaen and Granada, would be made with salt cod or wild hare. I like it made with chicken. The "rags" are made from a very simple flour and water paste, cut in squares or circles. Use any favourite pasta dough or substitute packaged lasagne or cannelloni squares.

50	ml. oil		1	clove
1	onion, chopped		1/4	teaspoon cumin
1	clove garlic, chopped		1/2	litre stock
2	tomatoes, peeled, seeded and chopped		400-800	grams boned and shredded chicken or rabbit, or desalted dried cod
1	teaspoon paprika			salt
1/4	teaspoon saffron		100	grams dry pasta squares
10	peppercorns			chopped parsley

Heat the oil in a pot or casserole and sauté the chopped onion and garlic. Then add the prepared tomatoes and fry for several minutes. Stir in the paprika. (If using salt cod, add it — soaked overnight and shredded — at this time.) In the mortar crush the saffron, peppercorns, clove and cumin and dissolve in a little of the stock. Add to the casserole with the stock. When it comes to a boil, lower heat and add the shredded chicken or rabbit and the squares of pasta. Cook until they are tender. Serve in the same casserole, garnished with chopped parsley. The pasta "rags," when home-made, are sometimes pulled apart while they cook with a fork, giving them a tattered look.

BREAD

Sin pan, no se puede comer — "you can't eat without bread," says a Spanish proverb. Bread in Spain is not just food. It symbolizes all food. Before breaking bread, village folk will make the sign of the Cross on the loaf and kiss it. A loaf dropped on the floor is quickly retrieved and kissed with a blessing. Children are not allowed to snatch bread, but are taught to treat it with respect. Stabbing the bread with a knife causes shudders among the devout — they will remind you that you are stabbing the body of Christ. Bread is, even in these days of abundance, the staff of life.

Every *barrio* has its *panadería* where fragrant, crusty loaves are produced daily. At breakfast time the small *bollos,* rolls, are hot from the ovens, just right for spreading with marmalade. By late morning, in time for the midday meal, the large round loaves are ready. Spanish bread with no fat and no sugar, does not keep well — it's meant to be consumed fresh, the same day it's baked. Day-old bread is never wasted, however, but is cut up to make *sopas,* filler for soups, or breadcrumbs for breading croquettes and fish. Spanish bakeries also produce excellent sandwich loaves, so there's really no reason to buy packaged, texturized, additive-laden breads.

In days — not really so long ago — when country folk mightn't go to the village more than once a week, bread was baked at home in clay ovens fuelled with scraps of wood, rosemary and vine prunings to be found on the farm. Though nowadays country people go off to town in a Land-Rover to buy bread and the ovens are converted into chicken coops and storage bins, there are still many whose eyes get misty as they tell you about that wonderful, home-baked bread.

One of my friends, who grew up in the country, taught me to make country bread. Here is her recipe. If at all possible, use stone-ground, unbleached white flour, still available at mills in Spain. You could also use any good recipe for French bread, moulding it into a round circle instead of a French-style loaf.

PAN CATETO
Country Bread

"Hay que tener suerte," she said — with bread-making, you have to be lucky.

From a bakery buy *levadura de masa,* about 150 grams. This is the "mother dough" which contains the yeast starter. If you don't have access to a Spanish bakery, substitute two cakes of compressed yeast, about 50 grams. Heat a big earthenware bowl slightly, just to take the chill off. The bread dough should never touch a cold surface or it will "catch a cold." Use a wooden tabletop, never tile or marble.

Dissolve the yeast dough or pressed yeast in 200 ml. very warm water. Place 2 kilos of flour in the warmed bowl with 2 tablespoons of salt. Mix the yeast mixture into it. Then begin adding water, little by little, working it into the flour with the hands. The bread should contain as little water as possible (500 to 750 ml.) only enough to hold the dough together. It is customary to place the bowl on the floor while mixing in the water, to get better leverage. Then turn the dough out onto a floured board or table and knead it for 10 or 15 minutes until very smooth and elastic. Cover the dough with a blanket and let it rest for about an hour in a warm place.

To shape the dough, divide it into two parts for the traditional round loaves, or three or four parts for short Vienna loaves. Roll out and shape them, perfectly smooth, seams on the bottom. Vienna loaves are slashed diagonally. Cover the wooden table with the heavy blanket. Place the loaves on top and completely wrap them up or, as they say, "put them to bed." Leave them to rise about two hours. The dough should almost double in size and leave an imprint if pressed lightly with a finger.

Place unglazed clay tiles *(lozas)* in the bottom of the oven. Heat the oven to hot (220°C/430°F). Slide the loaves onto tiles and bake for 10 minutes, then reduce heat to moderate (180°C/350°F) and bake until loaves are golden. To keep the crusts crispy, either brush the loaves with water part way through the baking or put a pan of boiling water on an oven rack. Cool the bread completely before storing.

PAN CON TOMATE Y JAMON
Bread with Tomato and Ham

This Catalan speciality, certainly a forerunner of today's sandwich, is a tasty way to use slightly stale bread. Cut the bread in thick slices. It can be slightly toasted on a grill, if desired. Rub it with a cut tomato, brush with good olive oil and sprinkle with a very little salt. Top the bread slices with thinly sliced *serrano* ham and serve with more sliced tomato.

COSTRADA MANCHEGA
Manchego "Rarebit"

6	slices day-old bread	1	clove garlic
250	grams aged Manchego cheese, grated	4	tablespoons chopped parsley
50	ml. white wine	6	eggs
	salt and pepper		

Toast the bread slices lightly. Mix the grated cheese with the white wine to make a thick paste. Season with salt and pepper. Spread the toast with the cheese mixture and place in an oiled oven dish. Mince the garlic and mix it with the chopped parsley and a little salt. Set aside. Break one egg on top of each of the toast slices and put the dish in a hot oven for 2 minutes. Sprinkle with the garlic-parsley and return to the oven just until the eggs whites are set, another 3 minutes. Serve from the same oven dish.

EMPAREDADOS
Fried Sandwiches

Slice sandwich loaf fairly thinly. Spread one side of slices with butter or oil. Layer with thinly sliced *serrano* ham and semi-cured Manchego cheese. Press the bread together tightly. Cut off crusts and cut the sandwiches into four triangles or squares. Dip them into milk, then into beaten egg and then into fine bread-crumbs. Fry the breaded sandwiches in oil, turning to brown both sides.

COQUETES
"Pizza," Costa Blanca Style

If as many people had emigrated from Alicante as from Naples, perhaps all of today's pizza parlours would instead be serving *coquetes*. Though these are typically made from bread dough, use prepared pizza bases or any favourite pizza dough. Top the rounds of dough — flattened out to about 30 cm. rounds — with spoonfuls of pisto, sautéed spinach or chard. Add chunks of tuna and bits of olives or capers. Bake until bread is slightly toasted, about 25 minutes in a medium-hot oven. Nobody says you can't add grated cheese before baking.

SAVOURY PASTRIES

Variously called *empanadas, pasteles* and *tortas,* these pies and pastries are a cross between a pot pie and a pizza. The empanadas are made with either a bread dough or a puff pastry *(hojaldre).* The *pasteles* and *tortas* not unlike quiches are more usually made with a shortcrust pastry. Frozen puff pastry, found in most supermarkets, is a great thing to have on hand in the freezer section of the refrigerator. Quickly thawed, it forms the basis of canapés and flaky pastries which can be put together in minutes with left-over cooked ingredients. For shortcrust dough, use your own favourite pie crust, the *empanadilla* wine pastry (Chapter 4 and Chapter 13) or the following flaky pastry. Unbaked bread dough can be purchased at *panaderías* — enquire as to what hour.

PASTA QUEBRADA
Flaky Pastry

100 grams butter, margarine or lard	2 teaspoons baking powder

150 ml. oil	150 ml. ice water
1 egg yolk	370 grams flour (approximate)
1 teaspoon salt	

Cream the butter with the oil. Beat in the egg yolk, salt and baking powder. The mixture should be smooth and as thick as cream. Then beat in the ice water. Add the flour gradually, adding only enough to make a dough which is not too sticky. Mix only enough to blend the flour into the fat; don't overwork. Chill the dough for 30 minutes. On a floured board, roll it out into a rectangle. Fold the top third down and the bottom third over it and turn the pastry and roll out again. Repeat this 3 more times. Then place the dough, covered with plastic wrap or a cloth, again in the refrigerator for 2 hours. It is now ready to be rolled out to line a flan tin or mould for *pastel* or *empanada*.

MASA PARA EMPANADA
Yeast Pastry

40 grams pressed yeast	500 grams flour
150 ml. very warm water	1 teaspoon salt
1/2 teaspoon sugar	75 grams lard (or butter)
3 tablespoons flour	1 egg

Place the yeast in a small bowl. Mix the water with the sugar and 3 spoonfuls of flour and add to the yeast. Let it set in a warm place for about 40 minutes. Meanwhile, place the flour in a bowl and add to it the salt and lard, mixing the fat into the flour with the fingers. Make a well in the centre and pour in the yeast water and beaten egg. With the hands or a wooden spoon mix the flour and liquid very well. Turn out onto a floured board and knead the dough until it is very smooth and elastic, at least 5 minutes. (Processors knead dough in short order.) Add more flour as needed to prevent dough from sticking. Now place it in a greased bowl, cover with a dampened cloth and set in a warm place to rise until double in bulk — about 1 hour depending on the temperature. Punch it down. The dough is now ready to be formed into the *empanada, coquetes* (pizza) or bread loaves. In Galicia a small quantity of cornmeal is often added to the wheat flour. Wholegrain flour might also be used.

EMPANADA DE LOMO A LA GALLEGA
Galician Pork Pie

The Galician *empanada* is also made with cooked and boned chicken, tuna, sardines, eel or minced meat. A "must" for picnics and fiesta days, the empanada is often served cold.

300 grams boneless pork loin, thinly sliced	3 onions, chopped
1/2 teaspoon paprika	3 tomatoes, peeled, seeded and chopped
2 cloves garlic	1 tablespoon chopped parsley
1/2 teaspoon oregano	salt and pepper
500 grams yeast pastry or bread dough	1 tin red pimentos

| 50 | ml. oil | 2 | hard-cooked eggs |
| 1 | large pepper, chopped | 1 | egg, beaten |

Put the slices of pork loin in a dish and sprinkle them with paprika, 1 clove chopped garlic, oregano and salt and pepper and let them set for 30 minutes. Heat the oil in a pan and fry the pork very quickly, removing the slices as they are browned. In the same oil sauté the chopped peppers, onions and remaining garlic until softened. Add the prepared tomatoes, parsley, salt and pepper and cook until the tomatoes are reduced and sauce is very thick. Divide the dough in half. On a floured board roll out one half to 2 cm. thickness. (If using bread dough which contains no fat, spread the rolled-out dough with softened butter or lard, fold into thirds; roll out again and spread with butter. Fold and roll it out a final time.) Line an oven tin with the dough (an all-metal paella pan makes a good mould). Spread this with half of the prepared sauce. Arrange the slices of pork loin on top. Cut the pimentos into strips and make a layer of them on top with the sliced eggs. Spoon on the remaining sauce. Roll out the remaining dough in the same manner. Cover the pie with it. Crimp the edges together and trim off any excess. Use scraps of dough to roll into long ropes to decorate the top of the pie, moistening them with just a little water so they stick. Make a hole in the centre for a steam vent. Put in a medium hot oven for 30 minutes. Brush the top with beaten egg and bake another 15 to 20 minutes. The crust should be golden and the pie loosened from the tin when lifted with a fork. Serves 6.

BOLLOS PREÑADOS
Pregnant Buns

Use bread dough, puff pastry or shortcrust pastry for these. They can be made fairly large or very tiny for canapés, a good use for scraps of leftover dough. Wrap chorizo sausage (or pieces of chorizo) in very thinly sliced ham. Roll out dough fairly thinly. Cut it into pieces just large enough to completely enclose the chorizo. Bake in a medium-hot oven until the pastry is lightly browned.

PASTEL A LA MURCIANA
Murcia Style Chicken Pie

This is typically made with a bread dough for the bottom crust and puff pastry for the top, making a wonderful contrast in textures. Instead of chicken, pieces of rabbit, hare, squab or partridge might be used. Omit the lamb's brains if preferred.

250	grams bread dough	1	tablespoon parsley
250	grams frozen puff pastry	3	tablespoons lemon juice
1	medium chicken, cut up		salt and pepper
50	ml. oil	200	ml. water
1/4	kilo veal, cut in small pieces	1	set lamb's brains
2	cloves garlic	200	grams chorizo
1	onion, chopped finely	3	hard-cooked eggs

Prepare the dough and pastry. Heat the oil in a pot and in it brown the chicken pieces, adding the veal, garlic and onion. Add the parsley, lemon juice and salt and pepper. Add enough water to just cover the chicken. Simmer until it is very tender. Remove the chicken pieces to a plate and when they are cool enough to handle, remove and discard all skin and bones. Cut the flesh into smallish pieces and return to the pan. Cook the brains in salted water, then cut them up and mix with the chicken and meat. Roll out the bread dough and line an oven tin with it. Cover with the chicken mixture. Slice the chorizo and place it on top. Peel and slice the eggs and place them on the filling. Top with the rolled out puff pastry. Bake in a hot oven for 15 minutes, then paint the top with beaten egg. Lower the heat to moderate and bake until pastry is golden. Serves 4 to 6.

EMPANADA DE ESPINACAS Y QUESO
Spinach and Cheese Pie

	flaky pastry or other shortcrust		grated nutmeg
1	kilo spinach (800 grams frozen spinach) or chard greens	1/2	small onion
		2	tablespoons oil
2	eggs, beaten	200	grams soft white cheese or dry cottage cheese *(requesón)*
	salt and pepper		

Wash the spinach well and cook until wilted. Drain it very well, pressing out excess water. Return it to the pan and chop it. Add the beaten eggs, salt and pepper and nutmeg. Sauté the finely chopped onion in the oil until softened and add to the spinach. Roll out about 3/4 of the pastry dough and line a 20 cm. flan tin. Spoon in a layer of spinach. Slice the cheese and place a layer of cheese on top of the spinach. Top with the remaining spinach. Use the remaining pastry to roll long cords and make a criss-cross topping for the pie (or cut rounds or stars, etc.) Put in a medium oven until the pastry is golden, about 25 minutes. Serves 8 as a starter or side dish.

GACHAS
Porridge

I resist calling *gachas* by the unappetizing name of gruel, which is really what it is. This is sturdy peasant fare, but ever-so-well flavoured with garlic, spices and ham. It has many variations, some sweet, some savoury and some both. The porridge can be made with garbanzo flour, vetch flour (not much found any more), ground broad beans, wheat flour, corn meal or lentil meal. In some places, made with white flour and spiced with anise and cinnamon and served with honey or molasses, it is a pudding. It can be garnished with grapes, cucumbers, olives, sardines, chocolate, sausage... You see, this is a versatile dish.

3	tablespoons oil		freshly ground pepper
100	grams salt pork or bacon, diced		few caraway seeds
100	grams serrano ham, diced		sprinkle of cloves
2	cloves garlic, chopped	1	teaspoon salt
50	ml. water		

100 grams corn meal or other meal	1/2 litre water
1 teaspoon paprika	boiling water

Heat the oil in a deep frying pan and in it fry slowly the diced salt pork and ham. Add the chopped garlic and fry. Meanwhile, soak the corn meal in the 50 ml. of water. Then stir it into the oil and season with the paprika, plenty of pepper, caraway, cloves and salt. Add the boiling water and cook the porridge, stirring with a wooden spoon, on a very low heat for about 20 minutes or until very thick. Serve in small earthenware bowls garnished with fried croutons of bread (in which case it's *con tropezones)* or sliced pork loin, fried, or fried chorizo or other sausage.

In the Canary Islands, a similar preparation, *gofio* or *frangollo,* is made with toasted corn meal. Serve it with fried bananas.

Fariñes, farrapes, pantruque and *boronchu* are other preparations made with corn meal, well flavoured with salt pork, ham or sausage, which might be cooked in a cabbage leaf — not unlike Mexican tamales — or combined with egg and made into a sort of dumpling to include in the cocido.

MIGAS
Croutons

This is one of those homely, satisfying dishes that you'll probably never find on restaurant menus. In Spain it might be served for breakfast or lunch. The flavourful croutons are a good base for fried eggs and sausage. They're excellent added to soups or turned into a stuffing for fish or fowl.

Cut 2-day-old bread, crusts and all, into very small dice. Sprinkle with salted water — enough to thoroughly dampen but not soak the bread. Wrap the croutons in a dampened tea towel and tie it tightly. Let set for a few hours or overnight. In a little oil or lard slowly fry salt pork, or bacon, cut in very small dice. Add chopped red pepper, chopped garlic, chopped parsley and a little chopped chili pepper, if desired. Add the bread cubes and sauté them, stirring constantly, until they are slightly toasted. Sprinkle with a little paprika to colour them, but don't allow to burn. If the *migas* are served with milk, they're *migas canas.* They can also be served with thick hot chocolate.

Fish & Shellfish

Seafood is absolutely the glory of Spanish cuisine. Spaniards will gladly pay prices for an exquisite sea bass, a pristine gilt-head or giant prawns which are considerably more than prices for pork fillet, beef entrecote or lamb chops. Not that every entrée from the fish market is so pricey — at the other end of the scale, inexpensive mackerel, sardines or grey mullet provide bargain protein plus flavourful eating.

The glory of Spanish seafood is its freshness and its incredible variety. I have tried to provide recipes here which show how best to prepare some of the less familiar fish as well as the old favourites in new ways. Spanish recipes seldom say, for instance, "fish in green sauce," leaving it to the cook to decide what kind of fish, so I have given recipes using the name of the fish. Of course, you can substitute one for another. Lots more information on buying, storing and cooking fish is to be found in Chapter 2 on marketing, along with a complete listing of the fish most commonly found in Spanish markets. Hopefully, this manual will give enough "user friendly" instructions to increase your enjoyment of the many exciting Spanish seafood dishes.

Most fishmongers will clean and often fillet fish for you. But if you are going to do it yourself, here's how. Place the fish on several thicknesses of newspaper on a flat surface. If it needs scaling, use a dull knife or a scaling tool and scrape the scales off from tail to head. This is a good chore to do outside, if convenient, as the scales do tend to fly. Then, with the knife point, slit all along the belly of the fish from the anal fin to just below the head. Pull out the entrails and discard with first layers of newspaper. You may want to save the roe *(huevas),* if there is any, and the liver of some fish.

Cut out the fins on the belly side, then slit along either side of the dorsal fin on top of the fish. Grasp it firmly and give a quick pull up and towards the head to release the fin and the bones attached to it. Fish vendors usually use scissors to trim fins and tails, but this operation doesn't release the attached bones. You can now remove the head (cut it off or snap it on the ege of the counter) if you wish, and the fish is ready for cutting into steaks or slices.

Because fish in Spain is so good, it's most frequently simply prepared whole — grilled, fried or baked. But there are other dishes for which you might want fillets of fish. Though not difficult, filleting is a little tedious until you get the knack. Lay the fish flat on the table and, starting either at the tail or just below the head, slice down at an angle until the knife blade reaches the backbone. Then turn the blade almost flat against the bone and slowly work down the length of the fish, freeing the top fillet. Turn the fish and repeat the operation. You now have two fillets. The thin and bony belly flaps can be cut out if desired. To skin the fillet, lay it skin side down, slice through the tail to the skin and with the blade taut against the skin, pull the skin away from the flesh. Flat fish such as sole are skinned by making an incision above the tail, holding the tail down firmly with one hand and with the other hand sharply pulling the skin up and towards the head. The skin peels off in one piece. A fish that is to be skinned needn't be scaled. Bones, head and skin can be saved for making flavourful fish stock, a basis for soups and sauces or a poaching liquid for the fillets.

The "magic touch" Spanish cooks have with fish is knowing not to overcook it. Fish is very quick cooking. To keep it moist and flavourful, don't overcook it. Probe the fish with a fork during cooking and remove from heat when the flesh is opaque and flaky.

RAPE EN SALSA DE ALMENDRAS
Angler Fish in Almond Sauce

3/4	kilo sliced angler fish	1/2	teaspoon saffron
65	ml. oil	50	ml. white wine or fish stock
	flour	1	medium onion, chopped
20	blanched almonds	1	medium tomato, peeled, seeded and
2	cloves garlic		chopped
1	sprig parsley	100	ml. fish stock or water
1	slice bread, crusts removed		salt and pepper

The large head of the angler fish can be used to make the fish stock. Boil it for an hour with onion, carrot, celery, parsley, bay leaf and a glass of white wine. Season with salt and pepper. Strain and reserve. Dust the fish steaks with flour. Heat the oil in a frying pan and very quickly brown the fish on both sides. Remove them to an oven casserole. In the same oil fry the blanched almonds, the peeled cloves of garlic, the parsley and the slice of bread until garlic is golden and bread crisp. Remove them to mortar or blender and crush with the saffron, adding the white wine to make a paste. In the same oil, fry the chopped onions until they are softened. Add the prepared tomato and fry for several minutes. Stir in the mortar mixture and simmer the sauce for several minutes, then add the fish stock or water. Season with salt and pepper and pour over the fish slices. Bake in a medium oven until fish flakes easily, about 15 minutes. Serves 6.

RAPE A LA MARINERA
Angler Fish, Fisherman's Style

500	grams sliced angler fish	3	scallions, thinly sliced
1	teaspoon salt	1	clove garlic, chopped
200	grams peeled prawns	1	hard-cooked egg
1	dozen clams	50	ml. tomato sauce
1	red pimento, chopped	50	ml. fish stock or white wine
3	tablespoons oil		

Place the fish slices in an oven dish and sprinkle with the salt. Arrange the peeled prawns and well scrubbed clams around it and sprinkle the chopped pimento on top. In a frying pan heat the oil and sauté the onions and chopped garlic. Pour this, oil included, over the fish. Chop the hard boiled egg and sprinkle onto fish. Mix the tomato sauce and fish stock and pour over. Bake in a medium oven until fish flakes easily and clam shells have opened, about 20 minutes. Serves 4.

RAPE A LA LANGOSTA
Fake Lobster

The angler fish has sweet tasting, slightly chewy flesh very similar to lobster, for which it can be substituted. Poach the angler fish in a well-seasoned court bouillon, or in a fumet made with lobster or prawn shells. Let it cool, then pull the meat into pieces with the fingers or using two forks. Serve on a bed of lettuce, covered with mayonnaise and garnished with quartered eggs, sliced tomato and lemon wedges.

SOLE AND OTHER FLAT FISH

Of all the flat fish (see Chapter 2 for descriptions), sole is certainly the most popular. The following recipes can be used for any of the flat fish.

RIZOS DE LENGUADO
Sole Curls

1/2	kilo sole	oil
	salt	parsley
1	egg, beaten	tomato sauce
100	grams breadcrumbs	

Have the fish vendor fillet the sole. (Each sole provides 4 fillets.) Salt them. Dip in beaten egg, then in breadcrumbs. Roll the fillet up and fasten it with a toothpick. Fry the rolls in oil, turning to brown and crisp on both sides. Drain on absorbent paper and serve hot, garnished with parsley and accompanied by a tomato sauce.

LENGUADO A LA GADITANA
Fried Sole, Cadiz Style

Cadiz is famous for its fried fish. The art is in shaking off excess flour and keeping the oil at the perfect temperature, so the fish turns golden and crispy and is scooped out with a skimmer while the flesh is still meltingly moist. Both Cadiz and Malaga are famous for their *fritura de pescados,* a mixed fish fry which includes, besides a small sole, fresh anchovies *(boquerones),* rings of squid *(calamares),* a slice of hake *(pescadilla* or *merluza)* and a few prawns. When all is cooked to perfection and served piping hot, it is one of the most perfect dishes of Andalusian cooking. So simple.

Soak the skinned sole in milk for a half hour. Then dredge the fish in flour. Put them in a coarse sieve and shake off excess flour. Fry the sole in hot oil until golden on one side, turn and brown the other side. Serve with lemon wedges.

GALLO AL LIMON
Whiff or Brill with Lemon

6	flat fish, skinned	100 ml.	oil
3	lemons	3	cloves garlic

Allow one fish per person. Slice the lemons very thinly and arrange half of them in a layer in a baking dish. Place the fish on top and cover with the remaining lemon slices. Put the fish in a hot oven for about 5 minutes. Meanwhile, heat the oil in a pan and in it toast the garlic, cut in slices. Pour this over the fish and return to the oven until they are flaky, about 10 minutes. Serves 6.

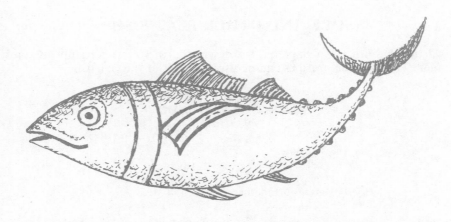

RUBIO A LA NARANJA
Gurnard in Orange Sauce

2	gurnards, each about 700 grams		1	chopped onion
2	oranges			flour
	salt		1/4	litre white wine
120	ml. oil		60	ml. orange juice
3	cloves garlic			

Clean the fish, but leave them whole. Rub them inside and out with salt and place in the cavity of each a few orange slices. Let them set for 30 minutes, then dust them with flour. Heat 50 ml. oil in a heatproof oven pan big enough to hold the fish. Add the chopped garlic and put the fish in. Turn to brown the reverse side, then put in a medium oven. Meanwhile, skin one of the oranges of the outer orange peel, with no white pith. Chop the peel and cook it in a little water for 5 minutes. Reserve the peel and the liquid. In a saucepan heat 4 tablespoons oil and sauté the onion until softened. Stir in 2 tablespoons flour and cook a few minutes without browning. Then add the white wine, the orange juice and the reserved, cooked orange peel. Cook, stirring, until the sauce is thickened. Remove the fish from the oven and place on a serving dish. Spoon a little of the sauce over the fish and garnish with additional orange slices. Serve the remaining sauce separately. Serves 4 to 6. Grouper *(mero)* can be prepared in the same manner.

CABRACHO EN SALSA VERDE
Scorpionfish, Redfish, Red Snapper or Rascasse in Green Sauce

1 1/2	kilos whole fish		4	tablespoons chopped parsley
	salt		600	grams potatoes (4 medium)
6	tablespoons oil		1/4	litre water
3	leeks, finely chopped			flour
2	cloves garlic, chopped		175	ml. white wine

Cut the fish into slices or fillets, salt the pieces and set aside. In a heatproof casserole heat the oil and fry the chopped leeks. Add the garlic, then the parsley and potatoes, peeled and very thinly sliced. Cover with the water, add 1 tablespoon salt and cook on a medium heat until the potatoes are almost tender, 25 minutes. Dredge the pieces of fish in flour and place them in the casserole. Pour in the wine. Cook the fish 5 minutes, turn the pieces of fish and cook another 10 minutes. Don't stir the potatoes after adding the fish, but shake the casserole to keep from sticking. Serves 4. Garnish, if desired, with a sprinkling of cooked peas.

CAP ROIG
Scorpionfish, Redfish, Red Snapper or Rascasse with Garlic

1 1/2	kilos whole fish		6	tablespoons oil
	salt		3	cloves garlic, sliced
100	ml. water or stock		1	tablespoon chopped parsley
50	ml. white wine			

Clean the fish but leave it whole. Rub it with salt and let set for 30 minutes. Place the fish in an oiled oven dish and pour over the water and the wine. Put in a medium oven until the fish flakes easily, about 25 minutes. Meanwhile, heat the oil in a saucepan and sauté the sliced garlic until lightly golden. Add the chopped parsley. Pour this sauce over the fish. Serves 4.

SALMONETES A LA PLANCHA CON ALIÑO
Grilled Red Mullet with Sauce

In my early days in Spain, while I was still getting a kitchen together and learning my way around the marketplace, I used to lunch every day in the same bar, where I always ordered the same thing — a salad and grilled red mullet with this simple sauce. I was straight out of Midwest America, where fresh seafood was unknown. The memory of that superbly fresh fish flavours all my impressions of Spain.

Red mullet is one of the few fish which can be cooked without gutting, as it has no bitter gall. At its simplest, lay the whole unscaled fish on a hot grill (griddle), brush with oil, and turn once. Or gut and scale it and cook under the broiler or over charcoal. For the sauce: mix 3 cloves chopped garlic with 3 tablespoons chopped parsley. Add 50 ml. oil and the juice of 1 lemon. Drizzle this over the grilled fish. Or serve with *romesco* sauce.

SALMONETES CON SALSA DE ANCHOAS
Red Mullet with Anchovy Sauce

6	red mullet	100	grams butter
	lemon juice	4	anchovy fillets, well drained
	salt	50	ml. water or stock
	oil	2	tablespoons white wine
	breadcrumbs		pepper
6	tablespoons tomato purée		chopped parsley

Clean the red mullet (one per person) and rub them with lemon juice and salt. Let them set for 15 minutes. Then dip them in oil and in breadcrumbs. Place them on an oven tin and bake in a moderate oven until the fish flakes, about 20 minutes. Place them on a serving platter and keep warm. To the juices in the pan add the tomato purée and the butter and let it heat, stirring. Mash the anchovy fillets in the mortar and add to the pan with the water and wine. Season with pepper (salt may not be necessary) and cook for several minutes. Pour the sauce over the baked mullet and garnish with chopped parsley. Serves 6.

CABALLA AL HORNO
Baked Mackerel

4	mackerel, about 300 grams each		salt
60	ml. oil	1	lemon, thinly sliced
4	small onions, sliced		

Clean the fish but leave them whole. Pour the oil into a baking dish large enough to hold the fish comfortably. Arrange the sliced onions on the bottom and place the fish on top of them. Sprinkle with salt and top with the sliced lemon. Bake in a medium oven until the fish flakes easily, about 25 minutes. Serve in the same dish. Serves 4.

CABALLAS RELLENAS
Stuffed Mackerel

This excellent preparation can be used for other fish as well. Try it with *lubina,* sea bass; *dorada,* gilt-head; salmon or trout.

6	medium mackerel or large fish	1	tablespoon brandy
300	grams boneless white fish		grated nutmeg
50	grams fine breadcrumbs	1	tablespoon chopped parsley
2	egg yolks	2	tablespoons oil
	salt and pepper	50	ml. white wine
1	chopped onion	1	tomato, sliced

The fish is boned and left whole. Not a difficult operation, but allow yourself time. Slit the fish along the belly from tail to head. Gut the fish and wash. Starting at the tail, ease the knife along the backbone, freeing the flesh of the top fillet all the way to the head. Turn the fish over and repeat the operation. Now cut the backbone free at the tail and head and remove it, leaving the whole, boned fish. Repeat with the remaining fish. Finely mince (can be done in processor) the boneless white fish (hake, angler, sole, etc.) and mix with the breadcrumbs, egg yolks, salt and pepper, minced onion, brandy, nutmeg and chopped parsley. Stuff the fish with this mixture. Sew up the cavity openings with needle and thread. Pour the oil into an oven dish and place the fish in it. Pour over the wine and top the fish with the slices of tomato. Bake in a medium oven until the fish flakes easily, about 35 minutes. Serves 6. (Note: leftover cooked fish or shellfish can be used in the filling.)

BONITO A LA BILBAINA
Bonito, Bilbao Style

1	bonito, about 1¼ kilos		sprigs parsley
1/2	litre water		slice onion
1	teaspoon salt	2	hard-cooked eggs
100	ml. white wine	1/2	onion, finely chopped
1	tablespoon vinegar	1	tablespoon chopped parsley
1	bay leaf	1	tablespoon chopped pickle or capers
1	clove garlic, slivered	2	tablespoons pickle juice
	peppercorns		lettuce

Clean the fish and cut it into thick slices. Place it in a pan with the water, salt, wine, vinegar, bay, garlic, peppers, parsley and slice of onion. Bring to a boil, lower the heat and simmer for 5 minutes. Remove the fish from the heat and let it cool in the liquid. Then remove it, draining well and discarding all skin and bones. Arrange on a serving dish. Chop the eggs and mix with chopped onion, chopped parsley, chopped pickle and pickle juice. Spread this mixture over the pieces of bonito and serve garnished with lettuce leaves, sliced tomato, cucumbers and lemon. Accompany with mayonnaise to which a spoonful of tomato sauce has been added. Serves 6 as an hors d'oeuvre.

FIAMBRE DE BONITO
Fish Pâté

1	bonito, about 1½ kilos	200	grams sliced ham or bacon
50	grams breadcrumbs	1	small tin red pimentos
50	ml. dry sherry or brandy	50	grams pitted olives, sliced
1/2	teaspoon thyme	1	onion, quartered
1 1/2	teaspoons salt	1	carrot
1/4	teaspoon pepper		bay, thyme, parsley, celery
	dash of cayenne	1	clove garlic
2	eggs	200	ml. white wine

Clean the fish and cut the flesh from the skin and bones. Chop the fish in a processor or meat grinder. Place in a bowl and add the breadcrumbs, sherry, 2 tablespoons chopped parsley, thyme and ½ teaspoon salt. Let the mixture sit for 30 minutes. Then mix in the beaten eggs. On a clean cloth or kitchen towel, dampened, spread a third of the fish paste in a layer. Arrange half of the sliced ham, strips of pimentos and chopped olives on it. Spread with another layer of paste and repeat with the ham, pimentos and olives. Spread the remaining paste. Wrap it tightly in the cloth, forming a rectangle about 18 × 14, and secure it with string or sew up with thread. In a pot put about 2 litres of water, one onion, carrot, herbs, garlic, white wine and 1 teaspoon salt. Bring to a boil and reduce heat to a simmer. Add the pâté and cook very slowly for about an hour. Drain it well, then place on a board with a weight on top and let it cool completely. Unroll from the cloth and cut in slices to serve cold or room temperature. Makes 12 hors d'oeuvre servings. This can be made with any fish.

ATUN CON TOMATE
Fresh Tuna Baked in Tomato Sauce

1	thick slice tuna (750 gm. to 1 kilo)	1	bay leaf
1	lemon		salt and pepper
1/4	cup oil	1	clove garlic
3/4	kilo tomatoes, peeled and chopped	1	teaspoon sugar
	(or tinned ones, drained)	1	tablespoon parsley, chopped

Sprinkle the tuna steak with salt and lemon juice and let it marinate 15 minutes. Then dredge in the flour and brown it on both sides in a frying pan. Remove it and place in an oven casserole. In the same oil, fry the tomatoes, peeled and cut up. Add the bay leaf, salt, pepper and sugar and let it cook on a high heat for five minutes. Pour over the tuna and sprinkle with the chopped garlic. Put in a medium hot oven until the tuna flakes easily, about 25 minutes. Sprinkle with parsley. Serves 6.

MARMITAKO
Tuna and Potato Casserole

There are dozens of versions of this Basque dish, all of them wonderful. Because it is originally a fisherman's stew, prepared aboard the boat, I have chosen the simplest version and, in my opinion, the tastiest.

1	kilo tuna or bonito	2	teaspoons paprika
50	ml. oil		salt and pepper
1	onion, chopped	1	small chili pepper
4	cloves garlic, chopped	1	kilo potatoes (7-8 medium)
2	sweet peppers, red and/or green	200	ml. white wine
1/2	kilo tomatoes (2 large)	100	ml. water

Cut the tuna into chunks, discarding the bone. If using bonito, cut it first into slices, then with a knife or fork pull off chunks of the flesh from the bone. Heat the oil in a heatproof casserole and in it sauté the chopped onions, garlic and peppers, cleaned of seeds and cut in strips. When they are soft, add the tomatoes, peeled, seeded and chopped, the paprika, salt and pepper and chili. When tomatoes are somewhat reduced add the potatoes, cut in dice. Stir for a few minutes, then add the wine and water. Cover the pot and cook on a high heat until the potatoes are nearly tender, about 20 minutes. Add the fish to the casserole, cover and cook another 5 minutes, or until fish flakes easily but is still juicy. Let the casserole rest, covered, for 5 to 10 minutes before serving. Serves 4 to 6. This dish can be cooked with more liquid, making a soupier stew which is served over a slice of bread. It can also be made with tinned tuna: drain it very well, rinse in water and add the tuna chunks to the casserole at the very end of cooking to heat thoroughly.

PATACO
Tuna, Catalan Style

100	ml. oil	1/2	kilo boned tuna
1	onion, chopped	3	dozen cooked snails
2	tomatoes, peeled, seeded and chopped	1	teaspoon salt
		1/4	teaspoon saffron
2	potatoes, peeled and cut in pieces	2	cloves garlic
1	courgette, sliced	1	tablespoon parsley
100	ml. sherry or *vino rancio*	12	almonds, blanched and toasted

Heat the oil in a casserole and sauté the chopped onion until soft. Add the prepared tomatoes and fry a few minutes, then add the cut up potatoes and sliced courgette. Add the sherry or the *vino rancio* and enough hot water to cover the vegetables. Cook until potatoes are nearly tender. Meanwhile, cut the tuna into chunks. Add it to the vegetables with the cooked snails and the salt. In the mortar or blender crush the saffron, garlic, parsley and almonds, dissolving this paste in some of the liquid from the casserole. Stir it into the casserole and cook slowly until the fish is cooked, about 10 minutes. Serves 4.

PEZ LIMON AL HINOJO
Charcoal Grilled Amberjack with Fennel

This is one of my favourites for charcoal grilling on the patio. Besides the meaty amberjack, sea bass, pompano, trout, mackerel or grey mullet are good choices for grilling.

2	amberjack (each about 1/2 kilo)		1	clove garlic, crushed
50	ml. oil			salt and pepper
50	ml. dry sherry		1	tablespoon chopped fennel
1	lemon			sprigs of fennel

Put the cleaned fish in a shallow dish and pour over them a marinade made with the oil, sherry, lemon juice, garlic, salt and pepper and chopped fennel. Let them marinate for an hour. Drain the fish and stuff the cavities with a few sprigs of fennel. Have charcoal prepared. Oil the grill and heat it before placing the fish on it. Grill the fish over the hot coals, basting with the marinade, until fish is done, about 5 minutes on each side. (A hinged grill makes turning the fish much easier.) A few sprigs of fennel can be laid on the fire as well — the aromatic smoke further flavours the fish. Serves 4.

PALOMETA FRITA
Fried Pompano

1	pompano (about 1 kilo)		1	egg, beaten
	salt		50	grams hazelnuts, ground
1	lemon		50	grams breadcrumbs
1	tablespoon chopped parsley			oil
	flour			

Fillet the fish and skin it. Cut the fillets into regular sized pieces and place them in a shallow dish. Sprinkle with salt, lemon juice and parsley and let them set for 30 minutes. Then dip them in flour, then beaten egg, then the finely ground hazelnuts mixed with the breadcrumbs. Fry the pieces of fish in oil, turning to brown both sides. Serves 4 to 6. Other fish fillets, such as John Dory or frozen fish, can be used in this recipe.

MORAGA DE SARDINAS
Sardines in a Row

Moraga is sometimes used to mean sardines grilled on spits at the beach more usually called *espetones*.

1	kilo fresh sardines		1	dozen clams, scrubbed
60	ml. oil		150	ml. white wine
	salt		4	cloves garlic, chopped
1	bay leaf		1	tablespoon chopped parsley
25	grams pine nuts			

Clean the fish, scale them, but leave them whole. Arrange them in a rectangular pan in rows, alternating the direction of heads and tails. Sprinkle them liberally with salt. Pour over the oil. Add the bay leaf, broken into several pieces, and the pine nuts. Arrange the well-scrubbed clams around the edges and between rows. Pour in the white wine and sprinkle with the chopped garlic and parsley. Cook on a medium heat (or in a hot oven) until the sardines are cooked and the clam shells have opened, about 15 minutes. Serve in the same pan. Serves 6.

SARDINAS RELLENAS
Stuffed Sardines

1/2	kilo fresh sardines	1	tablespoon pine nuts
2	tablespoons oil	1	tablespoon chopped parsley
2	tablespoons fine breadcrumbs	2	tinned anchovy fillets
1	tablespoon raisins, seeded and chopped		salt and pepper
			oil

Clean the sardines, scale them, cut off the heads and open them by slitting up the belly. Carefully remove the spines. Wash and pat dry. Heat the oil in a small pan and in it toast the breadcrumbs. Remove from heat and add the seeded and chopped raisins, the pine nuts, parsley and the anchovy fillets, well drained and chopped. Mix well and season with salt and pepper. Stuff the filleted sardines with this mixture, pressing them together and fastening with a toothpick. Place them in an oven dish, drizzle with oil and sprinkle with breadcrumbs. Bake in a medium oven until they are cooked, about 20 minutes. Serves 4. Grapes, seeded and chopped, can be used instead of raisins and chopped walnuts can be added in addition to the pine nuts. This extraordinary stuffing is equally good for mackerel. Either fish can be floured and fried instead of baked.

SARDINAS A LA MORUNA
Moorish Style Sardines

In the days of the Moorish kingdom, tomatoes wouldn't have entered in, though they are an excellent addition.

3/4	kilo sardines	1	chili pepper (optional)
400	grams onions (3 small)	1/4	teaspoon saffron
400	grams peppers	1/4	teaspoon cumin
400	grams tomatoes (2 large)	1/4	teaspoon paprika
2	cloves garlic		salt and pepper
2	tablespoons chopped parsley	2	tablespoons oil

Clean the sardines, scale them, remove heads and spines. Wash and pat them dry. Chop the onions, peppers, and the skinned and seeded tomatoes all very finely (processor does this quickly). Add the chopped garlic, chopped pepper, minced chili, crushed saffron, cumin, paprika, salt and pepper to the vegetables. In a casserole spread a layer of the chopped vegetables and on top a layer of the filleted sardines. Repeat the layers, ending with a layer of the vegetables. Drizzle with the oil and put the casserole on the stove. Cook fairly slowly until sardines are cooked, about 30 minutes. Serve hot. Leftovers make a delicious hors d'oeuvre, served cold or spread on bread.

BOQUERONES REBOZADOS
Fresh Anchovies in Batter

1/3	kilo fresh anchovies	4	cloves garlic, minced
130	grams flour	1/8	teaspoon saffron
100	ml. water	1	teaspoon salt
1	egg, beaten		oil
1	tablespoon chopped parsley		

Clean the fish, cut off the heads. To fillet them, grasp the top of the backbone firmly against the knife blade and pull it down sharply across the top of the fish. Cut off the bone at the tail, leaving the two fillets attached by the tail. Wash and pat them dry. Make the batter by beating together the flour, water, egg, parsley, minced garlic, saffron and salt. Let the batter set for an hour. Heat the oil. Dip the fish fillets in the batter and fry them in the hot oil until golden and crisp. Drain on absorbent paper and serve hot with lemon wedges. Serves 4.

LISA EN AMARILLO
Grey Mullet in Saffron Sauce

2	grey mullet, each about 450 grams	1	small onion, chopped
	salt	1/2	teaspoon saffron
	lemon juice	1	tablespoon chopped parsley
50	ml. oil	100	ml. water or fish stock
1	slice bread, crusts removed	1	lemon
2	cloves garlic		

Either fillet the fish or cut them into slices. Rub the pieces with salt and lemon juice and let them sit for an hour at room temperature or longer, covered, in the refrigerator. Arrange them in a *besuguera,* a rectangular, metal fish-cooking pan, or in a casserole. In a frying pan heat the oil and fry the slice of bread until it is golden and crisp. Remove. Then fry the garlic and chopped onion. Put the contents of the pan into a mortar, processor or blender with the fried bread, saffron, parsley and water and blend to a smooth paste. Pour this sauce over the fish with the juice of the lemon and place on a moderate heat until it begins to bubble. Then cover the pan with foil and cook until the fish flakes easily, about 10 minutes, adding a little more liquid if needed. Diced potatoes can be incorporated in this dish, adding them before the fish. Serves 4. *Pez espada en amarillo,* swordfish in saffron sauce, is prepared in the same manner.

LISA EN AJILLO
Grilled Grey Mullet with Garlic

Wonderfully simple, this preparation is equally good with sea bass, redfish, red mullet or any of the breams.

Clean the fish (needn't be scaled for grilling) and grill over charcoal or under broiler-grill or in oven, basting with oil, until fish is flaky. Serve with sauce made by frying 6 cloves of chopped garlic in 6 tablespoons oil with a piece of chili pepper. Remove from heat and add the juice of 1/2 lemon and 1 tablespoon chopped parsley.

BROCHETA DE PEZ ESPADA
Swordfish Kebab

1/2	kilo swordfish	1	lemon
2	tablespoons oil	1	tomato
2	tablespoons chopped parsley	1	onion
5	cloves garlic, chopped	1	green pepper

Cut the swordfish into cubes about 4 cm. square and place them in a bowl. Add the oil, parsley, garlic and lemon juice. Let marinate for 30 minutes. Cut the tomato, onion and green pepper each into eights. Thread the swordfish onto skewers, alternating with pieces of vegetables. Brush with marinade and grill over hot coals or on a griddle, turning frequently and basting with marinade until the fish is done, about 8 minutes. Angler fish, tuna and shark are all prepared in the same manner.

PEZ ESPADA A LA MALAGUEÑA
Swordfish, Malaga Style

This recipe is equally good with any large fish steak — tuna, haddock, cod, halibut, shark, etc.

219

1	medium onion, chopped	2	tomatoes, peeled, seeded and
4	cloves garlic, chopped		chopped
1	large green pepper, chopped	1	kilo swordfish steak
1	bay leaf	1	teaspoon salt
2	cloves	50	ml. oil
5	peppercorns	100	ml. white wine

Into a casserole large enough to hold the fish put the chopped onion, garlic, green pepper and tomatoes. Add the bay leaf, cloves and peppercorns. Place the fish on top, sprinkle with salt and add the oil. Place on a medium heat until it begins to sizzle. Then add the wine and just bring it to a boil. Then cover and simmer (or bake in a medium oven) until fish is done and flakes easily, about 25 minutes. If desired, the fish can be removed to a serving dish and the sauce boiled to reduce and thicken it. Serve garnished with parsley. Serves 6.

CAZON EN ADOBO
Marinated Dogfish

In Spain, instead of man-eating sharks, we have shark-eating men. The dogfish is one of several quite edible sharks. This tapa bar favourite is also a good way to treat frozen fish, as the marinade adds lots of flavour.

3/4	kilo dogfish	1/4	teaspoon ground pepper
50	ml. oil		pinch of cumin
50	ml. vinegar or lemon juice	1/2	teaspoon salt
1	tablespoon water		flour
3	cloves garlic, chopped		oil
1/4	teaspoon paprika		spring onions, carrots, etc.
1	teaspoon oregano		

Cut the fish into cubes about 4 cm. square, discarding any skin and bone. Put it in a glass or ceramic bowl. Mix together the oil, vinegar, water, chopped garlic, paprika, oregano, pepper, cumin and salt. Pour over the fish and toss it well. Marinate for at least 6 hours or overnight. Then drain the fish well, dredge it in flour and fry in hot oil until golden and crisp. Drain on absorbent paper and serve hot. In the remaining marinade, cook whole onions, carrots and other vegetables, adding just enough water to cover them. Drain well and serve as a garnish to the fried fish.

CORVINA EN SALSA DE ALCAPARRAS
Meagre in Caper Sauce

A very bland fish, meagre or corb profits from the sharp taste of capers. Spain is the world's largest producer of this piquant condiment. Use this preparation for *mero,* grouper; *cherna,* wreckfish; *brótola,* forkbeard; *merluza,* hake, and any frozen fish.

500	grams fish steak	1	head garlic, roasted
50	ml. white wine	20	almonds, blanched and toasted

4	tablespoons capers (50 grams)		salt and pepper
1	tablespoon minced scallion or onion		

Rub the fish steak with salt and let it set for 30 minutes. Place it in an oiled oven dish with the white wine and cover the casserole. Bake in a medium oven until the fish flakes easily, about 25 minutes. Drain off the cooking liquid and keep the fish warm while making the sauce. In mortar or blender mash the roasted and peeled garlic with the almonds, capers and scallions. Beat in the cooking liquid from the fish and season with salt and pepper. Serve the fish in the same dish, covered with the sauce. Serves 4.

HAKE

When, years ago, I acquired the typical traveller's malady after a sojourn in another country, the village doctor prescribed some strong medicine and a diet of white fish and white rice — with only red wine. At the local restaurant I presented my menu prescription. A few minutes later the waiter brought for my inspection, a whole hake *(merluza),* about 50 cm. long and gleamingly fresh. I nodded my approval. I was served a thick slice of the flaky, white fish, perfectly poached, with a serving of white rice, a sprig of parsley and a slice of lemon. So moist and flavourful was that fish, that for all the stupendous fish dishes I've enjoyed since, perhaps none were as good as that one. I like to think I was cured on the spot and certainly recommend this invalid's diet to even the most demanding gourmet.

Hake may be Spain's favourite fish, particularly on the north and the south coasts, where several quite different ways of cooking it are to be found. It's a good choice for "fish and chips," simple and straightforwardly fried, but lends itself to many fancier preparations. Where not available, try substituting cod, haddock, whiting or coley in these recipes.

MERLUZA A LA VASCA
Hake, Basque Style

This dish is also called *koskera* or *salsa verde* and may only include the parsley, with no peas or asparagus.

1	kilo hake steaks	2	dozen asparagus tips, cooked or tinned
	flour		
50	ml. oil	3	hard-cooked eggs
6	cloves garlic, chopped		salt and pepper
100	ml. white wine	3	tablespoons chopped parsley
75	grams cooked peas		

The fish should be cut in fairly thick steaks or in bone-free medallions. Salt them and let set for 15 minutes. Then dredge them in flour. In a heatproof casserole heat the oil. Add the pieces of hake and very quickly brown the fish on both sides. Add the chopped garlic and immediately the white wine. Don't stir, but shake the casserole, adding water, stock or liquid from peas and asparagus, drop by drop, until the sauce is the consistency of thick cream. Add the cooked peas and garnish with the cooked asparagus tips and quartered eggs. Season with salt and pepper and add lots of chopped parsley. Total cooking time for the fish should be less than 15 minutes, the sauce thickening while the fish cooks. Serves 4 to 6 and is often made in individual earthenware dishes. For those who prefer a "saucier" dish, sprinkle the fish with a tablespoon of flour, then "shake" more liquid into the mixture. Instead of liquid from the asparagus, you can add clam broth, adding the shelled clams to the finished dish.

MERLUZA A LA ANDALUZA
Hake, Andalusian Style

50	ml. oil	50	grams hazelnuts
3	cloves garlic	25	grams pine nuts
1	slice bread	100	ml. water
750	grams sliced hake	100	ml. white wine
2	tomatoes, peeled and chopped		salt and pepper
1	tablespoon chopped parsley		

Heat the oil in a frying pan and in it toast the peeled garlic and the slice of bread. Remove them when golden. Sprinkle the slices of fish with salt. Brown it in the same oil in which the garlic was fried, adding the prepared tomatoes when the fish slices are turned. Add the chopped parsley and cook on a medium heat. In the mortar or blender crush the fried garlic and bread with the hazelnuts and pine nuts. Dilute in the water and add to the fish with the wine and salt and pepper. Simmer until the fish is done. Serves 4 to 6.

MERLUZA A LA BILBAINA
Hake, Bilbao Style

1/2	kilo sliced hake (4 steaks)	2	large red peppers, roasted and skinned, or tinned peppers
50	ml. oil		
1	onion, chopped	1	bay leaf
2	cloves garlic, chopped		salt and pepper
		50	ml. white wine

Sprinkle the fish steaks with salt and let them sit while preparing the sauce. Heat the oil in a frying pan and sauté the chopped onion, chopped garlic and skinned peppers, cut in dice. Season with bay leaf and salt and pepper and cook until very soft, adding a few drops of water if necessary. Purée this mixture in the blender or sieve it. Oil an ovenproof dish and put the fish steaks in it. Pour over the white wine and put in a medium hot oven until the fish is partially cooked, about 10 minutes. Spread the puréed pepper sauce on top and bake another 5 minutes or until the fish flakes easily. This lovely sauce can also be spooned onto the plate and a slice of poached fish put on top. Serve with boiled potatoes and garnish the plate with chopped parsley.

MERLUZA CON UVAS
Hake with Grapes

4	fillets of hake, cut in half	2	tablespoons butter
100	grams ham, sliced	100	grams grapes, seeded
	flour	1	orange, peeled and sectioned
	oil	50	ml. champagne or wine

Sprinkle the fillets with salt. Put a slice of ham on half a fillet and fold it over. Dredge the "sandwiches" in flour and sauté them in oil, turning to brown both sides. Remove and keep warm. Add the butter to the pan and very gently sauté the grapes, peeled and seeded, and the sections of orange. Add the champagne and cook a few minutes. Spoon the fruits over the fried hake and serve with a lemon wedge.

MERLUZA CON MAYONESA
Poached Hake with Mayonnaise

1	whole fish, about 1400 grams	1	bay leaf
1 1/2	litres water	50	ml. white wine
2	leeks	1	piece lemon peel
1	tablespoon salt	200	ml. mayonnaise
1	carrot, peeled and sliced		parsley and lemon
2	sprigs parsley		

Put the water in a pot large enough to hold the whole fish. Bring to a boil and add the sliced leeks, salt, sliced carrot, parsley, bay leaf, white wine and lemon peel. Boil this *court bouillon* for 40 minutes. Place the cleaned fish on a clean cloth or kitchen towel and put it into the poaching liquid. Reduce heat so the liquid just simmers and cook until the fish flakes easily, about 20 minutes. Remove the fish to a platter and let it cool slighty. Then place it on a serving platter, skinning it if desired, and garnish with parsley and lemon. Spoon the mayonnaise over it and serve cold. Serves 4 to 6. The liquid in which the fish poached makes a wonderful basis for a soup.

KOKOTXAS EN SALSA VERDE A LA DONOSTIARRA
Hake Morsels in Green Sauce, San Sebastian Style

This is, inevitably, the priciest item on any menu where it is available. The tiny morsel of flesh from the fish's throat, so delicate and so perishable, is more commonly gobbled up by the fishermen. In northern markets, cods' cheeks can be used in this dish. Clams can be added to the *kokotxas* to extend the portions.

1	kilo kokotxas	2	tablespoons chopped onion
100	ml. oil	100	ml. water
6	cloves garlic, chopped		freshly ground pepper
1	chili pepper (optional)	2	tablespoons chopped parsley

Heat the oil in an earthenware casserole and sauté the chopped garlic, chopped chili pepper and chopped onion. Add the hakes' cheeks and fry for a minute. Then add the water very slowly, swirling the casserole to combine it. Season with pepper. Cook about 5 minutes, garnish with parsley and serve. Serves 8 as a starter.

RAYA EN PIMENTON
Skate in Paprika Sauce

3/4	kilo cleaned skate	1	teaspoon paprika
70	ml. oil	1/4	teaspoon saffron
6	cloves garlic	1	teaspoon oregano
1	sprig parsley	2	teaspoons vinegar
	dash cayenne		salt and pepper

Cut the fish into pieces. Heat the oil in a pan and fry the garlic and remove when golden. Add the skate to the pan and sauté it on a hot fire. Meanwhile, in the mortar or blender crush the garlic with the parsley, cayenne paprika, saffron, oregano and vinegar. Add this to the fish with salt and pepper to taste and cook a few more minutes. A little water can be added if desired to dilute the sauce. Serves 4. Any solid-fleshed fish, such as gar and angler, or shellfish such as prawns, mussels or scallops, can be prepared in this manner.

BREAMS

Spanish markets offer a variety of different breams (porgy) in various hues of pink and grey, from the small and cheap to the big and very expensive. They can all be used in the following recipes fairly interchangeably, though the named fish is the preferred choice. *Besugo* may be the favourite in Spain, a good fish for grilling or baking. A *besuguera* is a rectangular metal pan, just right for holding a *besugo,* which goes from gas burner to oven.

BESUGO A LA MADRILEÑA
Baked Bream, Madrid Style

1	whole fish (about 750 grams)	3	tablespoons breadcrumbs
	salt	50	ml. oil
8	cloves garlic	1/4	litre white wine
4	tablespoons chopped parsley		chopped olives

Clean and scale the fish and rub it inside and out with the salt and let sit for 15 minutes. Chop the garlic and mix with the chopped parsley and breadcrumbs. Heat the oil in a heatproof oven pan and put the fish into it. Sprinkle the garlic-crumb mixture on top of the fish and add the white wine. When the liquid starts to simmer, put the pan in a medium oven. Bake the fish until it flakes easily, about 20 minutes, basting frequently with the liquid in the pan. Sprinkle with a few chopped olives. Serves 3 or 4.

PESCADO AL HORNO
Baked Bream

A large bream, such as gilt-head or dentex, is excellent for this dish, but any large fish — bass, salmon, grouper — could be used. This is a speciality of the beachside restaurants on the Cadiz and Malaga coasts.

1	whole fish (about 1¼ kilos)		salt and pepper
100 ml. oil		1	onion, sliced
1	kilo potatoes, thinly sliced	2	tomatoes, sliced
5	cloves garlic, chopped	100	ml. white wine
3	tablespoons chopped parsley	1	bay leaf
2	small green peppers, chopped		

Rub the fish inside and out with salt and let it sit 15 minutes. Pour the oil into the bottom of a heat-proof oven dish and add a layer of half the thinly sliced potatoes. Sprinkle half the chopped garlic and parsley and peppers over them and sprinkle with salt and pepper. Then place a layer of the sliced onions and tomatoes. Add the rest of the potatoes, the remaining garlic, parsley and peppers and sprinkle with salt and pepper. Lay the fish on top of the potatoes and top it with a few remaining slices of tomato. Put pieces of bay leaf around it. Pour the wine over and when it begins to simmer, cover with foil, put the pan into a medium oven until potatoes and fish are done, about 30 minutes. Remove the foil during the last 15 minutes of baking. If using smaller fish, it will be necessary to put the potatoes in to bake before adding the fish. Serves 6.

BESUGO ASADO A LA DONOSTIARRA
Grilled Bream, San Sebastian Style

1	whole fish, about 1 kilo	6	cloves garlic
	salt	3	tablespoons lemon juice
100 ml. oil		1	chili pepper, minced

Rub the fish inside and out with the salt and oil and let it sit for an hour. Prepare charcoal or a griddle (plancha) for cooking the fish. Preheat the grill, brush it with oil and place the fish on it. (If using a griddle, brush it with heavy brine and heat until the salt turns white.) Brush the fish with oil as it cooks, turning it to toast both sides. The skin should be quite crisp. When done, place it on a platter and serve with sauce made by frying the chopped garlic in the remaining oil. Add the lemon juice and minced chili pepper. Serves 4.

PARGO ENCEBOLLADO
Bream in Onion Sauce

1 or 2 whole fish	1 lemon
salt	3 tablespoons parsley
2 onions	75 ml. oil
4 cloves garlics, chopped	25 grams almonds or pine nuts

Clean the fish, rub with salt and let them sit for a while. Chop or shred the onions (processor works well — no tears) and mix with the garlic and parsley. Put the oil in the oven dish and put the onion mixture on the bottom. Place the fish on it and squeeze over it the juice of the lemon. Put in a medium oven until fish is done, about 20 minutes, spooning the onion mixture over the fish occasionally while it bakes. Fry the almonds or pine nuts in a little oil until toasted. Sprinkle them over the fish before serving.

URTA A LA ROTEÑA
Fish, Rota Style

1 kilo fish	4 small green peppers, cut in strips
salt	1 large tomato, peeled and puréed
flour	1/2 teaspoon thyme
110 ml. oil	1 bay leaf
50 ml. brandy	salt and pepper
1 onion, chopped	50 ml. white wine

Cut the fish into crosswise slices, then cut each slice into two, removing the bone. Sprinkle lightly with salt and dredge in flour. Heat 60 ml. oil in a heatproof casserole and brown the pieces of fish on both sides. Pour in the brandy, set it alight and gently swirl the casserole until flames subside. Meanwhile, in another pan, heat the remaining oil and sauté the chopped onions and the peppers, cut in strips. Add the puréed tomato, thyme, bay leaf, salt and pepper and white wine. Simmer this sauce until it is somewhat reduced, about 10 minutes. Add it to the fish, combine well, and simmer until the fish is flaky, about 10 minutes more. Serves 4.

DORADA A LA SAL
Gilthead Baked in Salt

The salt forms an encasement for the fish, sealing in all the delicious juices. It is peeled away with the skin and the white flesh scooped out with a spoon to be served with the sauces. Because it's not possible to probe the fish while it bakes, timing the fish is fairly important. Measure it at the thickest part and allow 15 minutes in a fairly hot oven for every 2 cm, or about 20 minutes for a fish weighing 750 grams.

Oil a metal oven pan and put a layer of coarse rock salt on the bottom. Gut the fish, but do not scale it. Wash the fish and dry it well. Place it on top of the salt and completely cover the fish with more salt. Place it in a preheated hot oven. Remove when done. Crack the salt crust and very carefully peel it off (the skin usually adheres to the salt). Serve the fish onto individual plates and accompany with garlic mayonnaise or any other sauce (I like a mustard-flavoured hollandaise). Sea bass *(lubina)* is also baked *a la sal.*

SEA BASS

This is my own personal favourite, which I'd rather eat than steak or lamb chops any day. I prefer it very simply grilled: I place it on a preheated, oiled broiler pan and put under the broiler until the top is browned, about 8 minutes, and serve it without turning. However, because it is such an expensive fish, it merits fancier preparations.

LUBINA A LA ASTURIANA
Sea Bass, Asturias Style

1	kilo sea bass	150 ml. cider or white wine	
	salt and pepper	2	dozen clams
2	tablespoons oil		fried bread
1	small onion, chopped		parsley
1	teaspoon paprika		

Cut the fish in crosswise slices, season with salt and pepper and place in an oven dish. Pour over the oil, the chopped onion and sprinkle with the paprika. Add the cider and bake in a medium oven until the fish is cooked, about 20 minutes. While it is baking, steam the clams open and discard the shells. Reserve them in a little of their strained liquid. Place the fish on a serving platter and keep warm. Pour the juices in the pan through a sieve and add the clams. Pour this sauce over the fish and serve with triangles of fried bread and sprigs of parsley. Serves 4.

LUBINA CON SALSA DE CANGREJOS DE RIO
Sea Bass With Crayfish Sauce

4	small bass	1	dozen river crayfish
100	ml. oil	50	ml. brandy
6	cloves garlic	150	ml. white wine
	flour	1/2	teaspoon thyme

Clean the fish (one per person, each about 300 grams) and rub them with salt. Heat the oil in a pan large enough to hold the fish. Dredge the fish in flour and put them into the hot oil. Lower the heat and fry gently until they are browned on one side, about 5 minutes, then turn to cook the other sides. Add the crayfish which have been washed and split in half lengthwise, to the pan. When the bass have cooked, remove them to a serving dish and keep warm. Add the brandy to the pan, set it alight and shake the pan gently until the flames subside. Now add the white wine and thyme and cook the sauce for several minutes. Put the contents of the pan into a processor and chop it finely, then sieve the sauce, pressing hard on the crayfish shells. Reheat the sauce and pour it over the fish. Serves 4.

LUBINA CON GIBELURDIÑAS
Sea Bass with Wild Mushrooms

1	whole fish (about 1½ kilos)	50 ml. oil	
	salt and pepper	150 ml. white wine	
250	grams Chanterelles or other wild mushrooms, wiped clean	1 tablespoon parsley	

Clean the fish, scale it and rub with salt and pepper and let it sit for 30 minutes. Place it in an oiled oven dish and put in a moderately hot oven for 10 minutes. Then add the cleaned mushrooms to the pan (saving 2 of them) and pour over the oil. Return the fish to the oven to bake until it flakes easily, about 30 minutes in all. Baste it frequently with the liquid in the pan. Put the white wine, parsley and reserved mushrooms in the blender and whirl until puréed. Put it in a small saucepan and simmer. Place the fish on a serving dish with the cooked mushrooms and add the liquid in the pan to the saucepan. Heat thoroughly and pour over the fish. Serves 6.

SANCOCHO CANARIO
Fish with Canary Islands Red Sauce

This is typically made with *sama,* a Canary Islands fish for which either sea bass or a large sea bream can be substituted. The fish could be grilled instead of boiled and served with a *mojo verde,* green sauce in addition to the *mojo colorado,* red sauce.

1	kilo bass or bream	1	chili pepper
1/2	kilo potatoes	1/2	teaspoon cumin
2	cloves garlic	1	teaspoon paprika
	salt	2	tablespoons vinegar

Cut the fish into slices or into bone-free chunks. Peel the potatoes and, if small, quarter them, or cut into regular-sized chunks. Put them to cook in salted water to cover. When they are half cooked, about 10 minutes, add the pieces of fish and simmer about 8 minutes. Drain the fish and potatoes, reserving the liquid. In the mortar or blender crush the garlic with salt and the chili pepper, cumin, paprika and vinegar. Add 2 or 3 pieces of cooked potato and enough of the reserved cooking liquid to make a smooth sauce. Put the cooked fish and potatoes on a serving dish and pour some of the sauce over. Serves 4.

MERO A LA VINAGRETA
Grouper in Vinaigrette

This wonderful fish can be substituted in almost any of the preceding recipes. It seems especially good served cold with piquant sauces.

Poach a whole fish or steaks in a flavourful *court-bouillon,* to which have been added orange and lemon peels. Remove when flesh flakes easily and let cool. Chop hard-cooked eggs, onions, olives, capers or pickles and parsley. Stir in vinegar, oil, salt and pepper to taste. Serve the fish cold, accompanied by the sauce.

ANGULAS EN CAZUELA
Baby Eels with Garlic

This dish approaches mystique in Spain. No special occasion or holiday meal is complete without sizzling bowls of these tiny, almost transparent, baby eels. They are purchased already cooked (and often frozen), having been parboiled in water with tobacco to cleanse them.

For 1 serving: place 3 tablespoons oil in a small earthenware casserole with 1 clove garlic, sliced, and a small piece of chili pepper or dried sweet pepper. Heat it until the oil is very hot. Add 150 grams of *angulas* and toss them in the oil only until they are thoroughly heated and the oil is bubbling. They are not supposed to "fry" or they will dry out. Add 1 teaspoon water and serve immediately, while the oil is still bubbling.

ANGUILA AL ALL I PEBRE
Valencian Eel Stew

1 1/2	kilos eel	3	cloves garlic	
100	ml. oil	1	tablespoon parsley	
1	tablespoon paprika	1	dozen blanched and toasted almonds	
1/2	litre hot water		or 8 toasted walnuts	
1/4	teaspoon saffron		salt and pepper	

Clean and skin the eel and cut it into 8 cm. lengths. Season with salt and pepper. In an earthenware casserole, heat the oil. When it is hot, remove the casserole from the heat and stir in the paprika. Then add the hot water and return to the heat, letting it cook for several minutes. Then add the pieces of eel, adding more water if necessary so they are just covered. In the mortar or blender crush the saffron, garlic, parsley, almonds or walnuts and salt and pepper. Dissolve this paste in some of the liquid from the casserole and add it to the stew. Cook several minutes more until the eel is done. Cooked vegetables in season — peas, broad beans or green beans — can be added to the stew. Garnish with parsley. Serves 6.

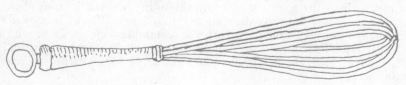

CONGRIO A LA RIOJANA
Conger Eel, Rioja Style

1 1/4	kilos conger eel	2	tomatoes, peeled and puréed
100	ml. oil	500	ml. red wine
	flour		salt and pepper
1/4	kilo sweet red peppers	1	chili pepper (optional)
6	cloves garlic, sliced		

Clean the conger and cut it into slices. Rub them with salt and pepper and dredge in flour. Heat the oil in a casserole and fry the peppers, which have been seeded and cut in wide strips. Remove them to a plate when softened. Add the garlic and when it is just golden, add the floured slices of conger. Brown them on both sides, then add the puréed tomatoes, fried peppers, wine, salt and pepper and chili pepper, if desired. Cook for 15 minutes until the conger is cooked.

SEAFOOD STEWS

Some are more like soups, others like casseroles, but all have two or more kinds of fish and shellfish. Savouring them is like touring all the coastlines of Spain.

ABAJA DE ALGECIRAS
Seafood Stew, Algeciras Style

1 1/2 to 2	kilos fish — hake, angler, grey mullet, skate, tuna, grouper, etc.	1	tomato, peeled and chopped
100	ml. white wine	2	tablespoons chopped parsley
	salt	150	grams day-old bread
100	ml. oil	1/2	teaspoon saffron
1	onion, chopped	6	peppercorns
1	clove garlic, chopped	5	clove garlic, whole

Clean the fish and cut it into slices, fillets or pieces, according to the type and size of fish. Put 2 litres of water into a large pot with the white wine, salt. Bring to a boil and lower heat so it simmers. Add the pieces of fish and cook them just until done, about 12 minutes. Remove them with a skimmer to a separate plate (or strain through a colander, reserving the broth). Heat 50 ml. oil in another pot and sauté the chopped onion and garlic until softened. Add the tomato and the parsley and fry until tomato is reduced to a sauce. Now add about half the broth in which the fish cooked, or enough to provide 1 bowl of soup for each person to be served. Crumble the bread with the fingers and add it to the soup and let it cook. In the mortar crush the saffron, peppercorns and 1 clove of garlic. Dissolve in a little of the soup and stir into the soup. Add salt to taste. Let this cook another 5 minutes and serve the soup as a first course. Place the cooked fish in a casserole. In mortar or blender crush the remaining 4 cloves garlic with the rest of the oil and a little salt. Beat in about 100 ml. of the remaining broth and pour over the fish. Heat the fish in this sauce and serve with a garnish of parsley and lemon. Serves 6 to 8.

TUMBET DE PESCADO MALLORQUIN
Mallorcan Fish and Aubergine Casserole

This can be made with any combination of fish or with frozen fish fillets.

3/4	kilo fish fillets	1	onion, chopped
1	lemon	1	clove garlic, chopped
100	ml. oil		bay leaf
50	ml. white wine		salt and pepper
1/2	kilo potatoes, sliced	3	large tomatoes, peeled, seeded and
2	aubergines		chopped
	flour	1/2	teaspoon cinnamon
2	large sweet red peppers	1	teaspoon sugar

Put the fish in an oven dish, salt it and squeeze the juice of the lemon over it. Drizzle with 1 tablespoon oil and pour in the white wine. Bake the fish until partially done, only about 10 minutes, and remove. Meanwhile, prepare each of the vegetables. Put the sliced potatoes in a frying pan with 2 tablespoons of oil, fry them for a few minutes, then cover the pan and let them cook, turning occasionally, until almost done. Peel the aubergines and slice them. Dredge in flour and fry in oil (or, to decrease oil in this dish, brush the slices with oil, put them on a tin and bake until they are tender). Roast the peppers, peel them and cut in wide strips. In a saucepan, heat remaining oil and sauté the chopped onion and garlic until softened. Add the prepared tomatoes, bay leaf, salt and pepper, cinnamon, sugar, and the liquid from the pan in which the fish baked. Cook this sauce for about 15 minutes, then sieve it or purée in processor. It should be fairly thick. In a *greixonera*, an oval, earthenware casserole, or other oven dish place a layer of half the potatoes, half the fish and half of the aubergine and peppers.

231

Repeat the layers and cover with the prepared sauce. Put in a medium hot oven until bubbly, about 15 minutes. Serves 4 to 6.

CALDERETA ASTURIANA
Asturian Fish Stew

2 to 3 kilos solid-fleshed fish — angler, mullet, redfish, scorpionfish, gurnard, bass
1 kilo shellfish — prawns, clams, mussels, razorshells
1 kilo onions, thinly sliced
4 tablespoons chopped parsley

1 small tin pimento
freshly ground pepper
grated nutmeg
cayenne
200 ml. oil
50 ml. sherry
250 ml. white wine

Clean the fish. Leave small ones whole and cut large ones into pieces. Scrub the clams; scrape and wash the mussels well; leave prawns unpeeled. In a large pot or fish kettle with a tight-fitting lid, put a layer of the sliced onions, then a layer of fish. Put the scrappiest, least good fish in the bottom layers and the best fish at the top. Continue layering onions and fish, sprinkling them with the chopped parsley. Purée the pimentos in the blender with a little water. Drizzle this sauce onto the fish (or substitute paprika). Sprinkle with pepper, nutmeg and cayenne. When the pot is filled, pour over the oil, sherry and wine and just a little water. Cover the pot, bring to a boil, then simmer gently for 15 minutes. Serve the stew in the same pot. Serves 8. Instead of the sherry and white wine, a *vino rancio* can be used, or cider or champagne.

ZARZUELA
Seafood Operetta

4 servings each of 3 or 4 different kinds of fish, for example: "meaty" fish such as angler, conger or lobster; flaky fish such as bass, grouper, bream, meagre, gurnard, and lean, delicate fish such as hake, sole, turbot. The servings can be cut into fillets or steaks.
1/2 kilo squid, cleaned and cut in rings and dredged in flour
1/2 kilo mussels, cleaned, steamed open and empty half-shells discarded
1/2 kilo clams scrubbed, steamed open and half-shell discarded (strain and save liquid from cooking mussels and clams)
8 large prawns, or 4 prawns and 4 Dublin Bay prawns (sea crayfish). The large red prawns, *carabineros*, are a good choice

100 ml. oil
1 onion, finely chopped
3 large tomatoes, peeled, seeded and finely chopped
50 ml. sherry or white wine
50 ml. brandy, rum or, for those who like the taste, anise brandy
1 bay leaf
1/2 teaspoon saffron
2 cloves garlic
6 blanched and toasted almonds
2 plain biscuits (*galletas Maria*)
salt and pepper
dash of cayenne
chopped parsley
lemon wedges
triangles of fried bread
pitted black olives or anchovy-stuffed green olives (optional)

This is an opera in three acts, a lavish but simply staged production if all the ingredients are prepared before starting to cook. The dish is usually served in a shallow earthenware casserole or a paella pan. A separate frying pan is used to sauté all the ingredients first. They are then combined to finish cooking in the casserole.

Heat some of the oil in the frying pan and fry the floured pieces of squid (the flour keeps the oil from splattering) until they are golden and transfer them to the casserole. Next add the pieces of angler, conger or lobster, sautéing them very slowly, turning once to brown the other side. The pieces of flaky fish (bass, grouper, etc.) can be added while the first are still cooking, as they take less time. Remove them as they are done to the casserole. Then fry the pieces of delicate fish, which only need quick browning on either side. Add more oil to the pan as needed. Now sauté the prawns and crayfish (prawns can be peeled, leaving tails and heads intact). Place them in the casserole and add the prepared mussels and clams. In the remaining oil in the frying pan sauté the finely chopped onions just until soft. Add the prepared tomatoes and fry for a few minutes. Then add the sherry or wine and the brandy, rum or anise and the bay leaf. In the mortar or blender crush the saffron, garlic, almonds, biscuits, salt and pepper and cayenne. Dissolve in a little liquid and add to the tomatoes with the strained broth from the mussels and clams. Cook a few minutes, then pour this sauce over the fish and shellfish in the casserole. Shake the casserole to distribute the sauce and continue cooking for about 10 minutes. Serve the casserole garnished with chopped parsley, lemon wedges, fried bread and a sprinkling of olives, if desired. Serves 4. The *suquillo del pescador,* fisherman's stew, is a similar Catalan dish, soupier and without the tomatoes.

SALT COD

It used to be in the small pueblo where I live that there were no supermarkets. Staples like sugar, flour and garbanzos were purchased in tiny shops, often the front room of someone's house. Sugar was scooped from bins, oil poured from jugs into a bottle that was perpetually recycled and wine was measured into the drinking glass, later to be set at the father's place. If you bought from the tiny selection of tinned foods — tuna, sardines and marmalades — the shopkeeper offered to open the tin, as no one had can openers in their homes. On my first forays into these shops, there were a few things I managed to avoid. One was the ropes of evil-looking sausages hanging from the beams, sweating and dripping a little in the summer heat. Another was the chunks of salt pork which gave a rancid pungency to the shop. The third was some strange-smelling stuff which looked like grey bats hanging on a line. This was *bacalao,* dry salted cod, and, village women bought a lot of it. I first ate bacalao on *Viernes Santo,* Good

Previous page, Baby eels with garlic, a Basque speciality (recipe, page 229)

Facing page, Hake, Basque style (recipe, page 221).

Friday, while processions were wending their way through village streets; while penitents, many barefoot with candles followed the images and the sombre throbbing drums. In a tapa bar — which, as on any Spanish holiday, was doing a brisk business — I was served two fishy tapas, one in a sauce, the other a croquette. They were both made of bacalao.

Since then I've learned to prepare it in many more ways, all of them quite delicious.

Though the Basques seem to have the most and the best recipes for bacalao, some others of interest are *a la manchega,* with anise brandy; *soldaditos de Pavía,* fried in a crisp batter; *porrusalda,* with leeks.

Salt cod is the "in" dish on fancy menus these days, though it's still dearly loved by simple village people all over Spain, especially during Holy Week. Today you can buy it in supermarkets, cut in pieces and packaged in plastic. Quality and price vary. The larger the fish, the better it is and, though dry, it should never be stiff as a board, but slightly pliable. The best bacalao has a thin skin and is grey rather than yellowish.

Clean bacalao in running water. Then put it to soak in water to cover for 12 to 24 hours, changing the water 2 or 3 times. Drain it, then cut into pieces, removing all skin and bones. Do not salt a dish made with salt cod until tasting it at the end of cooking time.

BACALAO A LA VIZCAINA
Salt Cod, Biscay Style

There are those who say this dish should be made only with dried peppers and no tomatoes and others who say that tomatoes must be included. In either case, the sauce is a deep ruddy red. The dried peppers *(ñoras* or *pimientos choriceros)* are first soaked in boiling water.

1	kilo salt cod, soaked overnight	1	kilo tomatoes, chopped
12	dried peppers (not chili), soaked overnight	2	slices toasted bread
			chili pepper or cayenne
150	ml. oil	2	sweet red peppers
2	onions, chopped	6	cloves garlic

Put the fish, soaked overnight, in a pot with fresh water and heat it almost to boiling. Remove from the heat and take out the fish, saving the liquid. Cut it into regular sized pieces, discarding all bone. Heat 100 ml. oil in a saucepan and sauté the chopped onions. Add the chopped tomatoes and fry for several minutes, then add the soaked peppers, the bread and chili pepper. Add some of the liquid from the fish and let this sauce cook for several minutes on a hot fire. Add more liquid and simmer for 30 minutes adding extra liquid as needed. Purée the sauce in a processor then pass it through a fine sieve. Spread some of the sauce in an earthenware casserole, place the pieces of cod on top and cover with the remaining sauce, adding a little more liquid if sauce seems too thick. The peppers can either be roasted or cleaned of seeds, cut in wide strips and sautéed in oil until very soft. Garnish the top of the casserole with these strips of pepper and put in a medium-hot oven until bubbly, about 15 minutes. Meanwhile, fry the garlic, slivered, in the remaining oil. Drizzle the top of the fish with the garlic and serve. Serves 6.

BACALAO AL PIL PIL
Sizzling Cod

1	kilo salt cod, cut in 12 pieces and soaked 12 to 24 hours	10	cloves garlic
		1	chili pepper
150	ml. oil	2	teaspoons flour

Put the soaked cod in a pan with water to cover and heat until it almost boils. Remove from heat and drain, saving the liquid. Remove any bones and scales, but do not skin the fish. Pat it dry on a clean cloth. Put the oil in a flameproof casserole and heat it. Add the garlic, cut in crosswise slivers, and the chili pepper, seeds removed and broken into several pieces. Fry until the garlic is toasted lightly and skim out with the chili. Reserve. Put the pieces of cod into the oil in one layer, skin side down and cook for a few minutes. Then sprinkle with the flour and, grasping the casserole with pot-holders, swirl it gently from side to side, lifting it off the stove slightly. Add a spoonful of the water in which the fish heated and swirl it in. The gelatinous quality of the skin causes the oil and liquid to amalgamate into a sauce the consistency of cream. Add a few more spoonfuls of liquid and cook the fish about 10 to 15 minutes. Sprinkle with the reserved garlic and chili, and serve. Serves 6.

BACALAO AL AJO ARRIERO
Salt Cod, Muledrivers' Style

Before the days of modern transport, the muleteers who carried fresh seafood inland from the coasts were vital to the economy. Obviously, like modern-day truckers, they ate very well in the *posadas* and *ventas* en route, excellent and unpretentious dishes like this one. So good is this that the same preparation is used for lobster!

1	kilo salt cod, cut in thin strips and soaked	2	red peppers, cut in strips
		1	teaspoon paprika
100	ml. oil	200	ml. tomato sauce
8	cloves garlic		parsley
1	chili pepper		

Put the fish in a pot with water bring it almost to a boil and drain. Remove all skin and bones and, with the fingers, tear the cod into thin strips. Pat dry. Heat the oil in a casserole and fry the chopped garlic and chili pepper, broken into small pieces. Add the red peppers and fry a few minutes, then the pieces of cod. Continue frying this mixture for several more minutes, then add the paprika and the tomato sauce. Depending on the consistency of the tomato sauce more liquid might be required. Simmer for 15 minutes and serve garnished with chopped parsley. Serves 6.

ALBONDIGAS DE BACALAO
Codfish Balls

350 grams salt cod, soaked	pinch of cinnamon
1 bay leaf	grating of nutmeg
1 thick slice bread	1 tablespoon chopped parsley
1 egg, beaten	flour
pepper	oil

Cook the desalted cod in water with the bay leaf for 5 minutes without letting it boil. Remove and drain, squeezing out all the liquid. Remove all skin and bones and put the cod in the processor (or mortar). Soak the slice of bread in milk until softened. Squeeze it out and add to the processor with the pepper, cinnamon, nutmeg, parsley and 1 tablespoon of flour. Process until smooth. Make small balls of the paste, roll them in flour and fry in oil until nicely browned. They may be served as is or added to an almond or hazelnut sauce.

SALMON A LA GALLEGA
Salmon, Galician Style

Boil equal parts of *aguardiente de orujo,* clear brandy distilled from grapes (or use French *marc* or Italian *grappa),* and water with bay leaves, peppercorns, clove and onion. Reduce heat and poach salmon steaks in the liquid. Remove from heat and let cool in the liquid. Marinate, refrigerated, for several days.

SALMON A LA RIBEREÑA
Salmon, Asturias Style

4 salmon steaks	100 grams diced ham
flour	1 tablespoon flour
4 tablespoons butter	100 ml. cider or champagne
2 tablespoons oil	salt and pepper

Salt the salmon steaks, let them sit for 30 minutes, then dredge them with flour. Heat the butter and oil in a frying pan and put in the fish, moderating the heat so the fish cooks in the time it takes to brown both sides, about 10 minutes. Remove to a platter and keep warm. In the same fat sauté the diced ham. Stir in the flour, then add the cider or champagne and salt and pepper. Simmer, stirring, until the sauce is thickened, adding a small quantity of fish stock if needed to thin the sauce. Pour over the salmon (or reheat the fish in the sauce) and serve with sprigs of parsley.

TRUCHAS A LA ASTURIANA
Trout, Asturias Style

Melt lard in a frying pan and fry a little chopped salt pork or bacon. Clean the trout, dredge them in flour and fry in the lard, turning to brown both sides. Garnish with fried salt pork.

TRUCHAS A LA NAVARRA
Trout, Navarre Style

Slit fairly large trout (350 grams) along the belly, removing the backbone, but leaving head and tail intact. Wash and pat dry. Put a thin slice of *serrano* ham inside the cavity. Salt the fish and let it sit for 15 minutes. Then dredge it in flour and sauté it gently in oil until nicely browned on both sides. Serve with lemon.

TRUCHA A LA ZAMORANA
Trout, Zamora Style

4	trout, cleaned	2	tablespoons vinegar
4	tablespoons oil	100	ml. water
4	cloves garlic	5	peppercorns
2	tablespoons chopped parsley		

Salt the trout and let them sit for 15 minutes. In a pan large enough to hold the fish put the oil, slivered garlic, chopped parsley, vinegar, water and peppercorns. Bring to a boil, reduce the heat so the liquid just simmers, and add the trout. Cover the pan and steam the trout just until done, about 8 minutes. Remove from heat. Serve hot or let the fish cool in the liquid.

TENCAS EN ESCABECHE
Marinated Tench

Clean the fish and fillet it or cut into slices. Put it into a bowl and cover with the following marinade. Mix 100 ml. oil, 50 ml. vinegar, 1 sliced onion, 2 crushed cloves of garlic, 1/2 teaspoon paprika, 1 sprig parsley, 1 sprig fennel, 1 bay leaf, 10 peppercorns and salt. Marinate for 2 hours. Drain well. Then flour the pieces of fish and fry them in oil. The fish can also be poached in equal parts of the marinade and water. Other lake fish — *carpa,* carp; *barbo,* barbel; *sábalo,* shad — can be prepared in the same manner.

HUEVAS DE PESCADO
Fish Roe

The roe, or eggs, of many different fish are used, though those of hake are considered a delicacy.

Wash the roe, encased in its membrane, gently. Bring a pot of water to a boil and add a bay leaf, slice of onion, salt and a slice of lemon. Lower the heat to a simmer and poach the roe very gently for about 10 minutes. Drain.

To fry: cut into lengthwise strips or slices, dredge them in flour, dip in beaten egg and again in flour. Sauté in butter or oil until golden on both sides. Serve with parsley and a lemon wedge.

As an hors d'oeuvre: Slice the roe and arrange it on lettuce leaves. Make a vinaigrette with chopped onion, chopped tinned pimento, chopped parsley, chopped hard-cooked egg, oil and vinegar and salt and pepper. Spoon this over the roe.

PRAWNS

These being, perhaps, my favourite food in the world, I was all set to put down lots of recipes for their preparation. However, as I combed through my collections of Spanish recipes, I found only a few! Prawns are served, if they are beautifully fresh, in their pristine glory — boiled for an instant in sea water and adorned with nothing more than lemon wedges. The floors of *tapa* bars are crunchy with the shells. They're also much appreciated for their baroque beauty as garnish — on paella, zarzuela or plate of hors d'oeuvres. Additionally, here are a few very Spanish ways of cooking prawns.

GAMBAS AL PIL PIL
Sizzling Prawns

This dish, favourite tapa bar fare, is supposed to arrive at the table *pil-pileando,* a word that sounds like spluttering oil. It is traditionally made in individual earthenware ramekins and topped with a plate of chunks of bread for sopping the savoury juices. One daren't remove the plate nor taste the first morsel until the oil stops sizzling, for fear of singeing the tongue.

Per serving: Put 3 tablespoons oil, 1 chopped clove of garlic, 1 minced piece of chili pepper and a pinch of paprika, into an earthenware ramekin. Put it on the heat until the oil is quite hot. Add 10 peeled prawns and cook only until they turn pink and curl slightly. Serve immediately.

GAMBAS A LA PLANCHA
Grilled Prawns

Select the largest prawns for this preparation. Wash them, drain well and pat dry. Brush a grill (griddle) with oil then with salted water and heat it until the salt shows white. Lay the unpeeled prawns on the grill and cook them, brushing with oil, until they turn pink. Turn and grill the other side. Serve with an alioli sauce or a romesco and a tomato sauce (Chapter 12). Don't forget the "lemon soup" — fingerbowls with a slice of lemon floating in them.

LANGOSTINOS SALTEADOS
Sautéed Prawns

1	kilo large prawns	2	tablespoons tomato sauce
50	ml. oil	1/4	teaspoon thyme
2	tablespoons chopped onion		salt and pepper
1	clove chopped garlic		chopped parsley
50	ml. dry sherry		

Peel the prawns, leaving heads and tails intact. Wash and dry them. In a pan heat the oil and sauté the chopped onion and garlic. When it is softened, add the prawns and turn up the heat. Stir-fry briefly, then add the sherry, tomato sauce, thyme and salt and pepper, with a little additional water as needed. Cook just until the prawns are pink and curled slightly. Serve garnished with chopped parsley. Freshwater crayfish, *cangrejos de río,* can be prepared in the same way.

ALMEJAS A LA MARINERA
Clams, Fisherman Style

This dish appears, with little variation, in all the countries bordering the Mediterranean — a little oil, garlic, wine and clams and a sprinkling of parsley. This version, very simple, adds the tang of tomatoes.

1	kilo clams, well scrubbed	1	bay leaf
75	ml. oil		pepper
1	small onion, minced		chopped parsley
4	cloves garlic, minced	50	ml. white wine
1	kilo tomatoes, peeled, seeded and finely chopped		

Heat the oil in a deep frying pan or casserole. Add the minced onion and garlic and fry. Then add the prepared tomatoes, bay leaf, pepper and white wine and simmer the sauce until the tomatoes are reduced, about 10 minutes. Then add the clams. On a high heat cook the clams just until the shells open, shaking the pan or stirring constantly. Serve in small bowls garnished with chopped parsley.

ALMEJAS CON ALUBIAS BLANCAS
Clams and Beans

250	grams white beans, soaked overnight	1	teaspoon salt
	onion	1	kilo clams
	garlic	1	2 teaspoon saffron

bay, thyme, parsley   1   tablespoon breadcrumbs
3   tablespoons oil   salt and pepper

Put the beans to cook in water to cover with the onion, cut in quarters, the clove of garlic, and the bay, thyme and parsley. When the beans are half-cooked, about 40 minutes, add the oil and salt. Meanwhile, scrub the clams very well and put them in a pot with a very little water and steam them open over a high heat, shaking the pan until the clam shells open. Remove them immediately from the heat. Strain the liquid and reserve it. Shuck the clams, discarding the shells. In the mortar, crush the saffron with a clove garlic and breadcrumbs. Dissolve in a little of the liquid from the beans. Now add the shucked clams to the beans with the mortar mixture. Simmer for a minute and let sit for a few minutes before serving. Serves 4 to 6.

MUSSELS

An extraordinarily inexpensive source of excellent protein and delicious basis for many dishes. Use mussels in any way suitable for pricier shellfish such as oysters or scallops; add them to pasta sauces; star them in seafood cocktails; use in soups. Mussels sold in Spanish markets are farmed in mussel beds and are safe to eat year round — as long as they are alive and shells tightly closed when tapped (see chapter 2 for more information on marketing and storing). Mussels come tangled in a seaweedy-looking growth called the beard. Pull it down to the hinge and cut it off with a knife. Use a dull knife to scrape off the various protuberances and scum on the mussels' shells. Wash them very well in running water or several changes of water.

To steam mussels open, put the cleaned mussels in a deep frying pan or pot. Add very little water (about 50 ml. for 1 kilo of mussels), as they will release quite a lot of liquid when they open. Cover the pot and put it on a hot fire. When the liquid begins to boil, shake the pot vigorously back and forth or remove the lid and, with a long-handled skimmer, stir them well. The shells should open within minutes. Remove them as they open or remove the whole pot from the heat.

Mussels served plump and juicy are a delight. Allowed to overcook and they are not very appetizing. Discard any mussels that do not open. Mussels can be served at this point. Or they may be shucked, both shells discarded, or, if to be served on the half-shell, only the empty shell discarded.

Strain the liquid in the pan through a sieve lined with dampened paper towelling. It can be incorporated in sauces, and soups. It is quite salty, so don't add salt to a sauce without tasting first. To store mussels, pour the strained broth over them in a bowl or jar, cover tightly and refrigerate. Use within two days. The whole mussel is edible, but, in large specimens, the mantle, or dark outer rim, which is quite chewy, can be removed. For those who are lesser *aficionados* of mussels, try chopping them before adding to sauces and soups.

MEJILLONES A LA MARINERA
Mussels, Sailors' Style

1	kilo mussels, cleaned	50 ml. water	
2	tablespoons oil	2	tablespoons fine breadcrumbs
4	cloves garlic, chopped		freshly ground pepper
50	ml. white wine	2	tablespoons chopped parsley

Put the oil, chopped garlic, wine and water into a pot big enough to hold the mussels. Bring it to a boil and add the mussels. Cover the pot and shake it until shells open. Sprinkle in the breadcrumbs, pepper and chopped parsley and cook for another minute. Serve mussels and their broth in soup bowls. For a soupier version, increase wine and water. If broth seems sandy, remove mussels before adding breadcrumbs. Strain the broth, then reheat. Serves 4.

SCALLOPS

These shells don't close tightly, so they're very easy to open by inserting a knife between the shells and cutting the muscle at the hinge. Or they can be steamed open (as for mussels, above) or opened in a hot oven. They will probably need rinsing to remove grit. Cut away the mantle, which is tough, and the black stomach sac. Both the white muscle and the coral "foot" are edible.

VIEIRAS A LA GALLEGA
Scallops, Galicia Style

12-16 scallops (coquilles St. Jacques)		salt and pepper	
3	tablespoons oil	1/8 teaspoon cinnamon	
1	onion, finely chopped		pinch of cayenne
1	clove garlic, chopped	3	tablespoons fine breadcrumbs
1	teaspoon paprika		oil
100	ml. white wine	1	tablespoon chopped parsley
50	ml. Galician *aguardiente de orujo* (or *marc* or *grappa*, the French and Italian equivalents) or use brandy		lemon wedges

Open the scallops as described. Cut off and reserve the coral. Clean 4 of the shells and oil them. Place 3 or 4 of the white scallop muscles in each and set on an oven tin. In a frying pan heat the oil and sauté the chopped onion and garlic. Chop the corals and add to the pan with the paprika. Then add the wine and *aguardiente,* salt and pepper, cinnamon and cayenne. Cook this sauce until it is reduced. Spoon it over the prepared scallops. Top with breadcrumbs which have been mixed with the parsley and drizzle with a little oil. Put under the broiler or at the top of a hot oven just until the crumbs are lightly browned. Serve immediately with lemon wedges. Serves 4 as a starter.

CRAB

Crabs should be purchased live and cooked immediately. They may be cleaned and then cooked or cooked and then cleaned. The latter is probably the simplest approach. Bring a large pot of salted water (150 grams salt to 4 litres of water) or sea water to a boil. Put in the crabs, bring the water again to a boil, then simmer for 15 minutes. Remove crabs and plunge them in cold water to stop the cooking.

To clean and extract the crab meat, place the cooked crab on its back and twist off the legs and claws. With thumbs under the tail flap, push upwards until the body snaps away from the shell. Remove and discard the mouth, stomach bag and spongy gills. Scrape all soft brown meat from the shell and reserve it. Save the liquid in the shells. Discard hard, finger-like protuberances, and extract remaining meat. Scoop white meat from leg sockets. Crack the claws and legs and remove meat from them. The shells may be trimmed, scrubbed and oiled for use as a casserole.

TXANGURRO
Basque Crab Casseroles

4	spider crabs	1	tablespoon chopped parsley
50	ml. oil		salt and pepper
1	onion, finely chopped		dash cayenne
250	ml. tomato sauce	4	tablespoons fine breadcrumbs
100	ml. brandy or white wine		butter

Cook the crabs and extract the meat as described above. Four crabs provide enough meat for 2 servings. However, the crab can be "extended" with the addition of a flaky fish to the casserole. In a frying pan sauté the onion in the oil until soft. Add the tomato sauce, the brandy or wine, parsley, salt and pepper and cayenne and simmer about 15 minutes, adding a little water or stock if the sauce seems too thick — it should be the consistency of thick cream. Add the crabmeat to the sauce (and cooked fish, if you are using it). Spoon the mixture into 2 or 4 of the cleaned and oiled shells. Top with the breadcrumbs and dot with butter. Put under the broiler or in the top of a hot oven just until slightly browned. This dish can, of course, be made with tinned crab meat. Put it in scallop shells or ramekins to gratin it.

LOBSTER

Most common in markets is the *langosta,* or clawless, spiny lobster. Buy them live. To cook, place in a large pot of cold water and bring them very slowly to a boil. Then simmer for about 20 minutes. Drain. While still hot (use a cloth to protect hands), place the lobster on its back and with sharp scissors split the underside of the tail shell lengthwise and extract the tail meat. Discard the stomach, a sac near the head; the dark, intestinal vein which runs through the tail meat, and the spongy lungs. Save the eggs or coral, if there are any, and the green liver or tomalley. Cooked lobster meat is usually served cold with mayonnaise.

Lobster which is to be grilled, baked or sautéed needs to be cleaned before cooking. Kill it by inserting the knife between the head and the body and severing the spinal cord. Slit the undershell lengthwise and remove stomach sac and vein. Or, cut the whole lobster in half lengthwise and remove viscera.

LANGOSTA A LA MALLORQUINA
Grilled Lobster, Mallorca Style

2	lobsters (each about 750 grams)	1/2	teaspoon pepper
100	ml. oil		ajoaceite or mayonnaise
50	ml. vinegar		lemon wedges

Cut the lobsters in half lengthwise, allowing 1/2 lobster per person. In a blender whisk the oil, vinegar and pepper together. Brush the lobster halves with this and grill them over charcoal, brushing them with more of the basting sauce, until done, about 12 minutes. Serve with the garlic sauce or mayonnaise and lemon wedges. The liver and roe can be mashed and combined with the sauces if desired.

LANGOSTA A LA COSTA BRAVA
Lobster, Costa Brava Style

2	lobsters, each about 3/4 kilo	1	teaspoon paprika
100	ml. oil	1	dozen almonds or hazelnuts,
1	onion, finely chopped		skinned, blanched and toasted
1	bay leaf	1	tablespoon parsley
1	teaspoon thyme	3	ladyfingers *(bizcochos secos)* or use
1	piece orange peel		toasted bread
1/2	teaspoon saffron	50	grams dark chocolate
2	cloves garlic		dash of cayenne

After severing the spinal cord, open the lobsters and cut the meat from the shell into chunks. Save all the liquid as well as the liver and roe, if there are any. Heat the oil in a casserole and sauté the finely chopped onion. Add the pieces of lobster and sauté briefly on a high heat with the bay leaf, thyme and orange peel. Meanwhile in mortar or blender crush the saffron, garlic, paprika, nuts, parsley, ladyfingers, chocolate and cayenne. Add the juices from the lobster and the liver and roe. Dissolve in a little white wine or a stock made by boiling the lobster shell. Pour into the casserole and cook the lobster in the sauce for about 15 minutes. Add additional liquid as needed. Serves 4.

Snails, already cooked, can be added to this dish with the sauce.

BOGAVANTE A LA GALLEGA
Lobster, Galician Style

1	large lobster (1½ kilos)	1	tomato, peeled and chopped
	salt and pepper	100 ml. white wine	
100 ml. oil		1	bay leaf
1	onion, finely chopped	1	teaspoon paprika
2	cloves garlic, chopped		

Cut the spinal cord of the lobster, open it and cut the meat into chunks and remove from the shell. Crack the claws and extract the meat from them. Save all the liquid and the liver and roe. Heat the oil in a frying pan or casserole and sauté the chopped onion and garlic. When they are softened, add the chopped tomato and fry for a few minutes. Then add the pieces of lobster. Stir in the wine, bay leaf, paprika and the liquid from the lobster as well as the chopped liver and roe. Cook, covered, about 15 minutes. Serves 3 to 4.

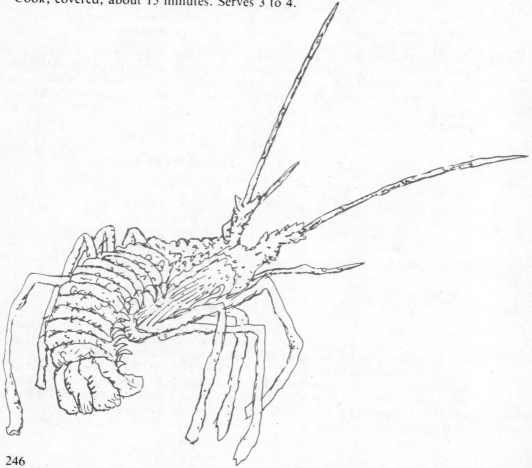

SQUID, CUTTLEFISH AND OCTOPUS

The great tentacle adventure needn't be scary. The squid, *calamar,* is the most delicate of this trio. Its body is a slender pouch out of which protrudes a head with short tentacles. Grasp the head and pull gently. It will come away from the body pouch bringing the innards with it. Still inside is the cartilage, which just looks like a strip of transparent plastic. Grasp the top of it and pull and it should come out in one piece. Rinse out the pouch and pull off the purple-coloured membrane covering it. The wing flaps will come off too. Save them and the pouch. Now, cut off the tentacles just above the eyes. Save the tentacles, pulling off their outer membrane. Discard the remaining head and innards — unless you need the ink. The ink is enclosed in a tiny silver sac, like a dot of mercury, along the innards. Cut it free without breaking. (Tiny plastic envelopes of squids' ink can be purchased in many markets, useful for making squid in ink sauce with frozen squid, which contain little ink.) The squid is now ready for cooking. Whether fried, poached or braised, it cooks in little time.

Cuttlefish *(jibia)* is often found already dressed. If not, the fish vendor will usually do it for you. Otherwise, slit the wide body section open, remove and discard the cuttlebone and innards. The flesh is usually cut into pieces for slow braising.

Octopus, *pulpo,* needs long, slow cooking. To avoid unnecessary queasiness about cooking it, simply dump it whole into a pot of boiling water and cook for 15 minutes. Drain it and put in a fresh pot of water with salt, bay, onions and celery and cook it until tender, about 3 hours. Drain. Then use kitchen scissors to cut the flesh and tentacles into pieces, discarding the stomach, eyes and mouth beak.

CALAMARES A LA ROMANA
Fried Squid Rings

A la romana, Roman style, means floured and fried. Prepare squid as described above. With scissors cut the body pouch into rings about 1½ cm. wide. Dry them well. Dredge in flour, then put in a sieve and shake lightly to remove excess flour. Fry the rings and tentacles in deep hot oil until they are golden and crisp. Serve with lemon wedges.

CALAMARES EN SU TINTA
Squid in Inky Sauce

This dish is also made with *chipirones,* tiny cuttlefish.

1	kilo small squid	100 ml. tomato sauce	
4	tablespoons fine breadcrumbs	100 ml. white wine	
2	cloves garlic	1	bay leaf
	flour		salt and pepper
50	ml. oil		dash of cayenne
1	onion, finely chopped		chopped parsley

Clean the squid as described, saving the ink sacs in a cup. Finely chop the wing flaps and tentacles and mix with the breadcrumbs and 1 clove minced garlic. Stuff the squid with this mixture and close them with toothpicks. Dredge in flour, shake off excess and sauté them in the hot oil until they are lightly browned. Remove them to a casserole. In the oil (or use fresh oil if flour bits have blackened in the pan) sauté the chopped onion and remaining clove garlic until soft. Add the tomato sauce, wine, bay leaf, salt and pepper and cayenne. Simmer for a few minutes, then pour over the squid in the casserole. Cover and cook until they are very tender, about 25 minutes, adding additional stock if necessary. A few minutes before they are done, break the ink sacs with the back of a spoon and dilute the ink in a little white wine. Stir into the casserole and cook another few minutes. Garnish with chopped parsley and serve accompanied by white rice or pieces of fried bread.

CALAMARES RELLENOS
Stuffed Squid

1	kilo medium squid	50	ml. oil
200	grams minced beef		flour
50	grams ham, chopped	1	onion, chopped
	grated nutmeg	1	green pepper, chopped
1 1/2	teaspoons salt	1	clove garlic, chopped
1	clove garlic, minced	5	tomatoes, peeled, seeded and
3	tablespoons breadcrumbs		chopped (or large tin tomatoes)
1	teaspoon lemon juice		pepper and dash of cloves
1	egg, beaten	100	ml. white wine

Clean the squid. Finely chop the tentacles and wing flaps and mix in a bowl with the minced beef, chopped ham, nutmeg, ½ teaspoon salt, minced garlic, breadcrumbs, lemon juice and beaten egg. Mix well with hands or a wooden spoon and stuff the squid. Fasten them with toothpicks. Heat the oil in a pan and flour the squid and fry them until golden. Remove them and add the chopped onion, pepper and garlic. Then add the prepared tomatoes, remainder of salt, pepper, cloves and wine. Bring to a boil, reduce to a simmer and return the squid to the pan. Cover and simmer until they are quite tender, about 45 minutes. Serves 6.

CHOCOS CON HABAS
Squid with Broad Beans

A speciality of the Atlantic coast by Cadiz and Huelva.

1	kilo squid	salt
100	ml. oil	freshly ground pepper
4	cloves garlic, slivered	chopped parsley
1/4	kilo shelled broad beans	

Clean the squid and cut them into rings or pieces. Heat the oil in a casserole and add the slivered garlic and the pieces of squid. Cook for 10 minutes, then add the shelled beans and about 100 ml. of water, the salt and pepper. Cover and cook until the beans are tender and most of the water has evaporated, about 15 minutes. Sprinkle with parsley. Serves 6.

JIBIA EN SALSA
Sauced Cuttlefish

3/4	kilo cuttlefish	1/2	teaspoon saffron
50	ml. oil	10	peppercorns
1	slice bread	2	potatoes, cut in dice
3	cloves garlic		salt
10	blanched almonds		parsley
1	green pepper		cooked peas (optional)
100	ml. white wine		

Clean the cuttlefish and cut into pieces. Heat the oil in a pan and fry the bread, garlic and almonds until they are toasted. Remove. Add the pieces of cuttlefish to the oil with the chopped green pepper and fry for several minutes. Then add the white wine. In mortar or blender crush the saffron and peppercorns with the toasted bread, garlic and almonds. Dissolve in a little water and add to the pan, stirring it in well. Add salt and cook the cuttlefish, covered, about 20 minutes. Then add the diced potatoes and continue cooking, adding water if needed, until everything is tender, another 20 minutes. Serve garnished with parsley and cooked peas, if desired. Serves 4.

PULPO A LA GALLEGA
Octopus, Galicia Style

With scissors cut cooked octopus into pieces about 2 cm. square. Put them in a wooden bowl with boiled potatoes. Sprinkle with salt, minced garlic, paprika and plenty of oil.

OSTRAS FRITAS
Fried Oysters

Pry open the oyster shells and scoop them out of the shells. Drizzle them with lemon juice, then dip in beaten egg, dredge in cornmeal and fry in hot oil until crisp. Drain briefly on absorbent paper, then stack the fried oysters in a pile and garnish with lemon wedges. Accompany them with a tomato sauce.

OSTIONES A LA GADITANA
Oysters, Cadiz Style

Ostiones are the so-called Portuguese oyster. Open the oysters and put them on an oven tin. Mix breadcrumbs, chopped parsley, minced garlic and ground pepper and spoon over the oysters. Drizzle them with oil and put in a hot oven just until the edges curl. Serve with lemon.

CANGREJOS DE RIO AL JEREZ
River Crayfish Jerez Style

1	kilo live crayfish	1	tablespoon chopped parsley
100 ml. oil			salt and pepper
1	small onion, chopped		dash of cayenne
6	cloves garlic, chopped	100 ml. dry sherry	
1 2 teaspoon thyme			

Wash the crayfish in several changes of water. To eviscerate them, grasp the middle of the three tail flaps and give it a sharp pull and twist. The vein will pull out with the fin. Heat the oil in a large pot or casserole and sauté the chopped onion and garlic. On a high heat add the crayfish and turn them in the oil for a few minutes. Sprinkle with the thyme, parsley, salt and pepper, and cayenne. Then pour in the sherry and cook just until the crayfish turn red and curl. Ladle them into individual bowls and serve with bread, spoons and a side dish for the shells. Follow with fingerbowls. Serves 6.

SNAILS

Snails are quite popular in Spain, a speciality of simple bars and restaurants, rather than a home-cooked delicacy. They're often strongly spiced or else combined in all sorts of interesting ways — with fish or eel in paella, with rabbit in a country stew, with ham and sausage.

Either fast the snails for two or three days or feed them cornmeal or wheat flour. This is so they are purged of any foods they have eaten which might possibly be harmful to the one who consumes them. Another method is to sprinkle them liberally with salt and let them froth for a while. In either case, wash them in several changes of water, then let them soak in a basin of water for about 30 minutes. This, supposedly, coaxes them to poke their heads out, making the cooked snail much easier to extract from its shell. Plunge them into a pot of boiling water for 5 minutes and drain. Then bring a well-flavoured *court-bouillon* (onions, parsley, wine, fennel, thyme, etc.) to a boil and put the snails into it. Simmer them for about two hours then drain. In Spanish preparations, the snails are not previously removed from the shell — each person extracts the snails with a toothpick. Eating snails is a "hands on" experience, and licking the fingers is part of the pleasure. Allow between two and four dozen per person.

CARACOLES A LA LEVANTINA
Snails, Levante Style

12	dozen snails	2	teaspoons paprika
100 ml. oil		1/2 teaspoon cumin	
1	onion, chopped		cayenne or chili pepper
4	cloves garlic, chopped		salt and pepper

150 grams diced ham
1 tomato, peeled and chopped

dash of cloves
1/2 teaspoon thyme
200 ml. white wine
chopped mint, fennel or parsley

Cook the snails according to the preceding directions. In a casserole heat the oil and sauté the chopped onion, garlic and ham. Then add the chopped tomato, paprika, cumin, chili, salt and pepper, cloves, thyme and white wine. Add the snails and cook, covered, for 30 minutes, adding water or stock as needed to keep the sauce just a little thick. Serve in the same casserole sprinkled with chopped mint, fennel or parsley. Serves 4.

CARACOLES A LA PATARRALLADA
Grilled Snails, Catalan Style

Prepare the snails for cooking as described above. Cook them on a grill over charcoal, placing with the openings uppermost so each one forms its own cooking pot. Serve with alioli.

CHAPTER 10

Poultry & Game

Going through my collection of Spanish cookbooks, I made a surprising discovery — there are more classic recipes for rabbit and partridge than for chicken! This is a reflection of less prosperous times, when hens were kept for laying, not the stew pot, but small game birds, rabbit and hare were free for the taking on scrubby hillsides and in dry ravines.

Today chicken is, with seafood, Spain's most consumed protein food. Both rabbits and partridge are now farm-raised, and there's very good reason to try some of these tempting ways of preparing them. Please see Chapter 2 on marketing for more information on buying and storing chicken and other poultry, game birds and rabbit.

Serving sizes are very approximate — a small chicken (1½ kilos) in some households will easily serve four; in others, that's a meal for two or three. With cut-up chickens, a piece — thigh, breast — is considered one serving, but most people will eat two servings.

POLLO ASADO
Roast Chicken

The village *feria,* in honour of the town's patron saint, marked with religious processions and plenty of merrymaking, is heralded by the pop of rockets and the arrival of the roast-chicken vendors and *turrón,* nougat, sellers. The roast chickens turning on big rotisseries waft a tantalizing aroma throughout the fairgrounds.

To rotisserie-roast chicken, choose small ones, about 1½ kilos. For oven roasting, any size is acceptable. Regulate oven heat so a large chicken does not brown before it is thoroughly cooked.

Rub cleaned chicken inside and out with salt, lemon juice and crushed garlic. Place inside the cavity a few sprigs of thyme, bay, rosemary and celery leaves. Rub the chicken all over with lard (or butter or oil). Place it in a very hot oven for 5 minutes. Then lower the heat to moderate and roast the chicken, basting frequently with the drippings. If it browns too quickly, cover with foil or greased paper. Allow about 20 minutes' roasting time per 1/2 kilo of chicken (weighed without feet or head). Serve the chicken immediately, *en su punto.* Leaving in a warm oven will only cause it to dry out. Skim fat from the pan juices, add a little white wine and boil briefly. Serve in a sauce bowl with the chicken. Roast partridge and squab in the same way, barding them with thinly sliced pork fat to prevent the birds from becoming too dry.

POLLO RELLENO
Stuffed Chicken

1 roasting chicken, capon or small turkey — about 2½-3 kilos	1/2 teaspoon oregano
200 grams ham, chopped	1/2 teaspoon salt
1/4 kilo minced pork and/or beef	pepper
50 grams salt pork, blanched and diced	3 tablespoons lemon juice
100 grams breadcrumbs	1 egg, beaten
2 tablespoons chopped parsley	50 ml. oil
2 cloves garlic, minced	1/4 litre white wine
grated nutmeg	50 ml. water

Clean the chicken well and rub it inside and out with salt and pepper and lemon juice. In a bowl combine the chopped ham, minced meat, blanched and diced salt pork, breadcrumbs, chopped parsley, minced garlic, nutmeg, oregano, salt and pepper and lemon juice. Add the beaten egg and work the stuffing well with the hands to mix it. Stuff the chicken with this mixture. Truss it with string, tying the legs and wings close to the body. In a large pot, heat the oil and very slowly brown the chicken on all sides. Then add the wine and water. Cover and simmer until chicken is very tender, about 1½ hours. Remove to a serving platter. Skim off excess fat and serve the sauce in a saucebowl. Serves 6 to 8. The stuffed chicken can also be oven roasted.

POLLO EN PEPITORIA
Chicken Fricassee

There are many variations on this recipe, which is a Christmas favourite, prepared with chicken or turkey. Most recipes call for almonds though, as one of my sources — an ancient lady — insisted, the real *pepitoria* should be made with pine nuts, because "obviously," *pepitoria* means *pepitas* and *pepitas* are pine nuts, not almonds. Using this logic, I have also tried shelled sunflower seeds, which are wonderful. Another variable is eggs. In some dishes they are hard-cooked and chopped and in others, beaten eggs are blended into the sauce to thicken it. Also, in some preparations the chicken is fried, then simmered; in others, boiled, then fried. Here is one version.

1	large chicken or small turkey	6	peppercorns
40	grams lard (or 50 ml. oil)	1/2	teaspoon saffron
20	blanched almonds	1/4	litre chicken stock
1	thick slice bread, crusts removed	50	ml. white wine
6	cloves garlic		bay leaf and thyme
1	tablespoon chopped parsley	1	teaspoon salt
	grated nutmeg		lemon juice (optional)
	dash of ground cloves	2	eggs

Cut the chicken or turkey into serving pieces. In a big pot heat the lard or oil and in it fry the blanched almonds, slice of bread, garlic and parsley. When they are crisped and golden, remove to mortar or blender. In the same fat, slowly brown the pieces of chicken. Crush the fried almonds, etc., in the mortar or blender with the nutmeg, cloves, peppercorns and saffron. Dilute this in a little of the chicken stock and add to the pot with the browned chicken, the remaining stock, white wine, herbs and salt. Cover and simmer until the chicken is very tender, about an hour and a half, adding additional liquid as needed to keep the sauce from scorching. Add the lemon juice, if desired. Either garnish the chicken with chopped hard-cooked eggs, or mash the hard-cooked yolks and dissolve in stock or wine and stir into the sauce, or stir beaten eggs into the sauce and cook gently until thickened Serves 6 to 8.

POLLO AL AJILLO
Chicken with Garlic

1	chicken, cut in serving pieces	10	cloves garlic, chopped
	salt, pepper, paprika	75	ml. brandy, sherry or Montilla
50	ml. oil	1	bay leaf

Rub the chicken pieces with salt, pepper and paprika and let them sit for 15 minutes. Heat the oil in a pot and in it very slowly brown the chicken. When it is turned to brown the other side, add the garlic, very coarsely chopped (many cooks don't peel them, in order to prevent their scorching). When chicken is browned, remove the pot from the fire and add the brandy or sherry and bay leaf. Cover the pot and simmer until the chicken is tender, about 20 minutes more. Serves 4 to 6.

POLLO AL CHILINDRON
Chicken with Peppers

2	chickens, legs and breasts only	200	grams ham
	salt and pepper	1	onion, finely chopped
4	red bell peppers	5	large tomatoes, peeled, seeded and
50	ml. oil		chopped
4	cloves garlic		

Rub the chicken pieces with salt and pepper. Roast the peppers under the broiler flame, turning them, until blistered and charred. Remove and let them set, covered. Then peel them and cut the flesh into wide strips. Heat the oil in a pot or casserole and brown the chicken pieces in it, a few at a time. Add the garlic, cut in slivers, the ham, cut in thin strips, and the chopped onion. When this has fried several minutes, add the strips of peppers and the prepared tomatoes. Cook the chicken, partially covered, until quite tender. The sauce should be considerably reduced and thick. Serves 6 to 8.

POLLO A LA LEVANTINA
Chicken, Levante Style

1	small chicken		pepper
3	tablespoons lard or bacon fat		grating of nutmeg
1	finely chopped onion		dash of cloves
3	cloves garlic	150	ml. white wine
1	teaspoon salt	1	tablespoon vinegar
1	teaspoon oregano	6	small green peppers

Cut the chicken into serving pieces. Melt the lard in a pot or casserole and put in the chicken, regulating the heat so it sautés without browning too quickly. Add the chopped onion, then the chopped garlic. Sprinkle with the salt and oregano, freshly ground pepper, cloves and nutmeg. Then add the white wine and vinegar. Cover and cook for 15 minutes. Then add the peppers, cleaned of seeds and cut in half lengthwise. Cook until chicken is tender, about 15 minutes more. Serves 4.

POLLO GRANADINA
Chicken, Granada Style

I have a friend who collects recipes with six or fewer ingredients. This is one of her favourite dishes.

50	ml. oil	200	grams diced *serrano* ham
6	cloves garlic	100	ml. sherry
1	chicken, jointed		salt and pepper

Heat the oil in a large frying pan. Add the whole, peeled garlic cloves and fry until golden. Remove. Fry the chicken in the same oil, turning occasionally until nicely browned on all sides, adding the diced ham part way along. Then add the sherry and salt and pepper and the toasted garlic. Cover and simmer until chicken is fork-tender, about 25 minutes more. Serves 4-5.

POLLO EN SAMFAINA A LA CATALANA
Chicken with Vegetables, Catalan Style

1	chicken, jointed	2	onions, thinly sliced
	salt and pepper	3	cloves garlic, chopped
2	medium aubergines	2	tomatoes, peeled and finely chopped
100	ml. oil or lard	75	ml. white wine
2	green or red peppers		salt and pepper
1	small marrow, diced (courgette)		bay, thyme, parsley

Rub the chicken pieces with salt and pepper. In a frying pan heat half the oil or lard and in it fry the aubergines, which have been peeled and diced. Add the peppers, cut in large pieces and then the diced marrow. In another pot heat the remaining fat and sauté the chicken pieces with the sliced onions. Add the chopped garlic, then the prepared tomatoes. Fry a few minutes more, then add the wine, salt and pepper, bay, thyme and parsley. Cover and cook until chicken is nearly tender, then add the fried aubergines, peppers and marrow and cook another 15 minutes. Serves 4 to 6.

POLLO CON TOMATE
Chicken with Tomato

So absolutely simple. No, don't add onions, garlic, peppers or fancy herbs. Fresh, ripe Spanish tomatoes are highly flavourful.

1	large chicken	8	tomatoes (2 kilos), peeled, seeded and chopped coarsely
	salt, pepper and paprika		
50	ml. oil	2	bay leaves
		1	teaspoon salt

Rub the chicken with salt, pepper and a little paprika. Heat the oil in a pot and brown the chicken pieces slowly on both sides. While they are browning, dip tomatoes in boiling water, peel, seed and chop them. Add to the pot with the bay leaves and salt. Simmer, uncovered, until tomatoes are reduced to a thick sauce and chicken is tender, about 30 minutes. Serves 6.

POLLO AL VINO
Chicken Braised in Wine

1	chicken, jointed	50	ml. oil
	salt and pepper	50	ml. water
1	head garlic, roasted	200	ml. white wine
1	bay leaf		chopped parsley
1	medium onion		

Rub the chicken pieces with salt and pepper. Put them in a pot or casserole with the roasted cloves of garlic, bay leaf, onion cut in quarters, oil, water and wine. Cover and simmer until chicken is very tender, about 45 minutes. Garnish with chopped parsley. Serves 6.

POLLO AL JEREZ
Chicken with Sherry

1	chicken, jointed	200	ml. sherry
	salt and pepper	100	ml. water
50	ml. oil	1	bay leaf
3	spring onions or 1 onion	100	grams mushrooms
50	grams salt pork, diced		chopped parsley
1	tablespoon flour		

Rub the chicken pieces with salt and pepper. Heat the oil in a frying pan and brown the pieces, transferring them to a casserole as they are done. In the same oil sauté the spring onions, sliced, and the diced salt pork. Stir in the flour and cook a minute, then add salt and pepper, the sherry and water. Cook for a few minutes, stirring up the browned bits from the bottom of the pan, and pour over the chicken pieces. Add the bay leaf, cover and simmer (or bake) until chicken is tender, about 25 minutes longer. Meanwhile, clean the mushrooms, slice them and sauté in a little oil. Add them to the chicken during the last few minutes and garnish with chopped parsley. Serves 6.

MAR I TERRA
Chicken with Lobster

This Catalan dish reminds me of an American one, "surf 'n' turf," which is steak with lobster. Somehow I think the chicken is a better companion to the lobster than beef — at least you don't have to argue about whether to drink white or red wine.

50	ml. oil	200	ml. white wine
30	grams lard	50	ml. anise brandy or brandy
1	chicken, cut in serving pieces	2	teaspoons flour or fine bread-
	salt and pepper		crumbs
	cinnamon		water or stock
1	chicken liver	1	lobster of about 1 kilo

1 onion, chopped
   bouquet garni of bay, thyme, oregano, leek, parsley and orange peel
4 tomatoes, peeled, seeded and chopped

1/2 teaspoon saffron
2   cloves garlic
30   grams almonds and hazelnuts, blanched and toasted
25   grams grated chocolate or cocoa powder

Heat the oil and lard in a large earthenware casserole. Season the chicken pieces with salt, pepper and cinnamon and brown them in the fat with the chicken liver. Remove the liver when browned. When nicely golden, add the chopped onion. Sauté a few minutes, then add the bouquet garni, chopped tomatoes, wine and anise brandy. Cover and let the liquid reduce by half. Then add the flour or breadcrumbs mixed in a little water. Add water or stock to just barely cover the pieces of chicken. Simmer, covered. Cut the lobster into 8 pieces (see Chapter 9 for how-to). Heat a little oil in a separate frying pan and sauté the pieces of lobster and the green lobster liver briefly. Transfer the lobster meat to the casserole with the chicken. In the mortar or blender crush the saffron, garlic, toasted almonds and hazelnuts, grated chocolate and the chicken and lobster livers. Add reserved lobster juices to make a smooth paste. Add this mixture to the casserole and cook a few minutes more to blend the flavours. The sauce shouldn't be too soupy. Garnish with triangles of fried bread and sprinkle with chopped parsley. Serves 4 to 6.

PECHUGA DE POLLO A LA SEVILLANA
Chicken Breast, Seville Style

1   boned chicken breast (about 250 grams)
2   tablespoons oil
1/2 onion, chopped
1   red pepper, chopped
1   clove garlic, minced

1   large tomato, peeled
50   ml. sherry
50   ml. water
     salt and pepper
10   anchovy stuffed olives.

Split the chicken breast in half, making 2 fillets. Flatten them slightly. Heat the oil in a frying pan and put in the chicken. Let them just firm in the oil, without browning, turning once. Then remove them to a plate. In the same oil sauté the chopped onion and pepper until softened. Add the chopped garlic, then the prepared tomato. Fry for a few minutes, then add the sherry and water, salt and pepper. Cook on a medium heat about 10 minutes. Return the chicken breasts to the pan and cook them very slowly until done, about 10 minutes. Transfer to a heated serving dish and garnish with the sliced olives. Makes 2 servings.

PAVO TRUFADO
Truffled Turkey

A dish for special occasions, lovely on the buffet table. Boning a whole bird requires patience, but is not a difficult operation — I've watched country women do it by the light of an oil lamp! Start with a slit all along the backbone, work the

legs and wings loose first, holding the knife close to the bone. Then work around the breast bone. Any cuts in the skin should be repaired with needle and thread.

1	young turkey, about 4 kilos	1/2	teaspoon cinnamon
1/2	kilo pork		salt and pepper
1/2	kilo veal	2	eggs, beaten
1/4	kilo ham	50	ml. brandy
3	hard-cooked eggs	1	truffle, diced
100	grams olives, chopped	40	grams butter and/or oil
2	tablespoons chopped parsley	1	litre white wine
80	grams walnuts or pecans		carrot, onion, celery
50	grams pine nuts		cloves, peppercorns, bay
100	grams fine breadcrumbs		

Have the butcher bone the turkey or do it yourself, as described above. Ask the butcher to grind together the pork, veal and ham. Put the minced meat in a bowl and mix with the chopped eggs, the turkey's giblets, finely minced, the chopped olives, chopped parsley, chopped walnuts, pine nuts, breadcrumbs, cinnamon, salt and pepper and beaten eggs. With the hands mix the stuffing thoroughly. Chop the truffle, soak it in the brandy and add to the stuffing mixture. Spread out the boned turkey on a flat surface and spread the stuffing over it.

Bring the edges together, as if reconstructing the bird, and sew tightly along the slit. The result looks a bit like a stuffed shirt. Melt the butter or oil in a roasting pan and slowly brown the turkey on all sides until golden. Then add part of the wine, the carrot, onion, celery, cloves, peppercorns and bay leaves. Cover and simmer slowly, turning the turkey occasionally, until it is quite tender, about 3 hours. Add additional wine as needed. The turkey may be served hot accompanied by the sauce, skimmed of fat, or it can be pressed under a weight for 2 days and served cold. Makes about 12 servings.

PAVO ASADO A LA CATALANA
Roast Turkey, Catalan Style

1	turkey, 4-5 kilos	25	grams pine nuts
50	grams lard	10	chestnuts, roasted, peeled and chopped
1/4	kilo pork or ham, chopped		
6	pork sausages	1/2	teaspoon cinnamon
50	grams prunes, soaked, pitted and chopped		salt and pepper
		50	grams breadcrumbs
50	grams dried apricots, or peaches, soaked, pitted and chopped	100	ml. *vino rancio* or amontillado sherry
25	grams Malaga raisins, seeded		pork fat
2	apples, peeled, cored and diced		thyme, oregano, bay, rosemary

Clean the turkey and rub it inside and out with salt and a little of the wine or sherry or with lemon juice. Heat the lard in a large pan and in it sauté the turkey liver until it is browned on all sides. Remove it and chop it. To the fat add the chopped pork or ham and the sausages, chopped. When they are browned, add the chopped liver, the chopped prunes and apricots, raisins, apples, pine nuts, chopped chestnuts, cinnamon, salt and pepper and breadcrumbs. Stir in the wine or sherry and cook for a few minutes until the mixture is "dry." Stuff the turkey with this mixture. Sew up the openings and truss the bird with string, tying the legs and wings close to the body, and covering the breast with thin slices of pork fat. Put the turkey in a roasting pan with the bouquet garni of herbs. Put in a very hot oven for 10 minutes, then reduce heat to moderate and roast the bird, basting frequently. After an hour's roasting, add a glassful of wine and continue adding wine as it is cooked away. Allow about 25 minutes per 1/2 kilo of turkey (weighed unstuffed, without head and feet). Remove turkey to a serving platter. Remove excess fat from the pan drippings and serve the sauce with the turkey. Makes about 12 servings.

PAVO EN ESCABECHE A LA EXTREMEÑA
Marinated Turkey

I once knew a Spanish lady who lived deep in the country, far from electricity. One year for Christmas I gave the family a turkey, never thinking what one did with the leftovers with no refrigerator. On a visit to their home a week later I found out — *escabeche,* a marinade. Try it next time you have leftover holiday bird.

1	kilo cooked turkey	1/4	litre vinegar
1	egg		parsley
75	grams flour	1	lemon
75	grams lard or oil	1	orange
3/4	litre turkey or chicken stock		

Remove the bones from the turkey. Dip the pieces of turkey in egg and flour and fry them until crisp in lard. Place in bowl, alternating with sprigs of parsley and slices of lemon and orange. Add vinegar to the turkey broth and pour over the turkey. Chill 2 days. Serve as hors-d'oeuvres.

DUCK

Try this bird with figs — fresh or dried — or with *membrillo,* quince jelly.

PATO A LA SEVILLANA
Duck, Seville Style

The classic duck *a l'orange* is, of course, made with Seville bitter oranges. This dish, however, is made with olives.

2	ducklings, each about 2 kilos	1	sprig parsley
80	ml. oil	1	bay leaf
1	onion, sliced	2	carrots, peeled and quartered
1	tablespoon flour		salt and pepper
1/2	litre white wine		water or stock
1	bitter orange or 1 orange plus 1 tablespoon vinegar	150	grams olives, drained, rinsed and chopped.

Cut the duck into quarters. Heat the oil in a large casserole and brown the pieces of duck in it with the sliced onion. Remove the duck when browned and pour off excess fat. Stir the flour into the drippings. Let it begin to brown, then add the wine. Return the duck to the casserole with the quartered orange, parsley, bay leaf, carrots, salt and pepper and enough water or stock to nearly cover the duck. Cover the casserole and cook until the duck is fork tender, about 1½ hours. Strain the sauce and return to pot with the chopped olives. Serve the duck from the same casserole or cool it, chill overnight, and remove the congealed fat from the sauce. Reheat before serving. Serves 6.

PERDICES A LA CASERA
Partridges, Home Style

2	partridges (or squab, Cornish game hens), cleaned	100	ml. Malaga wine
		100	ml. brandy
50	ml. oil	50	ml. water
2	medium onions, chopped	2	bay leaves
5	cloves garlic	5	cloves
3	tomatoes, peeled	5	peppercorns
		2	teaspoons salt

Allow 1 partridge per person for a main course dish. Heat the oil in a pot large enough to hold the birds. Brown them very slowly. Then add the chopped onions and peeled garlic cloves. When golden, add the peeled and quartered tomatoes. Fry for a few minutes, then add the remaining ingredients. Cover and simmer until the partridges are tender, about an hour. Place them on a serving dish, pass the sauce through a sieve and spoon some of it over the partridges. Accompany with slices of fried bread. Serves 2.

PERDICES EN ESCABECHE A LA TOLEDANA
Marinated Partridge, Toledo Style

4	partridges (or other bird)	10	peppercorns
75	ml. oil	3	cloves
8	small onions		salt
3	cloves garlic, crushed	100	ml. white wine
2	carrots, peeled	100	ml. vinegar
2	bay leaves	100	ml. water
1	teaspoon thyme		lemon
1	teaspoon oregano		parsley
1	teaspoon paprika		

Clean the partridges and rub them inside and out with salt and pepper. Truss them with string so they keep their shape. Heat the oil in a frying pan and slowly brown them, one or two at a time. When golden, transfer the birds to a casserole. Peel the very small onions and cut a slit in their stem end (helps to keep them from opening out) and add them to the oil with the crushed garlic and the carrots, peeled and halved lengthwise. Then add the bay, thyme, oregano, paprika, peppercorns, cloves, salt and white wine. Pour this over the partridges in the casserole and add the vinegar and water. Bring to a boil, then cover and cook very slowly until the birds are very tender, about 1 hour, adding more water as needed so there is always plenty of liquid in the casserole. When the birds are done, remove the pan from the heat and let cool thoroughly. Then remove the partridges and discard the string. Place them in a glass or crockery bowl. Strain the cooking liquid and pour it over the partridges, which should be covered by the liquid. Slice the carrots and add them and the onions to the bowl. Cover tightly and chill for at least 2 days. Serve at room temperature or reheat very gently. Garnish with sliced lemon and parsley. Serves 4 or 8, depending on whether the birds are split.

PERDICES CON COLES A LA CATALANA
Partridge with Cabbage, Catalan Style

4	partridges, split in half		bay, thyme, oregano
	salt and pepper	100	ml. Malaga wine or medium sherry
	cinnamon	100	ml. veal stock
	ground nutmeg	1	cabbage
2	tablespoons oil or lard	1	egg, beaten
100	grams unsmoked bacon		flour
2	onions, chopped	100	grams *butifarra* (white) sausage
1	carrot, chopped		

Rub the cleaned and split partridges with salt and pepper, cinnamon and nutmeg. In a pot heat the oil or lard and very slowly brown the partridges, adding the bacon, cut in strips, the chopped onion and chopped carrot. When the birds are nicely browned, add the herbs and the wine and stock. Cover and simmer until the partridges are quite tender, about an hour, depending on their size. Meanwhile, cut the core out of the cabbage and blanch the cabbage in boiling water for 5 minutes. Drain and very carefully separate the leaves from the head of cabbage. Spread out 4 or 5 leaves overlapping on a flat surface. Place a half partridge on them and fold over to enclose the partridge in a packet. Do this with the remaining partridge halves. Dip them in beaten egg and roll in flour and place in an oven casserole. Pour over the sauce from the pot in which the birds cooked, adding more liquid if necessary. Add sliced *butifarra*. Cover the casserole and bake in a medium oven for 25 minutes. Serves 8.

PERDICES A LA NAVARRA
Partridge, Navarra Style

4	partridges	1	bay leaf
	salt and pepper	1	teaspoon thyme
	brandy	1/4	teaspoon cinnamon
	flour	1	tomato, peeled
4	tablespoons oil or lard	1/4	litre water or stock
1	onion, chopped	1	teaspoon salt
1	green pepper, chopped	1	tablespoon vinegar
4	cloves garlic, chopped	50	grams dark chocolate, grated
2	tablespoons chopped parsley		

Clean the partridges and rub them inside and out with salt and pepper and brandy. Let them sit for 30 minutes, then dredge them in flour and brown them slowly in the hot oil or lard. When they are browned, add the chopped onion, chopped pepper and garlic. Fry a few minutes more, then add the parsley, bay, thyme, cinnamon, whole peeled tomato, and water or stock. Add the salt and vinegar. Cover and simmer until the birds are tender. Remove them to a serving dish. Pass the sauce through a sieve and return to the pan. Add the grated chocolate and cook very slowly until it is completely dissolved, adding more stock as needed to make a smooth sauce. Pour over the partridges. Serves 4.

CODORNICES EN HOJAS DE PARRA
Quail in Grape Leaves

8	quail	100 ml. sherry	
8	thin slices ham or bacon	8	slices fried bread
16	grape leaves, blanched		lemon and watercress for garnish
50	ml. veal stock, boiling		

Clean the quail, and wrap each in a slice of ham or bacon. Place a quail on 2 overlapped grape leaves, fold the leaves around the bird and tie with twine. Put the wrapped quail in an oven pan with the stock and roast in a hot oven for about 20 minutes. Remove the grape leaves and place each quail on a slice of fried bread on a serving platter. Keep it warm. Add the sherry to the pan juices and reduce by half on a hot fire. Pour some of the sauce over the birds and serve the rest separately. Garnish with lemon slices and watercress. Serves 4. The leaf-wrapped quail can also be grilled over charcoal.

CODORNICES EMBORRACHADAS
Drunken Quail

8	quail	100 ml. brandy	
1	tablespoon lard	1	egg
100	grams salt pork, diced	1	teaspoon sugar
1/2	litre white wine	50	ml. milk

Clean the quail, rub them with salt and brown them in the lard with the diced salt pork. Add the white wine and brandy, cover and cook them gently until tender, about 25 minutes. Remove the quail to a plate. Beat the egg with the sugar and milk. Whisk a little of the hot liquid from the pot into the egg, then whisk the egg into the liquid in the pot. Stir until the sauce is thickened. Return the quail to the pot to reheat and serve. Serves 4.

PICHONES, PALOMA O TORTOLA
Squab, Dove or Turtledove

Finely mince the liver, heart and cleaned gizzard of the birds. Sauté briefly in a little oil. Add fine breadcrumbs and enough brandy to moisten. Stuff the birds with the mixture and truss them. Brown them well in oil with a little minced garlic. Add sherry or white wine, cover, and simmer until tender.

CONEJO EN ADOBO
Marinated Rabbit

1	rabbit, cut in serving pieces	3	tablespoons lemon juice or vinegar
6	cloves garlic, chopped	1/4	litre white wine
1	onion, thinly sliced		piece of lemon peel
1/2	teaspoon ground pepper		salt
1	teaspoon thyme		flour
1	bay leaf		oil

Place the rabbit in a bowl and add the garlic, sliced onions, pepper, thyme, bay, lemon juice and peel, white wine and salt. Marinate at least 6 hours or up to 24 hours. Drain the pieces of rabbit, dip them in flour and fry slowly in oil until nicely browned. Transfer the pieces to a casserole, add the marinade and cook until the rabbit is tender, about 30 minutes for small, farm-raised rabbits. Wild rabbit or hare may take longer cooking. Serves 4.

CONEJO A LA CAZADORA
Rabbit, Hunter's Style

1	rabbit, cut in pieces	200	ml. white wine
3	tablespoons oil	100	ml. water
100	grams diced serrano ham	3	tablespoons tomato paste
50	grams diced salt pork	1 1/2	teaspoons thyme
1	onion, chopped		salt and pepper
2	cloves garlic, chopped	200	grams mushrooms
50	ml. brandy		chopped parsley

Rub the rabbit pieces with salt and pepper and set aside. Heat the oil and sauté the diced ham, salt pork, chopped onion and garlic. With a skimmer, transfer it to a casserole. In the same fat brown the pieces of rabbit, placing them as they are browned in the casserole. Add the brandy, wine and water to the pan and bring to a boil, scraping the pan to deglaze it. Add the liquid to the casserole with the tomato paste, thyme and salt and pepper. Cover and simmer slowly until the rabbit is tender, about 30 minutes for young, domestically-raised rabbit. Slice and sauté the mushrooms and add them to the casserole during the last 15 minutes. Sprinkle with chopped parsley. Serves 4.

Roast chicken (recipe, page 253).

CONEJO EN SALSA DE ALMENDRAS
Rabbit in Almond Sauce

1	rabbit, cut in pieces	10	peppercorns
50	ml. oil	2	cloves
1	onion, chopped	1/2	teaspoon saffron
5	cloves garlic	1	teaspoon salt
20	almonds, blanched and skinned	50	ml. water
1/4	teaspoon cinnamon	1/4	litre white wine
1	tablespoon chopped parsley	2	bay leaves

Rub the pieces of rabbit with salt and pepper and set aside. Heat the oil in a pan and fry the onions, 4 cloves garlic and almonds with the rabbit liver, if available, just until they are toasted. Remove them to mortar or blender and crush with the cinnamon, parsley, raw garlic, peppercorns, cloves, saffron and salt. Dissolve in the water. Meanwhile, in the oil in the pan slowly brown the rabbit pieces. Add the mortar mixture to the rabbit with the white wine and bay leaves. Cover and simmer until rabbit is very tender, 30 minutes to an hour, depending on size of rabbit, adding water or light stock if more liquid is needed. Serves 4.

CONEJO TARRACONENSE
Rabbit, Tarragona Style

1	rabbit, (about 1 kilo) cut in pieces	3/4	kilo new potatoes
100	ml. oil	1/2	teaspoon saffron
1	onion, chopped	1	dry chili pepper (or more)
4	tomatoes, peeled, seeded and chopped	2	cloves garlic
		1	square chocolate
150	ml. red wine	1	tablespoon toasted flour
	bay, thyme, parsley and rosemary		chopped parsley
	salt and pepper		
	grated nutmeg		

Heat the oil in a casserole or pot and slowly brown the rabbit pieces and the liver. Remove the liver and reserve it. When partially browned, add the chopped onion. Continue frying, then add the prepared tomatoes, then the red wine, herbs, salt and pepper and nutmeg. Cover the pan and let the rabbit cook very slowly. Meanwhile scrub the small new potatoes very well and parboil them for 5 minutes. Drain, then cut them in half. (If using regular-sized potatoes, cook them until nearly tender, then cut in quarters.) In a mortar or blender crush the saffron, fried liver of the rabbit, chili pepper, which has been seeded, garlic,

Lacon con grelos — *cured pork shoulder with turnip tops* — *a typical Galician dish (recipe, page 292)*

chocolate and toasted flour. (To toast flour, put it in a frying pan with no fat and no liquid and stir it over a low flame just until it is slightly coloured. Do not let it scorch or it will be bitter.) Dissolve this mixture in about 100 ml. of boiling water and stir it into the casserole with the parboiled potatoes. Cover and cook another 20 minutes, or until rabbit and potatoes are very tender. Garnish with chopped parsley. Serves 4 or 5, depending on the size of the rabbit.

LIEBRE ESTOFADO A LA CASTELLANA
Stewed Hare, Castilian Style

1	hare, cut up	150	ml. white wine
1/4	kilo white beans, soaked overnight	2	tablespoons vinegar
2	onions, sliced	50	ml. water
3	cloves garlic, slivered	75	ml. oil
2	green peppers, cut in strips		salt and pepper
	bouquet garni of bay, parsley, thyme and cinnamon stick	1	chili pepper

Season the pieces of hare with salt and pepper and a little wine. Put the soaked beans to cook with a few slices of the onion and a bay leaf. Simmer them until tender, about 1½ hours, adding the salt to taste when they are partially cooked. Meanwhile, put the hare, sliced onions, garlic, green peppers, bouquet garni, wine, vinegar, water, oil, salt and pepper and chili pepper cut into small pieces into a pot. Bring to a boil, then reduce heat and simmer until the hare is quite tender, adding a little of the liquid from the beans as needed. Then add the drained beans to the hare and cook another 15 minutes to combine the flavours.

GAZPACHOS MANCHEGOS
Shepherd's Stew, La Mancha Style

This dish, concocted by shepherds and hunters is also called *galianos*. The plural, *gazpachos,* distinguishes it from the Andalusian cold gazpacho. Though typically containing several partridges and rabbits, a home version can be made with chicken and squab or domesticated rabbit. A *torta*, a flat, unleavened bread baked on the hearth stone, is added to the soup to thicken it and another is used as a spoon. Indian *chapati* or Hebrew *matzoh* can be substituted for the torta (no, they are not the same, but I have seen both used in Spain). Traditionally gazpachos would be made in a wide and deep two-handled frying pan and everyone eats from the pot in which it is cooked.

3	partridges or squab		salt and pepper
2	rabbits	3/4	litre white wine
100	ml. oil	1	litre water
1	slice bread or *torta*	1/2	teaspoon cinnamon
3	cloves garlic	1/2	teaspoon saffron
1	onion, sliced		*tortas*
1	tomato, peeled and cut up		
2	green peppers, cut in half bay, thyme, rosemary		

Cut the partridges in half and the rabbits in quarters and rub the pieces with salt. Heat the oil in a large frying pan and first fry the rabbit livers, the slice of bread and the garlic and remove them when browned. Add the birds and rabbit to the oil and fry slowly, adding the sliced onion. When the meat is browned, add the cut up tomato, peppers, herbs, salt and pepper, wine and water. Bring to a boil, cover the pan and simmer. In the mortar or blender crush the fried livers, bread and garlic with the cinnamon and saffron. Dissolve in a little liquid and add to the pan. When the meats are tender, cut 2 or 3 tortas into small pieces and add to the pot. Cook another 5 minutes and remove from heat. Let set, covered, for 10 minutes before serving. Serve additional tortas for dunking. Serves 8 to 10.

LARGE GAME

Bear stew, once a favourite dish in Asturias, is in short supply since bears became a protected species in Spain. However other large game — in particular, venison and wild boar — is widely taken and much enjoyed by connoisseurs. Their meat is usually marinated, then braised. Deer meat is very lean and needs barding with fat to keep it moist. Boar is like pork, but not nearly so fatty.

Here is one method for preparing any piece of wild game.

JABALI O VENADO A LA MONTAÑESA
Boar or Venison, Cantabrian Style

2	kilos boar or venison	10	peppercorns
1/2	litre red wine	100	grams salt pork, diced
1	tablespoon sugar	100	grams serrano ham, diced
1	leek, split	1	dozen tiny onions
1	carrot, split lengthwise	1/4	kilo mushrooms
	bay, thyme, parsley, rosemary and	2	tablespoons oil
	mint sprigs	2	tablespoons flour
	a few juniper berries	100	ml. meat stock
1	clove garlic, crushed	100	ml. tomato sauce
150	ml. oil		

The meat can be cut into pieces, as for stew, or left whole as for pot roast. Saddle of venison or loin of boar, the most tender sections, can be roasted, after marinating, as for beef or pork. Other cuts should be braised. Put the meat into a glass or crockery bowl and add the wine, sugar, leek, carrot, herbs, juniper berries, crushed garlic, 50 ml. oil and peppercorns. Marinate 24 hours for pieces, 48 hours for a whole piece. Drain the meat and pat it dry, reserving the marinade. Heat the 100 ml. oil in a pot and brown the meat on all sides. Remove it. Add the diced salt pork and diced ham, whole small onions and cleaned and quartered mushrooms. Sauté for a few minutes, then return the meat to the pan. Add half the strained marinade, along with the bouquet garni of herbs. Cover and simmer.

In a saucepan heat the tablespoons of oil, stir in the flour and let it cook until lightly browned, about 2 minutes, stirring so that it does not scorch. Then add the meat stock, the tomato sauce and a little of the marinade. Stir until the sauce has thickened. Add this to the meat and continue cooking until the meat is fork tender, adding additional marinade as needed.

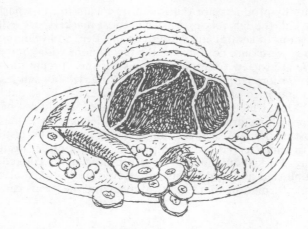

CHAPTER 11

Meat

There are those feast days which appear on the calendar, like Christmas and Easter. There are those feast days that mark special events — a wedding, a baptism, a first communion. And then there is the *matanza,* the greatest of the secular holidays and an excuse for some serious feasting.

The *matanza* is a hog slaughtering, and far from being a dying custom in modern-day Spain, is still practised the length and breadth of the country.

During the cool winter months several families will gather, usually at a country cottage far from electric lights and mains water. Once the pig is "sacrificed" (that is the verb in Spanish), great cauldrons of fresh pork are put to cook in flavourful sauces. The liver is fried up and the ribs barbecued to be served to the assembled people, from small children to old *abuelas*. And the work begins. The hams are rubbed down with salt, the first step in curing. The belly fat also is salted. The blood is added to spices, rice and pine nuts for black puddings; lean and fat are ground together and macerated with garlic and paprika for making *chorizo* and other sausages, depending on the regions, sausage casings are prepared. Late at night, while the women take turns stirring the pots and everyone has eaten and drunk his fill, someone starts strumming a guitar and the dancing starts. The work goes on till dawn and sometimes the dancing does, too.

Meat in Spain has never been plentiful. Perhaps that is why its "sacrifice" is cause for celebration. I used to marvel at the village butcher shop when Spanish housewives would walk away with a big package of meats to feed a family of six for considerably less money than what I paid for two not-very-tender *filetes de ternera,* thin veal cutlets. Their package would include a chunk of boiling beef, a quarter of stewing hen, a piece of salt pork, a ham bone, a few pork ribs, and black pudding and red sausage. It all went into the *cocido* (see chapter 5) with garbanzos and vegetables and provided a nutritious and filling meal for a whole family.

Pork and its by-products are the favourite meats in most parts of Spain. Lamb and baby kid, though very expensive in most markets, are still traditional in the grazing regions of central and western Spain. Beef and veal, though of very good quality now, were once confined to the few regions with good grazing. For that reason there are so few traditional recipes for their preparation.

Bring meat to room temperature before cooking. Do not salt it. Meat which is to be breaded and fried or braised in its own juices can be salted immediately before cooking. Meat which is to be grilled or roasted should not be salted until after cooking, as salting draws out the juices which keep the meat moist. In general, the most tender cuts of meat can be cooked on the hottest heat for the shortest length of time (served rare) and the least tender pieces need very gentle and long cooking. Pork should always be served thoroughly cooked; pale meats such as baby lamb, kid and veal are usually served well-cooked also.

Much more information about kinds of meat and meat cuts can be found in Chapter 2.

BEEF AND VEAL

In Spain *ternera,* veal, generally means young beef. In the following recipes either beef or veal can be used.

FILETE A LA CASERA
Veal Cutlets, Home Style

4 thin veal cutlets	5 cloves garlic, chopped
salt and pepper	lemon wedges
50 ml. oil	chopped parsley

Pound the cutlets thin with a wooden mallet or pestle. Rub them with salt and pepper. Heat the oil in a frying pan and put in one cutlet at a time with some of the chopped garlic. Fry the meat very quickly on both sides. Remove and reheat the oil. Fry the remaining cutlets in the same manner. Serve with lemon wedges and chopped parsley. Makes 4 servings.

GRANADINA DE TERNERA
Veal Cutlets, Granada Style

4 thin veal cutlets	flour
100 grams serrano ham or bacon	150 grams mushrooms

salt and pepper	50 grams diced ham
50 ml. oil	1 clove garlic
	50 ml. sherry

Pound the cutlets thin with a mallet or pestle and trim them to an even shape. Cut the thinly sliced ham into four strips. Cut 3 slits in each cutlet and thread the slice of ham through it. Rub with salt and dust with flour. Heat the oil and fry the cutlets one at a time. Remove and keep them warm. In the same oil sauté the sliced mushrooms, diced ham and chopped garlic for a few minutes. Add the sherry and cook for 5 minutes. Pour over the cutlets and serve with a garnish of parsley or watercress. Four servings.

PULPETAS
Veal Rolls

1/2 kilo veal cutlets	flour
4 slices cooked ham	oil
1 clove garlic, minced	1 onion, chopped
salt and pepper	50 ml. sherry
1 sprig mint	100 ml. stock
grated nutmeg	sprigs of parsley or mint

Trim the cutlets into 8 strips about 8 by 16 cm. Pound them thin with a wooden mallet or pestle. Place a strip of ham on top of each. Grind the trimmings (about 100 grams) with the minced garlic and chopped mint leaves. Season with salt and pepper and nutmeg. Spread a little of this on each cutlet. Roll up the cutlet in a thin roll and tie with twine or secure with toothpicks. Dredge them in flour and sauté in oil until browned on all sides. Remove. In the same oil, sauté the chopped onion until softened. Add the sherry and stock and put the veal rolls back in the pan. Cover and cook them gently about 20 minutes. Garnish with parsley or mint. Four servings.

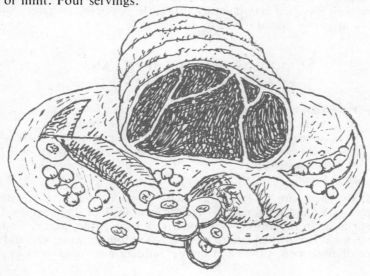

TERNERA MECHADA
Veal Pot Roast

Mechada refers to larding or threading with strips of pork fat which helps keep the meat juicy during cooking. Classically it's done with a larding needle. The village cooks I watched simply use a sharp knife, cutting deep gashes into the meat which are plugged with thin strips of salt pork. The *redondo* or round, a long, roundish piece of meat, is most favoured for this dish, but any "roast beef" would be suitable.

1 1/2	kilos veal or beef in one piece	4	tablespoons oil or lard
5	peppercorns	1	onion, quartered
1	clove	3	carrots, cut in half
1/4	teaspoon grated nutmeg	2	tomatoes, quartered
2	tablespoons chopped parsley	1	head roasted garlic
2	cloves garlic	1	bay leaf
1	hard-cooked egg	100	ml. sherry or Malaga wine
2	teaspoons oil	150	ml. stock or water
50	grams salt pork, cut in thin strips		

Wipe the meat with a cloth. In the mortar grind together the peppercorns, clove, nutmeg, parsley, garlic cloves, egg and 2 teaspoons oil to make a paste. Cut the salt pork into very thin strips. With a sharp knife cut deep gashes into the piece of meat and with the knife blade insert some of the paste and a piece of salt pork. Continue, spacing the gashes regularly on the meat's surface. Tie the meat with twine, giving it a good shape (thin slices of pork fat can be used to bard it, if desired). Heat the oil or lard in a pot big enough to hold the piece of meat and brown the meat, very slowly, on all sides. Add the quartered onion, carrot, tomatoes, and roasted garlic cloves. Put in the bay leaf, sherry and stock and cook the meat very slowly until fork tender, about 2 hours, adding additional stock as needed. Remove the meat to a serving dish, discard the string and slice it. Sieve the sauce and spoon it over the meat. Serve with potato purée or potatoes which have been browned in lard with a little garlic. Cooked vegetables — carrots and peas — are often added to the meat. Serves 6.

CARNE ASADA A LA SEVILLANA
Pot Roast, Seville Style

1 1/2	kilos beef pot roast	100	ml. Montilla or sherry
	flour		salt and pepper
4	tablespoons oil or lard		cinnamon stick
3	cloves garlic	100	grams pitted olives
2	tablespoons parsley	1	small tin red pimento
1	lemon		

If desired, the meat can be larded as in the previous recipe, using slivers of almonds and garlic and salt pork. Dredge the meat in flour, then brown it slowly in the oil or lard. In the mortar or blender crush the garlic, parsley and lemon juice. When meat is browned add to pot with the Montilla wine, salt and pepper and a piece of cinnamon. Cover and simmer, adding water and stock as needed, until the meat is quite tender, about 2 hours. Remove the meat to a serving platter. Rinse the olives in water, drain them well and add them to the sauce in the pot. Pour over the meat and garnish with strips of red pimento. Serves 6.

ROPAVIEJA
"Old Clothes" (Beef with Aubergines)

A good dish for leftover roast beef or boiled beef.

3/4	kilo cooked beef	2	teaspoons flour
2	medium aubergines	100	ml. tomato sauce
75	ml. oil	100	ml. beef stock
1	onion, chopped		salt and pepper
1	clove garlic, chopped	1	red pepper, roasted or tinned

Cut the meat into slices or strips. Peel the aubergines and slice them. Fry them slowly in the oil until they are slightly browned and soft. Remove and set aside. In the same oil sauté the chopped onion and garlic until softened. Then stir in the flour and let it cook briefly. Add the tomato sauce and stock, the salt and pepper, the red pepper cut in pieces, the cut up meat and the fried aubergines. Stir and let cook for 10 minutes. Serves 4.

FALDA RELLENA
Stuffed Flank

1 1/2	kilos beef or veal flank, skirt or boned breast	3	hard-cooked eggs
		1	tinned red pimento
100	grams cooked ham, finely chopped		salt and pepper
1	slice bread, soaked in milk	1	egg, beaten
1	dozen pitted olives, chopped	75	ml. oil
1	tablespoon finely chopped onion	1	onion, quartered
3	cloves garlic	100	ml. tomato sauce
2	tablespoons parsley, chopped	200	ml. white wine

Have the butcher trim the piece of meat so it is an even rectangle. Grind the trimmings. Mix the minced meat with the chopped ham. Squeeze out the soaked bread and add to the meat with the chopped olives, chopped onion, 1 clove garlic, minced, chopped parsley, chopped eggs, chopped pimento, salt and pepper and beaten egg. Spread this mixture on top of the meat. Starting at a short end, roll up the meat as tightly as possible. Either sew it closed or fasten with skewers. Wrap securely in string. Heat the oil in a pot large enough to hold the roll and very slowly brown it on all sides. Add the quartered onion, 2 cloves slivered garlic, the tomato sauce and white wine. Cover and simmer until the meat is very tender, about 2 hours, adding more liquid as needed. Remove it to a serving platter. Sieve the sauce. Let the meat rest for 10 minutes, then remove strings and cut it in slices. Serve with the sauce. Serves 6 to 8.

ESTOFADO DE BUEY A LA ASTURIANA
Asturian Beef Stew

1	kilo stewing beef	2	turnips, peeled and quartered
1	calf's foot, split	1/4	litre red wine
50	grams lard	50	ml. vinegar
2	onions, quartered		bay, thyme, parsley, celery
100	grams bacon, diced		beef stock
2	carrots, halved lengthwise		salt and pepper

Heat the lard in a pot and brown the piece of meat very slowly on all sides. Add the onion, bacon, calf's foot, carrots and turnips. When these ingredients are slightly browned, add the wine, vinegar and bouquet of herbs. Cover and simmer the meat, adding beef stock to keep sufficient liquid, until it is very tender, about 2 hours. Season to taste with salt and pepper. Place the beef on a serving platter and slice it. Remove the bone from the foot and cut the meat into pieces. Put it around the sliced beef with the carrots and turnips. Strain the sauce and pour over all. Serves 4 to 6.

ESTOFADO A LA ANDALUZA
Andalusian Veal Stew

1	kilo stewing beef or veal	1/4	teaspoon cinnamon
1	large green pepper	100	ml. water
1	large tomato, peeled	50	ml. oil
2	onions, sliced	2	bay leaves
2	carrots, halved lengthwise	1	sprig parsley
1/2	teaspoon saffron	2	teaspoons salt
8	peppercorns	1/4	litre white wine
2	cloves	4	potatoes, peeled and cut up
1	head garlic, roasted		

Cut the meat into cubes of about 3 cm. Place it in a stew pot with the green pepper, cut in strips, the tomato cut in quarters, the onions and carrots. In the mortar crush the saffron, peppercorns, cloves, roasted garlic, cinnamon and dissolve in the water. Add this to the pot with the oil, bay leaves, parsley, salt and white wine. Cover and cook about 1 hour, adding more water or stock as needed to keep the meat just covered with liquid. Then add the potatoes and cook another 30 minutes. Serves 4 to 6. Other vegetables — peas, pumpkin, artichoke hearts, broad beans, etc. — can be added to this stew and it's perfectly acceptable to add quartered pears or apples as well.

PICADILLOS ALMERIENSES
Chopped Beef, Almeria Style

1/2	kilo beef, cut into dice	1/4	teaspoon crushed saffron
150	grams salt pork or bacon, diced	1/2	teaspoon ground pepper
50	ml. oil	1	teaspoon salt
1	onion, finely chopped	100	ml. white wine
2	tomatoes, peeled, seeded and chopped	100	ml. water
			hard-cooked eggs
40	grams pine nuts		chopped parsley
1/2	teaspoon cinnamon		fried bread
1/4	teaspoon grated nutmeg		

The meat and salt pork should be cut into dice of the same size. Heat the oil in a casserole and in it brown the meat and pork or bacon. When browned, add the onions and fry for a few minutes. Then add the prepared tomatoes, pine nuts, cinnamon, nutmeg, saffron, pepper, salt, wine and water. Cover and cook until the meat is tender, about 45 minutes, adding additional water to keep the mixture just juicy. Serve in the same casserole garnished with sliced eggs, chopped parsley and triangles of fried bread. Serves 4.

GRILLED MEATS

The most tender cuts of beef — fillet, entrecote, chateaubriand, tournedo — are best enjoyed simply grilled or pan fried and served medium to rare. Use tongs or spatula to turn the meat, so as not to pierce with a fork. As grilled meats are pretty much the same in any language, no recipe is given for their preparation. However, in serving them, try some of the Spanish sauces (see chapter 12) as an accompaniment. Especially good are *romesco,* pepper sauce; olive sauce; Cabrales blue cheese; and *mojo,* a paprika sauce.

CHULETON A LA VASCA
Beef Chops, Basque Style

4	rib steaks, thickly cut	5	cloves garlic, chopped finely
100	ml. oil	3	tablespoons chopped parsley
1	lemon	1	dozen fried green peppers
	pepper		

Trim the steaks of fat and place them on a platter. Pour over the oil and the juice of the lemon. Let them macerate for 2 or 3 hours. Drain them, sprinkle with pepper and grill on a hot griddle or under broiler or over charcoal. Sprinkle the steaks with the chopped garlic and parsley while they are grilling. Serve accompanied by the fried peppers. Serves 4 big eaters.

PORK

Cutlets *(filetes)* and chops can be interchanged, adjusting the cooking time. Other boneless pork roasts can be substituted for the loin *(lomo)*.

FILETES A LA PLANCHA
Grilled Pork Cutlets

4 pork cutlets (or thin pork chops)
5 cloves garlic, coarsley chopped
2 tablespoons chopped parsley

1 lemon
salt and pepper

Put the cutlets in a shallow bowl. Sprinkle them with the chopped garlic, parsley and juice of the lemon. Let them marinate for 2 hours. Heat a griddle or a heavy frying pan and brush it very lightly with oil. Place the cutlets on the griddle and cook, turning once, until browned on both sides. Sprinkle with salt and pepper. Serve with lemon wedges. Makes 4 servings. Cut into small pieces (about 6 × 4 cm.) these are the *planchitas* served at tapa bars.

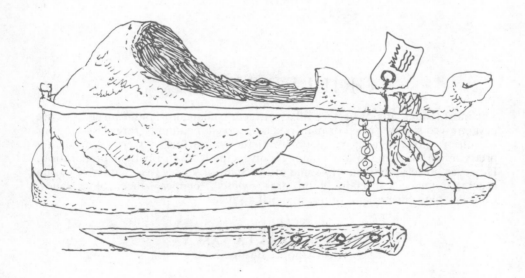

EMPANADOS DE CERDO
Breaded Pork Cutlets

4   pork cutlets (or chops, thinly cut)
4   cloves garlic, chopped
1   tablespoon chopped parsley
1/2 teaspoon crushed thyme
    salt and pepper

1   lemon
1   egg, beaten
50 grams fine breadcrumbs
60 ml. oil

Place the cutlets in a shallow bowl and sprinkle them with the chopped garlic, parsley, thyme and salt and pepper. Squeeze over the juice of the lemon and let them marinate for 1 hour. Then dip the cutlets into the beaten egg, then breadcrumbs. Fry slowly in oil until browned on both sides. Serves 4.

CHULETAS DE CERDO A LA MADRILEÑA
Baked Pork Chops, Madrid Style

6	pork chops	1/2	teaspoon thyme
6	tablespoons oil	1	bay leaf
3	cloves garlic, chopped	1/2	teaspoon paprika
2	tablespoons chopped parsley		salt and pepper

In a shallow pan large enough to hold the chops in one layer, mix the oil, chopped garlic, parsley, thyme, bay leaf, paprika and salt and pepper. Place the chops in the marinade and let them set for 2 hours, turning them frequently. Then put them in an oiled oven tin and bake in a medium oven, basting frequently with the remaining marinade until done, about 25 minutes. Serve with chips. Makes 6 servings.

LOMO EN ADOBO
Marinated Pork Loin

3/4	kilo boned pork loin	1/2	teaspoon salt
4	cloves garlic	1	teaspoon paprika
1	teaspoon oregano	150	ml. vinegar
1/4	teaspoon saffron	2	tablespoons oil
10	peppercorns		

Put the pork loin in a deep bowl. In the mortar crush the garlic, oregano, saffron and peppercorns with the salt and paprika. Dissolve the paste in a little of the vinegar. Pour over the meat with the rest of the vinegar. Cover and marinate, refrigerated for about 48 hours, turning the meat 2 or 3 times a day. Then drain the piece of meat and pat it dry. Place it in an oiled oven tin and rub with the oil. Place in a very hot oven for 5 minutes, then reduce heat to moderate and roast the pork until done, about 40 minutes. (In roasting pork, allow 25 to 30 minutes for each 500 grams of meat.) Baste with pan drippings. Makes 4 servings. Instead of roasting, the pork loin can be thinly sliced and the pieces fried in oil.

LOMO A LA SAL
Pork Loin Baked in Salt Crust

This method seals in the juices. Time the roasting as in the preceding recipe.

1 1/2	kilo boned pork loin	3	kilos coarse salt

Pat the piece of meat dry. In an oven pan just big enough to hold the piece of meat put a layer of salt about 2 cm. thick. Place the pork loin on top of it and completely cover it with a thick layer of salt. Put in a preheated hot oven for 5 minutes, then reduce to moderate and bake until the meat is done. Remove from the oven and break open the salt crust. Place the meat on a serving platter and slice it. Garnish with strips of roasted peppers and parsley sprigs. Serves 8.

LOMO A LA MALAGUEÑA
Pork Loin with Malaga Wine

1	kilo boned pork loin	1	piece cinnamon stick
50	ml. oil	25	grams Malaga raisins
200	ml. Malaga muscatel wine	25	grams almonds, blanched

Heat the oil in a large pot and very slowly brown the piece of meat on all sides. Place it in a roasting pan and pour over the wine. Put the piece of cinnamon in the pan and put the pan in a very hot oven for 5 minutes, then reduce the heat and bake until meat is done, about 50 minutes. Meanwhile, seed the raisins and plump them by soaking in a little hot water. Sliver the blanched almonds and toast them lightly in the oven or in a frying pan. When meat is done, place on a serving dish and slice. Pour over a little of the pan juices and sprinkle with the raisins and almonds. Serve the remaining juice in a sauce bowl. Serves 6.

LOMO CON LECHE
Pork Loin with Milk

1	kilo boned pork loin	1/2	teaspoon coarsley ground pepper
	lard or oil	1	teaspoon salt
1	clove garlic	1/4	teaspoon cinnamon
1/2	litre milk		

Trim the piece of meat of excess fat and melt the fat in a large pot, adding lard or oil to make enough in which to brown the meat. Rub the meat with the garlic and slowly brown it on all sides. Then add the milk, pepper, salt and cinnamon. Bring to a boil, then simmer very slowly until the meat is very tender, about 1 hour. Remove the loin to a serving platter and slice it. Reduce the sauce by boiling it. Pour over the meat and serve. Serves 6. Good served with potato purée and fried peppers.

LOMO DE CERDO RELLENO A LA GADITANA
Stuffed Pork Loin, Cadiz Style

1 1/2	kilos boned pork roast	2	tablespoons lard or oil
200	grams cooked ham, thinly sliced	1	teaspoon thyme
2	hard-cooked eggs, chopped	1	head garlic
75	grams almonds, blanched, and/or walnuts, chopped finely	10	peppercorns
2	cloves garlic	1/2	teaspoon salt
1	egg, beaten	100	ml. dry sherry
			water

Cut the piece of meat open lengthwise, opening it up like a book. Arrange a layer of half the ham slices on one half. Mix the chopped eggs, chopped almonds, 2 cloves chopped garlic and beaten egg and spread on top. Place on top the remaining sliced ham. Close the meat and sew up with thread and tie with string to make an even-sized roll. Rub it with lard or oil and sprinkle with thyme. Place in an oven tin with head of garlic, peppers and salt. Put in a hot oven for 5 minutes, then reduce the heat to medium. Pour over the sherry and roast the meat until done, about 1 hour and 15 minutes, adding water so there is always liquid in the bottom of the pan. (The meat can also be cooked, covered, on top of the stove.) When tender, remove to a serving platter. Let the meat sit for 5 or 10 minutes, then remove string and thread. Slice the meat. Sieve the sauce in the pan and spoon it over the sliced meat. Serves 8.

SOLOMILLO DE CERDO AL JEREZ
Pork Fillet with Sherry

2	pork fillets (about 750 grams)	1-2	dozen small onions
50	grams serrano ham	100	ml. sherry
2	tablespoons lard		sprig of rosemary
1	head garlic		

Lard the fillets with strips of ham or lay strips of ham over the "tail" end of the fillets, double them over the ham and secure with string. Rub them with lard and put in a baking dish. Put in a preheated hot oven for 5 minutes, then add the garlic and onions which have been peeled and parboiled in boiling water for 2 minutes, and the sherry and rosemary. Lower the heat to moderate and roast about 45 minutes, basting occasionally. Remove to a serving dish and slice the fillets. Serve covered with the pan juices and surrounded by the onions. Serves 4.

ASADO DE CERDO A LA CATALANA
Roast Pork, Catalan Style

Any piece of pork can be prepared in this manner — a whole, fresh ham, cuts from the leg or shoulder, or the unboned loin.

1 1/2 kilo pork roast	1	bay leaf	
4	cloves garlic	1	sprig parsley
2	tablespoons lard	1	stalk celery
1	piece cinnamon stick	1	teaspoon coarsely ground pepper
1	teaspoon thyme		pinch of cloves
1	teaspoon oregano	50	ml. brandy or anise
1	onion, sliced	100	ml. medium dry sherry or dry Malaga wine

In the mortar crush the cloves of garlic to a paste and rub the piece of pork all over with it. Let sit for an hour. Melt the lard in a casserole or flameproof oven dish and brown the meat on all sides. Add the cinnamon, thyme, oregano, onion, bay, parsley, celery, pepper and cloves. Put in a very hot oven for 5 minutes, then reduce the heat and add the brandy or anise and the sherry or Malaga wine (or a *vino generoso).* Roast the meat until done, about 1 3/4 hours, adding small

283

quantities of water as needed so there is always some liquid in the roasting pan. Remove to a serving platter and let sit for 10 minutes before carving. Strain the pan juices and serve in a sauce bowl. Garnish the meat with cooked vegetables and potatoes. Serves 6.

COCHINILLO ASADO
Roast Suckling Pig

1	whole pig, 3 to 4 weeks, weighing		thyme
	3 1/2 to 4 kilos	1	tablespoon salt
100	grams lard	1	tablespoon vinegar or lemon juice
4	cloves garlic	1/4	litre water
	bay leaves		

Buy an oven-ready suckling pig and have the butcher split it in half lengthwise (it can also be roasted whole). Crush the garlic cloves and mix them with the lard. Spread the pig with about half the lard and place, skin side down, on a bed of bay leaves and thyme in a large roasting pan or earthenware platter. Put in a preheated medium oven for about 1 hour, basting frequently (if browning too fast, partially cover with foil). Then turn the pig skin side up. Raise the oven temperature to hot. Prick the skin with a fork and brush with lard. Mix the salt, vinegar and water and brush over the skin. Return the pig to the oven and roast it another 45 minutes, brushing frequently with the water to crisp the skin. The meat should be tender enough to be "carved" with the edge of a plate. Serves 8.

CERDO Y PATATAS A LO EXTREMEÑO
Pork and Potato Casserole, Extremadura Style

3/4	kilo potatoes	50	grams ham or bacon, diced
	bay leaf	2	cloves garlic
50	grams butter	8	thin pork cutlets or sliced loin (about
50	ml. milk		350 grams)
50	grams salt pork, diced		salt and pepper

Peel the potatoes and cook them in salted water with the bay leaf. Drain and put them through a ricer or whip them smooth, adding half the butter and the milk. Season with salt and pepper. In a frying pan lightly sauté the diced salt pork and ham and remove. In the same fat fry the pork cutlets on both sides and remove. Use the fat in the pan or a little lard to grease an oven casserole. Rub the casserole with the crushed garlic cloves and place half the fried salt pork and ham in it. Spread with the potato purée and put the fried pork cutlets on top with the remaining salt pork and ham. Dot with butter and put in a medium oven until browned on top, about 30 minutes. Serves 4 to 6.

MAGRO CON TOMATE
Pork with Tomato

A tapa bar speciality, this is simple and flavourful. Made with fresh, ripe tomatoes, it really needs no extra spices or herbs.

1/2	kilo pork, cut in cubes	2	teaspoons salt
50	ml. oil	1	bay leaf
1	kilo tomatoes, peeled, seeded and chopped		

Fry the pork cubes in oil until browned. Add the chopped tomatoes, salt and bay leaf. Fry on a high heat for a few minutes, then simmer until pork is cooked and tomatoes reduced to a sauce, about 20 minutes. This makes a good "barbecue" sandwich when served on bread rolls. Serves 4.

COSTILLAS AL HORNO
Baked Spare Ribs

1 rack spare ribs, about 1 3/4 kilos

Make up the stuffing as in the recipe for Stuffed Turkey, Catalan Style (Chapter 10). Put the stuffing in a roasting pan and put the rack of spare ribs on top of it. Cover with foil and bake in a medium oven until the meat is tender, about 1½ hours. Remove the foil during the last 15 minutes and let the ribs brown slightly. Serves 4.

COSTILLAS A LA PARRILLA
Grilled Spare Ribs

100	ml. water	1	bay leaf
1	teaspoon salt		freshly ground pepper
3	tablespoons chopped parsley	1	lemon
1	teaspoon oregano	1 3/4	kilos spare ribs
1	teaspoon thyme		

Mix together the water, salt, parsley, oregano, thyme, bay leaf, pepper and quartered lemon. Cut the ribs into 3-rib segments and place them in a shallow pan. Pour over the marinade and let set for 4 hours. Grill them very slowly over charcoal or on a griddle, brushing with the marinade, until they are thoroughly cooked, about 15 minutes on each side. Serve with *alioli* and *picante* sauces (see chapter 12). Serves 4.

PINCHITOS
Kebabs, Moroccan Style

Cooked over charcoal braziers at fiestas and in tapa bars, these kebabs are relatives of the ones made in Tangier just across the Straits of Gibraltar. The difference is that in Morocco, a Moslem country, they are made with lamb and in Spain they are usually made with pork. The *especias para pinchitos,* a mixture of spices, can be purchased in many markets. Where not available, use a curry powder to which is added extra cumin. These are usually served as snacks, accompanied by bread.

1 kilo pork, lamb or veal	1/2 teaspoon cayenne or red pepper flakes
4 tablespoons chopped parsley	1 teaspoon salt
10 cloves garlic, minced	
2 lemons	
1 tablespoon Moroccan spices *(especias para pinchitos)*	

Cut the meat into quite small cubes (about 2 cm. square). In a deep bowl, glass or crockery, put a single layer of meat. Sprinkle with chopped parsley, minced garlic, a pinch of salt, a teaspoon of spice and a tiny pinch of cayenne. Squeeze the juice of a half-lemon over it. Add another layer of meat and other ingredients. Continue until all the meat is used. Cover and marinate in the refrigerator 6 to 12 hours, turning the mixture 2 or 3 times. Thread 4 or 5 pieces of the meat on thin, metal skewers and grill over charcoal or under broiler grill until browned on all sides. Makes about 20 kebabs.

LAMB AND KID

Milk-fed, baby lamb and kid are much appreciated in Spain and can be used in the following recipes fairly interchangeably. Except when roasted whole, the meat is usually hacked into even-sized pieces, which, unfortunately, makes for bone splinters. You can instead have the meat jointed, but then allow longer cooking time. In markets outside of Spain where the suckling animals are not available, use small lamb chops, well-trimmed, or slices from a leg of lamb for these dishes. In general, Spaniards like their meat well-cooked, so spring lamb is usually braised rather than roasted and is never served still pink.

CAZUELA DE CHIVO
Baby Kid in Casserole

I first had this dish at a wedding feast in the country, where two kids were cooked in a huge cauldron, almost a metre in diameter, which went into the domed bread oven to cook for many hours. I've made the casserole on a much smaller scale in my gas oven, using lamb chops instead of the kid. It's an easy dish and wonderfully spiced.

1 1/2-2	kilos baby lamb or kid or use lamb chops	4	bay leaves
150	ml. oil	2	teaspoons salt
8	medium potatoes, peeled and sliced	2	cloves garlic
6	medium tomatoes, sliced	10	peppercorns
2	large onions, sliced	4	cloves
3	small green peppers, cut in strips	1	teaspoon cinnamon
2	tablespoons parsley, chopped	1	teaspoon saffron
1	head garlic, roasted	1/2	litre white wine

Have the butcher cut the lamb or kid into even-sized pieces. Pour the oil into the bottom of a large roasting pan or deep casserole. Put a layer of sliced potatoes on the bottom and alternate with layers of sliced tomatoes and onions. Then put in the meat. Cover with strips of green pepper, chopped parsley, cloves of roasted garlic, bay leaves and another layer of sliced potatoes, tomatoes and onion. In the mortar crush the salt, 2 cloves of garlic, peppercorns, cloves, cinnamon and saffron. Dissolve in a little white wine and add to the pot with the rest of the wine. Put the casserole in a hot oven for 10 minutes, then reduce the heat to moderate and cook until meat and potatoes are very tender, about 3 hours. Serves 6 to 8.

COCHIFRITO A LA NAVARRA
Lamb Sauté, Navarra Style

1	kilo boned lamb	1/4	teaspoon pepper
3	tablespoons lard or oil	300	ml. water
1	onion, chopped	1/2	teaspoon salt
2	cloves garlic, chopped	1	lemon
2	teaspoons paprika		parsley

Cut the lamb into small cubes. Heat the lard in a heavy frying pan and on a high heat sauté the meat. When it is partially browned, add the chopped onion and garlic. Keep stirring the lamb while it browns. Then add the paprika and pepper and immediately add the water. Continue cooking on a hot fire until the liquid is evaporated and the meat begins to fry again, then add the juice of the lemon and the parsley. Cover the pan and cook slowly another 15 minutes. Serves 4.

CHOTO AJILLO A LA GRANADINA
Baby Kid with Garlic, Granada Style

1 1/2	kilos baby lamb or kid or use lamb chops	1	teaspoon oregano
	the animal's liver or 150 grams chicken livers		pinch of cayenne
		1	teaspoon paprika
75	ml. oil	1/2	teaspoon salt
7	cloves garlic	1	tablespoon vinegar
1	slice bread	2	bay leaves
10	peppercorns	1/2	litre white wine

Cut the lamb or kid into even-sized pieces. Cut the liver in several pieces. Heat the oil in a frying pan and sauté the liver until lightly browned and remove it. In the same oil fry 5 cloves garlic and the bread until they are toasted, and remove. Continue browning the meat in the same oil. Meanwhile, in mortar or blender crush the peppercorns, oregano, cayenne, paprika, salt and 2 cloves raw garlic with the fried garlic, bread and liver. Add the vinegar and a little wine to make a smooth paste. Place the meat in a deep pot or casserole. Add the remaining wine to the frying pan and scrape up all the browned bits. Dissolve the paste from the mortar in the wine and pour over the meat with the bay leaves. Cover and simmer until the meat is tender, about 1½ hours. Serves 6. The *caldereta extremeña,* a lamb stew from Extremadura, is prepared similarly.

CORDERO AL CHILINDRON
Lamb with Peppers

A speciality of Aragon, this dish is prepared as for Chicken with Peppers *(Pollo al Chilindrón)* in Chapter 10. Though baby lamb should be used, it's a very good dish made with lamb chops instead.

CORDERO A LA PASTORA
Lamb, Shepherd's Style

1 1/4	kilos baby lamb		thyme, rosemary, bay leaf, mint and parsley
5	peppercorns		
1	clove	1/2	litre water
2	cloves garlic	3/4	kilo small potatoes
2	tablespoons vinegar	1/4	litre milk
50	ml. white wine		salt and pepper
75	ml. oil		chopped parsley
1	tablespoon flour		

Cut the lamb into regular-sized pieces. In the mortar crush the peppercorns, clove, garlic and ½ teaspoon salt. Mix with the vinegar and wine and rub the pieces of meat with this mixture. Marinate overnight. Put the oil in a pot or casserole and warm it. Turn the meat in the oil just to seal it, without letting it brown. Stir in the flour and blend well, then add the bouquet of herbs and the water. Peel the potatoes, but if they are small, leave them whole. Add to the casserole and cover and simmer until the liquid is reduced, about 1 hour. Then add the milk, salt and pepper to taste, and cook until the sauce is smooth, about 15 minutes more. Serve in the same casserole sprinkled with chopped parsley. Serves 4.

CALDERETA DE CORDERO
Lamb Stew

1 kilo boned lamb	50 ml. oil
1 onion, quartered	6 peppercorns
2 tomatoes, quartered	1 clove
4 small peppers, cut in half	1 teaspoon paprika
1 head garlic, roasted	1/2 teaspoon cumin
bay leaf, parsley, thyme	1 slice bread, soaked in water
1/2 teaspoon salt	

Cut the lamb into cubes and put in a pot. Add enough water to just cover the meat. Bring to a boil, skim the froth and reduce to a simmer. Add the onion, tomatoes, peppers, roasted garlic, bouquet of herbs, salt and oil. Cover and simmer until the meat is tender, about 45 minutes. In the mortar or blender crush the peppercorns, clove, paprika, cumin and soaked bread. Dissolve in a little water and add to the lamb. Cook another few minutes and serve. Serves 4 to 6.

PIERNA DE CORDERO ASADA
Roast Leg of Lamb

Restaurants which specialize in baby lamb will usually serve one leg per person. Except for very hearty eaters, the portion will usually serve two very nicely. Where baby lamb is not available, use a leg of spring lamb weighing about 1½ kilos.

2 or 3 legs of baby lamb or kid	100 ml. white wine
3 cloves garlic	1 dozen small potatoes
salt and pepper	2 carrots, sliced
1 teaspoon oregano	1 bay leaf
50 grams lard	

With a sharp knife cut slits in the surface of the meat and insert slivers of garlic. Rub the meat with salt and pepper and crushed oregano. Let it sit for an hour then rub it with the lard, put in an oiled roasting pan and place in a hot oven. Let the meat brown, about 15 minutes, then reduce the heat to medium and pour over the wine. Add the potatoes, peeled, the sliced carrots and bay leaf to the pan. Roast until the meat is done, about 1 hour for baby lamb (or allow 20 minutes per 500 grams for a larger leg of lamb). Baste frequently with the pan juices and add additional water or wine as needed, so there is always some liquid in the pan. Strain the pan liquid and serve in a sauce bowl. Serve the meat garnished with the potatoes and carrots. Serves 4 to 6.

PIERNA DE CORDERO GUISADA CON JUDIAS BLANCAS
Braised Leg of Lamb with White Beans

1	leg of lamb or mutton, about 1½ kilos	4	carrots
	salt and pepper	1/2	litre meat stock
4	tablespoons oil, lard or butter		salt and pepper
4	cloves garlic	1/4	kilo white beans, soaked overnight
1	dozen tiny onions	1	slice onion
		1	bay leaf

Have the butcher bone the leg of lamb and roll and tie it. Rub it with salt and
pepper. In a large pot, heat the oil and very slowly brown the meat on all sides.
Add the garlic cut in slivers, the whole, peeled onions, the carrots, peeled and cut
in chunks. Let them brown in the fat for a few minutes, then add the meat stock.
Cover and simmer the meat until it is very tender, about 1½ hours. While the
meat is cooking, put the soaked beans in another pot with the onion and bay leaf
and plenty of water to cover. Bring to a boil, then simmer until tender, about 1
hour. Add salt when the beans are partially cooked. Drain them and add to the
pot in which the lamb is cooking. Cook another 20 minutes and serve the lamb,
sliced, on a platter surrounded by the beans, potatoes and carrots. Serves 6.

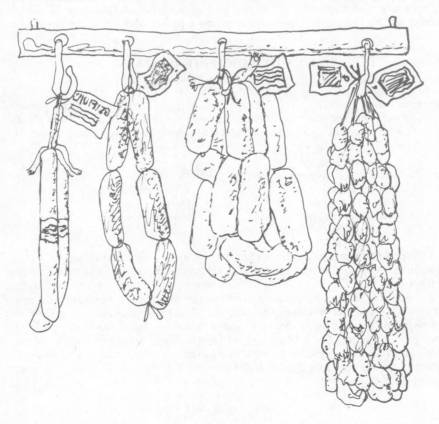

LECHAZO ASADO AL CASTELLANO
Roast Baby Lamb, Castilian Style

Choose a lamb of about 4 weeks. Split it in half lengthwise. Rub it inside and out with salt and pepper. In a bowl mix finely chopped thyme, parsley, garlic and onion with a little paprika. Rub the meat with this mixture and let it sit for 2 hours. Then grease it with lard and place in a roasting pan. Put in a very hot oven, skin side up, until browned, basting with the fat in the pan. Then reduce the heat and pour over a little white wine. Roast the lamb until tender, about 45 minutes, adding extra wine as needed. Remove to a serving platter and cut into serving pieces. Add a little extra wine to the pan and boil it briefly. Serve the sauce with the lamb. Serves about 8.

CHULETAS DE CORDERO AL JEREZ
Lamb Chops with Sherry

8	lamb chops	2	bay leaves
	salt and pepper		pinch of ground cloves
50	ml. oil	1/2	teaspoon ground pepper
2	medium onions, chopped	1/2	teaspoon salt
4	carrots, diced	1/4	litre sherry

Sprinkle the lamb chops with salt and pepper. Heat the oil in a large frying pan and brown the chops on both sides. Remove them to a plate. In the same oil sauté the chopped onions and diced carrots until softened. Return the chops to the pan and add the bay leaves, clove, pepper, salt and sherry. Cover and simmer, adding a little water if necessary, until chops are tender and sauce reduced, about 40 minutes. Serves 4.

CHULETAS DE CORDERO A LA PAMPLONA
Lamb Chops, Pamplona Style

12-16	baby lamb chops	3	tomatoes, peeled and chopped
2	tablespoons oil	1	teaspoon sugar
2	tablespoons lard		salt and pepper
100	grams diced ham	1/4	kilo Pamplona chorizo sausage
1	onion, chopped		

Heat the oil and lard in a frying pan and fry the lamb chops. As they are browned, transfer them to an oven casserole. In the same fat fry the diced ham and chopped onion. Then add the tomatoes, sugar, salt and pepper. Let cook for several minutes, then pour the sauce over the lamb chops. Put in a medium oven until the meat is tender, about 20 minutes. Cover the casserole with a layer of sliced *chorizo* and return to the oven to cook for several minutes. Serve in the same casserole. Serves 4.

HAM

Two kinds of ham are used in Spanish cookery — the salt-cured *jamon serrano,* which is most usually served raw, and *jamón cocido,* or cooked ham, which might be baked English style or fried and sauced with sherry. The raw ham is used in small quantities to flavour beans and pottages. Soften it before cooking by soaking in water.

MAGRAS CON TOMATE
Sliced Ham with Tomato Sauce

12	slices serrano ham	1	kilo tomatoes, peeled, seeded and
150	ml. milk		chopped
	flour	1	teaspoon sugar
4	tablespoons oil or lard		salt and pepper to taste
4	slices bread		

Put the slices of ham in a shallow dish and pour over the milk. Let it soak for an hour. Remove the ham and pat it dry. Flour the ham and fry it in oil or lard until lightly browned. Remove and set aside. Cut each slice of bread into 4 triangles. Dip them quickly into the milk and fry in the remaining oil until toasted. Remove and set aside. Add the prepared tomatoes to the pan with the sugar and cook them until reduced to a sauce, about 10 minutes, seasoning with a very little salt as the ham is salty. Return the fried ham to the sauce and simmer another 10 minutes. Serve with the fried bread. Serves 4.

JAMON A LO GITANILLO
Gypsy Style Ham

12	slices serrano ham	75	ml. vinegar
3	tablespoons lard	75	ml. water
	freshly ground pepper	1	teaspoon sugar
1	tablespoon flour		

Soak the ham for 24 hours in water, changing it several times. Drain it and pat dry. Fry the ham in the lard and remove. Season it with pepper. Stir the flour into the fat and let it cook, stirring, for a few minutes. Then add the vinegar, water and sugar and stir until the sauce is thickened. Return the ham to the pan and cook to reheat for a few minutes. Serves 4.

LACON CON GRELOS
Cured Pork Shoulder with Turnip Tops

The *grelos* in this Galician speciality are the flowering stalks of the turnip. If not available, use turnip leaves, cabbage or other greens. *Lacón* is salt-cured pork hand or shoulder. (Ham can be used instead.) Other salted meats — the feet, ears and cheeks — are usually added to this tasty brew. Soak all of the salted meat in water to cover for 24 hours, changing the water several times.

1	kilo *lacón,* soaked	1/2	kilo chorizo (red sausage, preferably Galician)
200	grams ear, cheek, etc.		
1	pig's foot, split	12	small potatoes
1 1/2 kilo *grelos*			salt and pepper

Put the soaked *lacón,* pig's ear, cheek and foot to cook in plenty of water to cover. Bring to a boil, skim, then simmer until the *lacón* is tender, about 1½ hours. Remove to another pan with a little of the liquid to cover. Wash the *grelos,* chop them into pieces and blanch in boiling water and drain. Then add to the same broth in which the *lacón* cooked. Add the chorizo and let cook 10 minutes, then add the potatoes, peeled and left whole. Add salt if necessary and pepper. Cook until potatoes and greens are tender, about 20 minutes. With a skimmer, remove the *grelos* to a serving platter. Cut the meat into pieces and put on top and arrange the chorizos and potatoes around the side of the platter. Serves 6.

JAMON AL JEREZ
Ham with Sherry

1	kilo cooked ham	75	grams dried apricots
100	ml. cream sherry		*huevos hilados,* candied egg yolk
50	grams butter		threads

Rub the piece of ham with the softened butter and put it in an oven tin. Place in a hot oven for 5 minutes, then reduce heat to medium and pour sherry over the meat. Soak the apricots in hot water to cover for 20 minutes. Drain them and add to the ham. If more liquid is needed, use the juice in which the apricots soaked. Roast the ham, basting frequently, for about 50 minutes (allow approximately 25 minutes per 500 grams). Place the ham on a serving platter and surround with the candied egg yolk threads. Makes 6 servings.

MINCED MEAT, PÂTÉS AND SAUSAGE

Minced — ground — pork or a combination of pork and veal is more widely used in Spanish dishes than minced beef. Pork, of course, must be thoroughly cooked. Sometimes chopped ham or pork fat is added to the mixture both to flavour it and to keep it juicy.

ALBONDIGAS
Meatballs

Spanish style meatballs are usually added to a sauce to simmer for another 20 minutes after frying. Use either almond sauce or tomato sauce (see chapter 12).

This same mixture is used to stuff peppers, tomatoes, marrow, aubergine, onions, etc. If made with minced pork, it should be partially cooked before adding the egg and stuffing the vegetable.

1/2 kilo minced pork and/or veal	1/2 teaspoon salt
2 slices bread, soaked in milk or water and squeezed out	1/4 teaspoon ground pepper
	1/4 teaspoon grated nutmeg
1 clove garlic, finely minced	1 egg, beaten
1 tablespoon finely chopped onion	flour
2 tablespoons chopped parsley	oil

If you have a processor, put the soaked bread, garlic, onion, parsley, salt, pepper, nutmeg and egg in the work bowl and process until smooth. Then add the minced meat and process a few seconds longer. Otherwise, put all the ingredients in a large bowl and knead them well with the hands to make a homogenous mixture. Form into small 3 cm. balls. Roll them in flour and fry them slowly in oil until browned on all sides. Remove. Then add the meatballs to the sauce and simmer about 20 minutes, adding water or stock to the sauce to keep it from scorching. If made of beef, the fried meatballs can be served as is, accompanied by a sauce for dipping. Makes about 3 dozen.

ROLLO DE CARNE
Meat Roll

1/2	kilo minced veal	1	chicken breast, boned and cut in thin strips
1/2	kilo minced pork	150	grams sliced ham
50	grams breadcrumbs		flour
2	eggs, well beaten		oil
1	teaspoon salt		onion, carrot, celery
1/4	teaspoon ground pepper		thyme, bay leaf, parsley
1	clove garlic, minced	1/2	litre white wine
	grated nutmeg	1/4	litre water
2	tablespoons brandy		
1	tablespoon chopped parsley		

Mix the minced veal and pork with the breadcrumbs, beaten eggs, salt and pepper, minced garlic, grated nutmeg, brandy and parsley. Knead until very smooth. Spread a sheet of foil on a flat surface and flour it lightly. Spread half the minced meat on top of it, shaping it into a rectangle. On top of the minced meat place the strips of chicken breast and the sliced ham. Spread the remaining minced meat on top. Using the foil as an aid, roll the meat up, patting it into shape. Flour the roll. Heat oil in a pan large enough to hold it and brown it very slowly on all sides. Then add slices of onion, carrot, celery and bouquet of herbs. Pour over the wine and water and simmer the meat, turning it carefully, for an hour. It can be served hot with the strained sauce or removed to a platter and pressed with a weight on top to be sliced and served cold garnished with salad. Six servings.

BITOKES
Beef Patties

1	kilo minced beef or veal	75	ml. milk
2	cloves garlic, finely minced	2	tablespoons breadcrumbs
	salt and pepper	2	eggs
1	tablespoon oil		flour
1	tablespoon flour		oil

Put the minced meat in a bowl and season it with the minced garlic and salt and pepper. Let it macerate for 30 minutes. Meanwhile in a saucepan heat the oil and stir into it the flour. Cook, stirring, for a few minutes, then whisk in the milk. Stir until this sauce is thickened. Remove and let it cool slightly, then work it into the meat along with the breadcrumbs and 1 egg, beaten. Divide the meat into 8 pieces. Form balls and flatten them into patties. Dip them into beaten egg, then into flour and sauté them gently in oil until browned on both sides. Makes 8 patties. Serve on toasted bread, the Spanish version of hamburger.

HORNAZO A LO CASTELLANO
Castilian Baked Lamb Roll

3/4 kilo minced lamb or veal	1 egg, beaten
50 grams chopped ham	flour
50 grams chopped salt pork	75 ml. oil
2 slices bread	1 onion, chopped
300 ml. white wine	1/2 teaspoon oregano
grated nutmeg	1/2 teaspoon thyme
1/4 teaspoon cinnamon	salt and pepper
cabbage, chard, spinach or grape leaves	

Put the minced lamb in a bowl with the chopped ham and chopped salt pork. Put the bread to soak in 50 ml. wine until softened. Squeeze it out, reserving the wine, and add the bread to the meat. Season with salt and pepper, nutmeg and cinnamon. Blanch cabbage, chard, spinach or grape leaves in boiling water until wilted, drain and cut out the stem. Make an overlapping layer of them on a flat table. Form the meat into a roll and place it on top of the leaves. Roll the leaves around the meat and tie with string. Dip the roll in beaten egg, then dredge in flour. Fry it in oil, turning to brown on all sides. Add the chopped onion, the oregano, thyme, reserved white wine and enough additional wine to partially cover the roll. Season with salt and pepper. Bake in a medium oven until done, about 1 hour. Serves 6.

FIAMBRE
Pâté

1/2 kilo veal	50 ml. brandy
1/2 kilo calf's liver	2 eggs, separated
200 grams salt pork	1 teaspoon salt
3 tablespoons breadcrumbs	1/2 teaspoon freshly ground pepper
1 onion, finely chopped	1/2 teaspoon thyme
1 clove garlic, minced	grated nutmeg
1 tablespoon parsley, finely chopped	200 grams ham, thinly sliced
80 ml. white wine	

Have the butcher grind the veal, liver and salt pork two or three times. Put it in a bowl and mix with brandy and the yolks of the eggs. Season with salt, pepper, thyme and nutmeg. Whip the whites of the eggs until stiff and fold them into the meat mixture. Grease a loaf pan and line it with the sliced ham. Put in the pâté mixture, patting it down. Place the mould in an oven tin, add boiling water to half the depth of the pan, and put in a medium-hot oven until a knife comes out clean, about 1½ hours. Let cool in the pan for 30 minutes. Drain off the liquid, then unmould the meat on to a serving plate. Let cool and serve sliced.

MORTERUELO
Meat Conserve

In the days before refrigeration, minced meats would be packed in clay pots and sealed with lard to conserve them. The *morteruelo* can be served cold like pâté, spread on bread, or hot, in which case it resembles hash.

1	chicken (or 1/2 stewing hen)	300	grams breadcrumbs, toasted
1	wild hare or rabbit	2	teaspoons salt
1	partridge	1	teaspoon pepper, coarsely ground
1/4	kilo serrano ham	1	tablespoon paprika
1/2	kilo pork liver	1	teaspoon cinnamon
1/4	kilo streaky belly pork *(panceta)*	1/4	teaspoon ground cloves
100	ml. oil or 65 grams lard	1	teaspoon caraway seeds

Clean all the meats and put them together in a very large pot. Add water to cover. Bring to a boil and skim off the froth. Cover and simmer for 3 hours. Remove the meats from the pot and save the broth. Remove and discard all skin, bones, tendons and gristle. Finely chop all the meats (with a knife, mincer or processor). Heat the oil or lard in a pot and add the breadcrumbs and the spices. Stir in about 1/4 litre of the reserved broth and all the minced meat, adding additional broth if needed. The mixture should be very thick. Cook it very slowly for 30 minutes to thicken it (an asbestos pad is useful to avoid scorching). Cool and refrigerate for several days before serving.

RELLENO
Sausage Stuffing

This is cooked, like a sausage, inside a casing made from the cleaned stomach. If you don't have sausage casings, place the prepared meat mixture in the centre of a clean cloth or square of cheesecloth. Gather the ends together and tie them, forming the mixture into a round ball. After cooking let it cool completely before unwrapping.

1/2	kilo pork	2	tablespoons chopped parsley
1/4	kilo ham	1	lemon
1/4	kilo chicken or turkey breast	6	eggs, beaten
2	cloves garlic	200	grams breadcrumbs
1/2	teaspoon saffron	1	onion
1	teaspoon pepper	1	bay leaf
2	teaspoons salt		ham bone
1/4	teaspoon cloves		

Have the butcher mince together the pork, ham and turkey breast or chop them all finely with a knife. Place the meat in a bowl. In a mortar crush the garlic, saffron and pepper. Mix with the salt, cloves and chopped parsley and add to the meat. Add the juice of the lemon, the beaten eggs and the breadcrumbs. Work the mixture with the hands to blend very well, adding additional breadcrumbs if needed to keep the mixture stiff enough to hold its shape. Fill the casing and stitch up or tie in a cloth. Put into boiling water for 2 minutes and drain. Then bring a pot of water to boil with the sliced onion, bay leaf and ham bone. Put the meat sausage into it and simmer for 2 hours. Drain well. Serve cold, thinly sliced. Makes 15 hors-d'oeuvre servings.

OFFAL (VARIETY MEATS)

Though pork and lamb liver are most frequently used, calf or beef liver can be used in these dishes if preferred. Lamb and veal kidneys are considered the most delicate in flavour but, again, any can be used. Pork tongues are the most usual; if substituting beef tongue, which is much larger, increase cooking time.

HIGADO CON SALSA DE ALMENDRAS
Liver in Almond Sauce

1/2	kilo liver	8	peppercorns
50	ml. oil	1	clove
1	clove garlic	1/2	teaspoon salt
1	dozen almonds, blanched and skinned	100	ml. white wine
1	slice bread	1	bay leaf
1/4	teaspoon saffron	2	tablespoons chopped parsley

Cut the liver into 3 cm. cubes. Heat the oil in a frying pan and in it fry the garlic, almonds and bread until toasted. Remove and set aside. In the same oil sauté the pieces of liver until they are browned. Meanwhile, in the mortar crush the saffron, peppercorns, clove and salt with the garlic, almonds and bread. Dissolve this paste in a little water and add to the pan with the wine and bay leaf. Return the liver to the sauce and cook gently for 20 minutes. Garnish with chopped parsley. Serve accompanied by potatoes cut in dice and fried until browned. Four servings.

HIGADO EN ADOBO
Liver in Sour Sauce

1	kilo liver	100	ml. water
50	ml. oil	1/2	teaspoon salt
4	cloves garlic	1	teaspoon paprika
	piece of chili pepper	1/2	teaspoon pepper
50	ml. vinegar	1	teaspoon oregano

Cut the liver into strips. Heat the oil in a pan and sauté it. In the mortar or blender crush the garlic, chili pepper, vinegar, water, salt, paprika, pepper and oregano. Pour this over the liver and cook until liquid is reduced by half. Serves 6.

CHANFAINA
Liver Sauté

1/2	kilo stale bread			salt and pepper
1/2	kilo liver		1	bay leaf
100	ml. oil		6	walnuts
1	large onion, thinly sliced			chopped parsley
3	cloves garlic			

Remove crusts from the bread and cut it into strips. Cut the liver into similar-sized pieces. Put a little of the oil in a frying pan and fry the pieces of bread and remove them. Add more oil and put in the liver, the sliced onion, the chopped garlic, salt and pepper and bay leaf. While the liver is sautéing, crush the walnuts in the mortar. When the liver is done, add them to the liver with the pieces of fried bread and cook a few minutes more. Sprinkle with chopped parsley. Makes 4 servings.

HIGADILLOS SALTEADOS
Sautéed Chicken Livers

3	tablespoons oil	100	ml. dry sherry
1/4	kilo chicken livers, cut up		salt and pepper
150	grams salt pork or bacon, diced	1/2	teaspoon thyme
1/2	onion, finely chopped		chopped parsley
1	clove garlic, minced		strips of red pimento

Heat the oil in a frying pan and sauté the pieces of chicken liver with the diced salt pork. Add the onion and garlic, then the sherry, salt and pepper and thyme. Cook 10 minutes. Sprinkle with parsley and garnish with strips of pimento. Good served in a rice ring. Makes 2 servings.

HIGADO AL VINO TINTO
Liver with Red Wine

1/2	kilo calf liver		salt and pepper
3	tablespoons oil	1	tablespoon lemon juice
1	tablespoon flour		chopped parsley
100	ml. red wine		

Cut the liver in strips. Sauté it in the oil until lightly browned and remove. Stir in the flour, then add the wine, salt and pepper and lemon juice, stirring well. Return the liver to the pan and cook until the sauce is thickened slightly. Sprinkle with chopped parsley. Four servings.

RIÑONES AL JEREZ
Sautéed Kidneys with Sherry

Very fresh lamb or veal kidneys should not need soaking or blanching. Pork or beef kidneys can be blanched for 15 minutes in simmering water to which has been added lemon juice or vinegar. Peel off the thin membrane which encases the kidney and cut out the core of fat. Small lamb kidneys may be sliced crosswise; the larger veal kidney should be cut in quarters and sliced.

1/2	kilo kidneys, prepared for cooking	1	bay leaf
4	tablespoons oil or lard	100	ml. dry sherry
1/2	onion, finely chopped	100	ml. meat stock
1	clove garlic, chopped		salt and pepper
1	tablespoon flour		chopped parsley

Heat the oil or lard in a frying pan and sauté the kidneys very gently — high heat and overcooking cause kidneys to harden. When they are lightly browned, remove them and reserve. Add the chopped onion and garlic to the fat and sauté until softened. Stir in the flour and cook for a minute, then add the bay leaf, sherry and stock. Season with salt and pepper and simmer the sauce for 10 minutes. Return the kidneys to the pan and heat them gently for a few minutes. Serve sprinkled with chopped parsley. Makes 6 first-course portions.

RIÑONES CON CHAMPIÑONES
Kidneys with Mushrooms

1	dozen lambs' kidneys	50	ml. red wine
25	grams butter	1	tablespoon tomato sauce
2	scallions, chopped	1/2	teaspoon oregano
1/4	kilo mushrooms, sliced		salt and pepper
100	grams bacon, diced		chopped parsley
100	ml. dry sherry		

Cut the kidneys in quarters. Heat the butter in a frying pan and sauté them very gently. Remove when they are lightly browned. Add the chopped scallions, sliced mushrooms and diced bacon to the pan and sauté briskly. Then add the sherry, red wine, tomato sauce, oregano, salt and pepper. Cook this sauce about 10 minutes, then return the kidneys to the pan to reheat gently. Do not overcook, or the kidneys will toughen. Sprinkle with chopped parsley. Serves 6.

CRIADILLAS
Fries

I first encountered this dish in a Seville restaurant where it was translated into English as "the moo cow's delight." *Criadillas* is kitchen terminology for the testicles of bulls or sheep, in English called "fries," "mountain oysters" or "animelles." It is a delicate meat, not unlike brains but a little more solid.

4	calves' or lambs' fries	50	grams fine breadcrumbs
2	teaspoons vinegar	75	ml. oil
1	egg, beaten		lemon slices
1/2	teaspoon salt		

Blanch the fries in boiling salted water for 5 minutes. Remove and let them cool. Then peel off the layers of skin. Slice them thickly and put in a bowl. Add enough water to cover and the vinegar. Soak for 2 hours. Then drain well and pat the slices dry. Place the beaten egg and salt in one bowl and the crumbs on another plate. Dip the slices first into egg, then into breadcrumbs and sauté in oil until golden on both sides. Serve garnished with lemon slices. Serves 6 as a starter.

SESOS HUECOS
Scatterbrains

These make tasty hors-d'oeuvres or starter. Calf's or lamb's brains are the best, but pork or beef brains are also eaten. A half-kilo should make appetizer nibbles for about eight people.

1/2	kilo brains	75	grams flour
2	teaspoons vinegar		salt and white pepper
2	teaspoons salt	100	ml. white wine
1	sliced onion	2	egg whites
	bay leaf and parsley		oil for deep frying
1	tablespoon lemon juice		parsley sprigs and lemon wedges
2	teaspoons oil		

Soak the brains in cold water for 2 hours, changing the water frequently. Gently pull off the outer membranes, then soak 2 hours more in water to which the vinegar has been added. Bring a litre of water to a boil with the salt, sliced onion, bay leaf, parsley and lemon juice. Reduce the heat so the water just barely simmers and blanch the brains for 15 minutes. Drain and cool. (If not to be used immediately, refrigerate.) While the brains are soaking, prepare the fritter batter, which needs to set several hours (or overnight). In a bowl mix the oil, flour, salt and pepper and white wine, beating well to make a smooth batter, adding a spoonful of water to make the consistency of thick cream. Let it rest, refrigerated. Whip the egg whites with a drop of lemon juice until they are stiff. Fold them into the batter until well mixed. Cut the blanched brains into small pieces (3 cm.). Put them in a dish and add enough of the fritter batter to cover them generously. Scoop up spoonfuls of the batter with brains and drop into the hot oil. Remove when they are puffed and golden. Serve with parsley sprigs and lemon wedges.

MOLLEJAS AL OLOROSO
Sweetbreads with Sherry

1/2	kilo sweetbreads	50	ml. chicken broth
50	grams butter	1	tablespoon lemon juice
50	grams ham, diced		salt and pepper
1	tablespoon chopped onion	50	ml. cream.
50	ml. oloroso sherry		

Soak, clean and blanch the sweetbreads as for brains (see preceding recipe). Then cut them in slices. Melt the butter in a pan and sauté the diced ham and onion. Add the sweetbreads and sauté gently for several minutes. Add the sherry, stock lemon juice, salt and pepper and simmer, covered, for 20 minutes, adding stock if necessary. Remove the sweetbreads, stir in the cream and heat thoroughly. Pour over the sweetbreads and serve. Makes 4 servings.

ESTOFADO DE LENGUA
Braised Tongue

1	kilo pork tongues	6	cloves garlic
1	onion, quartered	1	slice bread
1	carrot, cut in half	1/2	teaspoon saffron
3	bay leaves	10	peppercorns
	salt and pepper	2	cloves
75	ml. oil	100	ml. dry sherry
1	dozen almonds, blanched and peeled	8	medium potatoes

Scrub the tongues under running water then put them to soak in a basin of salted water for 2 hours. Rinse again. Put them in a lidded pot with water to cover, the quartered onion, carrot, a bay leaf, salt and pepper. Bring to a boil, skim off the froth, and simmer the tongues for 40 minutes. Remove them from the water, reserving the broth. As soon as they are cool enough to handle, but while still warm, slit the skin and peel it off. Then cut the tongues crosswise into thick slices, discarding any bone and fatty parts from the thick ends. Heat the oil in a pot and in it fry the almonds, garlic and bread until toasted and crisp. Remove. In the mortar or blender crush the saffron, peppercorns and cloves with the fried almonds, garlic and bread. Dissolve in the sherry. Add the sliced tongue to the oil and sauté it, turning with a fork, for a few minutes. Add the almond mixture, ¹⁄₂ teaspoon salt, potatoes peeled and cut in small pieces, the 2 bay leaves and enough of the reserved broth to just cover the meat and potatoes. Cover and simmer until the tongue is very tender, about 1 hour. Serves 6.

LENGUA CON NUECES
Tongue with Walnut Sauce

1	veal tongue, trimmed (about 1 kilo)	10	peppercorns
50	ml. oil or lard	2	cloves
1	carrot, chopped	100	ml. white wine
1	onion, chopped	1	tomato, quartered
1	stalk celery, chopped	1	dozen walnuts
1	clove garlic, slivered	1/4	litre milk
2	bay leaves		salt and pepper

Clean the tongue as in the preceding recipe. Put it in a pot with water to cover and a spoonful of salt. Bring to a boil, then simmer for 40 minutes. Drain it reserving the broth and when cool enough to handle, slit the skin and peel it off. Heat the oil in a large pot and put the whole tongue into it with the chopped carrot, onion, celery and garlic. Turn the tongue in the oil to brown it on all sides. Then add the bay leaves, peppercorns, cloves, 1 teaspoon salt, white wine and quartered tomato. Add enough of the reserved broth to partially cover the meat. Cover and simmer until the tongue is very tender, about 2 hours. Meanwhile, crush the walnuts in mortar or blender with the milk. Heat in a saucepan. Remove the tongue to a serving platter and slice it. Strain the pan juices and add to the saucepan with the ground walnuts. Simmer the sauce until it is somewhat reduced and spoon some of it over the sliced tongue. Serve the remaining sauce in a bowl. Accompany the tongue with fried potatoes. Serves 6.

LENGUAS CON SALSA DE GRANADAS
Tongue with Pomegranate Sauce

This Mallorcan sauce reminds me of ancient Persian dishes, in which the tart juice of the pomegranate lends a piquant flavour. Where fresh pomegranates are not available. use a little grenadine syrup with several spoonfuls of lemon juice.

4	pork tongues, trimmed (about 900 grams)	100 ml. dry sherry	
50	grams lard	200 ml. meat stock	
1	onion, chopped	salt and pepper	
2	pomegranates	fried potatoes	

Clean the tongues as in the recipe for braised tongue. Put them in a pot with water to cover and bring to a boil. Simmer for about 25 minutes, then drain and, when cool enough to handle, peel the skin from the tongues. Heat the lard in a pot and put in the tongues. Brown them slowly on all sides, adding the chopped onion. Cut the pomegranate in quarters and with a knife loosen the seeds from the membrane. Add them to the meat with the sherry, stock and salt and pepper. Cover and simmer until the tongue is very tender, about 1 hour. Remove the meat to a serving platter and slice it. Sieve the sauce and serve over it, garnished with a few reserved kernels of pomegranate. Accompany the meat with thickly sliced potatoes fried slowly in lard. Serves 4.

CALLOS A LA MADRILEÑA
Stewed Tripe, Madrid Style

I had never eaten tripe in my life — nor ever expected to — until one chill night in one of Madrid's *tascas,* when friends ordered plates of a hot and fragrant pottage, full of rich, deep flavours. So satisfying was the experience, that I have loved tripe ever since. Though time-consuming, it is not a difficult dish to prepare at home.

To clean and prepare the tripe: first wash it well under running water, scraping it with a knife to clean off bits of fat clinging to the surface. Then spread the tripe out and sprinkle it with coarse salt. Use a half lemon to "scrub" the tripe well on both sides, adding more salt and another lemon as needed. Rinse well. With scissors, cut the tripe into 4-cm. squares. Put the tripe in a bowl, sprinkle with salt and pour over it a glass of vinegar. Let it set for an hour, turning occasionally. Rinse again. Put it in a pot and cover with water. Bring to a boil, skimming off the froth, and boil 5 minutes. Drain. Put the pieces of tripe in fresh water with bay leaf, chili pepper, peppercorns, an onion stuck with cloves and several cloves of garlic. Bring to a boil, skim, then simmer until the tripe is tender, about 3 hours for veal tripe, 5 hours if it is cow's tripe. A calf's foot is often cooked with tripe. It should be skinned, split, well scrubbed and blanched with the tripe. After cooking, remove bones and cut the meat into pieces similar to the tripe. The tripe can be prepared up to this point and refrigerated, with the broth, until the following day.

1	kilo veal tripe, cooked	1	tablespoon paprika
1	calf's foot, cooked	100	ml. tomato sauce
75	ml. oil	1	teaspoon freshly ground pepper
1	onion, chopped		cayenne or chili to taste
1	carrot, chopped	1/2	teaspoon cumin
100	grams ham, diced		salt to taste
1	tablespoon flour	200	grams chorizo or longaniza
4	cloves garlic		

Drain the tripe, saving the broth. Put the tripe and cut-up calf's foot into a casserole. In a pan heat the oil and sauté the chopped onion, carrot, diced ham and garlic. Stir in the flour and the paprika, then the tomato sauce and about 1/4 litre of the reserved broth. Season with pepper, cayenne, cumin and salt. Pour over the tripe and add the chorizo. Cook slowly for an hour, adding additional broth as needed. The sauce should be thick. Before serving, cut the chorizo into slices and arrange on top of the tripe. Serves 6.

CALLOS A LA ANDALUZA
Andalusian Style Tripe

In Seville this is prepared similarly to Madrid tripe, with the addition of garbanzos and chopped mint. In the village where I live it is usually made with pig tripe instead of veal, and includes the trotter, ears and tail. Because it contains all the parts of the pig, it is a favourite dish for the festival of San Anton, St. Anthony Abbot, patron of farm animals.

1	kilo pig tripe	15	peppercorns
2	pig trotters, split	4	cloves
2	pig ears	1	chili pepper
1	pig tail	2	cloves garlic
1/4	kilo pork	2	teaspoons paprika
100	grams salt pork	2	teaspoons salt
300	grams garbanzos, soaked overnight	3	tablespoons oil
1	head garlic, roasted	1	onion, chopped
3	bay leaves	1	tomato, peeled and chopped
2	sprigs parsley	100	grams *morcilla* (black pudding)
1/2	teaspoon saffron	150	grams *chorizo* (red sausage)

Clean and blanch the tripe, trotters, ears and tail as in the previous recipe. Drain and put all of them to cook in water to cover for just 1 hour. Drain again. Cut the tripe into pieces, remove bones from the trotter and dice the meat, cut the ears and tail into pieces. Place them in a pot with the piece of pork, the salt pork, the soaked garbanzos, the roasted garlic, bay leaves and parsley. Cover with water, bring to a boil and simmer, partially covered. In the mortar or blender crush the saffron, peppercorns, cloves, chili pepper, raw garlic, paprika and salt. Dissolve in a little liquid from the pot and add to the tripe. Heat the oil in a frying pan and sauté the chopped onion. Add the chopped tomato and continue frying for 10 minutes until reduced to a sauce. Add this to the tripe with the black pudding and red sausage. Continue simmering until the tripe is done, about 3 hours. Cut the sausages, the pork and salt pork into pieces. Serves 8.

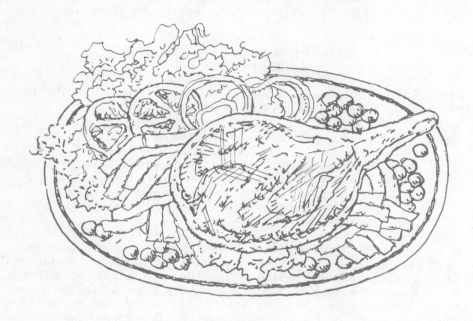

ESPARRAGOS MONTAÑESES
Mountain "Asparagus" (Lambs' Tails)

In the sheep-raising regions of Aragon it is customary to cut off the tails of the ewes to facilitate lambing — hence this dish. The preparation works very well with lamb riblets — the "spare ribs" — cut into single rib sections.

1	kilo lambs' tails or ribs	salt and pepper
2	onions	flour
	bay leaf, parsley	oil
4	large peppers	
3	tomatoes, peeled, seeded and chopped	

If using lambs' tails, cut off the tip and split the tail in half lengthwise. Cut into 10-cm. lengths. Soak in salt water for an hour. Put the tails or ribs in a pot, cover with water and add 1 onion, quartered, bay leaf and parsley. Season with salt and pepper and bring to a boil. Simmer until the meat is tender, about 40 minutes. Drain the tails and pat dry. Roast the peppers under the broiler until charred, cover with a cloth and let them set until cool enough to handle, then peel off the skin and cut the peppers into strips. Heat 50 ml. oil and fry the peppers for several minutes with a chopped onion. Add the prepared tomatoes and season with salt and pepper. Simmer until the sauce is reduced, about 10 minutes, adding a little of the broth in which the lamb cooked. Meanwhile, season the lambs' tails or ribs with salt and pepper. Dredge them in flour and fry in oil until crisp. Serve on a platter accompanied by the pepper sauce. Serves 4.

RABO DE TORO A LA SEVILLANA
Seville Braised Ox Tails

After a bullfight, *corrida de toros,* this is, indeed, made with bulls' tails. Otherwise, the butcher's oxtails will do nicely.

1	oxtail, about 1¼ kilos	75	ml. brandy
50	ml. oil	100	ml. red wine or sherry
1	onion, chopped		bay leaf, parsley, thyme
1	leek, chopped		salt, pepper, cloves
3	carrots, chopped	1	piece chili pepper or cayenne
2	cloves garlic, chopped	1	tomato, peeled and chopped
50	grams ham, diced		

Have the butcher cut the tails into segments of about 7 cm. Blanch them in boiling water and drain. In a pot heat the oil and add the chopped onion, leek, carrots, garlic and ham. Sauté until softened, then add the blanched pieces of oxtail and sauté on a high heat. Add the brandy, set it alight, and stir with a long-handled spoon until the flames subside. Then add the red wine or sherry, the herbs and the spices, the chili pepper and chopped tomato. Simmer until the meat is very tender, about 2 hours, adding stock or water as needed. When cooked, the sauce should be fairly thick from reduction. If not, thicken it with a little flour mixed in water. Serves 4.

CHAPTER 12

Sauces & Salad Dressings

Few Spanish cookbooks include a chapter on "sauces." In Spanish cookery, a sauce is an integral part of a dish rather than a separate preparation. There are, of course, some notable exceptions — mayonnaise and romesco are two — plus some others too good to be relegated exclusively to the dishes in which they are cooked.

SOFRITO
Fried Tomato

This is the backdrop of many Spanish dishes. A *sofrito* is not exactly a sauce, it's a procedure — the ingredients are fried in oil, then added to meat, fish, vegetables, eggs to finish cooking together. After frying, the sauce can be sieved or puréed in a blender if a smooth consistency is desired. More often it is left as is to reduce slowly during cooking.

50	ml. oil	1	kilo tomatoes (4 large), peeled, seeded and chopped
1	small onion, chopped	1/2	teaspoon salt
1	clove garlic, chopped		pinch of paprika, cumin and pepper
1	green pepper, chopped (optional		bay leaf, parsley
50	grams ham, diced (optional)		

Heat the oil in a frying pan and sauté the chopped onion, garlic and pepper until they are softened. Add the diced ham, if used, then the prepared tomatoes. "Fry" the tomatoes on a high heat for several minutes. Season with salt, spices and herbs and continue cooking briskly until the tomatoes "sweat" out their liquid and it has evaporated. Mash the tomatoes with the back of a fork as they fry. The tomatoes need to cook only about 12 minutes. At this point they can be sieved or the *sofrito* added to food to continue cooking. Makes about 300 ml. sauce.

SALSA DE TOMATE
Tomato Sauce

This is a smooth tomato sauce, also called *tomate frito.*

50	ml. oil	1/2	teaspoon sugar
1	small onion, chopped	1/4	teaspoon cumin
1	clove garlic, chopped	1/4	teaspoon pepper
2	kilos tomatoes, peeled, seeded and chopped		bay leaf and parsley
1	teaspoon salt	100	ml. white wine, stock or water

Heat the oil in a pot and sauté the chopped onion and garlic until softened. Add the prepared tomatoes and fry, as for a *sofrito,* on a high heat for several minutes. Then add salt, sugar, cumin, pepper, bay leaf, parsley and liquid. Simmer, covered, about 45 minutes. Pass the sauce through a sieve or purée in a blender. Makes about 750 ml. of sauce.

SAMFAINA
Catalan Aubergine Sauce

This is basically a *pisto* (see chapter 7), to which chicken, meat, fish or eggs are added. Wonderfully versatile, it is one of the classic Catalan sauces. The others are *picada, romesco, sofrito* and *alioli.*

ROMESCO
Tarragona Pepper Sauce

A good deal of mystique accompanies this sauce, which is said to have hundreds of variations plus a "secret" ingredient personal to each cook. It may be served as a sauce added to grilled meats, fish and vegetables (in particular, grilled onions); or as a salad dressing, or as a cooking medium for shellfish such as prawns, crayfish, lobster. The sauce is named for the *romesco,* dried sweet red peppers. These are either soaked, fried or roasted and, preferably, their pulp scraped out so the flecks of skin don't appear in the finished sauce. If dried peppers are not available, use paprika and add tomato sauce or a roasted tomato for substance.

1/4	litre oil	1/2	teaspoon strong paprika
2	dried red peppers	1/2	teaspoon salt
1	chili pepper (optional)	1/4	teaspoon pepper
1	dozen skinned hazelnuts and/or almonds	1	tablespoon red wine
		1	tablespoon vinegar
1	slice bread	1	tablespoon tomato sauce (optional)
3	cloves garlic		

Heat the oil in a heavy saucepan. Put in the red peppers and chili and fry until they are toasted and remove. Add the skinned nuts to the oil, toast them and remove. Then fry the bread until crisp and remove. Let the oil cool. With a spoon, scrape the pulp from the fried peppers. Place the toasted nuts, bread and garlic in the mortar, blender or processor and crush to a smooth paste. Add the pulp from the peppers, the paprika, salt, pepper, wine, vinegar and tomato sauce and blend until smooth. Then whisk in the oil in a slow stream until the sauce is the consistency of thick cream. For a perfectly smooth sauce, pass through a sieve. Let it set, preferably refrigerated, for several hours before serving. Makes about 300 ml. sauce.

PICADA CATALANA
Catalan Minced Sauce

Like the *sofrito,* the *picada* is a preparation added to foods to flavour them while they are cooking. And, like *romesco,* it has hundreds of variations. Use *picada* with chicken, fish, eels, eggs, stewed meat, etc.

40 grams skinned hazelnuts and/or almonds, toasted	1/4 teaspoon cinnamon
1/2 teaspoon saffron	1/4 teaspoon salt
2 cloves garlic	100 ml. sherry or white wine
2 biscuits	100 ml. water
1 sprig parsley	25 grams chocolate (optional)
	a few pine nuts (optional)

In the mortar or blender crush the toasted nuts with the saffron, garlic, biscuits, parsley, cinnamon, salt, sherry and water, adding the chocolate and pine nuts if desired. Add this to cooked chicken, fish, etc., with some of the cooking liquid and simmer another 10 minutes.

MOJO COLORADO
Canary Island Red Sauce

2 cloves garlic	3 tablespoons oil
1 chili pepper	2 tablespoons vinegar
1 teaspoon paprika	100 ml. water
1/2 teaspoon cumin	salt and pepper
1/2 teaspoon oregano	

In the mortar or blender crush the garlic and chili pepper with the paprika, cumin, oil and vinegar. Add water to dilute the mixture and season with salt and pepper. Serve with fish, drizzle over boiled potatoes and cooked vegetables. *Mojo verde,* green sauce, is made by omitting the paprika and adding chopped coriander and parsley leaves.

SALSA DE ACEITUNAS
Olive Sauce

100 grams pitted green olives	1 tablespoon lemon juice
1/2 small onion	salt and pepper
2 cloves garlic	3 tablespoons oil
2 tomatoes, peeled, seeded and chopped	100 ml. water or stock
50 ml. white wine or sherry	1 teaspoon flour

In the blender or processor whirl the olives, onion, garlic, prepared tomatoes, wine and lemon juice until finely minced. Add the salt and pepper, oil and flour. Put the mixture in a saucepan with the water or stock and simmer, stirring, for 10 minutes. Serve with grilled or fried meat or fish; with vegetables; on pasta. Black olives or capers may be substituted for the green olives in this sauce.

SALSA ANDALUZA
Andalusian Pumpkin Sauce

This is typically served as an accompaniment to the *cocido* or boiled dinner, but it is interesting — and mysterious — enough to be served in a number of other ways — try it with chicken or duck, with stuffed aubergines or peppers, with savoury pasties or vol-au-vents.

1/2	kilo pumpkin	1	clove garlic
2	tablespoons vinegar		salt and pepper
1	tomato		grated nutmeg

Peel the pumpkin, cut it in chunks and steam it with a very little water until tender. Drain, reserving some of the liquid. Meanwhile grill the tomato under the broiler until the skin splits and it is softened. Peel it and discard seeds. Put the tomato and cooked pumpkin in blender or processor with the vinegar, garlic, salt and pepper and nutmeg. Purée the pumpkin, adding a little of the reserved liquid to make a fairly thick sauce.

SALSA DE ALMENDRAS
Almond Sauce

15	almonds, blanched and skinned	1/2	teaspoon saffron
1	slice bread	1	clove
2	cloves garlic	1/2	teaspoon salt
50	ml. oil	100	ml. white wine
5	peppercorns	1/4	litre stock or water

Fry the almonds, bread and garlic in the oil until toasted and remove. In mortar or blender crush the peppercorns, saffron, clove and salt. Add the toasted almonds, bread and garlic and mash to a smooth paste. Dilute with the wine and stir into the oil in the pan. Fry it for a minute, then add the stock or water. Cook for 10 minutes. Add to the sauce sliced hard-cooked eggs, meatballs, cooked chicken, sautéed liver, etc. Finish the sauce with a squeeze of lemon juice and a sprinkling of parsley.

SALSA DE PIÑONES
Pine Nut Sauce

200	grams pine nuts	50	ml. water
1	clove garlic		salt and pepper
100	ml. oil	2	tablespoons chopped parsley
1	lemon		

In blender or processor purée the pine nuts and garlic. Beat in the oil, lemon juice and water. Season with salt and pepper and stir in the chopped parsley. Serve with fish, vegetables, pasta.

SALSA MAYONESA
Mayonnaise

I lived for several years in a beautiful mill house in the country, where the sound of running water was a constant backdrop, but where there was no electricity, thus no modern appliances like blenders. Making mayonnaise by hand became one of my favourite rituals — a big stone mortar, olive oil measured into the egg shell, and a particular patience in stirring that indicated one really had nothing more important to do than confect a perfect mayonnaise. When I built a new house and put in electricity, I bought a blender the day I moved in. I still make mayonnaise regularly, but now it takes minutes.

The most flavourful mayonnaise is made with olive oil. However, if you wish the mayonnaise as a sandwich spread or a bland salad dressing, other vegetable oils can be used instead of, or in addition to, olive oil. Likewise, vinegar or lemon juice or both can be used, adjusting the quantity to taste. Some people like a very tart mayonnaise.

2 egg yolks	3 tablespoons vinegar and/or lemon
1/4 litre oil	juice
	1/2 teaspoon salt

Have the eggs and oil at room temperature. In the winter, it is helpful to rinse out the bowl in very hot water and dry it well and very slightly warm the oil near the stove. Place the yolks in the bowl or in in a large mortar. Beat them until mixed, then add a few drops of vinegar or lemon juice and a few grains of salt. Have the oil in a small pitcher. Stirring the yolks with a wooden spoon or the pestle, begin adding the oil, a drop at a time. Stir in the same direction until the oil is completely absorbed before adding another drop of oil. When about half the oil has been incorporated, beat the rest of it in in a slow stream. By this point the mayonnaise should be thickened. Add the remaining vinegar and salt to taste. If necessary, thin with a little milk or water. If the mayonnaise should "break," it can be reconstituted by placing a fresh yolk in another bowl and adding the first sauce to it, drop by drop, until emulsified. Makes about 300 ml. mayonnaise. Store refrigerated.

Blender Mayonnaise

1 egg	2 tablespoons vinegar or lemon juice
175 ml. oil	1/2 teaspoon salt
pinch of mustard and cayenne	

Put the whole egg in the container of blender or processor with a spoonful of oil and the mustard and cayenne. Whirl until the egg is mixed. With the motor running add the oil in a very slow stream until the mayonnaise is thick. Add the vinegar or lemon juice and salt and whirl again. Store refrigerated.

MAYONESA A LA ANDALUZA
Andalusian Mayonnaise

Add 1 tablespoon tomato purée or 2 tablespoons tomato sauce to 150 ml. of mayonnaise with 25 grams finely chopped tinned pimento, 1 clove of garlic, minced, and 2 tablespoons chopped parsley. Season with pepper and additional lemon juice. Serve with seafood cocktail, cold vegetables, cold cuts and as a sandwich spread.

ALIOLI
Garlic Mayonnaise

Alioli just means "garlic oil," and is variously called *ajiaceite, ajoaceite* and *all-i-oli*. At its simplest — the original formula — the sauce is crushed garlic to which oil is added, drop by drop. Today, it is usually made with egg yolk as well. Serve it with grilled lamb chops, grilled fish, snails, rabbit, chicken, squab, prawns, lobster.

Crush 4 to 6 cloves garlic in mortar, then proceed as for handmade mayonnaise. For blender *alioli,* whirl 4 cloves garlic with the egg, then proceed as for blender mayonnaise.

SALSA VINAGRETA
Vinaigrette

Spanish green salads are usually served accompanied by cruets of oil and vinegar. A vinaigrette sauce would more likely be used on vegetable salads, such as potatoes or beans, or drizzled over fish or served with many cold foods.

2	hard-cooked egg yolks (optional)		freshly ground pepper
1	clove garlic	50	ml. wine vinegar
1/4	teaspoon salt	150	ml. olive oil

In a mortar or bowl crush the egg yolks with the garlic and salt. Add the pepper, then beat in the vinegar until creamy. Add the oil, drop by drop, beating well, until it is all incorporated. Makes 200 ml. Can also be made in the blender.

SALSA GALLEGA
Galician Sauce

This is served with boiled potatoes, grilled octopus, prawns, fish, meat and also makes a good salad dressing.

1	clove garlic, crushed		pinch of white pepper
1	teaspoon paprika	3	tablespoons vinegar
	pinch of cayenne	100	ml. oil
1/2	teaspoon salt		

In a bowl mix the crushed garlic, paprika, cayenne, salt, pepper and vinegar. Beat in the oil until blended.

SALSA DE CABRALES
Blue Cheese Sauce

Beat Cabrales blue cheese with a wooden spoon or in the blender, adding just enough cider, white wine or cream to make it of spreading consistency. For a thinner, pouring sauce, add more liquid until the cheese is about the consistency of cream. Serve it with crisp bread as a dessert course; as an hors-d'oeuvre with crudités for dipping; as a salad dressing, as a steak sauce. Crushed garlic, minced onion, mustard, herbs or butter can be incorporated in the sauce as desired.

CHAPTER 13

Desserts

In Spain as in Arabic countries sweets of all kinds are a gesture of hospitality. Platters of small cakes and pastries are proffered to guests, usually accompanied by decanters of anise, brandy and sweet wine. They're also essential ingredients of every holiday, often with special puddings or sweet bread made in honour of a local patron saint. A feature of village fairs are vendors with push-carts laden with candies and other confections — *turrón,* nougat; sugared almonds and pine nuts, candied fruits moulded to look like real fruits; *yemas,* egg yolk candies; marzipan confections, and much more.

Many of the finest sweets are available only from Spanish convents from recipes used for centuries. Others are packaged and sold in *patiserías* and are favourites souvenirs for travellers. Be sure to sample them on your tours through Spain.

Though tarts, tortes, cakes, pastries, biscuits and confections are consumed at all hours of the day, perhaps with coffee or sweet wine, they are seldom served as dessert. Fruit, preferably fresh, is the preferred dessert everywhere in Spain, though a pudding, such as *flan,* caramel custard, is quite acceptable.

PASTRIES, CAKES AND BISCUITS

CASADIELLES
Galician Walnut Rolls

200 grams walnuts	1 teaspoon cinnamon
100 grams sugar	1 piece lemon peel
50 ml. sherry or anise brandy	500 grams puff pastry
100 ml. water	1 egg, beaten

Grind the walnuts or chop finely in processor. Put the sugar, sherry, water, cinnamon and lemon peel in a saucepan and bring to a boil. Cook 5 minutes. Remove the lemon peel and stir in the walnuts. Roll out the pastry and cut squares of about 10 cm. Spread a spoonful of the walnut mixture on the squares. Fold the top edge to the centre and the bottom edge to meet it and pinch together. Crimp the ends with the tines of a fork and put the packets, seam side down, on a lightly buttered oven tin. Brush them with beaten egg and bake in a hot oven until they are golden. Makes about 15. Shortcrust pastry or *empanadilla* dough can be used instead of puff pastry. The *casadielles* can be fried instead of baked.

SOPLILLOS GRANADINOS
Almond Meringue Puffs, Granada Style

150 grams almonds, blanched and skinned	1 tablespoon lemon juice
1 teaspoon butter or oil	grated lemon peel
3 egg whites	1 teaspoon vanilla
200 grams sugar	

Toast the skinned almonds with the butter in a frying pan or in the oven until lightly golden. Grind them or chop very finely and set aside. In a mixing bowl, beat the egg whites until stiff. Beat in the sugar a little at a time and fold in the lemon juice, grated lemon peel and vanilla. Fold in the ground almonds. Spoon small mounds of the meringue onto a well-greased oven tin and bake in a slow oven until the puffs are very slightly coloured, about 20 minutes. Makes about 40 meringues. These can also be baked in small fluted paper cups.

POLVORONES
Crumble Cakes

300 grams flour, sifted	150 grams sugar
140 grams butter or lard	pinch of aniseed or cinnamon

Garlic mayonnaise, a great accompaniment for many dishes (recipe, page 313).

Cream the butter with a wooden spoon until soft. Blend in the sugar gradually, then add the sifted flour and the aniseed or cinnamon. Knead very lightly just to blend. Form balls of the dough, about the size of a small plum. Flatten them slightly and place on an ungreased baking tin. Bake in a medium oven until lightly golden, about 25 minutes. Makes about 2 dozen small cakes.

MANTECADOS
Lard Cakes

1/2 kilo flour	1/2 teaspoon cinnamon
125 grams almonds	1 tablespoon sesame seeds, toasted
1/4 kilo lard (or butter)	icing sugar, for dusting
200 grams icing (powdered) sugar	

Spread the flour in an oven tin and toast it in the oven until lightly coloured, stirring it so it browns evenly. Meanwhile, scald the almonds in boiling water and skin them. Toast them lightly, then grind or chop very finely. When the flour is cooled, mix with the ground almonds. Beat the lard until it is very creamy. Beat in the sugar and cinnamon, then add the flour-almond mixture a little at a time and the toasted sesame seeds. Roll or pat the dough to a thickness of 1 cm. Cut into rounds about 5 cm. in diameter and place them on an oven tin. Bake in a slow oven until the cakes are dried, about 30 minutes. Let them cool several minutes before removing from tin. They are fragile. When completely cool, dust with icing sugar. Good with fruit and ices. Makes about 3 dozen small cakes.

MEDIAS LUNAS
Half Moons

100 grams butter	1/2 teaspoon cinnamon
75 grams sugar	1 egg white, beaten
3 egg yolks	sugar
200 grams flour, sifted	

Cream butter and sugar. Gradually beat in the egg yolks, then the flour and cinnamon. Blend well. Roll out on a lightly floured board and cut in half moon shapes (or circles cut in half). Place them on an ungreased oven tin, brush with beaten egg white and sprinkle with sugar. Bake in a medium oven until lightly browned, about 15 minutes. Makes about 3 dozen small biscuits.

Flan and, bottom left, **Crema Catalana** (recipes, pages 327 and 329).

GALLETAS DE PEPA NIEBLA
Pepa Niebla's Biscuits

1/2 kilo coarse flour *(harina recia)*	100 ml. dry anise brandy
pinch of salt	200 ml. oil
100 grams sugar	

Put the flour in a bowl and add the salt and sugar to it. Make a well and mix in the anise brandy, using the fingers to mix it. Heat the oil until it is smoking and add to the dough. Turn out onto a pastry board and knead the dough just until it is compact. Roll or pat it out very thinly and cut the dough into strips about 3 by 5 cm. Place the biscuits on a lightly oiled baking tin and bake in a hot oven just until they are lightly golden, about 5 minutes.

PAN DE BIZCOCHO
Sponge Cake

To increase or decrease this recipe, weigh the eggs, take the same weight of sugar, minus a few spoonfuls for the shells, and half the weight of flour. Modern versions include baking powder.

6 eggs, separated	1 teaspoon grated lemon rind *or* 1/2
375 grams sugar	teaspoon cinnamon
185 grams flour	

In a deep mixing bowl beat the egg whites until stiff. Add the yolks one by one, beating well after each addition. Gradually beat in the sugar until well blended. Then blend in the flour, a little at a time, and the lemon peel *or* cinnamon. Beat well by hand or electric mixer, until batter is light and frothy. Butter a sponge cake mould (18 to 20 cm.) and line with a round of paper, well buttered. Pour in the batter and bake in a medium oven. The cake is done when an inserted knife comes out clean, about 40 minutes. Let it set a few minutes, then unmould to cool on a rack. If the cake is to be served as is, dust it with icing sugar. Good with fruit compotes and fruit purées. The sponge may also be split horizontally into 2 or 3 layers and filled with any cream filling.

BORRACHOS
Drunken Cakes

1 sponge cake, cut in squares	100 ml. water
100 grams sugar	100 ml. medium sherry or Malaga wine

Bake the sponge cake (see preceding recipe) in a rectangular pan. Cut the cooled cake into squares. Put the sugar and water in a saucepan and boil 5 minutes. Remove from heat and when partially cooled add the sherry or Malaga wine. Drizzle the wine syrup over the squares of cake. Place each one in a paper cup and dust the tops with cinnamon. Good served topped with cream.

BRAZO GITANO
"Gypsy's Arm" Cake Roll

6 eggs, separated	4 tablespoons icing (powdered) sugar
75 grams sugar	200 ml. *cremadina* (cream filling, recipe
75 grams flour, sifted	follows)
1 teaspoon grated lemon rind	

Beat the egg whites until stiff. Beat in the yolks one at a time, then the sugar. Add the flour gradually, then the grated lemon rind. Butter a shallow oven tin or jelly-roll pan (about 28 by 34 cm.) and line it with paper, well buttered. Pour in the batter and bake in a medium-hot oven until the cake is springy, about 10 minutes. While still hot, unmould the cake onto a sheet of paper sprinkled with the icing sugar. Spread it with the cream filling, reserving a few spoonfuls for the top. With the help of the paper, roll up the cake. Place on a platter, seam side down and spread the top with the remaining cream. Sprinkle with icing sugar.

CREMADINA
Custard Filling

2 egg yolks, beaten	piece cinnamon
2 tablespoons sugar	vanilla bean or 2 teaspoons vanilla
1 tablespoon flour	extract
salt	2 tablespoons water
225 ml. milk	1 tablespoon (or more) butter

In the top of a bain marie (double boiler) beat the egg yolks, sugar, flour and a pinch of salt until smooth. Place over boiling water and beat in the milk which has been scalded with the cinnamon stick and vanilla bean. Whisk the sauce until mixture begins to bubble, then beat in the water. Lower the heat and continue cooking, stirring constantly, for 10 minutes. Remove from heat and beat in the butter until the cream is smooth and satiny. Cool. Use as a pastry filling.

Chocolate cream filling: Melt 60 grams bitter-sweet chocolate with the milk. A tablespoon of instant coffee will give a mocha flavour.

TARTA HELADA
Frozen Torte

150 grams semi-sweet chocolate	1/2 teaspoon cinnamon
150 grams sugar	5 teaspoons sugar
125 ml. milk	200 grams plain biscuits *(galletas María*
65 grams butter	or similar)
100 ml. brandy	sweetened whipped cream
1 egg yolk	

In a saucepan place the chocolate, broken into pieces, 50 grams sugar and 75 ml. milk. Cook on a low fire, stirring constantly, until the chocolate is melted. Cool completely. In a bowl, cream the butter until soft and fluffy. Gradually beat in remaining sugar, then 50 ml. brandy, a few drops at a time, beating well after each addition. Beat in the egg yolk, then add 50 ml. of the melted chocolate, reserving the rest. Into a shallow bowl put the remaining milk, brandy, cinnamon and sugar. Dip the biscuits, one at a time, quickly into the milk mixture. Arrange a layer of them in the bottom of a buttered loaf pan. Spread the biscuits with a layer of the butter cream, then add another layer of biscuits dipped in the milk mixture. Continue until all the biscuits and all the cream filling have been used, ending with a layer of the biscuits. Put the mould in the freezer for at least 5 hours. Run a knife around the edges and dip the mould briefly into hot water. Unmould the torte onto a serving platter. Cover it with a frosting of the sweetened whipped cream (it can be decorated with rosettes piped with a pastry gun). Use the reserved melted chocolate to drizzle a decorative pattern on the cream. Return to the freezer, covered in plastic wrap, until firm. Let set at room temperature a few minutes before slicing.

Variation: After 2 layers of the biscuits and cream filling, spread a layer of softened ice cream, 3 or 4 cm. thick, and follow with 2 more layers of biscuits and filling. Freeze, unmould and frost the torte as described above.

Addition: Blanch and skin 75 grams almonds. Chop them coarsely. In a frying pan toast them with 1 tablespoon butter and 2 teaspoons sugar, stirring constantly to prevent their scorching. Sprinkle a layer of the toasted almonds between layers of the biscuits.

MOSTACHONES
Crispy Pine Nut Biscuits

3 eggs	1/4 teaspoon cinnamon
1/4 kilo sugar	100 grams pine nuts, toasted
1/4 kilo flour, sifted	icing sugar
pinch of salt	

Beat the eggs in a saucepan with the sugar until thick. Heat whisking constantly until sugar is dissolved. Remove from heat and beat well. Beat in the flour, cinnamon and toasted pine nuts. Drop tiny spoonfuls onto a buttered oven tin. Sprinkle with icing sugar and bake in a moderate oven about 15 minutes. Makes about 6 dozen small biscuits.

FILLOAS
Galician Dessert Crêpes

3 eggs	200 grams *queso fresco* or *requesón*
100 ml. milk	(soft cheese or cottage cheese)
100 ml. water	200 ml. cream
6 tablespoons flour	50 grams sugar
pinch of salt	1 teaspoon grated lemon peel
1 tablespoon butter, melted and cooled	1 teaspoon vanilla extract

Beat together the eggs, milk, water, flour, salt and melted butter. The batter should be the consistency of thick cream. Rub a frying pan with a little pork fat or butter and pour in a little of the batter to make a thin film. Fry on both sides, as for crêpes. The edges will crisp slightly. Remove and stack on a plate. They can be served, as is, sprinkled with sugar as an accompaniment to fruit. Or, beat the soft cheese or cottage cheese until soft. Whip the cream and fold in the sugar and lemon peel and vanilla and whip it into the softened cheese. Spoon this mixture onto the crêpes and roll or fold them. Serve with strawberry purée or apples sautéed in butter and sprinkled with cinnamon.

FRIED PASTRIES

This is a very special category in Spanish cookery, especially in regions such as Andalusia where few homes had ovens but where oil was plentiful. There are several types of pastry doughs, each with its particular texture and flavouring. Many of these pastries are especially beloved at Christmas time — *roscos, empanadillas* and *pestiños,* in particular — but any of them makes a nice tea-time snack. I especially enjoy them as an accompaniment to fruit compotes. Many can be baked instead of fried — though they are emphatically not the same. Please read the section about *fritos* in Chapter 4.

EMPANADILLAS
Fruit Pasties

25 grams lard	100 ml. *cabello de angel, dulce de batata*
25 grams butter	or any fruit jam
100 ml. white wine	oil
200 grams flour	100 ml. honey
1/4 teaspoon salt	50 ml. brandy
1/2 teaspoon aniseed (optional)	sugar
flour	

Melt the lard and butter in a saucepan. Add the wine, then beat in enough of the flour with the salt and aniseed if desired to make a smooth dough. Knead very briefly and let it rest, refrigerated, for at least 2 hours. Meanwhile, put the fruit jam in a saucepan and boil until very thick. *(Cabello de angel* is a preserve made from a squash called *cidra;* it is available tinned. *Batata* is sweet potato, cooked with sugar to a paste.) Roll out the pastry dough quite thinly. Cut in very small circles (about 6 cm.). Place a half teaspoon of the fruit paste on each circle, fold over, and seal the edges by pressing with a fork. Fry the tiny pies in deep, hot oil until golden. Remove and drain on absorbent paper. Boil the honey, water and brandy until thickened, about 15 minutes. Dip the fried pies in the honey syrup and place them on a serving platter. Sprinkle with sugar. Makes about 50 tiny *empanadillas*.

PESTIÑOS
Sweet Fritters

These are frequently made with the scraps of dough left from making the above empanadillas. Roll out the dough and cut into 5 cm. squares. Fold 2 opposite corners to the middle and pinch them together. Slip a fork under the fold and drop into hot oil and fry until golden. They will puff up like pillows. Drain on absorbent paper and dip into honey syrup, as above recipe. Sprinkle with sugar.

ROSCOS DE HUEVO
Egg Doughnuts

300	ml. oil	2	tablespoons cinnamon
30	grams aniseed	3	eggs, separated
	grated peel of 1 lemon	3	teaspoons baking soda
675	grams sugar	1 1/2	kilos flour
300	ml. milk (or 1/2 milk and 1/2 orange juice)		oil for frying

Put the 300 ml. oil in a saucepan and heat until hot, but not smoking. Add the aniseed and cook for a few minutes just until the spice is fragrant. Remove and cool the oil. In a large bowl mix the lemon peel, 275 grams sugar, milk and juice, cinnamon and the oil and aniseed. Add 2 cups of the flour, then beat in the egg yolks and baking soda. Beat the whites until stiff and fold them into the batter. Add flour, using the hands to work it in. At first the dough will be very sticky. Continue adding flour until the dough is just stiff enough to roll without sticking to the hands. Take a small ball of the dough and roll it into a thick cord about 12 cm. long. Pinch the ends together to form a circle. Continue forming the *roscos*.

Heat deep oil until hot but not smoking and add the *roscos,* a few at a time. Fry until they are golden brown. Remove with a skimmer, drain briefly and, while still hot, dredge them in sugar on both sides. Makes about 10 dozen.

To increase or decrease the quantity: for each egg use 8 tablespoons oil, milk and sugar and 1 teaspoon baking soda.

Though not typical, I happen to like the substitution of poppy seed or sesame seed for the aniseed. Try it.

BORRACHUELOS
Wine Doughnuts

200 ml. oil	100 ml. white wine
1 tablespoon aniseed	50 ml. juice of bitter orange
2 tablespoons sesame seed	1/2 kilo flour
100 ml. Malaga wine	honey or icing (powdered) sugar

Heat the oil in a saucepan with the aniseed and sesame. Cool it. Put it in a bowl with the two kinds of wine and the orange juice. Add enough flour to make a soft dough. Let it rest, covered and refrigerated, at least 2 hours. Roll the dough into thick cords about 8 cm. long and pinch the ends together to make a circle. Let them rest for an hour. Either fry them, as in the preceding recipe, or bake in a medium oven about 20 minutes. If fried, dip them in a honey syrup, as in the preceding recipe. If baked, dredge them in icing sugar.

BUÑUELOS DE VIENTO
Puffs of Wind

225 ml. milk	125 grams flour
70 grams butter	4 eggs
1 tablespoon anise brandy (optional)	oil for frying
2 tablespoons sugar	icing sugar
1/4 teaspoon salt	

Place the milk, butter, anise, sugar and salt in a saucepan and heat just until it boils. Lower the heat and add the flour all at once, beating it hard with a wooden spoon until it forms a smooth ball of dough. Remove from the heat and beat in the eggs one at a time. Dip spoons into oil and use them to drop balls of dough into deep hot oil. Fry until golden and puffed. If the oil is too hot, the *buñuelos* will not puff. Make caramel sauce (as in recipe for *flan*) using 200 grams sugar and 8 tablespoons water. Pour over the *buñuelos* and serve. The puffs can also be split in half with a knife and filled with a cream filling or spoonful of jam, then pressed together again and dusted with icing sugar.

TORTILLITAS DE PASAS
Raisin Pancakes

75 grams raisins	1/2 teaspoon cinnamon
2 tablespoons brandy	1/4 teaspoon grated nutmeg

2	eggs, separated	50	grams almonds, blanched, skinned
125	grams flour		and shredded
1	teaspoon baking powder	50	ml. oil for frying
1/4	teaspoon salt		icing (powdered) sugar or
150	ml. milk		honey syrup
2	eggs, separated		

Soak the raisins in the brandy for 15 minutes. Sift together the flour, baking powder and salt. Beat the milk with the egg yolks, cinnamon and nutmeg. Add the raisins and brandy then the dry ingredients. Fold in the almonds. Let the batter set for an hour. Beat the egg whites until stiff and fold into the batter. Heat the oil in a frying pan and drop spoonfuls of the batter into the pan. Fry the pancakes until browned on the bottom and slightly bubbly on top, then turn them and fry the reverse sides. Remove to a serving dish and sprinkle with icing sugar or drizzle with honey syrup. Serves 6.

HUESOS DE SANTO
Saints' Bones

Edible reliquiae, this confection is a speciality for the holiday All Saints Day, *Todos los Santos,* on Nov. 1. The "bones" might be made from an almond-potato paste or fried dough rolled around a stick of cane and the hollows filled with a cream filling.

1	egg, separated	1/2	teaspoon baking soda
3	tablespoons sugar	125	grams flour
3	tablespoons milk		oil for frying
	grated lemon peel		custard or cream filling
1/4	teaspoon cinnamon		sugar and cinnamon

Beat the egg white until stiff, then beat in the egg yolk and sugar until thick. Beat in the milk, lemon peel, cinnamon, baking soda and flour to make a smooth dough. Let it rest refrigerated for several hours. Roll out on a floured board and cut into 10 cm. squares. Roll the pieces around short lengths of oiled cane or bamboo, about 2 cm. diameter. Do not use wood dowels, as dough will stick to them. Fry in hot oil until golden. Remove and take out the cane pieces. Fill the hollows with custard or cream filling and roll the "bones" in sugar and cinnamon. Makes 6 "bones."

CHURROS
Breakfast Fritters

Churros, typically, either start the day or finish it. At the end of a village *feria,* after the last fireworks and rockets have died down and the band is packing away the instruments, the last stall still open is the *churrería,* where these crisp strips of fried dough are served with thick, hot chocolate. And so to bed. Then, very early in the morning at cafés near big marketplaces, great cauldrons of oil are put to heat to serve *churros* to the wholesalers bringing fresh produce, meat and fish to the markets. Later, shoppers can stop for a breakfast of *churros* with *café con leche* while doing the day's marketing. On Sundays when no one has to hurry off to work or school, papa gets up first and takes the littlest child with him to buy churros for the family — the earlier the better, to avoid a long queue. They may be fried in rings and these strung, a dozen or more, on a loop of reed for carrying home. By the time he gets back, mama has the chocolate ready. Churros, by the way, were invented for the sole purpose of dunking. They must be eaten fresh and hot.

250	ml. water	1/2	teaspoon salt
1	piece cinnamon	200	grams flour
75	ml. oil		oil for frying
1	piece lemon rind		sugar

Put the water in a saucepan with the 75 ml. oil and salt. Bring to a boil. Add the flour all at once and beat hard with a wooden spoon, working it on a low fire for a minute or two until if forms a ball. The batter will be quite stiff. Put it in a pastry bag and pipe long strips or rings of the batter into deep, hot oil. It takes a bit of muscle to push it through. Fry until golden brown and remove and drain. With scissors, cut long strands into short lengths. Sprinkle generously with sugar. Makes about 30 strips.

PUDDINGS

FLAN
Spanish Caramel Custard

In Spanish shops you can by *flan* mixes, complete with ready-mix caramel.

175	grams sugar	2	egg yolks
1/2	litre milk	2	whole eggs
	cinnamon and lemon peel or vanilla		

In a heavy saucepan melt 100 grams sugar until it is a golden caramel colour. Remove from heat and pour it into a single mould or 4 individual custard cups, tilting to coat the mould. Scald the milk with the cinnamon and lemon peel or vanilla. Beat the egg yolks and whole eggs until mixed and beat in remaining sugar. Whisk in the hot milk, then pour the custard through a sieve into the mould or moulds. Set them in a pan and add hot water to half their depth. Put in a medium oven until the custard is set, about 40 minutes. Cool the custards, then unmould onto serving plates. Serves 4 to 6.

Variations: toasted coconut or toasted and finely chopped almonds can be added to the custard.

PIJAMA
Pyjamas

I don't know how this concoction got its name, but it's a favourite child-pleaser and man-teaser in many family-style resturants. Unmould a *flan* onto a serving plate. Surround it with 3 or 4 scoops of different flavoured ice creams. Add a selection of tinned fruit — half peaches and sliced pineapples. Pipe whipped cream over the whole and top with a cherry.

NATILLAS
Creamy Custard With Meringue

1/2	litre milk	3	tablespoons milk
	cinnamon stick	2	egg whites
	lemon peel		pinch of salt
	vanilla bean	1/2	teaspoon lemon juice
4	egg yolks	1	teaspoon cinnamon
150	grams sugar		ladyfingers *(bizcocho soletilla)*
1	tablespoon cornstarch		

Place the ½ litre milk, cinnamon, lemon peel and vanilla in a saucepan, bring the milk to a boil and remove. Let it set until slightly cooled and strain it. Beat the egg yolks and 100 grams sugar in the top of a bain marie (double boiler) until they are thick. Whisking the yolks, pour in the hot milk. Dissolve the cornstarch in the 3 tablespoons milk and whisk it into the yolks. Set the pan over boiling water and cook, stirring, until the custard is thickened, about 10 minutes. It should be thick enough to coat a spoon. Remove and let it cool. Place ladyfingers or other biscuits in individual pudding bowls and divide the custard between them. Chill. The custard will be the consistency of very thick cream. Meanwhile whip the 2 egg whites until stiff. Beat in 4 tablespoons of sugar (if using more egg whites, use 2 tablespoons sugar for each white), the salt and lemon juice. Lightly butter an oven tin. Spoon the meringue into 4 "mountains" (or more if using additional egg whites). Sprinkle the tops with cinnamon. Place in a medium oven until the meringues are lightly coloured, about 10 minutes. Turn off the oven and let them dry in the oven until nearly cooled. Serve each *natilla* topped with a meringue. Four servings.

CREMA CATALANA
Catalan Custard

6	egg yolks		cinnamon stick
200	grams sugar	1/2	cup milk
3/4	litre milk	3	tablespoons cornstarch
	lemon peel		

Beat the egg yolks and 150 grams sugar in a bowl. Put the 3/4 litre milk in a saucepan with the cinnamon and lemon peel and bring it to a boil. Remove from fire and strain it into the eggs, whisking them constantly. Dissolve the cornstarch in the half-cup of milk and stir it into the custard mixture. Pour the mixture into the saucepan and cook it on a low heat, stirring constantly, just until it starts to bubble. Remove from the heat and strain into a shallow pudding bowl. Let the custard cool. Before serving, sprinkle the top with remaining sugar and caramelize it with a hot salamander (or use a metal spatula or small iron frying pan, heated red hot) or place under a broiler. Decorate the pudding with biscuits or squares of cake and rosettes of whipped cream. Serves 6.

LECHE FRITA
"Fried Milk"

140	grams butter		lemon peel
250	grams flour, sifted	4	eggs, separated
150	grams sugar		fine breadcrumbs (about 125 grams)
1/2	litre milk		oil
	cinnamon stick, 4 cm.		sugar

In a heavy saucepan melt the butter and add 175 grams sifted flour. Stir and let cook very gently. Then add the sugar. Meanwhile, scald the milk with the cinnamon and lemon peel. Strain it and add to the butter mixture, stirring hard to keep the mixture smooth. When it starts to bubble, remove from heat and add the egg yolks one by one, incorporating each before adding the next. Lightly oil a rectangular tin or dish and spread the mixture in it to a thickness of about 2 cm. Chill in the refrigerator until set, at least 2 hours. Cut the batter into squares or triangles of about 5 cm. Dip each into flour, then into lightly beaten egg whites, then into breadcrumbs. Fry in hot oil, turning to brown on both sides. Sprinkle with sugar. Serve hot or cold. Nice accompanied with fruit jam or fruit purée. Makes about 2 dozen 5 cm. triangles.

MENJAR BLANC
Almond Pudding

400	grams almonds, blanched and skinned	250	grams sugar
1	litre boiling water	1/4	teaspoon salt
1	piece cinnamon stick, 4 cm.	50	grams cornstarch (6 tablespoons)
1	piece lemon peel	3	tablespoons oil or butter
			whipped cream (optional)

Grind or finely chop the almonds and place them in a bowl. Pour the boiling water over them and let them set for 10 minutes. Place a sieve lined with cheesecloth over a bowl and pour through the liquid, squeezing the cloth to extract all of it. Place this almond milk in a saucepan with the cinnamon, lemon peel, 200 grams sugar and salt. Bring to a boil and simmer for a few minutes. Remove the cinnamon and lemon peel. Dissolve the cornstarch in a little cold liquid and whisk it into the almond milk. Stir constantly until the pudding is thickened. Pour into 6 or 8 individual pudding dishes or into a mould oiled with almond oil. Chill well. Toast the reserved chopped almonds in the oil or butter until they are golden. Add the remaining sugar and stir until it is dissolved. Cool, and top the puddings with the almonds.

ARROZ CON LECHE
Creamy Rice Pudding

1/4	kilo rice	75	grams sugar
250	ml. water	1/4	teaspoon salt
1	piece cinnamon stick, 4 cm.	1 1/4	litres milk
1	piece lemon peel		ground cinnamon

Put the rice, water, cinnamon stick, lemon peel, sugar and salt in a saucepan and bring to a boil. Cover and simmer on a low fire until the water is nearly absorbed, about 8 minutes. Then add the milk and continue cooking until the rice is very tender. There should be enough liquid left to give a creamy consistency to this dessert. Remove cinnamon and lemon rind. Serve dusted thickly with cinnamon. Serve hot or chilled. Makes 6 servings.

TORRIJAS
Sweet Bread Fritters

In America we call this French toast and serve it for breakfast. In Spain it's a dessert.

Cut stale bread into thick slices, remove crusts and trim into evenly-sized rectangles or circles. Dip them into white wine or sherry or Malaga wine or milk or water for a few minutes. Remove and dip into beaten egg, then fry the slices in oil or butter until browned on both sides. Sprinkle liberally with sugar and cinnamon or drizzle with honey. Serve hot or cold.

CUAJADA
Cheese Custard Tart

1/2	recipe for *mantecados* or any crumb crust	4	eggs
400	grams *requesón* (dry cottage cheese)	200	ml. milk
250	grams sugar		grated lemon peel
		1/4	teaspoon cinnamon

Line a pie tin or spring-form tin with the *mantecado* dough or crumb crust. Beat the cheese until soft, then beat in the sugar. Add the eggs, one by one. Beat in the milk, the biscuit crumbs, lemon peel and cinnamon. Pour into the pie tin and bake in a medium-hot oven until set, about 45 minutes. Sprinkle the top with sugar and cinnamon. Serve cool. Makes 8-10 servings. A layer of sliced apples or pears can be placed over the crust before adding the custard.

DULCE DE BATATA
Sweet Potato Pudding

Sweet potatoes come into season in the late fall, at the same time as chestnuts, and are often cooked together, sweet or savoury. This *dulce* in its original form is a sugary paste made by cooking puréed sweet potatoes with an equal quantity of sugar. Here is a lighter version that makes a very nice pudding.

300	ml. cooked and puréed sweet potatoes	2	eggs
75	grams sugar	1	teaspoon cinnamon
50	ml. Malaga wine	1/4	teaspoon salt
100	ml. milk		grated nutmeg

Beat the puréed sweet potatoes (chestnut purée can be combined with it) in a bowl with the sugar, wine and milk. Beat in the eggs, cinnamon, salt and nutmeg. Pour into a buttered oven dish and bake in a medium oven until set, about 1 hour.

TOCINO DEL CIELO
"Heavenly Bacon"

So-called because this caramel-topped custard looks remarkably like a slab of bacon. Very rich and sweet, it is best cut into small squares.

225	grams sugar	6	egg yolks
1/4	litre water	1	whole egg
	lemon peel or vanilla pod		

In a heavy pot melt 75 grams sugar until it is a pale caramel colour. Pour immediately into a mould, 14 cm square and let cool. Put the 1/4 litre water, lemon peel or vanilla and remainder of sugar in a pan and bring to a boil. Cook it to the thread stage (forms a thread of syrup when dropped from a spoon). Beat the yolks and whole egg until very smooth. Beating the eggs constantly, add the syrup in a slow stream. Strain this custard into the caramel-lined mould. Cover the pan with foil. Place it on a trivet or rack in a larger pan and add boiling water to just the depth of the custard pan. Cover the pan and steam the custard (or bake it) until a knife inserted comes out clean, about 20 minutes. Take it off the heat and let it set until completely cool. Then run a knife around the edge of the custard and unmould it onto a serving plate. Cut the custard into squares to serve. Makes 12 squares.

INTXAURSALSA
Walnut Cream Soup

A Basque Christmas Eve speciality.

150	grams walnuts	2	litres milk
4	slices bread, toasted	300	grams sugar

Finely chop the walnuts (don't grind them). Grind the toast or crumb it in the processor. Cook the milk, sugar, nuts and breadcrumbs together for about 40 minutes. Serve cold in small bowls or cups. Serves 8.

FRUIT DESSERTS

A slice of chilled melon in August, a bowl of glowing oranges in December, a dish of sweet strawberries in the spring — fresh fruit in season is the favourite dessert in Spain. There are, however, quite a few compotes, conserves and other fruit desserts which are very good. You'll find lots more information about fruits in Chapter 2 on marketing.

MACEDONIA DE FRUTAS DE PRIMAVERA
Spring Fruit Cup

Macedonia or *copa de frutas* is a delicious way to serve fresh fruit. It is freely varied according to what is available in the markets. Following are two possibilities, but any combination of fruits may be used.

4	bananas	200	grams cherries, pitted
300	grams strawberries	100	ml. water
3	oranges	200	grams sugar
5	apricots	50	ml. brandy or liqueur

Slice the bananas into a bowl with the hulled and sliced strawberries. Chop the oranges and apricots and add with the cherries. Mix the water and sugar in a saucepan and cook for 5 minutes and let it cool. Add to the fruit with the brandy or liqueur. Chill the fruit. Serves 8.

MACEDONIA DE FRUTAS DE VERANO
Summer Fruit Salad

1	ripe melon	100	ml. sweet sherry
3	peaches	1/2	lemon
1/2	kilo muscatel grapes		

Cut the melon and peaches into bite-size pieces or use a melon ball cutter to remove melon from its shell. Put in a bowl with the grapes, peeled and seeded. Add the sherry and the grated peel of the lemon and a little of the juice. Chill well. Serves 6.

MELON EN VINO TINTO
Melon in Red Wine

Cut melon into chunks or balls and put in a bowl. Cover with red wine and sprinkle with sugar. Macerate the fruit, refrigerated, for several hours. Pineapple chunks can be added.

POMELOS EN ALMIBAR
Grapefruit in Syrup

4	grapefruit	2	tablespoons brandy or medium
125	grams sugar		sherry
1/4	litre water	1	piece lemon peel
			cherries for garnish

Peel the grapefruit and cut into sections. Cut away the white pith. Put the sugar, water, brandy and lemon peel to cook in a saucepan for 5 minutes. Cool, then add the prepared grapefruit. Chill. Serve the grapefruit with a few cherries. Any fresh fruit can be poached in syrup in the same manner — try apricots, fresh figs, peaches, pears, cherries. Slices of orange can be added as can spices such as cinnamon, cloves, ginger, nutmeg. Hard fruits such as apples can also be poached in the syrup.

MEMBRILLO COCIDO
Quince Compote

4	quince	1	piece cinnamon stick, 2 cm.
1	orange, sliced	2	cloves
100	grams sugar	50	grams raisins, seeded
1/4	litre white wine		

Bake or steam the quince about 30 minutes. Then pare them and remove cores. Slice the fruit into a saucepan. Add the sliced orange, sugar, wine, cinnamon, cloves and raisins. Simmer the fruit until very soft, about 40 minutes. Very good served with duck, turkey, ham, pork or game.

ESPUMA DE FRUTA
Fruit Mousse

Innovative cooks are using some of the country's more exotic fruits — custard apple, loquat, prickly pear, persimmon, pomegranate — in new ways. This mousse works with custard apple, loquat or persimmon, and can be used for the more usual strawberries, apricots and peaches. If frozen, the mousse can be unmoulded. Otherwise it is spooned into serving dishes.

400	ml. fruit pulp	2	teaspoons powdered gelatin
2	tablespoons orange or lemon juice	2	tablespoons water
150	grams sugar	400	ml. cream
60	ml. water	1	teaspoon vanilla extract

Add the orange or lemon juice to the fruit pulp. Put the sugar and water in a saucepan and bring to a boil. Cook a few minutes. Meanwhile, sprinkle the gelatin into the 2 tablespoons of water until it is softened, then stir it into the hot sugar syrup until completely dissolved. Mix with the fruit pulp and let the mixture cool. Whip the cream with the vanilla. Fold into the fruit mixture. Either chill the mousse for several hours (it will not be solid) or else place it in a decorative mould, cover with foil and freeze it. To unmould, dip into hot water and turn out onto a serving dish. Serves 8.

CASTAÑAS CON LECHE
Chestnuts With Milk

Shell the chestnuts, then blanch them in boiling water for a few minutes. Drain and skin them. Put them to cook in water to cover with a sprig of fennel or aniseed and a pinch of salt. Cook them for 20 minutes and drain. Put a litre of milk and 150 grams of sugar in the pan, add the chestnuts and cook slowly until they are very soft. Pour into a serving bowl and sprinkle with sugar and cinnamon.

MANZANAS ASADAS AL VINO
Apples Baked in Wine

6	apples	6	teaspoons butter
6	tablespoons sugar or honey cinnamon	1/2	litre white or red wine, or cider

Remove the cores from the apples and put them in baking dish. Put a tablespoon of sugar or honey in each, sprinkle with cinnamon and top with a teaspoon of butter. Pour over the wine or cider and put in a hot oven until the apples are cooked, about 35 minutes, spooning some of the liquid over the apples from time to time. Serve hot or cold. Serves 6. Quince can be baked as for apples, allowing about an hour or more.

MANZANAS RELLENAS
Stuffed Apples

6	apples	50	ml. sweet sherry
40	grams walnuts	1/4	litre water
150	grams dates, figs or raisins	75	grams sugar

Remove cores from the apples. Chop the walnuts and the dates, figs or seeded raisins and stuff the centres of the apples. Place them in a baking dish, pour over the sherry and water and sprinkle with the sugar. Bake until done, about 35 minutes. Serve hot or cold. Serves 6.

PERAS AL HORNO
Baked Pears

1	kilo pears (8 to 10)	50	grams raisins, seeded
3	tablespoons orange juice	200	ml. Malaga wine or *oloroso seco*
100	grams sugar		sherry
2	cloves	50	grams almonds

Peel the pears, halve them and remove cores. Sprinkle with the juice and place them in a buttered oven dish. Sprinkle with the sugar and raisins. Pour over the wine and bake in a medium oven until the pears are quite soft, about 30 minutes. Meanwhile, blanch and skin the almonds, then sliver and toast them with a little butter. Sprinkle the pears with the almonds. Serve hot or cold. Serves 6. Can be served with sweetened meringue, whipped cream or sabayon sauce. Pumpkin *(calabaza),* peeled and cut in chunks, can be prepared in the same manner.

TORTAS DE PLATANO
Banana Cakes

3	firm bananas		grated lemon peel
2	eggs	1/2	kilo flour
150	grams sugar	2	teaspoons baking powder
2	tablespoons oil	1/2	teaspoon baking soda
200	ml. milk		oil
1/2	teaspoon cinnamon		sugar or honey
1/4	teaspoon aniseed or nutmeg		

Peel the bananas and cook them in boiling water with lemon juice for a few minutes. Drain them and mash smooth. In a bowl, beat the eggs with the sugar until thick. Then beat in the mashed banana, the oil, milk, cinnamon, aniseed and lemon peel. Add enough flour to make a smooth dough with the baking powder and baking soda. Chill the dough, then pat it to a thickness of about 2 cm. Cut into circles about 8 cm. Fry the cakes in hot oil until golden. Drain them. When cool sprinkle with sugar or drizzle with honey. Makes about 3 dozen.

HIGOS A LA MALAGUEÑA
Fresh Figs, Malaga Style

2	dozen ripe figs	50	grams sugar
1	tablespoon lemon juice	100	ml. Malaga wine

Peel the figs and cut them in half. Place in a fruit bowl and add the lemon juice, sugar and Malaga wine. Chill for several hours before serving. Makes 8 servings.

BUÑUELOS DE HIGOS
Fig Fritters

2	dozen firm ripe figs (about 1 kilo)		grated lemon rind
2	eggs, separated	125	grams flour
150	ml. milk	1	tablespoon sugar
1	tablespoon oil		oil for frying
	pinch of salt		

Wash and dry the figs. If they are large, halve or quarter them. In a bowl beat the eggs yolks with the milk, oil, salt and lemon rind. Stir in the flour and sugar and combine well. Refrigerate the batter for 2 hours. Beat the egg whites until stiff and fold them into the batter. Dip the figs into the batter and fry them in deep, hot oil until golden. Drain briefly and sprinkle sugar. Apricots, bananas and other fruits can be prepared in the same way.

HIGOS EN SALSA DE ALMENDRAS
Figs in Almond Sauce

2	dozen dried figs	2	tablespoons butter
50	ml. water	1	tablespoon flour
150	ml. honey	3	tablespoons sugar
50	grams almonds, blanched, skinned and lightly toasted	1/4	teaspoon cinnamon
		200	ml. milk.

Wash the figs and put them in a bowl. Boil the honey and water briefly and pour over the figs. Let them macerate for several hours or overnight to plump them. Grind the toasted almonds and set aside. In a saucepan, heat the butter and stir in the flour and cook briefly without letting it colour. Add the sugar, cinnamon and whisk in the milk. Cook, stirring, until the sauce is thickened. Add the ground almonds. Drain the figs (the honey-water can be saved for another use). Spoon the sauce onto 6 or 8 dessert plates and place 3 or 4 figs on each. Serve warm or chilled. If the sauce is chilled, it will need to be thinned with a little brandy, cream or honey-water.

PAN DE HIGO
Fig Roll

My neighbour and I used to make dozens of these rolls at Christmas time for giving to our friends. You can find *pan de higos,* nicely wrapped, in supermarkets around holiday time. It makes a nice souvenir for fig lovers back home.

The proportions can be freely varied — some people like an equal quantity of figs and nuts, some like a dominant anise flavour, etc. Here is one version.

1	kilo dried figs	1/2	teaspoon ground pepper
300	grams hazelnuts or peanuts		sesame seed, toasted
300	grams almonds	1	tablespoon grated lemon peel
1	teaspoon cinnamon	3	squares chocolate, melted
50	grams sugar		brandy or anise
1/2	teaspoon aniseed, ground		blanched almonds
1/4	teaspoon ground cloves		

Finely chop the figs or put them through a grinder. Chop the nuts and add to the figs with the sugar, cinnamon, aniseed, cloves, pepper, 2 tablespoons sesame seed and lemon peel. Mix well with the hands. Add the melted chocolate and just enough brandy or anise to moisten the mixture slightly. It should be quite stiff. When well mixed, form balls each of about 200 grams, and make each into a roll about 5 cm. in diameter and 20 cm. long. Roll them in sesame seed and stud each with 3 or 4 blanched almonds. Let them dry for a few hours, then wrap them individually in plastic wrap. Store in tightly closed tins or in the refrigerator — they keep very well. Makes 8-10 rolls.

CONFECTIONS AND CANDIES

As many of these take some expertise to make, it's better to buy them ready-made from those who specialize in their confection. However, for those far from Spain and yearning for some of these sweets, here are a few to try at home.

ALMENDRAS GARAPIÑADAS
Candied Almonds

These are sold by street vendors, who stir the almonds and sugar in a copper pan until the sugar makes a crunchy, caramelized coating around the almond. The aroma is delicious and so are the almonds.

> 1/4 kilo almonds
> 1/4 kilo sugar

Do not skin the almonds. Put them in a heavy pot or untinned copper pan and stir with a wooden spoon until they are heated. Then stir in the sugar and continue stirring then over a medium fire until the sugar adheres to the almonds. Don't stop stirring, or the sugar will scorch. When they are done, turn them immediately out onto a marble or other cool surface and break up the clusters. Let them cool.

YEMAS
Candied Egg Yolks

12	very fresh egg yolks	250 ml. water	
425	grams sugar	1	piece cinnamon stick, 3 cm.
1	teaspoon glucose	1	piece lemon peel

Put the egg yolks in a bowl with 1 tablespoon of water and beat them until they are thick and ribbony. Pass them through a very fine sieve. Put 175 grams sugar, glucose, 100 ml. water, cinnamon and lemon peel to boil. Swirl the pan to mix, but do not stir. Let it cook to the thick thread stage. Discard cinnamon and lemon rind. While beating the yolks, very slowly add this syrup to them. Put the yolks in a clean pan, put on the heat again and, stirring hard with a wooden spoon, cook just until the mixture comes away from the pan in a ball. Remove it immediately from the heat and turn out onto a marble slab which has been lightly sprinkled with sugar. Let it cool. Then take small pieces of the mixture and shape them into balls, cones, lozenges or cylinder shapes (different regions are known for their different shapes). Let them dry while making a syrup with the remaining sugar and water, boiled to the soft ball stage. Remove the pan from the heat and continue beating the syrup, scraping down the sides of the pan, until the syrup is very thick and white. Dip the candies in the syrup and place them in small papers which have been sprinkled with sugar. Let them dry then wrap individually in paper or plastic wrap. Store in tins.

HUEVOS HILADOS
Candied Egg Threads

These are combined with the above *yemas* in some versions, but can also be used as decoration for cakes, puddings, or a baked ham.

> 1 kilo sugar
> 1/2 litre water
> 12 egg yolks

Boil the sugar and water to the thick thread stage. Meanwhile, beat the yolks and sieve them several times to remove all trace of the whites. Warm them slightly in a double boiler over hot water. Then put them in a funnel with a very tiny spout, holding finger over opening so it doesn't run out (in Seville, a special *hilador* with

6 funnels is used). Bring the syrup to a boil and reduce heat so it just barely bubbles. Hold the spout about 15 cm. over the surface of the pan and let the egg yolks fall into the syrup. Move the spout in a slow circular motion to keep forming long threads. Let them cook 3 minutes, then remove with a skimmer and drop into a bowl of ice water to firm and drain immediately. Let the threads dry on a marble slab.

ICE CREAMS AND ICES

Ice cream used to be a purely seasonal phenomenon — Corpus Cristi day in early June marked the first day for eating ice cream and bathing in the sea. Now ice cream is available year-round and I have never seen it consumed with more gusto than in mid-winter at the ski station of the Sierra Nevada. Which is, of course, where it all started. Centuries ago Moorish kings, and later their Christian counterparts, sent runners to the snow-covered mountains to carry back snow, which was sweetened with syrups and fruits. What a marvel that icy-sweetness must have seemed in the languid heat of the city!

Ice creams are easily made at home, with or without an ice cream maker. The trick is to freeze the mixture, then break it up and beat it by hand or in a processor until it is slushy, then refreeze it, repeating the process if desired. This breaks down the ice crystals so the cream or sorbet freezes smooth — exactly what the paddle in an ice cream maker does. Another kind of ice made in Spain is the *granizado* — see the following chapter for how to make it.

SORBETE DE FRUTA
Fruit Sorbet

Use any kind of fruit pulp for this sorbet, fresh, frozen or in conserve (preferably unsweetened). If you have such exotica as *chumbos,* prickly pears; *chirimoyas,* custard apples or *nísperos,* loquats, in your garden, try this refreshing ice with any of these fruits. Any fresh fruit should be moistened with lemon juice to prevent its darkening.

450 ml. fruit pulp		200 grams sugar
2 tablespoons orange or lemon juice		250 ml. water

Peel the fruit, remove seeds and mash or purée it with the orange or lemon juice. Put the sugar and water in a saucepan and boil 5 minutes. Cool the syrup, then mix it with the fruit purée (it can be strained, if desired). Chill. Pour into a metal pan, cover and freeze until almost firm. Then break the ice into chunks and beat it in mixer or processor until slushy. Return to pan, cover and freeze until firm. Or freeze in electric ice cream maker according to directions. Makes 1 litre sorbet. Serve garnished with fresh fruit, or in dessert cups drizzled with a little liqueur or in tall flute glasses filled with champagne.

Variation: To make the sorbet with juice instead of pulp, such as orange, lemon, grapefruit, pomegranate, (try tomato!), substitute about 350 ml. juice for the fruit pulp.

HELADOS DE FRUTAS
Moulded Fruit Ices

125	grams sugar	200 ml. cream, whipped
1	piece lemon peel	150 ml. fruit purée
100	ml. water	1 teaspoon vanilla or liqueur
3	egg whites	

Put the sugar in a saucepan with the lemon peel and water, and boil until it makes a syrup which spins a fine thread. Meanwhile, beat the egg whites until stiff. With the mixer running, add the hot syrup to the meringue in a slow stream. Let it cool, then fold in the whipped cream, the fruit purée and the vanilla extract or liqueur. Spoon into small moulds such as hollowed orange shells or custard cups and put them in the freezer until solid. To unmould, dip them briefly into hot water and turn out onto dessert plates. Garnish with fruit and pastries.

HELADO OLOROSO
Sherry Ice Cream

250	ml. *oloroso seco,* medium sherry	pinch of salt
300	grams sugar	500 ml. cream
8	egg yolks (fewer can be used)	

Put the sherry and 250 grams sugar in a saucepan and cook it for 15 minutes. Meanwhile, beat the egg yolks with a pinch of salt and the remaining sugar until they are thick. Put in a bain marie (double boiler) over boiling water and cook, stirring, until they thicken. Now whisk in the wine syrup and continue cooking until thick enough to coat a spoon. Remove from heat and whisk until the mixture is creamy and cooled. Beat in the cream and chill the mixture. Mix again before freezing, preferably in an ice cream maker. Otherwise, freeze, beat, refreeze and beat again before letting the cream freeze finally. Makes about 1 litre.

HELADO DE TURRON
Nougat Ice Cream

Turrón, nougat candy, is famous in Spain. Buy it from push-cart vendors at village fairs and in any supermarket at Christmas time. The best nougat is made from almonds. Very good — and less expensive — types are made from peanuts and hazelnuts. *Turrón* comes in bars covered with rice paper, which is edible, and is of two main types, the hard, white Alicante, studded with almonds, and a soft, brown one, like a nut fudge, from Jijona. Use the soft *turrón* in this ice cream. Crush some of the hard *turrón* in a mortar to sprinkle over the top.

850 ml. milk or 1/2 milk and 1/2 cream	pinch of salt	
175 grams sugar	150 grams soft nougat candy	
6 egg yolks	1 teaspoon vanilla extract	

Scald the milk and/or cream with the sugar. Whisk the egg yolks with the salt until they are frothy, then slowly whisk in the hot cream. Cook this custard until it is thickened. Remove from heat and add the vanilla. Cool this mixture, then chill it before freezing. Put in ice cream maker and when the cream is partially frozen add the nougat cut in small dice.

HELADO MOSCATEL
Muscatel Ice Cream

One of the favourite ice cream flavours in Spain is *nata,* cream, like vanilla without the vanilla. It's a wonderful foil for fruits and other flavours. For this dish, scoop *nata* ice cream into coupes or tall glasses, sprinkle over each a spoonful of muscatel raisins and pour over a shot of Malaga wine.

SWEET BREADS AND BUNS

For breakfast, tea time or dessert, these are always good. Knead yeast doughs until they are smooth and elastic, adding only enough flour to keep them from being sticky.

ENSAIMADAS MALLORQUINAS
Mallorcan Buns

Saim is lard with which these are made, sweet or savoury.

10	grams pressed yeast	2	eggs
1	teaspoon sugar	100	ml. hot water
4	tablespoons warm water	80	grams sugar
1/2	kilo flour	2	tablespoon oil
1	teaspoon salt		icing sugar

Dissolve the yeast in the 4 tablespoons of warm water with teaspoon sugar, and mix with 100 grams of flour. Put in a bowl and cover with a damp cloth and leave to rise in a warm place. Meanwhile, melt the lard, strain it if necessary, and cool it. In a large bowl, mix 400 grams flour, salt, eggs, hot water and remaining sugar. Add the first yeast mixture to it, turn out onto floured board and knead until very smooth, adding the oil a little at a time. Divide the dough into pieces of about 50 grams. Roll each one out quite thinly, brush it with the lard, fold in quarters and roll out and brush again with lard. Then roll the piece of dough into a cord about 30 cm. long. Twist the cord into a spiral, pinching the end underneath so it does not unwind. Place on a lightly greased oven tin. Continue with the remaining pieces of dough, spacing them several centimetres apart. Cover with a damp cloth and put them in a warm place until they are nearly doubled in bulk. Then sprinkle them with cold water and put in a hot oven until golden, 10 to 12 minutes. Remove and sprinkle with icing sugar. Makes about 16 buns.

If they are to be served as a savoury, place slices of *sobrasada,* Mallorcan red sausage, on top of the dough before baking. As a dessert: form the dough into 2 or 3 large spirals. After baking, pipe whipped cream following the spirals and top with pieces of glacéed fruit.

SUIZOS
Sweet Rolls

Another typical sweet roll, *suizos,* can be made from the same recipe as ensaimadas using milk instead of water, and butter instead of lard. Form them into oval-shaped buns. Before baking, slash them deeply lengthwise, brush with beaten eggs and sprinkle with sugar. Bake in a hot oven.

TORTELLS
Catalan Almond Roll

1	recipe as for *ensaimadas* (no lard)	1	teaspoon grated lemon rind
1	small potato	50	grams butter
125	grams sugar	1	egg, beaten
125	grams ground almonds		sugar for sprinkling

Prepare the dough up to the point of rolling out. For the filling, cook the potato, put it through a ricer and whip it with the sugar. Add the ground almonds and the grated lemon rind. Divide filling into 6 portions. Divide the dough into pieces of about 150 grams. Roll each out on a lightly floured board into a rectangle and smear it with softened butter. Place a strip of filling across one end and roll the dough up. Bring the ends together, forming a circle, and pinch them together. Place on buttered baking sheet. Proceed to fill and roll the remaining dough. Cover with a damp cloth and put in a warm place to rise until nearly doubled in bulk (about 1 hour depending on temperature). Then brush with beaten egg and sprinkle with sugar and bake in a medium hot oven until golden, about 20 minutes. Makes 6 rolls.

ROSCON DE REYES
Kings' Day Cake

In Spain it isn't jolly old St. Nicholas who brings toys and sweeties to good girls and boys, but the Three Kings, los *Reyes Magos,* who arrive by camel from Bethlehem. And they don't come on Christmas Eve, either, but on the twelfth day of Christmas, January 6. This cake, which can also be purchased in pastry shops, always contains a tiny trinket — the one who finds it is assured a year's good fortune.

Needless to say, this makes a lovely tea cake any time of the year.

20	grams pressed yeast	1	tablespoon orange flower water
4	tablespoons warm milk		*(agua de azahar)*
200	grams sugar	1	teaspoon grated orange rind
1/2	kilo flour	1	teaspoon grated lemon rind
3	whole eggs	100	grams butter, softened
1	egg, separated	50	grams almonds, blanched, skinned
1	teaspoon salt		and slivered
1	tablespoon dark rum		candied fruits, orange peel, etc., for
			decoration (about 100 grams)

Dissolve the yeast in the warm milk with 1 tablespoon of the sugar. Add 50 grams of the flour and mix it to make a soft dough. Cover with a damp cloth and set in a warm place until doubled in bulk. Put the remaining flour in a large bowl. Make a well in the centre. Beat the eggs together with the egg yolk and pour into the flour with the salt, rum, orange flower water and the rest of the sugar. Add the grated orange and lemon rind. Work the flour into the liquids in the centre with the hands or a wooden spoon. Add the yeast dough and mix very well until the dough is no longer sticky. Divide the butter into 4 parts and sprinkle it with flour. Divide the dough into 4 parts. On a lightly floured board work a piece of butter into each of the pieces of dough, then knead them together again. Knead the dough until very smooth and elastic. Lightly butter a bowl, put the ball of dough into it, turn it, cover with a damp cloth and set in a warm place for 1 hour. Punch the dough down, turn out onto the board and knead again. Insert the trinket into the dough. Shape it into 1 or 2 rings by making a flattened ball, then inserting a finger into the centre and very gently easing the dough outwards to create a hole in the centre. Either stuff the hole with crumpled paper and place on a buttered oven tin or set the ring in a lightly buttered ring mould. Cover and set in a warm place to rise again. The dough will not double in bulk, but will rise substantially during baking. Lightly beat the remaining egg white (or use a whole egg). Brush the cake with the egg. Sprinkle on the slivered almonds and decorate with candied fruits. Sprinkle lightly with sugar and bake in a medum hot oven until nicely browned, about 35 minutes. Makes 1 large cake, or 2 medium ones.

CONSERVES AND PRESERVES

I once lived in an old house in the village with a garden behind it. There grew 10 different kinds of fruit trees in a very small space. I was delighted to see an orange tree — my first — heavily laden with fruit When the oranges looked sufficiently ripe and juicy, I picked one, peeled it and popped a section in my mouth. It was unbelievably bitter! I had a tree which had never been grafted. What to do with bitter oranges? I started making marmalade and wonderful marmalade it was, too. I made so much that I put a sign on the front door and sold it to passers-by.

Very small quantities of marmalades, jams and preserves can be stored refrigerated. To preserve in quantity, they must be packed in sterile jars. Canning jars can be purchased or ordinary jars recycled, as long as the lids are not scratched or dented. To sterilize jars, first wash them well in soapy water and rinse. Then set them in a large pan and partially fill them with water. Set their lids on top. Fill the pan with water to about three-quarters the height of the jars. Bring the water to a boil and boil for 15 minutes. Remove carefully, pour out water and drain the jars on a clean cloth. Fill them while still hot with hot contents.

MERMELADA DE NARANJA
Orange Marmalade

This is a 3-day procedure. For each kilo of fruit, allow 1 litre of water and 1 kilo of sugar. If you like a very bitter marmalade, use equal quantities of bitter oranges and sweet oranges, plus a couple of lemons. If you prefer a sweeter flavour, use more eating oranges and fewer bitter ones, and only 1 lemon.

Day 1: Wash the oranges, weigh them and soak them in fresh water for several hours. Then shred, chop or finely slice them, catching all the juice and reserving the seeds in a separate bowl. Add enough water to cover the seeds and add the required quantity of water to the oranges. Cover and let them set for 24 hours.

Day 2: Cook the oranges very slowly until they are tender, about 1 hour. Cover and let set overnight.

Day 3: Add the sugar and let the oranges set for 6 hours. Put the seeds and their liquid (it will be quite gelatinous from the pectin) into a strainer and strain the liquid into the oranges. Bring the oranges to a boil and regulate the heat so they just bubble gently. Cook until thickened. The marmalade is done when a small quantity dropped on a cold surface does not run. Stir occasionally to prevent scorching. Time depends on quantity of oranges, but the jelling can easily take an hour. Pack while hot into sterile jars, and seal.

MERMELADA DE FRUTA
Fruit Jam

Recipes for fruit jams generally call for equal weight of sugar and fruit. I find this excessively sweet and always use about 3/4 kilo sugar for each kilo of fruit. Lemon juice helps to give a tart flavour, and a pinch of salt enhances flavour. No water is added to soft fruits such as peaches, apricots, strawberries, figs, etc. The sugar is gently mixed with the fruit and left to set for several hours or overnight. The sugar draws out the fruit's juice and it is ready to cook. Low pectin fruits, such as strawberries and figs take a long time to set and benefit from the addition of high pectin fruits such as apples or quince.

CARNE DE MEMBRILLO
Quince Jelly

This can be purchased in any *tienda,* but the home-made product is so much better. In tightly sealed containers it will keep for months. Serve *membrillo* in thin slices for dessert, accompanied by white cheese and a few nuts. Delicious.

Wash the quinces, put them in a pot with water to cover and cook until they are quite tender, about 25 minutes. Drain, reserving a little of the water. Peel and core them and put the fruit through a sieve. Weigh the fruit pulp and add the same weight of sugar. Cook the fruit and sugar, adding just a little of the reserved liquid, until it is very thick, stirring constantly so it does not scorch. Pour the jelly into shallow rectangular moulds and let it cool. It should set solid enough to slice.

CABELLO DE ANGEL
Angel's Hair Jam

Made with a type of squash, *cidra,* which doesn't seem to be used for anything else, this preserve gets its name because the *cidra* cooks into fine strands. It is much used as a filling for *empanadillas,* little pies; cakes, pastries and simply as a jam. The *cidra* should be left to age for a year before using. Or make the jam with pumpkin or other hard-skinned squash. Apricot or orange marmalade can be substituted in recipes which call for *cabello de angel.*

   Cut the squash open and remove seeds and membranes. Cut it into chunks and put in a pot with a little water. Cover and steam until tender. Drain and peel the squash. Weigh the pulp and put the same weight of sugar into a pan with the peel of a lemon. Add enough water to moisten the sugar; bring to a boil. Shred the squash pulp and add to the sugar. Cook, stirring frequently, until it becomes the consistency of a thick jam or marmalade. Pack in sterile jars to conserve or keep a small quantity in the refrigerator for several weeks.

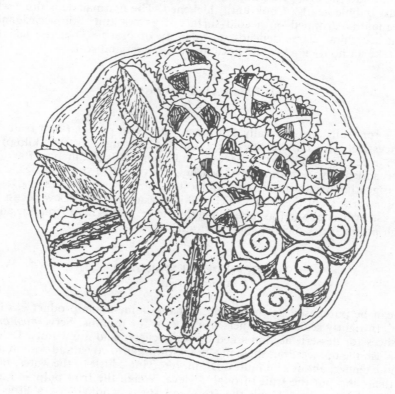

CHAPTER 14

Beverages

Spain is a wine-drinking country and no meal is complete without it. Except for special occasions and for special wines, its drinking is accompanied by no ceremony or ritual: the bottle is opened, the wine poured — in simple restaurants into ordinary water glasses — and the wine is drunk. Simple red wine, *vino común,* is frequently diluted with *gaseosa,* a slightly sweet, bubbly water, which makes it possible to return to work after a midday meal of three courses with wine. You'll find lots more about Spanish wines in Chapter 2 on marketing.

Like wine drinkers everywhere, Spaniards have never been overly imaginative with cocktails and mixed drinks. The best ones are based on wine — such as the concoction so adored by tourists, *sangría.* My own favourites are those based on sherry, which seems to have a special affinity to orange juice. A "screwdriver" or sherry and orange juice over ice, is a lovely, sunny brunch drink, and a sherry sour — sherry, lemon juice and sugar — is richer but less potent than its whisky counterpart. Of course, there are wonderful festive drinks like *coctel de champán,* champagne cocktail made with Spanish *cava.*

Refrescos, refreshers, is the word for cool, non-alcoholic drinks, which include lemonade, orangeade and other fruit drinks as well as bottled drinks. There are many bottled waters sold in Spain and those who don't drink wine with meals usually order a bottle of water, either *sin gas,* still, or *con gas,* fizzy. (Nobody in Spain would dream of drinking coffee with a meal, as do Americans.) A *batido* is a milkshake or flavoured milk, which you can buy bottled in cafés but is so much better freshly made. *Horchata* is an exotic summer drink which makes me think of Arabic *souks* and cushioned harem rooms. This is the orgeat of the Moors, originally sweetened almond milk. Today it is made with the *chufa,* tiger nut. The sweet, milky drink has a faint flavour of coconut. It's available bottled, but can be made at home with either *chufas* or almonds.

As much a part of Spanish life as wine is coffee. Indeed, how would any business get done or social engagements made if it were not for the café, a veritable social institution in Spain? Coffee begins the day; boiled in a *puchero* pot or made with a filter, served half and half with hot milk. And coffee ends the day: strong, expresso brew drunk black in tiny cups with plenty of sugar. In between are numerous expresso coffees with varying degrees of milk — a *sombra* is lots of milk, a *cortado* is a tiny bit of milk, and so forth. In cafés, coffee is very often served in small glasses, a very satisfying hand-warmer in the winter. In the summer, I order my *café con leche* with a glass full of ice cubes on the side and, after sweetening the brew, pour it over ice. Some cafés specialize in hot chocolate, thick and rich, for dunking *churros* into. At home it would be scented with cinnamon and liberally infused with sugar.

SANGRIA
Red Wine Punch

There are many versions of this favourite — which, by the way, is rather too sweet to be served with a meal, though it makes a nice afternoon or evening refresher. Some prefer the fruit macerated in brandy for several hours and others like crisp, fresh fruit added at the last minute. Some aficionados insist on only brandy with the wine, others mix a syrup of sugar and fruit liqueurs. Some say no soda water, others, wishing to be able to walk home afterwards, dilute the punch.

In a pitcher mix a litre of chilled red wine with 1/4 litre brandy or orange liqueur. Stir in 100 grams sugar until dissolved. Add a variety of sliced fruit — oranges, lemons, bananas, apples, strawberries are typical. Chill the punch. Before serving add ½ litre soda water or *gaseosa*.

ZURRA
Manchegan White Wine Cooler

1	litre white wine, chilled	1	stalk celery
200	ml. water	1	piece cinnamon, 4 cm.
50	grams sugar	1	sliced lemon
	several sprigs of mint	1	sliced orange

Boil the sugar and water for 5 minutes. Remove from heat and add the mint, celery, cinnamon, lemon and orange slices. Let steep until the syrup is cool. Strain into a pitcher and add the chilled wine and a few slices of lemon and orange. Dilute to taste with soda water and garnish with fresh mint sprigs.

ARDAURGOZATZA
Basque Lemonade

3	lemons, skinned	1/2	litre red wine
1/2	litre water	1/2	litre white wine
75	grams sugar		

Soak the lemon peel in the water for 24 hours. Add the sugar and red and white wines to the water with sliced lemons. Serve chilled.

SANGRI MENORQUI
Mulled Wine, Menorcan Style

2	litres red wine	lemon and orange peel
1	litre water	nutmeg
100	grams sugar	toast
	cinnamon stick	

Put the wine, water and sugar in a pot and add the cinnamon stick and peel of a lemon and an orange. Heat until the mixture begins to bubble, but do not boil.

Remove from heat and sprinkle with grated nutmeg. Squares of toasted bread can be added, to be consumed when nicely sodden.

PUNYS D'OUS
Menorcan Hot Egg Punch

6	egg yolks	1/2 litre milk	
8	tablespoons sugar	lemon peel	
300	ml. brandy or dark rum	3	egg whites

Beat the egg yolks until frothy, then beat in 6 tablespoons sugar and brandy or rum. Heat the milk with the lemon peel just until it begins to boil. Pour it into the yolk mixture slowly while beating constantly. Beat the egg white until stiff and whisk in the remaining sugar. Divide the hot drink between 6 cups and top each with a dollop of meringue. Serves 6.

PONCHE
Spanish Hot Toddy

Put a shot of brandy in a small glass with a lump of sugar. Fill the glass with hot water and add a slice of lemon. The drink may also be made with a bottled liqueur called "Ponche," omitting the sugar.

QUEIMADA
Galician Fire Drink

This is made with Galician *aguardiente de orujo,* a strong, clear brandy distilled from the pressed grapes left after the wine making. Sometimes called "firewater," it is powerful stuff and would probably make suitable fuel for a jet plane. If you can't get aguardiente, use French *marc,* Italian *grappa,* brandy or rum.

In the bottom of a warmed earthenware bowl mix 50 ml. *aguardiente* and 1 tablespoon sugar per person. Stir to blend. Turn off the lights. Dip up a spoonful, light it and add to the bowl. Continue stirring until the alcohol is more or less burned off. While still burning, you may add a few shots of brandy, Cointreau and crema de café. Serve as it is, while telling ghost stories, or extinguish the flames by adding a small pot of freshly made coffee.

Sangría, *Spain's famous wine cooler (recipe, page 349).*

GUINDAS EN ANIS
Cherries in Anisette

Fill clean jars with cherries, which have been well washed and stems removed. Put in a cinnamon stick, and 1/4 kilo of sugar for each 1 kilo of fruit. Fill the jars with anise brandy. Cap tightly. The fruit will keep for years as long as it is covered with anise. Serve the anise as a cordial and the fruit as a punchy addition to cakes, punches, ice cream and puddings. If you don't like the flavour of anise, try this with brandy or rum.

COPA DE NAVIDAD
Christmas Cup

Mix 1/2 kilo raisins, which have been well washed and dried, with 1 litre of sweet anise brandy. Let set 2 or 3 months. Serve in brandy snifters at Christmas — or any time.

LIMONADA DE MIEL
Honeyed Lemonade

Mix the juice of one large lemon with 2 tablespoons of honey. Dissolve in a little hot water, then add cold water to taste, about 400 ml. Chill.

NARANJADA
Orangeade

Cut the rind from 12 oranges, without taking any of the white part. Squeeze the oranges, strain the juice and set aside. Cut the peel into strips and put in a bowl. Pour a litre of boiling water over them, add 100 grams of sugar (or to taste), cover and let stand several hours. Strain and mix with the orange juice. Chill well. Lemonade can be made in the same way.

HORCHATA
Orgeat

Wash 1/4 kilo of *chufas* tiger nuts, and put them to soak in water for 24 hours (or use blanched and skinned almonds). Wash them again, drain and dry well in a towel, rubbing them to whiten them. Put the *chufas* through a grinder or finely chop in processor. Add 1 litre of water or milk to the pulp. Let it soak for several hours, then press the liquid through a sieve. Add 1/4 kilo of sugar and chill well. Sprinkle with cinnamon.

Spain is one of the world's major wine producers. Apart from being the perfect accompaniment to a Spanish meal, wine forms the basis of many typical mixed drinks.

GRANIZADO DE LIMON
Lemon Ice

Make 1 litre of lemonade, adding sugar and water to taste. Put it in metal pans and freeze. Before serving whirl the ice in blender or processor until it is slush. Serve in tall glasses with straws.

GRANIZADO DE CAFE
Coffee Ice

Make coffee, adding sugar and water to taste. Put in metal pans and freeze. Proceed as in the previous recipe. A tablespoon of brandy can be added to the coffee.

GRANIZADO DE VINO
Wine Ice

Mix 1 bottle of Malaga wine or medium sherry with 50 grams of sugar and 50 ml. orange juice. Put in metal trays and freeze. Proceed as above.

CHOCOLATE A LA ESPAÑOLA
Spanish Hot Chocolate

In the supermarket you'll find a bewildering array of chocolate bars. Besides eating chocolate there is *chocolate a la taza,* chocolate meant for making this hot drink. It contains starch which will thicken the chocolate as it cooks.

Allow 50 grams of chocolate for each cup. Chop or grate it and put in a pan with 1 cup of water or milk per person. Heat the mixture and whisk it continually to keep it very smooth. Remove the chocolate from the heat the instant it begins to boil and beat it hard for a few minutes. Pour into cups, adding sugar to taste and thinning as desired with cold water. Sprinkle with a little cinnamon. If you can't get Spanish chocolate, mix 2 tablespoons cornstarch for each 1 litre liquid and use any dark chocolate, grated.

CAFE
Coffee

For Spanish-style coffee brewed at home choose a dark roast, what in Spain is called *natural,* and have it ground very fine. Expresso coffee served in cafés is usually made with coffee beans which have been very darkly roasted with sugar, giving a slight caramel taste. This is called *torrefacto* and you can buy it in Spanish supermarkets. It also must be finely ground.

Whether you are making morning *café con leche* or after-dinner *café solo,* use 1 measure of coffee (a heaped tablespoon, about 8 grams) per cup, but change the quantity of water from 200-250 ml. for the big cup to 100 ml. for demitasse. Use either a filter pot or an expresso pot, which forces the water up through the coffee into the top section of the pot.

For café con leche, heat milk just to the boiling point, remove and strain it. Serve hot.

Spanish/English Glossary

A

Abadejo: (fish) pollack
Aceite: oil
Aceituna: olive
Acelga: chard, Swiss chard, spinach beet
Achicoría: chicory
Adobo: marinade
Agrio: sour
Agua: water
Aguacate: avocado
Aguardiente: distilled liquor; **aguardiente de anís,** anise brandy; **aguardiente de orujo,** clear grape brandy
Aguja: (fish) needlefish, gar
Ahumado, -a: smoked
Ajo: garlic
Ajoaceite, ajiaceite: garlic sauce
Ajonjolí: sesame seed
Albahaca: basil

Albaricoque: apricot
Albóndiga: meatball
Alcachofa: artichoke
Alcaparra: caper
Alcaravea: caraway seed
Alfalfa: alfalfa
Aliño: dressing, sauce, marinade
Alioli: garlic mayonnaise
Alitan: type of edible shark
Almeja: clam
Almendra: almond
Almíbar: syrup
Almirez: mortar and pestle
Almuerzo: lunch, midday meal
Alondra: lark
Alubia: bean
Amargo: bitter
Anacardo: cashew nut
Anca de rana: frog's leg
Anchoa: anchovy
Angelote: angel-fish

Anguila: eel
Angula: baby eel
Anís: aniseed
Añojo: year-old, yearling
Apio: celery
Araña: (fish) weever
Arándano: blueberry
Arbitán: (fish) ling
Arenque: herring
Arete: (fish) red gurnard
Armado: fish similar to gurnard
Arroz: rice
Asado: roast, roasted, from the verb "asar"
Atún: tunny
Ave: fowl, poultry
Avena: oats
Avellana: hazelnut
Azafrán: saffron
Azahar: orange blossom
Azúcar: sugar; **azúcar tamizado,** icing sugar; **azúcar moreno,** brown sugar

B

Bacaladilla: (fish) blue whiting
Bacalao: cod
Baila: (fish) type of bass
Barbo: (fish) barbel
Batata: sweet potato
Becada: woodcock
Bejel: (fish) tub gurnard
Berberecho: cockle
Berenjena: aubergine, egg plant
Berro: watercress
Berza: cabbage
Besugo: red bream
Bicarbonato sódico: sodium bicarbonate, baking soda
Bizcocho: sponge cake
Bocadillo: sandwich
Bocarte: young sardine
Bodio: (fish) type of wrasse
Boga: (fish) a small bream
Bogavante: lobster
Boleto: boletus mushroom
Bollo: bun, bread roll
Boniato: sweet potato

Borracho: drunken, as in **tarta borracha,** cake soused in wine or liqueur; also (fish) grey gurnard
Boquerón: fresh anchovy
Brasa: ember; **a la brasa,** charcoal grilled
Breca: (fish) a small bream
Brecol: broccoli
Breva: early fig
Broculi: broccoli
Brote: sprout, i.e. beansprout
Brótola: (fish) forkbeard
Brut: dry sparkling wine
Buey: ox; also, beef from older animal; also (shellfish) a type of crab
Buñuelo: fritter
Búsano: whelk
Butifarra: type of Catalan sausage

C

Caballa: mackerel
Cabeza: head, i.e. **cabeza de ajo,** head of garlic
Cabra: goat; also (fish) type of rascasse
Cabracho: scorpion-fish
Cabrillo: (fish) comber
Cabrito: kid, baby goat
Cacahuete: peanut
Cacerola: cooking pot, saucepan
Cachorreña: bitter orange
Cailón: type of edible shark
Calabacín: courgette, small marrow; zucchini
Calabaza: pumpkin, squash
Calamar: squid
Caldereta: stew
Caldo: broth, stock, consommé
Callos: tripe
Camarón: small prawn, shrimp
Canela: cinnamon
Canelones: cannelloni
Cangrejo: crab; **cangrejo de río,** crayfish
Capitón: (fish) type of grey mullet
Caqui: persimmon
Carabinero: large prawn
Caracol: snail
Caracola: sea snail
Carbonera: type of wild mushroom

Carbonero: (fish) coley, saithe, coalfish
Cardamomo: cardamom
Cardo: cardoon
Carne: meat; **carne picada,** minced meat, ground meat
Carnero: mutton
Carpa: carp
Cártamo: safflower
Castaña: chestnut
Cayena: chili pepper, cayenne
Caza: hunt, game
Cazón: dogfish
Cazuela: casserole
Cebada: barley
Cebado: fattened
Cebolla: onion
Cebollino: chive
Cecina: dried beef jerky
Cena: evening meal, supper
Centeno: rye
Centollo: spider crab
Cereal: cereal, grain
Cereza: cherry
Cerdo: pig, pork
Cerveza: beer
Chacina: cured meat
Chalota: shallot
Champiñón: mushroom, sp. cultivated
Chanquete: (fish) type of goby
Charcutería: the curing of meat; shop where cured meats are sold
Cherna: wreckfish, stone bass
Chicharro: (fish) horse mackerel, scad
Chicarro: (fish) horse mackerel, scad
Chipirón: small squid
Chirimoya: cherimoya, custard apple
Chirivía: parsnip
Choco: small cuttlefish
Chivo: kid, baby goat
Chopa: (fish) red bream
Chopito: small cuttlefish
Chorizo: red sausage
Choto: baby kid
Chufa: tiger nut
Chuleta: chop, cutlet
Chuletón: large beef chop
Chumbo: prickly pear
Churro: breakfast fritter
Cidra: a type of gourd
Ciervo: deer
Cigala: Dublin Bay prawn, sea crayfish

Cilantro: coriander
Ciruela: plum
Clavo: clove
Clementina: a type of tangerine
Cochinillo: suckling pig
Cocido: cooked, from the verb "cocer"; also, a type of meal-in-a-pot
Cocina: kitchen; cuisine
Coco: coconut
Codorniz: quail
Cogollo: heart, core, as in *cogollo de palmito,* palm heart
Col: cabbage
Col de Bruselas: Brussels sprout
Coliflor: cauliflower
Colza: rape seed
Comida: food; meal
Comino: cumin
Concha: (seafood) shell; **concha fina:** Venus shell clam
Conejo: rabbit
Confitura: jam, preserve
Congelado: frozen from the verb "congelar"
Congrio: conger eel
Coquina: wedge shell clam
Corazón: heart
Corcón: (fish) a type of grey mullet
Cordero: lamb
Corvina: (fish) meagre
Corzo: roe deer
Cosecha: harvest, vintage
Costilla: rib
Crema: cream; cream soup, as in **crema de espárragos,** cream of asparagus soup
Criadilla: testicle; **criadilla de tierra,** truffle
Cuajada: curd, rennet pudding
Cuajo: rennet
Cúrcuma: turmeric

D

Dátil: palm date
Dentón: (fish) dentex
Desayuno: breakfast
Diente: tooth; clove, as in **diente de ajo,** clove of garlic

Doncella: (fish) type of wrasse
Dorada: (fish) gilt head
Dulce: sweet; **dulce de membrillo,** quince jelly

E

Eglefino: (fish) haddock
Embutido: sausage
Empanada: pie
Empanadilla: little pie
Empanado, -a: breaded, from the verb "empanar"
Emperador: swordfish
Endibia: endive, chicory
Endrina: sloe berry
Enebro: juniper berry
Eneldo: dill
Ensalada: salad
Entremeses: hors-d'oeuvre
Erizo de mar: sea urchin
Escabeche: marinade; **en escabeche,** pickled
Escalonia: shallot
Escarola: escarole, endive
Escolano: (fish) ling
Escorpion: (fish) weever
Espagueti: spaghetti
Esparrago: asparagus
Especia: spice
Espinaca: spinach
Estofado: stew, stewed
Estornino: Spanish mackerel
Estragón: tarragon

F

Faba: type of dried bean
Faisan: pheasant
Falda: (meat) flank
Fesol: type of dried bean
Fiambre: pressed meat, pâté
Fideo: vermicelli noodle
Filete: (meat) slice of steak; (fish) fillet
Fino: fine; also (wine) type of dry sherry
Frambuesa: raspberry
Frejol: type of dried bean

Fresa: strawberry
Freson: strawberry
Frigüelo: black-eyed pea
Frijol: type of dried bean
Frisuelo: type of dried bean
Frito: fried, from the verb "freir"
Fruta: fruit
Fuerte: strong

G

Galleta: biscuit, cookie
Gallina: hen
Gallineta: redfish, bluemouth, Norway haddock
Gallo: (poultry) cock, rooster; (fish) whiff, megrim
Galludo: dogfish
Galupe: (fish) type of grey mullet
Gamba: prawn, shrimp
Ganso: gander
Garbanzo: garbanzo, chick pea
Garneo: (fish) piper
Gayano: (fish) type of wrasse
Germen: germ, as in **germen de trigo,** wheatgerm
Girasol: sunflower
Granada: pomegranate
Granadina: grenadine
Granel, al: in bulk
Gratinado: au gratin
Grelo: flowering turnip green
Grosella: currant
Guayaba: guava
Guinda: cherry
Guindilla: hot chili pepper
Guisante: pea

H

Haba: broad bean
Habichuela: green bean or dried bean
Harina: flour
Helado: iced; ice-cream
Hierba Buena: mint
Hierba Luisa: lemon verbena

Hígado: liver
Higo: fig
Hinojo: fennel
Hojaldre: puff pastry
Hongo: fungus; also, certain types of wild mushrooms
Horno: oven
Hueso: bone
Huevas: fish roe
Huevo: egg

I

Infusion: herbal tea

J

Jabalí: boar
Jamón: ham
Jarabe: syrup
Jengibre: ginger
Jerez: sherry
Jibia: cuttlefish
Judía: bean; **judía verde,** green bean; **judía seca,** dried bean
Jurel: horse mackerel

L

Lacon: cured pork shoulder
Langosta: spiny lobster, rock lobster
Langostino: large prawn
Laurel: bay leaf
Lechal: milk fed
Leche: milk
Lechuga: lettuce
Legumbre: vegetable, specially legume, pulse
Lengua: tongue
Lenguado: sole
Lenteja: lentil
Levadura: leavening; **levadura en polvo,** dry yeast, baking powder; **levadura prensada,** cake yeast
Liebre: hare

Lima: lime
Limanda: lemon sole
Limón: lemon
Lingote: a type of dried bean
Lisa: (fish) grey mullet
Llisera: flat fish similar to whiff or megrim
Lombarda: red cabbage
Lomo: loin, specially pork
Lota: (fish) ling
Lubina: sea bass
Lucio: (fish) pike

M

Macarrones: macaroni
Macis: mace
Magro: pork, lean
Maiz: corn
Malva: hibiscus flower
Mandarina: tangerine
Manojo: handful, bunch
Manteca: lard
Mantequilla: butter
Manzana: apple
Manzanilla: camomile; also (wine) a type of sherry
Maragota; (fish) a type of wrasse
Margarina: margarine
Marisco: shellfish
Maruca: (fish) ling
Masa: pastry or bread dough
Matadero: slaughterhouse
Matalahuva: aniseed
Mayonesa: mayonnaise
Mazapán: marzipan
Mejillón: mussel
Mejorana: marjoram
Melaza: molasses
Melocotón: peach
Melón: melon
Membrillo: quince
Menta: mint
Merlan: (fish) whiting
Merlo: (fish) a type of wrasse
Merluza: hake
Mermelada: jam, marmalade
Mero: grouper

Miel: honey; **miel de caña,** molasses
Mielga: type of edible shark
Mijo: millet
Mojama: cured tuna
Molleja: sweetbreads
Monjete: type of dried bean
Morcilla: blood sausage
Morena: (fish) moray eel
Mostaza: mustard
Mujol: type of grey mullet
Musola: type of edible shark

N

Nabo: turnip
Ñame: yam
Naranja: orange
Nata: cream
Navaja: (fish) razor clam
Nécora: small crab
Niscalo: type of wild mushroom
Níspero: loquat
Ñora: sweet dried pepper
Nuez: nut, walnut
Nuez moscada: nutmeg

O

Gblada: fish similar to dentex
Oca: goose
Olla: pot
Oloroso: (wine) type of sherry
Orégano: oregano
Orejón: dried apricot
Ostión: Portuguese oyster
Ostra: oyster

P

Pajarito: small bird
Paletilla: shoulder of an animal
Palmito: palmetto, palm heart
Paloma: squab, pigeon, dove
Palometa: (fish) pompano

Palometa negra: (fish) pomfret, Ray's bream
Palometón: (fish) pompano
Pan: bread; **pan rallado,** breadcrumbs
Panceta: streaked pork fat
Pardete: type of grey mullet
Pargo: fish similar to dentex
Parrilla: grill
Pasa: dried fruit, as in **uva pasa,** dried raisin, **ciruela pasa,** dried plum, prune
Pastel: pie, pastry
Pata: leg of an animal
Patata: potato
Pato: duck
Pavo: turkey
Pechuga: (poultry) breast
Peluda: scaldfish
Pepinillo: cucumber pickle
Pepino: cucumber
Pera: pear
Perca: (fish) perch
Percebe: barnacle
Perdiz: partridge
Peregrina: (shellfish) scallop
Perejil: parsley
Perifollo: chervil
Perlon: (fish) gurnard
Pescadilla: small hake
Pescado: fish
Pez: fish; **pez angel,** angel-fish; **pez espada,** swordfish; **pez limón,** amberjack
Picante: hot, spicy, piquant
Pichón: squab, pigeon, dove
Picota: cherry
Pierna: leg
Pijota: hake
Pimentón: paprika
Pimienta: (spice) pepper
Pimiento: (vegetable) pepper
Piña: pineapple
Piñón: pine nut
Pintada; guinea fowl
Pintarroja: dogfish
Plancha: grill, griddle
Plátano: banana
Platija: flounder
Pocha: type of dried bean
Pollo: chicken
Pomelo: grapefruit
Potaje: pottage
Puchero: stock pot, boiled dinner

Puerro: leek
Pulpo: octopus

Q

Queso: cheese
Quisquilla: small prawn

R

Rábano: radish; **rábano picante,** horse-radish
Rabo: tail
Rape: anglerfish, monkfish
Rascacio: rascasse
Rata: (fish) stargazer
Raya: (fish) skate, ray
Rebeco: chamois
Rebozado: batter-dipped and fried, from the verb **"rebozar"**
Redondo: (beef) round
Remojo: soaking
Remol: (fish) brill
Remolacha: beet
Reo: sea trout
Repollo: cabbage
Requesón: cottage cheese
Reserva: (wine) aged wine
Riñón: kidney
Rodaballo: (fish) turbot
Romero: rosemary
Rombo: (fish) brill
Rosada: ocean catfish, wolf-fish
Rosco: doughnut
Rubio: gurnard

S

Sábalo: (fish) shad
Sal: salt
Salado: salted, salty
Salchicha: fresh pork sausage
Salchichón: cured sausage
Salema: (fish) bream

Salmón: salmon
Salmonete: red mullet
Salsa: sauce
Salteado, -a: sautéed, from the verb **"saltear"**
Salvia: sage
Salvado: bran
Sandía: watermelon
Sangre: blood
San Pedro: John Dory
Sardina: sardine
Sargo: (fish) bream
Sarten: frying pan
Sebo: suet
Seco: dry, dried
Sepia: cuttlefish
Serandell: scaldfish
Serrano: mountain-style, as in **jamón serrano,** mountain-cured ham, **huevos serranos,** mountain-style eggs
Sesos: brains
Seta: wild mushroom
Sidra: cider
Soja: soy
Solla: (fish) plaice
Solomillo: (meat) fillet, tenderloin
Sopa: soup
Sortija: French sand sole
Suela: fish similar to sole

T

Tambor: fish similar to sole
Tarta: cake
Tenca: (fish) tench
Ternera: veal, young beef
Tienda: shop
Tigre: fish similar to sole
Tila: linden flower
Tocino: pork fat, salt pork
Tomate: tomato
Tomillo: thyme
Tordo: type of wrasse
Torta: round, flat bun or cake
Tortilla: omelette
Tórtola: turtle dove
Tostado: toast, toasted, from the verb **"tostar"**

Trigo: wheat
Trucha: trout
Trufa: truffle
Tuétano: bone marrow
Turrón: nougat

U~V~Y~Z

Uva: grape
Urta: fish similar to dentex
Urogallo: wood-grouse

Vacuno, carne de: beef
Venado: venison
Verdura: green vegetable
Vieira: (shellfish) scallop
Vino: wine; **vino rancio,** mellowed wine

Yema: egg yolk; also, a sweet made of yolks

Zanahoria: carrot
Zapata: fish similar to dentex
Zarzamora: blackberry
Zorzal: thrush

Index of Recipes

The following is an alphabetical listing of over 400 recipes that appear in this book. Recipes are listed under their Spanish name — for recipes in English, check individual ingredient in the general index that follows. A page number in **bold type** indicates a photograph.

Alcachofas rellenas (Stuffed artichokes) 154
Alcachofas salteadas con jamon (Sautéed artichokes with ham) 153
Alboronia (see **Pisto,** 184)
Alioli (Garlic mayonnaise) 313, **317**
Almejas a la marinera (Clams, fisherman's style) 241
Almejas con alubias blancas (Clams and beans) 241
Almendras garapiñadas (Candied almonds) 337
Almendras tostadas (Toasted almonds) 105
Amanida (Catalan salad) 112
Andrajos (''Tatters and rags'') 198
Anguila al alli i pebre (Valencian eel stew) 229
Angulas en cazuela (Baby eels with garlic) 229, **233**
Ardaurgozatza (Basque lemonade) 349
Arros amb crosta (Crusty rice, Alicante style) 193
Arros negre amb all i oli (Catalan black rice with garlic) 192
Arroz abanda (Rice and fish, fisherman's style) 191
Arroz a la marinera (Sailor's rice) **168,** 190
Arroz a la zamorana (Rice, Zamora style) 194
Arroz con leche (Creamy rice pudding) 330
Arroz en perdiu (Rice with ''partridge'') 194
Arroz rosetxat (Rice and lamb casserole, Valencian style) 193
Asado de cerdo a la catalana (Roast pork, Catalan style) 283
Atun con tomate (Fresh tuna baked in tomato sauce) 214

Bacalao a la manchega (see Salt Cod, 235-236)
Bacalao a la vizcaina (Salt cod, Biscay style) 236
Bacalao al ajo arriero (Salt cod, muledriver's style) 237
Bacalao al pil pil (Sizzling cod) 237
Berenjenas a la catalana (Aubergines, Catalan style) 157
Berenjenas a la morisca (Moorish aubergines) 159
Berenjenas al horno (Baked aubergines) 158
Berenjenas fritas (Fried aubergines) 157
Berenjenas rellenas a la mallorquina (Stuffed aubergines, Mallorcan style) 158
Berza de acelgas (Andalusian vegetable pot) 135
Besugo a la madrileña (Baked bream, Madrid style) 224
Besugo asado a la donostiarra (Grilled bream, San Sebastian style) 225
Bitokes (Beef patties) 295
Bollos preñados (Pregnant buns) 203
Bogavante a la gallega (Lobster, Galician style) 246
Bonito a la bilbaina (Bonito, Bilbao style) 213
Boquerones al natural (Marinated fresh anchovies) 107
Boquerones rebozados (Fresh anchovies in batter) 218
Borrachos (Drunken cakes) 320
Borrachuelos (Wine doughnuts) 325
Brazo de gitano (''Gypsy's arm'' cake roll) 321
Brazo de gitano de patatas (''Gypsy's arm'' potato roll) 178
Brocheta de pez espada (Swordfish kebab) 219
Buñuelos (see **Rebozados,** 103)
Buñuelos de batata (Sweet potato fritters) 183
Buñuelos de higo (Fig fritters) 336
Buñuelos de queso (Cheese puffs) 105
Buñuelos de viento (Puffs of wind) 325

Caballa al horno (Baked mackerel) 212
Caballas rellenas (Stuffed mackerel) 213
Cabello de angel (Angel's hair jam) 346

General Index

Following is a general index of ingredients, etc. followed by their translation into Spanish. A page number in **bold type** indicates a photograph or illustration.

BRILL *(Rombo, rémol)*, 50. See also **Flat-fish.**
  Recipe:
  With Lemon, see Whiff with Lemon, 210
BRISKET *(pecho)*, see **Meat cuts.**
BROAD BEAN *(haba)*, see **Bean**
BROCCOLI *(brecol)*, 41
  Recipes:
  Mousse, see Aubergine mousse, 156
BROTH *(caldo)*, 124
BROWN RICE *(arroz integral)*, 76
BRUSSELS SPROUT *(col de Bruselas)*, 41
BUCKWHEAT *(trigo sarraceno)*, 76-77
BUTIFARRA, 67
  Ingredient in:
  Catalan salad, 112
  Crusty rice, Alicante style, 193
BUTTER *(mantequilla)*, 68
CABBAGE *(col, berza, repollo)*, 41
  Recipes:
  Cabbage, Catalan style, 164
  Cabbage rolls, Seville style, 165
  Cabbage, Valencia style, 164
  Mallorcan cabbage soup, 125
  Partridge with cabbage, Catalan style, 264
  Red cabbage, Castilian style, 169
  Stuffed cabbage, 166
  White cabbage with garlic sauce, 164
CAKE *(bizcocho, pastel)*, 316-321
CAMOMILE *(manzanilla)*, 74
CANARY ISLANDS, 28-29
  Specialities:
  Mojo colorado, 310
  Puchero canario, 131
  Sancocho canario, 228
  Tortas de plátano, 335
CANDIES, 337-338
CANNELLONI *(canelones)*, see **Pasta**
CANTABRIA, 16-17
  Specialities:
  Cabracho en salsa verde, 211
  Jabalí o venado a la montañesa, 271
  Mejillones a la marinera, 243
CAPER *(alcaparra)*, 74, 220
  Recipe:
  Meagre in caper sauce, 220
CAPON, 57. See also **Chicken**
CARAMEL CUSTARD *(flan)*, 327
CARAWAY SEED *(alcaravea)*, 72
CARDAMOM *(cardamomo)*, 72
CARDOON *(cardo)*, 41
  Recipe, 169
CARP *(carpa)*, 54
  Marinated, see Marinated Tench, 239
CARROT *(zanahoria)*, 41
  Recipes:
  Carrots braised in Malaga wine, 169

Mousse, see Aubergine mousse, 156
Vegetable salad, 111
CASHEW *(anacardo)*, 36
CASTILE AND LEON, 18-19
  Specialities:
  Arroz a la zamorana, 194
  Chanfaina, 299
  Cochinillo asado, 284
  Hornazo a lo castellano, 296
  Lechazo asado al castellano, 291
  Liebre estofada a la castellana, 270
  Sopa de cangrejos de río, 123
  Trucha a la zamorana, 239
CATALONIA, 19-20
  Wine, 80
  Specialities:
  Amanida, 112
  Arros negre amb alli i pebre, 192
  Asado de cerdo a la catalàna, 283
  Berenjenas a la catalana, 157
  Canelones a la catalana, 196
  Cap roig, 211
  Caracoles u la patarrallada, 251
  Coles a la catalana, 164
  Conejo tarraconense, 269
  Costillas al horno, 285
  Fideos a la catalana, 198
  Habas a la catalana, 161, **167**
  Langosta a la Costa Brava, 245
  Mar i terra, 258
  Menjar blanc, 329
  Paella parellada, 191
  Pan con tomate y jamón, 200
  Panadons amb espinacs, 183
  Pataco, 215
  Patatas a la cerdeña, 178
  Pavo asado a la catalana, 261
  Perdices con coles a la catalana, 264
  Picada catalana, 309
  Pollo en samfaina a la catalana, 257
  Potaje a la catalana, 137
  Rape en salsa de almendras, 208
  Romesco, 309
  Rovellons a la brasa, 173
  Samfaina, 309
  Sopa de mejillones, 123
CAULIFLOWER *(coliflor)*, 42
  Recipes:
  Breaded cauliflower, 170
  Cauliflower, muledriver's style, 170
  Cauliflower with garlic sauce, 170
  Fritters, 103
  Vegetable salad, 111
CAYENNE *(cayena)*, see **Chili pepper**
CELERY *(apio)*, 42, 72
CEPE, see **Mushroom**

2

4

Also from Lookout Publications

GARDENING IN SPAIN
by Marcelle Pitt. 176 pages.

Your most valuable tool for successful gardening in Spain, from the author of Lookout Magazine's popular gardening column. How to plan your garden, what to plant, when and how to plant it, how to make the most of flowers, trees, shrubs, herbs. Illustrated with full-colour photographs.

NORD RILEY'S SPAIN
by Nord Riley. 272 pages.

The best of popular columnist Nord Riley's writing over 14 years, brought together in the funniest book ever published about expatriate life in Spain. If you're not one of those lucky expats living in Nord Riley's Spain, by the time you've finished this book you'll wish you were.

HERE IN SPAIN
by David Mitchell. 208 pages.

Spain seen through the eyes of famous travellers, from Borrow to Hemingway. This unique survey by David Mitchell, himself a respected observer of Spanish life, is a collection of the most outrageous, admiring, insulting, libellous, passionate, hilarious, thoughtful, bigoted, eloquent remarks ever made about any country. An invaluable key to understanding the Spanish character.

INSIDE ANDALUSIA
by David Baird. 200 pages (large format).

A travel adventure through Spain's most fascinating region, from the top travel writer in Spain today. David Baird invites you to explore an Andalusia you never dreamt of, to meet its people, and discover fascinating fiestas. Illustrated with brilliant colour photography.

404 SPANISH WINES
by Frank Snell. 140 pages.

From the author of the best-selling *202 Spanish Wines,* a guide to who's who on the wine shelf. What wines to buy, how to judge a wine, how to read the label, how to store your wine, how to serve it, and lots more.

YOU AND THE LAW IN SPAIN
By David Searl. 216 pages.

Thousands of readers have relied of Lookout Magazine's best-selling *You and the Law in Spain* to guide them through the Spanish legal jungle. Now, author David Searl brings you a new, completely revised third edition with even more information on taxes, work permits, cars, banking in Spain, buying property, Spain and the Common Market, and lots more. It's a book no foreigner in Spain can afford to be without.

On sale in bookstores in Spain, or by post from Lookout Publications SA, Puebla Lucía, 29640 Fuengirola (Málaga), Spain.

Quick Conversions

In the recipes in this book, quantities are given in metric measurements. The charts on this page show approximate equivalents between Imperial or American measures, and metric measures. For further information on conversions, see Chapter 3.

FLUID MEASURES
METRIC/BRITISH STANDARD

10 MILLILITRES = 1/3 OUNCE
50 MILLILITRES = 1 3/4 OUNCES
100 MILLILITRES = 3½ OUNCES
250 MILLILITRES = 8½ OUNCES
500 MILLILITRES = 17½ OUNCES
1 LITRE = 1 3/4 PINTS

1 TEASPOON = 5 MILLILITRES
1 TABLESPOON = 18 MILLILITRES
1 OUNCE = 28 MILLILITRES
1 PINT = 570 MILLILITRES
1 QUART = 1.14 LITRES
1 GALLON = 4½ LITRES

FLUID MEASURES
METRIC/U.S. STANDARD

10 MILLILITRES = 2 TEASPOONS
50 MILLILITRES = 3 TABLESPOONS
100 MILLILITRES = 3½ OUNCES
250 MILLILITRES = 1 CUP + 1 TABLESPOON
500 MILLILITRES = 1 PINT + 2 TABLESPOONS
1 LITRE = 1 QUART + 3 TABLESPOONS

1 TEASPOON = 5 MILLILITRES
1 TABLESPOON = 15 MILLILITRES
1 OUNCE = 30 MILLILITRES
1 CUP = 235 MILLILITRES
1 PINT = 475 MILLILITRES
1 QUART = 950 MILLILITRES
1 GALLON = 3 3/4 LITRES

OVEN TEMPERATURE

TEMPERATURE	DIAL NUMBER
VERY SLOW = 250F/120C.	= ¼
SLOW = 300F/150C.	= 1
MODERATE = 350F/180C.	= 4
HOT = 400F/200C.	= 6
VERY HOT = 450F/230C.	= 8

WEIGHT
METRIC/OUNCES & POUNDS

10 GRAMS = 1/3 OUNCE
50 GRAMS = 1 3/4 OUNCES
100 GRAMS = 3½ OUNCES
250 GRAMS = 8 3/4 OUNCES
500 GRAMS = 1 POUND + 1½ OUNCES
1 KILO = 2 POUNDS + 3¼ OUNCES

½ OUNCE = 14 GRAMS
1 OUNCE = 28 GRAMS
¼ POUND = 110 GRAMS
½ POUND = 230 GRAMS
1 POUND = 450 GRAMS

TEMPERATURE

F.	C.
500-	
	-250
475-	
	-240
450-	
	-230
425-	
	-220
	-210
400-	
	-200
375-	
	-190
350-	
	-180
	-170
325-	
	-160
300-	
	-150
275-	
	-140
	-130
250-	
	-120
225-	
	-110
200-	
	-100 (WATER BOILS)
	-90
175-	
	-80
150-	
	-70
125-	
	-60
	-50
100-	
	-40
	-30
75-	
	-20
50-	
	-10
	-0 (WATER FREEZES)
25-	
	- -10
0-	
	- -20
-25-	
	- -30
	- -40
-50-	
	- -50
F.	C.